SHAME PUDDING

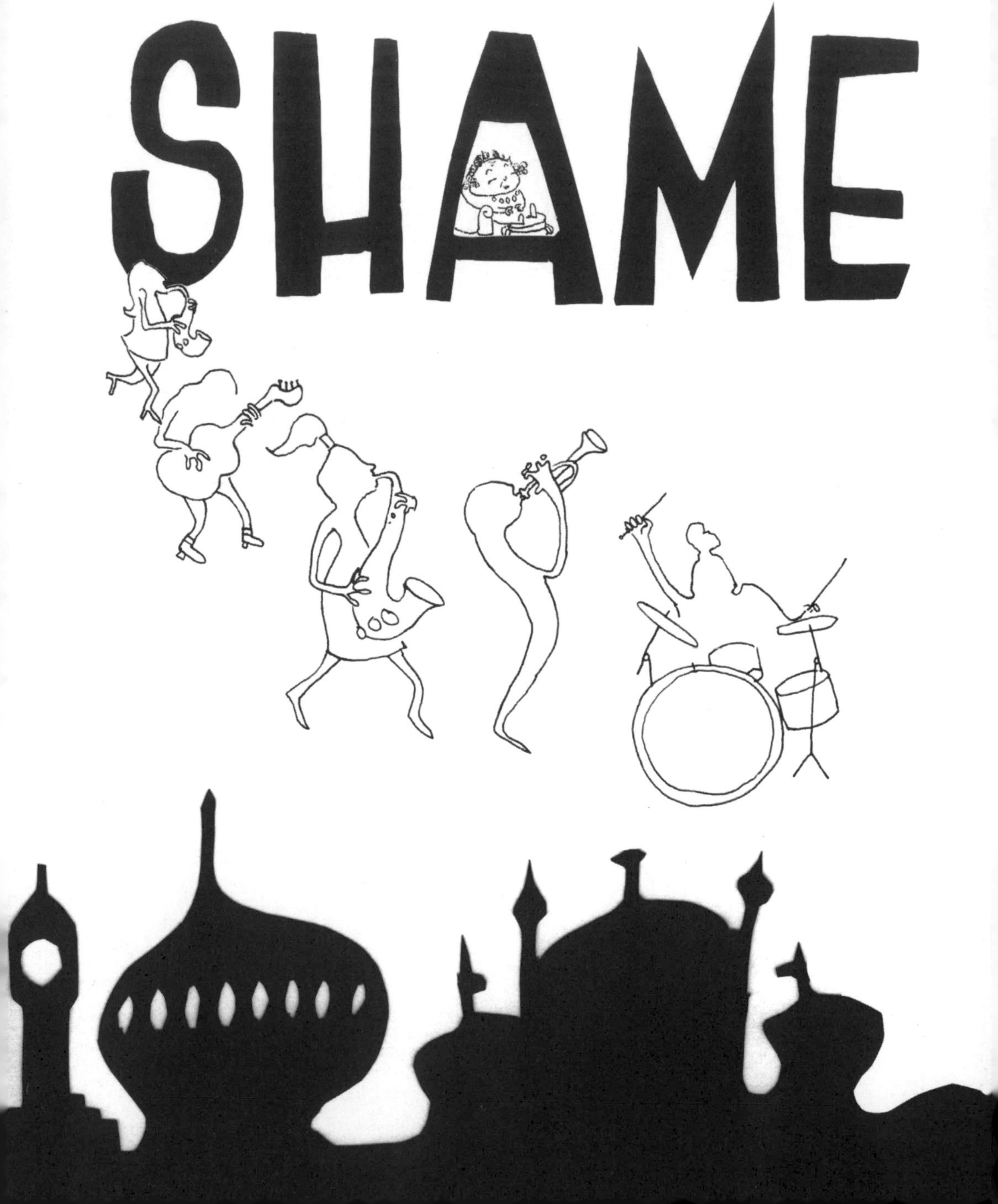
SHAME

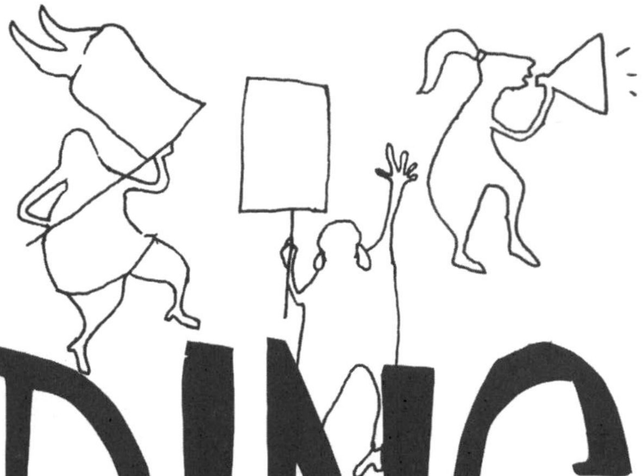

PUDDING

A GRAPHIC MEMOIR

BY DANNY NOBLE

Street Noise Books
Brooklyn, New York

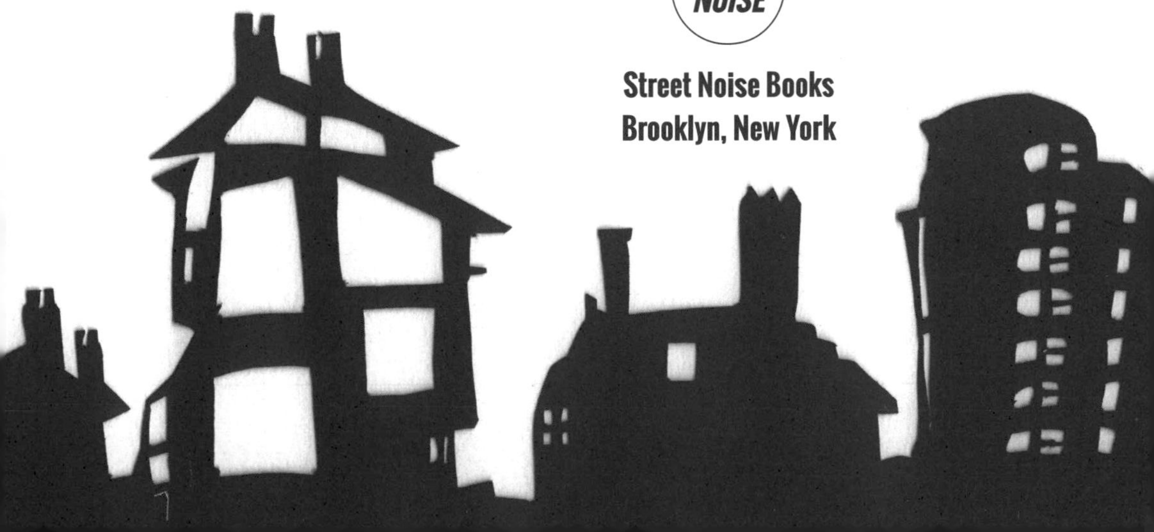

FOR NETTIE AND MINNIE... THE MAs

Library of Congress CIP data available.

ISBN 978-1-951-491-02-4

Edited by Ada Price
Book design by Liz Frances and Charice Silverman

Printed in South Korea

9 8 7 6 5 4 3 2 1

First Edition

CONTENTS

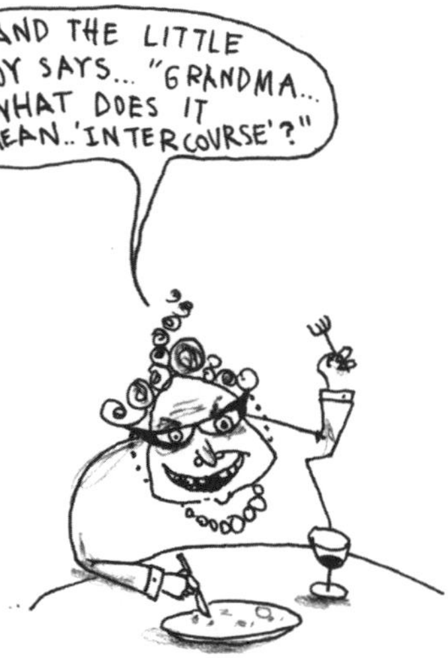
AND THE LITTLE BOY SAYS... "GRANDMA... WHAT DOES IT MEAN..'INTERCOURSE'?"

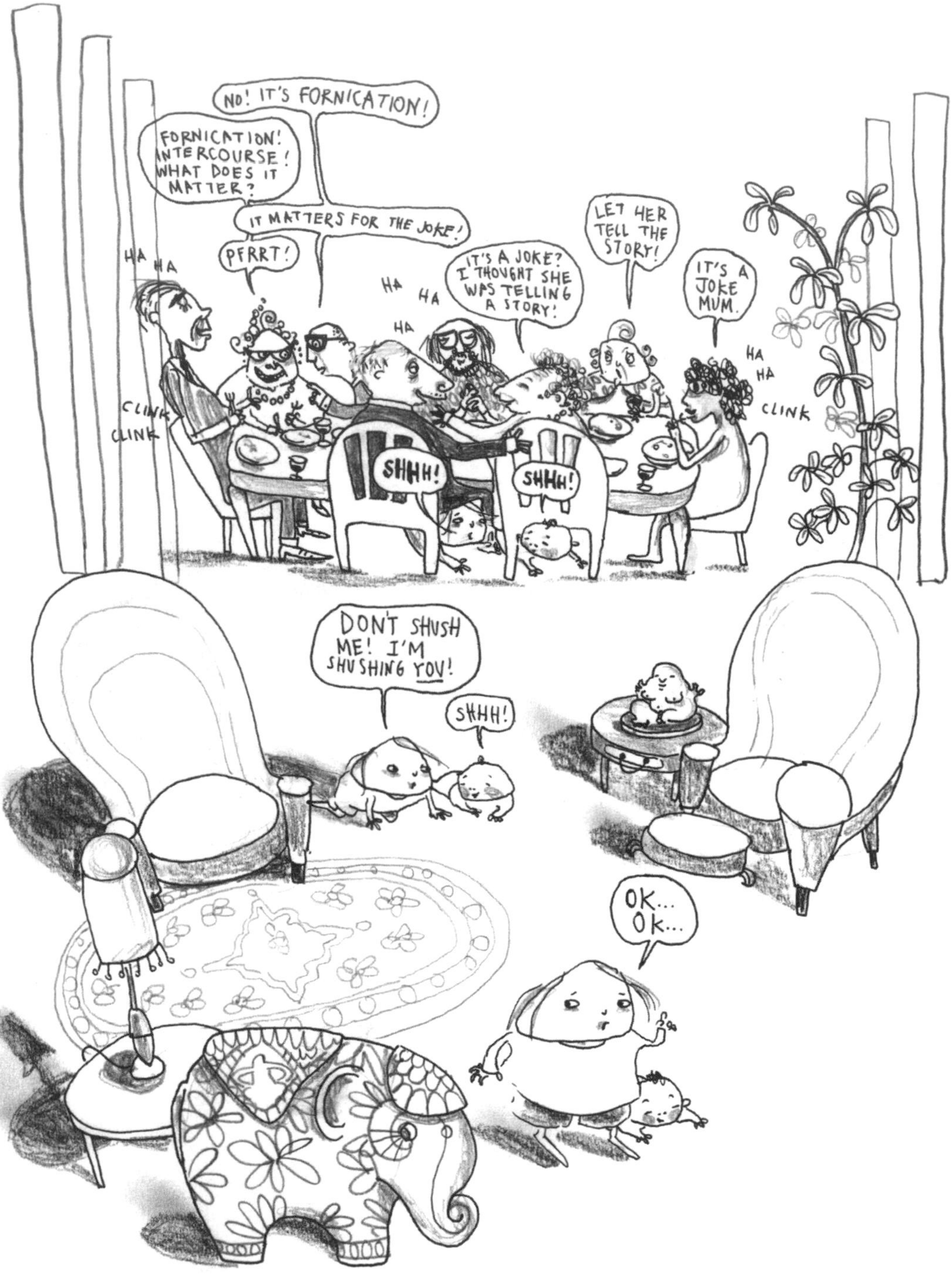
NO! IT'S FORNICATION!
FORNICATION! INTERCOURSE! WHAT DOES IT MATTER?
IT MATTERS FOR THE JOKE!
PFRRT!
HA HA
HA HA
HA
IT'S A JOKE? I THOUGHT SHE WAS TELLING A STORY!
LET HER TELL THE STORY!
IT'S A JOKE MUM.
HA HA
CLINK CLINK
CLINK
SHHH!
SHHH!
DON'T SHUSH ME! I'M SHUSHING YOU!
SHHH!
OK... OK...

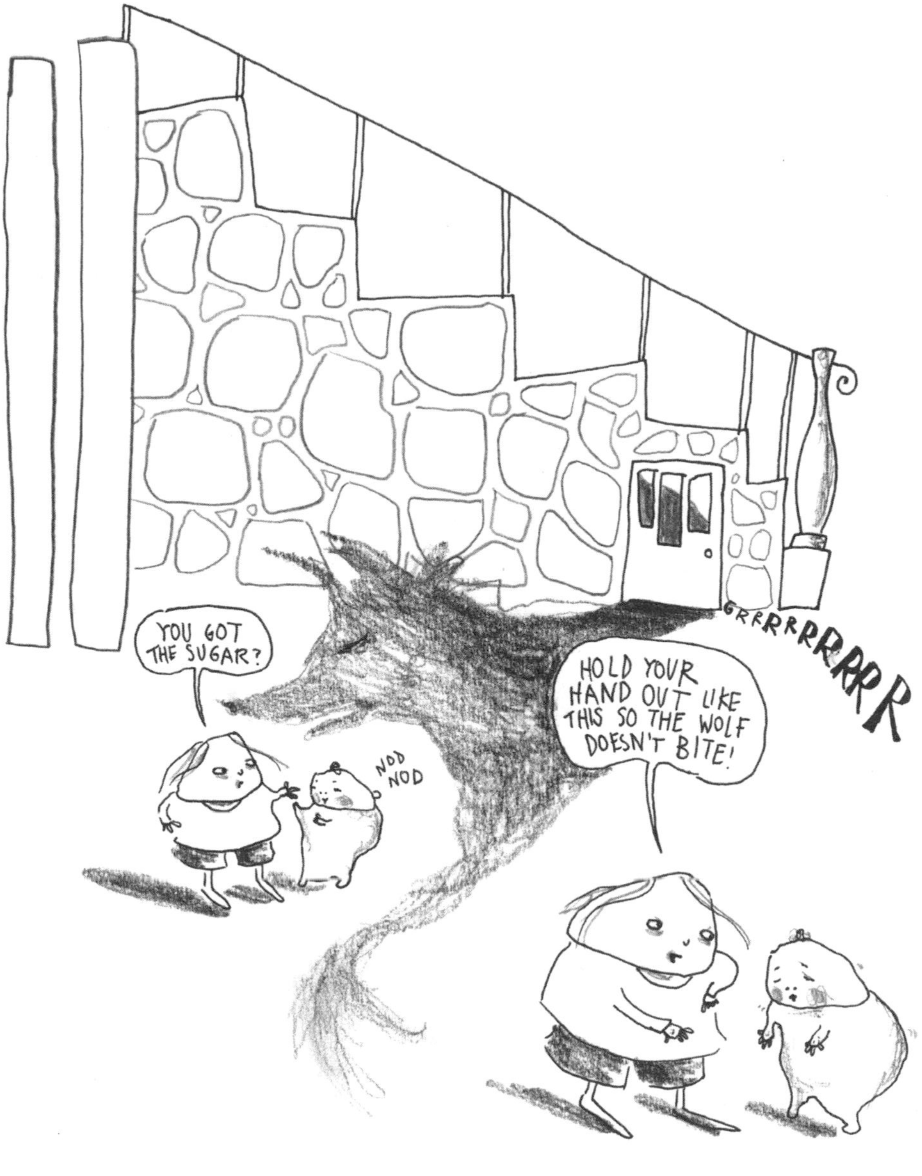
YOU GOT THE SUGAR?
NOD NOD
GRRRRRRRRRR
HOLD YOUR HAND OUT LIKE THIS SO THE WOLF DOESN'T BITE!

AN INVISIBLE WOLF LIVED IN GRANDMA MIN'S CUPBOARD. ME AND ADAM WERE THE ONLY ONES WHO KNEW SO IT WAS VERY IMPORTANT WE FED IT SUGAR...

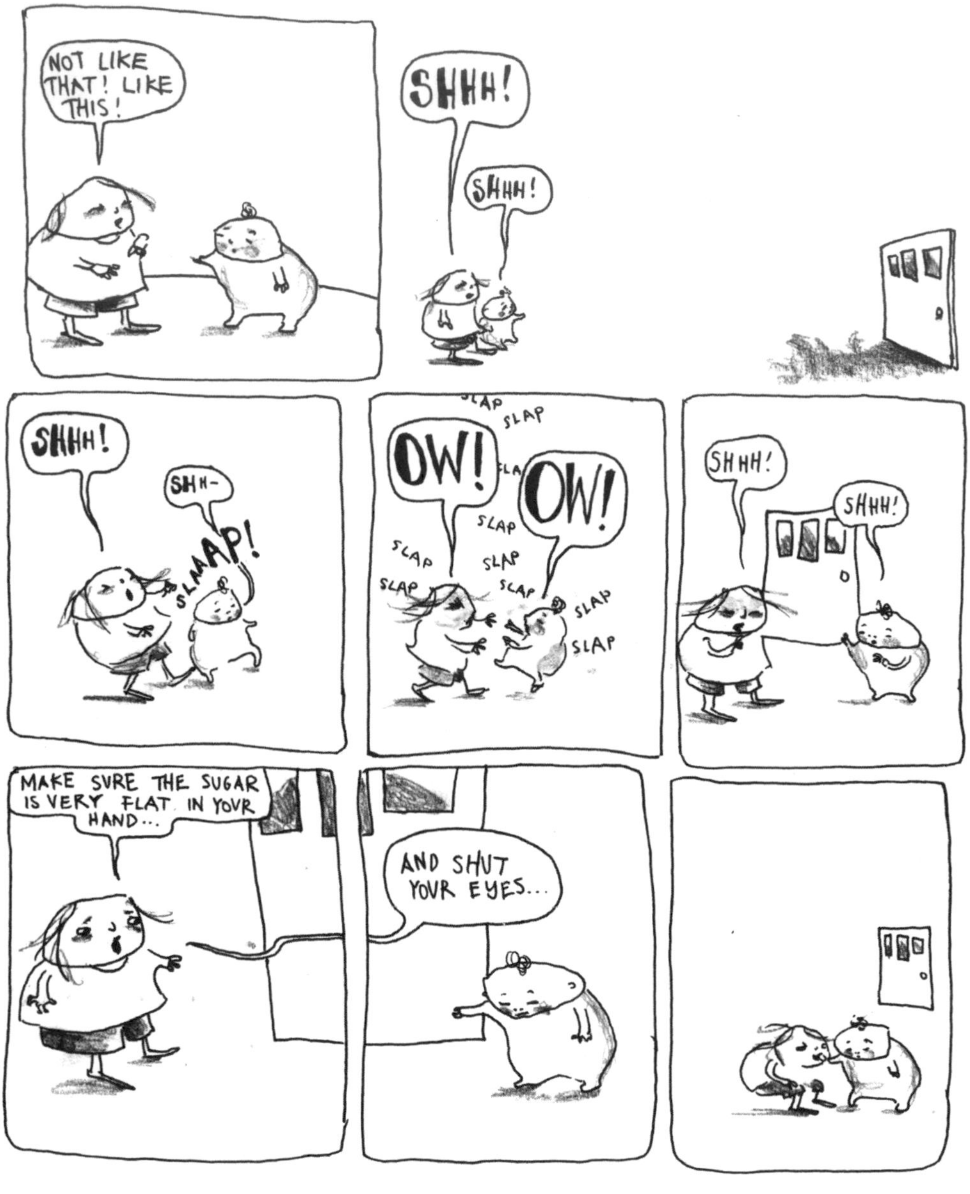
NOT LIKE THAT! LIKE THIS!
SHHH!
SHHH!
SHHH!
SHH-
SLAAAP!
SLAP SLAP
OW!
OW!
SLAP
SLAP
SLAP
SLAP
SLAP
SLAP
SLAP
SHHH!
SHHH!
MAKE SURE THE SUGAR IS VERY FLAT IN YOUR HAND...
AND SHUT YOUR EYES...

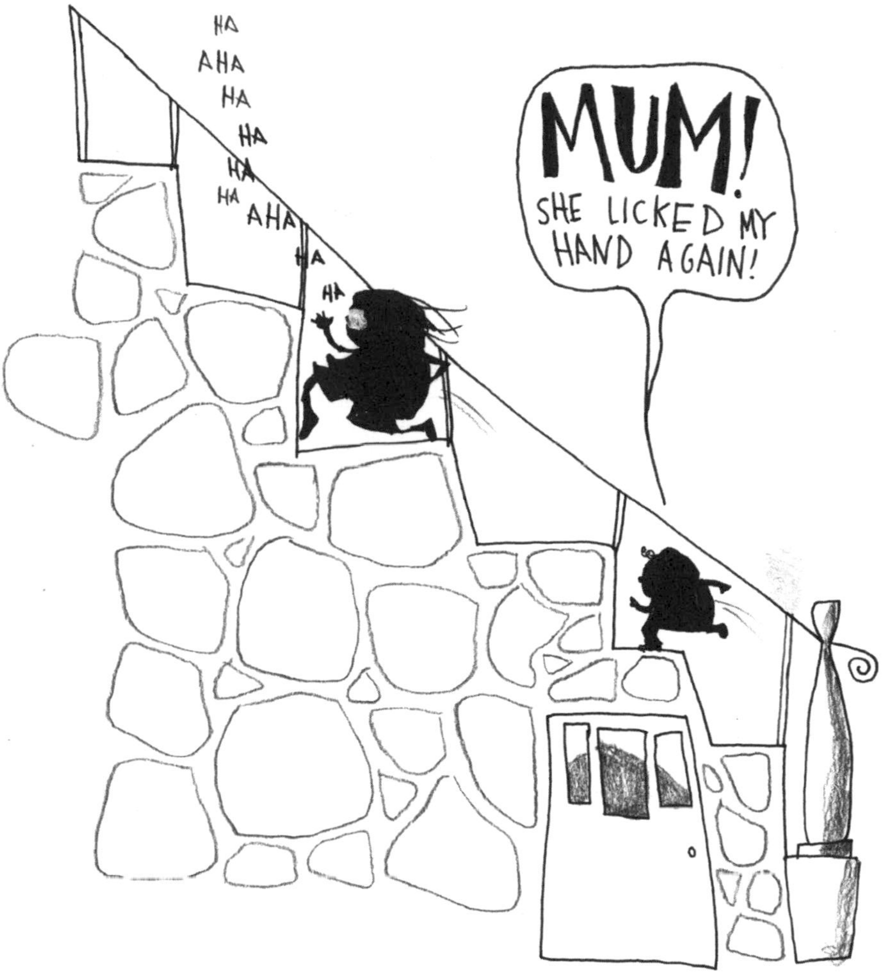
HA
AHA
HA
HA
HA
HA AHA
HA
HA
MUM! SHE LICKED MY HAND AGAIN!

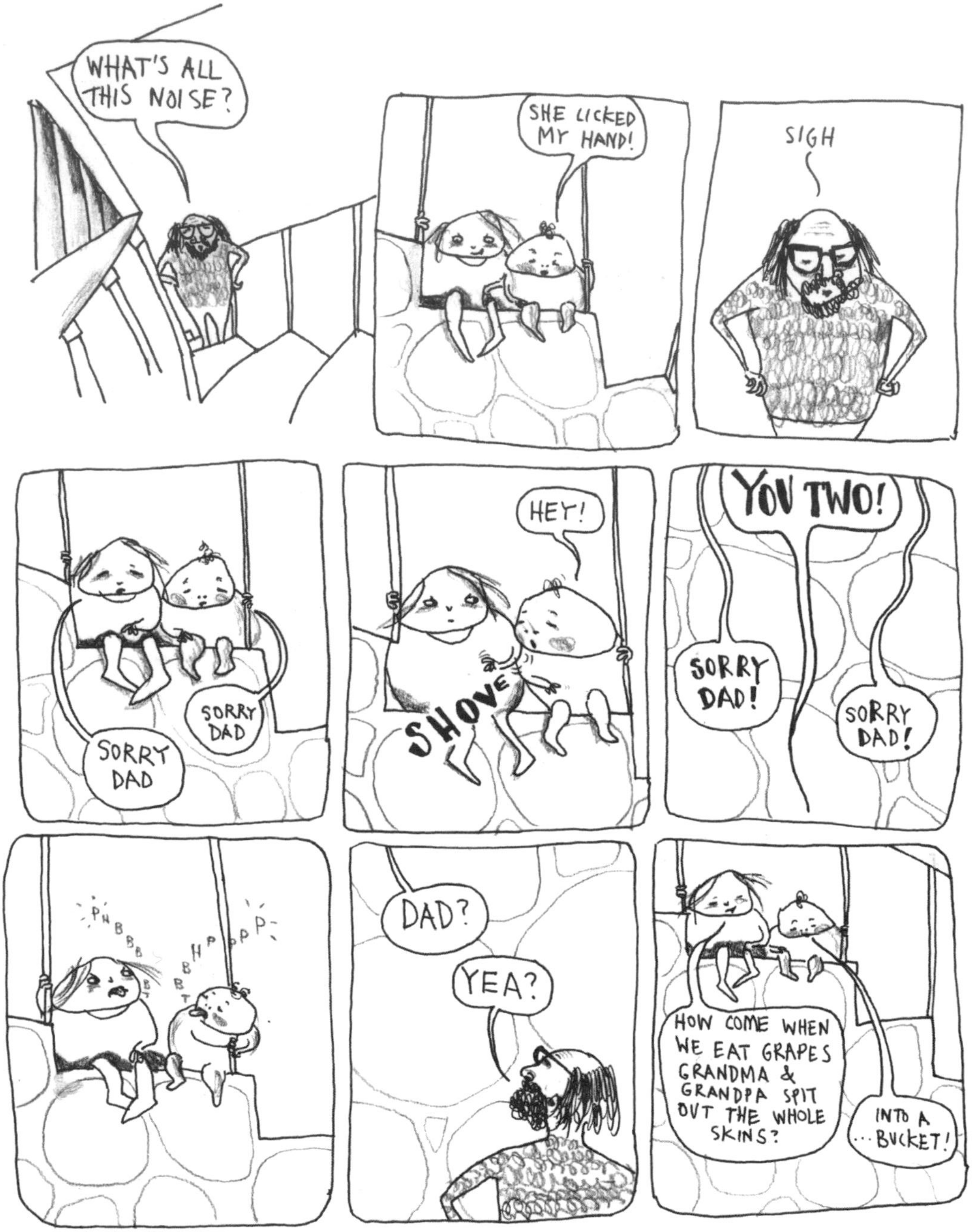
WHAT'S ALL THIS NOISE?
SHE LICKED MY HAND!
SIGH
SORRY DAD
SORRY DAD
HEY!
SHOVE
YOU TWO!
SORRY DAD!
SORRY DAD!
PHBBBBT
BHPPPP
DAD?
YEA?
HOW COME WHEN WE EAT GRAPES GRANDMA & GRANDPA SPIT OUT THE WHOLE SKINS?
INTO A ...BUCKET!

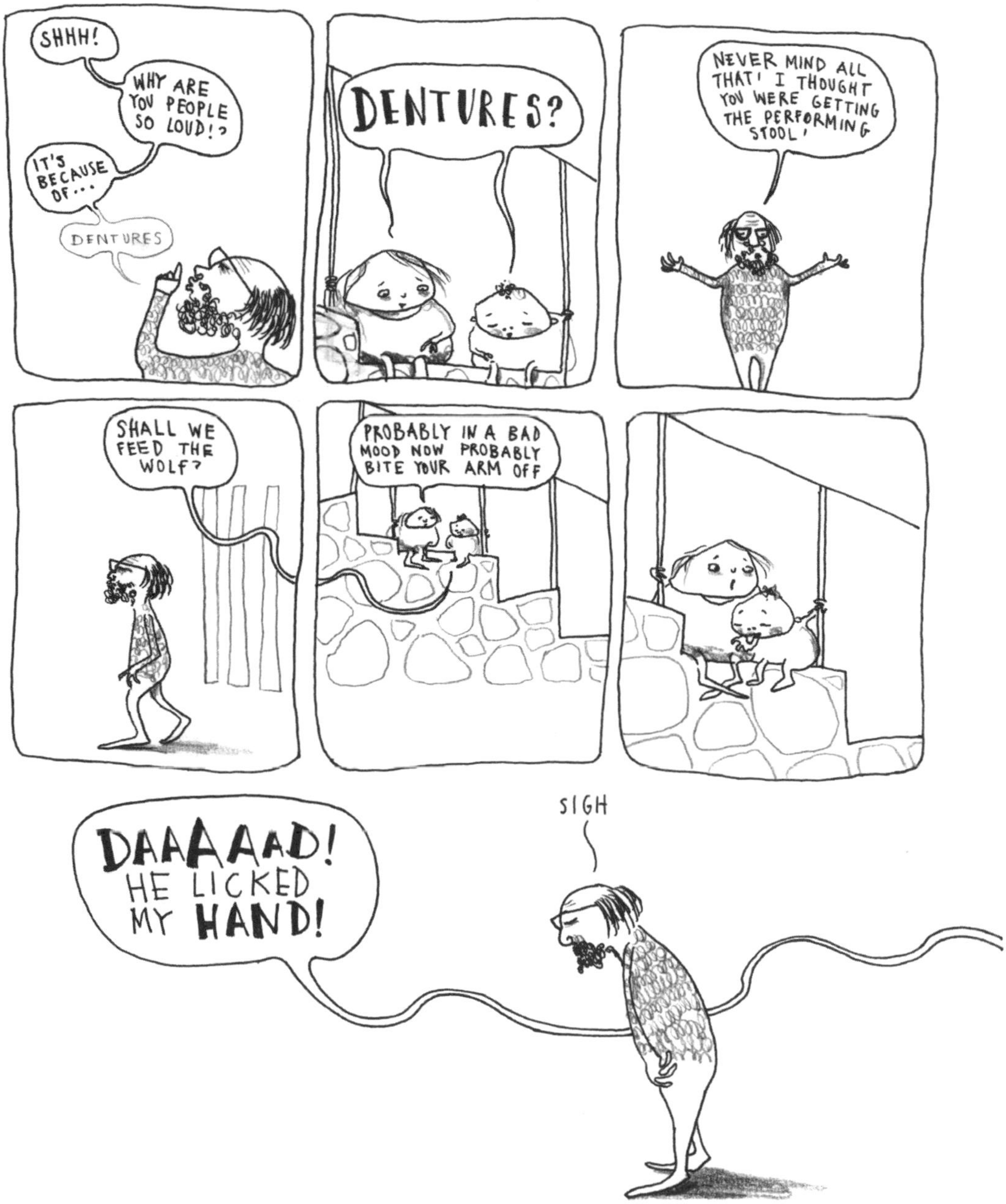
SHHH!
WHY ARE YOU PEOPLE SO LOUD!?
IT'S BECAUSE OF...
DENTURES
DENTURES?
NEVER MIND ALL THAT! I THOUGHT YOU WERE GETTING THE PERFORMING STOOL!
SHALL WE FEED THE WOLF?
PROBABLY IN A BAD MOOD NOW PROBABLY BITE YOUR ARM OFF
DAAAAAD! HE LICKED MY HAND!
SIGH

THE MAS

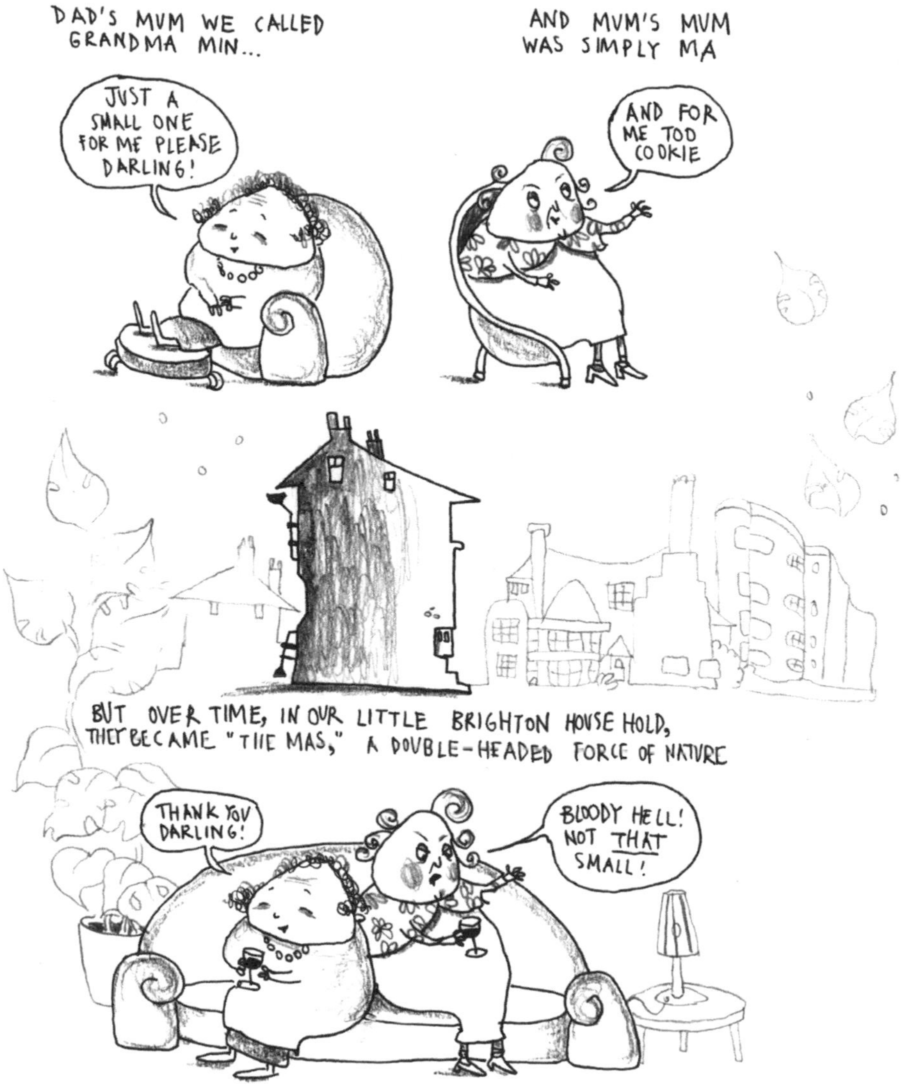

DAD'S MUM WE CALLED GRANDMA MIN...
JUST A SMALL ONE FOR ME PLEASE DARLING!
AND MUM'S MUM WAS SIMPLY MA
AND FOR ME TOO COOKIE
BUT OVER TIME, IN OUR LITTLE BRIGHTON HOUSE HOLD, THEY BECAME "THE MAS," A DOUBLE-HEADED FORCE OF NATURE
THANK YOU DARLING!
BLOODY HELL! NOT THAT SMALL!

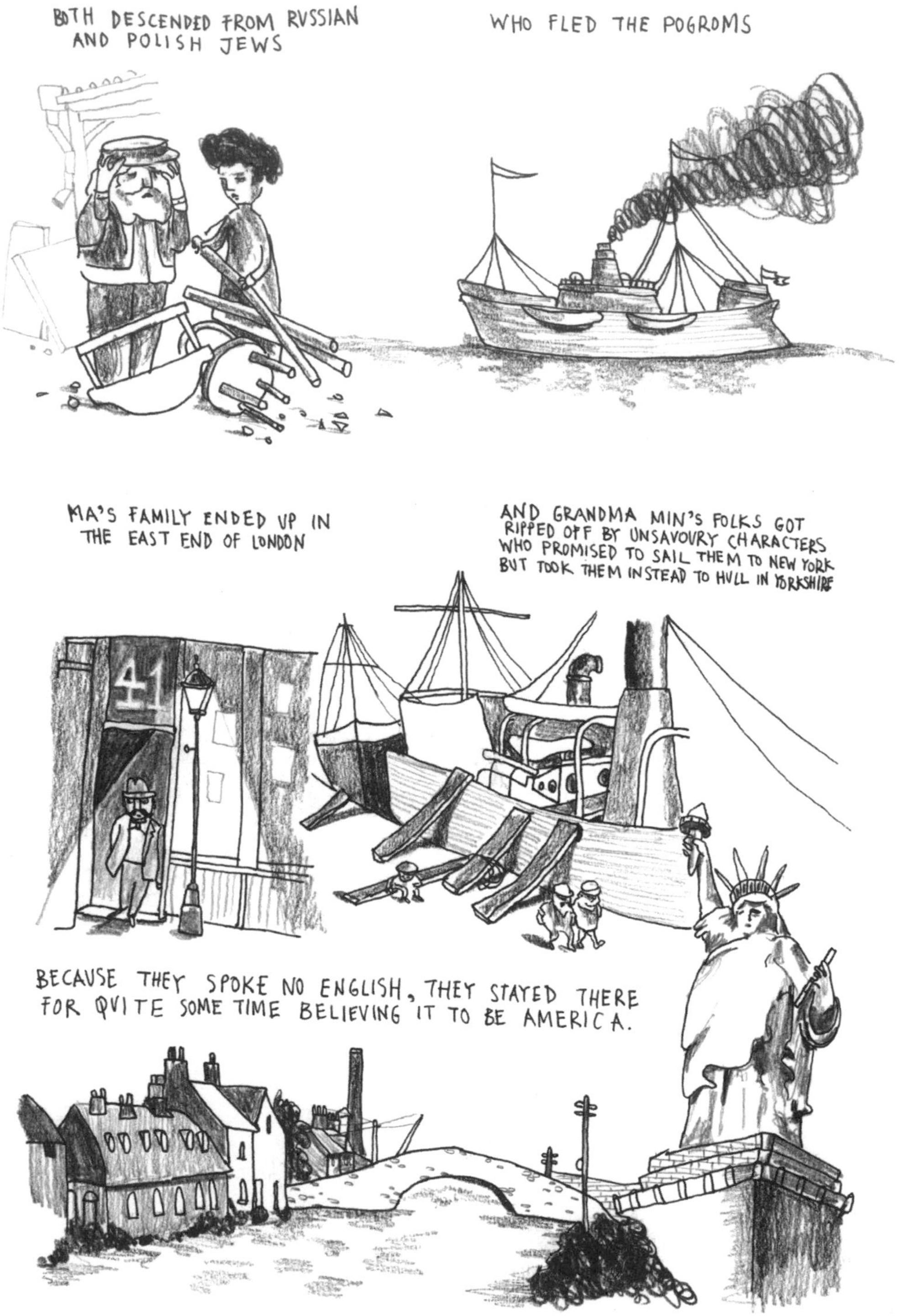
BOTH DESCENDED FROM RUSSIAN AND POLISH JEWS
WHO FLED THE POGROMS
MA'S FAMILY ENDED UP IN THE EAST END OF LONDON
41
AND GRANDMA MIN'S FOLKS GOT RIPPED OFF BY UNSAVOURY CHARACTERS WHO PROMISED TO SAIL THEM TO NEW YORK BUT TOOK THEM INSTEAD TO HULL IN YORKSHIRE
BECAUSE THEY SPOKE NO ENGLISH, THEY STAYED THERE FOR QUITE SOME TIME BELIEVING IT TO BE AMERICA.

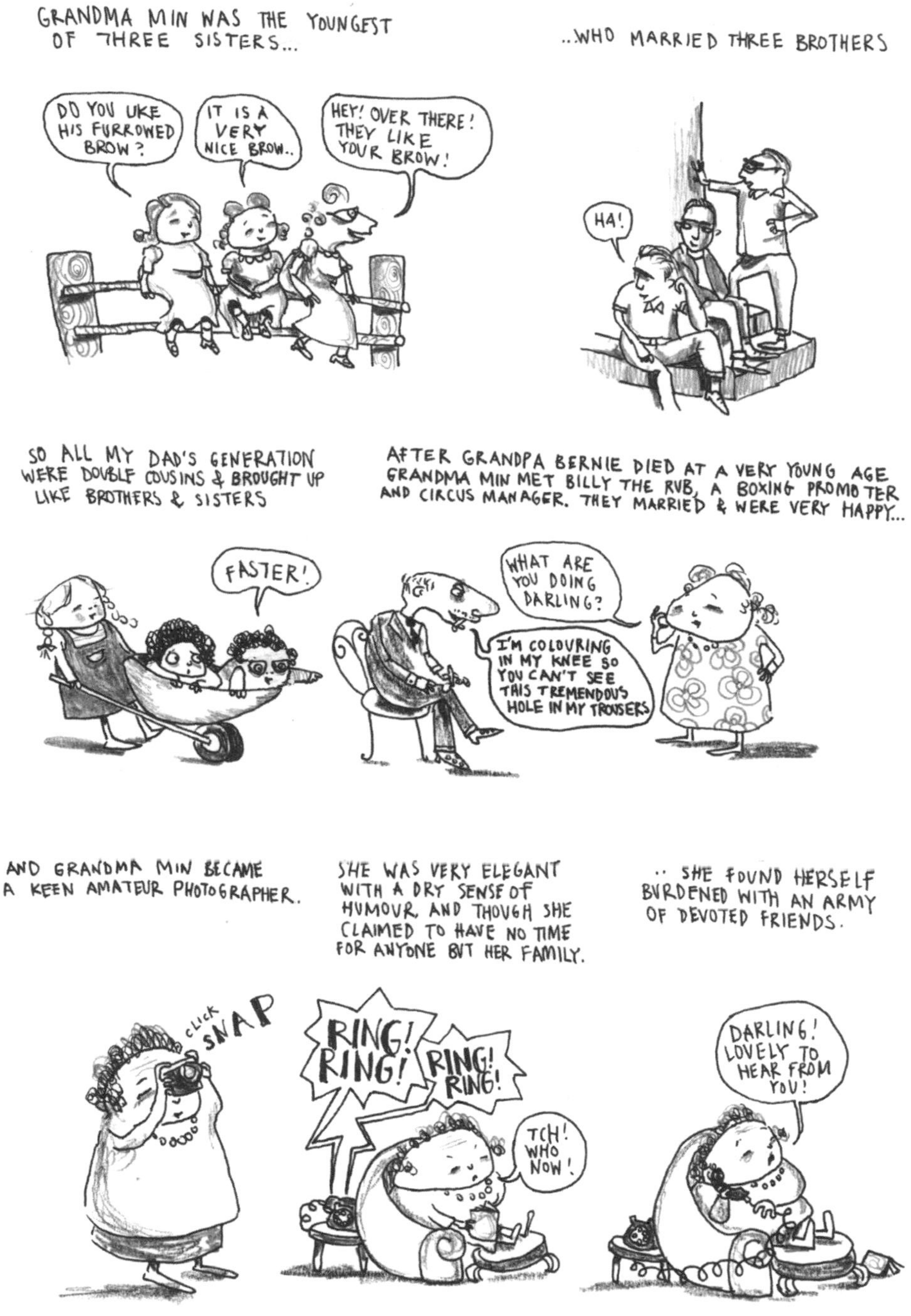
GRANDMA MIN WAS THE YOUNGEST OF THREE SISTERS...
DO YOU LIKE HIS FURROWED BROW?
IT IS A VERY NICE BROW..
HEY! OVER THERE! THEY LIKE YOUR BROW!
..WHO MARRIED THREE BROTHERS
HA!
SO ALL MY DAD'S GENERATION WERE DOUBLE COUSINS & BROUGHT UP LIKE BROTHERS & SISTERS
FASTER!
AFTER GRANDPA BERNIE DIED AT A VERY YOUNG AGE GRANDMA MIN MET BILLY THE RUB, A BOXING PROMOTER AND CIRCUS MANAGER. THEY MARRIED & WERE VERY HAPPY...
WHAT ARE YOU DOING DARLING?
I'M COLOURING IN MY KNEE SO YOU CAN'T SEE THIS TREMENDOUS HOLE IN MY TROUSERS
AND GRANDMA MIN BECAME A KEEN AMATEUR PHOTOGRAPHER.
CLICK SNAP
SHE WAS VERY ELEGANT WITH A DRY SENSE OF HUMOUR, AND THOUGH SHE CLAIMED TO HAVE NO TIME FOR ANYONE BUT HER FAMILY.
RING! RING!
RING! RING!
TCH! WHO NOW!
.. SHE FOUND HERSELF BURDENED WITH AN ARMY OF DEVOTED FRIENDS.
DARLING! LOVELY TO HEAR FROM YOU!

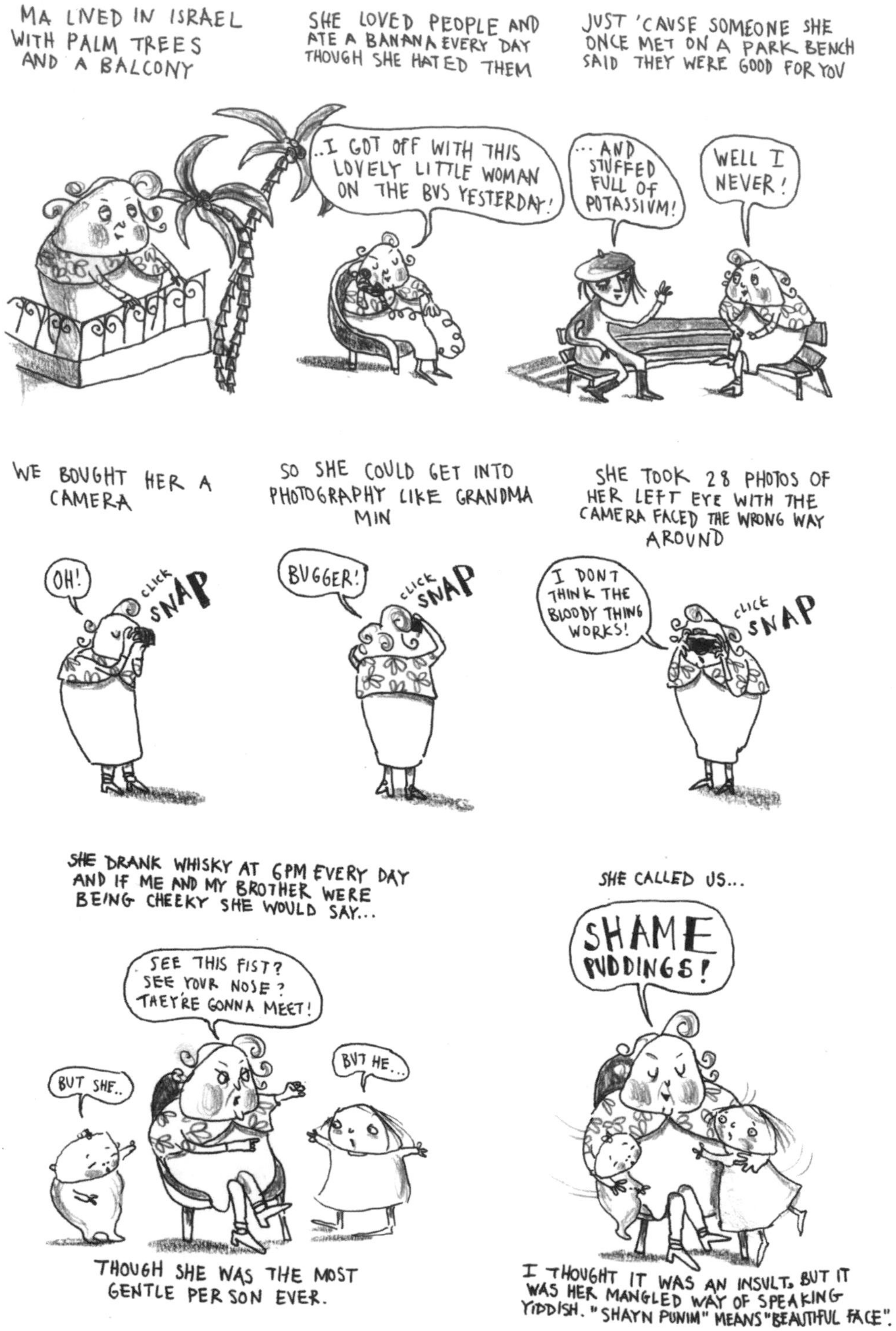
MA LIVED IN ISRAEL WITH PALM TREES AND A BALCONY
SHE LOVED PEOPLE AND ATE A BANANA EVERY DAY THOUGH SHE HATED THEM
..I GOT OFF WITH THIS LOVELY LITTLE WOMAN ON THE BUS YESTERDAY!
JUST 'CAUSE SOMEONE SHE ONCE MET ON A PARK BENCH SAID THEY WERE GOOD FOR YOU
...AND STUFFED FULL OF POTASSIUM!
WELL I NEVER!
WE BOUGHT HER A CAMERA
OH!
CLICK SNAP
SO SHE COULD GET INTO PHOTOGRAPHY LIKE GRANDMA MIN
BUGGER!
CLICK SNAP
SHE TOOK 28 PHOTOS OF HER LEFT EYE WITH THE CAMERA FACED THE WRONG WAY AROUND
I DONT THINK THE BLOODY THING WORKS!
CLICK SNAP
SHE DRANK WHISKY AT 6PM EVERY DAY AND IF ME AND MY BROTHER WERE BEING CHEEKY SHE WOULD SAY...
SEE THIS FIST? SEE YOUR NOSE? THEY'RE GONNA MEET!
BUT SHE..
BUT HE...
THOUGH SHE WAS THE MOST GENTLE PERSON EVER.
SHE CALLED US...
SHAME PUDDINGS!
I THOUGHT IT WAS AN INSULT, BUT IT WAS HER MANGLED WAY OF SPEAKING YIDDISH. "SHAYN PUNIM" MEANS "BEAUTIFUL FACE".

CHAPTER 1
BOY IN A BUBBLE

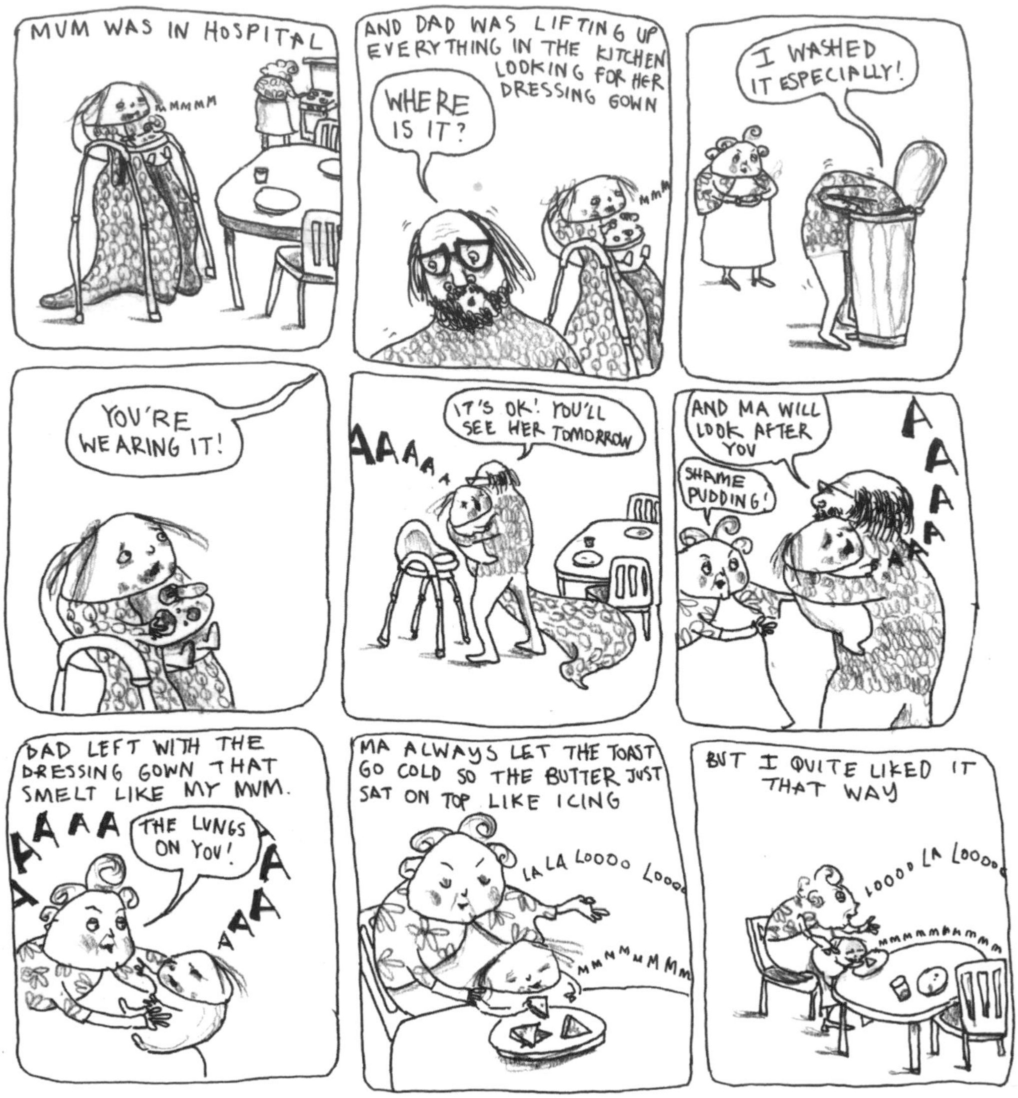
MUM WAS IN HOSPITAL
MMMMM
AND DAD WAS LIFTING UP EVERYTHING IN THE KITCHEN LOOKING FOR HER DRESSING GOWN
WHERE IS IT?
MMM
I WASHED IT ESPECIALLY!
YOU'RE WEARING IT!
IT'S OK! YOU'LL SEE HER TOMORROW
AAAAA
AND MA WILL LOOK AFTER YOU
SHAME PUDDING!
AAAAAA
DAD LEFT WITH THE DRESSING GOWN THAT SMELT LIKE MY MUM.
AAAA
THE LUNGS ON YOU!
AAAA
MA ALWAYS LET THE TOAST GO COLD SO THE BUTTER JUST SAT ON TOP LIKE ICING
LA LA LOOOO LOOOO
MMMMMMMM
BUT I QUITE LIKED IT THAT WAY
LOOOO LA LOOOO
MMMMMMMMMM

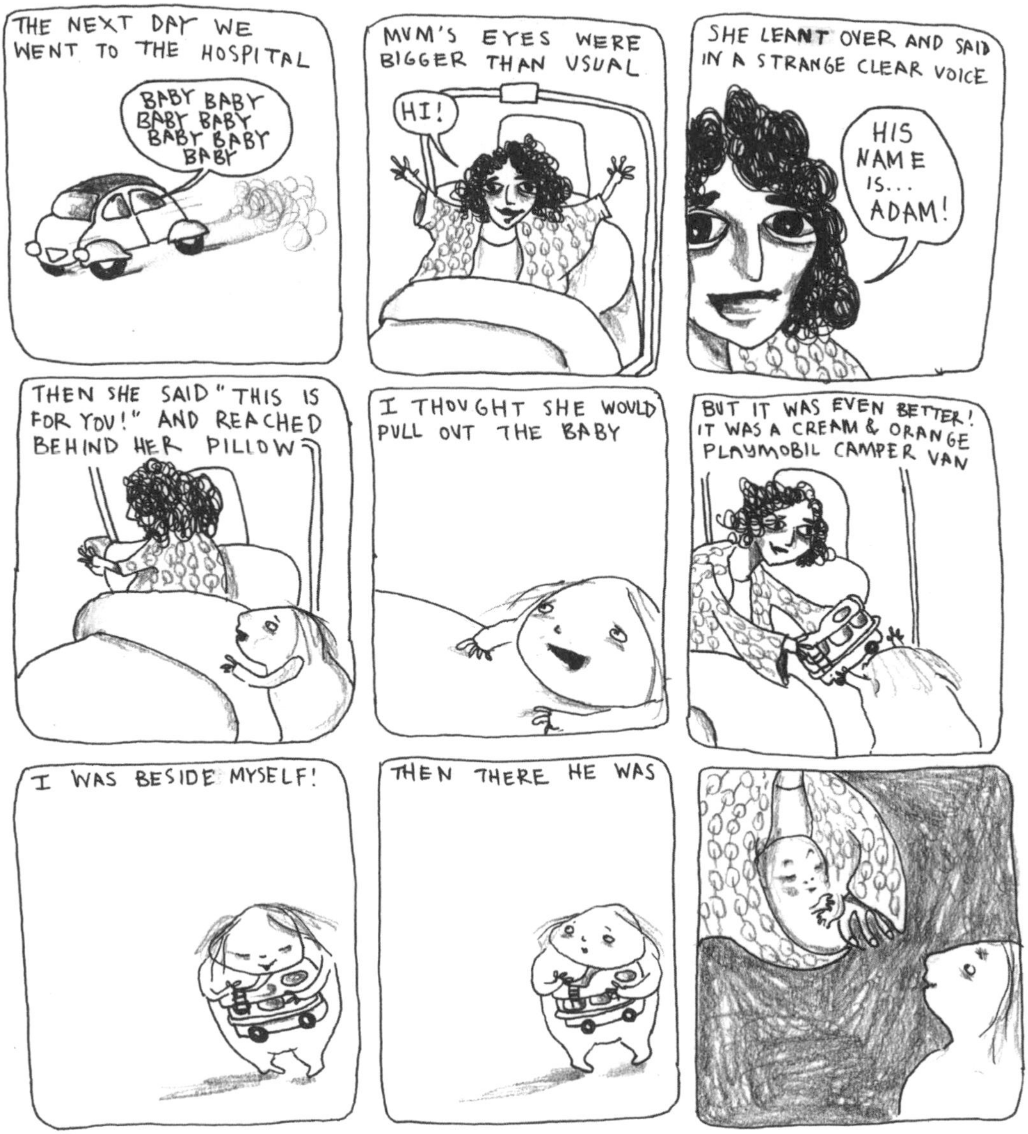
THE NEXT DAY WE WENT TO THE HOSPITAL
BABY BABY BABY BABY BABY BABY BABY
MUM'S EYES WERE BIGGER THAN USUAL
HI!
SHE LEANT OVER AND SAID IN A STRANGE CLEAR VOICE
HIS NAME IS... ADAM!
THEN SHE SAID "THIS IS FOR YOU!" AND REACHED BEHIND HER PILLOW
I THOUGHT SHE WOULD PULL OUT THE BABY
BUT IT WAS EVEN BETTER! IT WAS A CREAM & ORANGE PLAYMOBIL CAMPER VAN
I WAS BESIDE MYSELF!
THEN THERE HE WAS

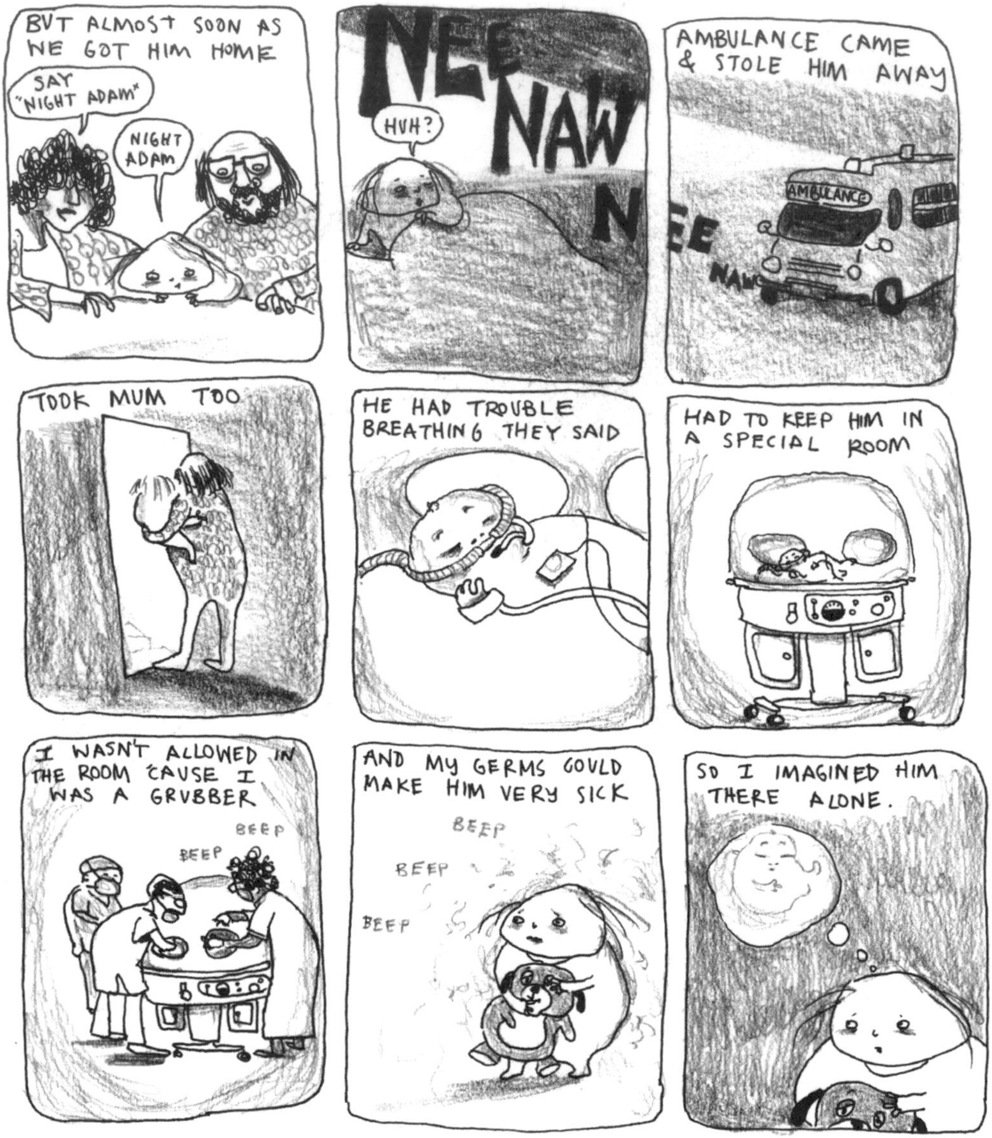
BUT ALMOST SOON AS WE GOT HIM HOME
SAY "NIGHT ADAM"
NIGHT ADAM
NEE NAW
HUH?
NEE NAW
AMBULANCE CAME & STOLE HIM AWAY
AMBULANCE
TOOK MUM TOO
HE HAD TROUBLE BREATHING THEY SAID
HAD TO KEEP HIM IN A SPECIAL ROOM
I WASN'T ALLOWED IN THE ROOM 'CAUSE I WAS A GRUBBER
BEEP
BEEP
AND MY GERMS COULD MAKE HIM VERY SICK
BEEP
BEEP
BEEP
SO I IMAGINED HIM THERE ALONE.

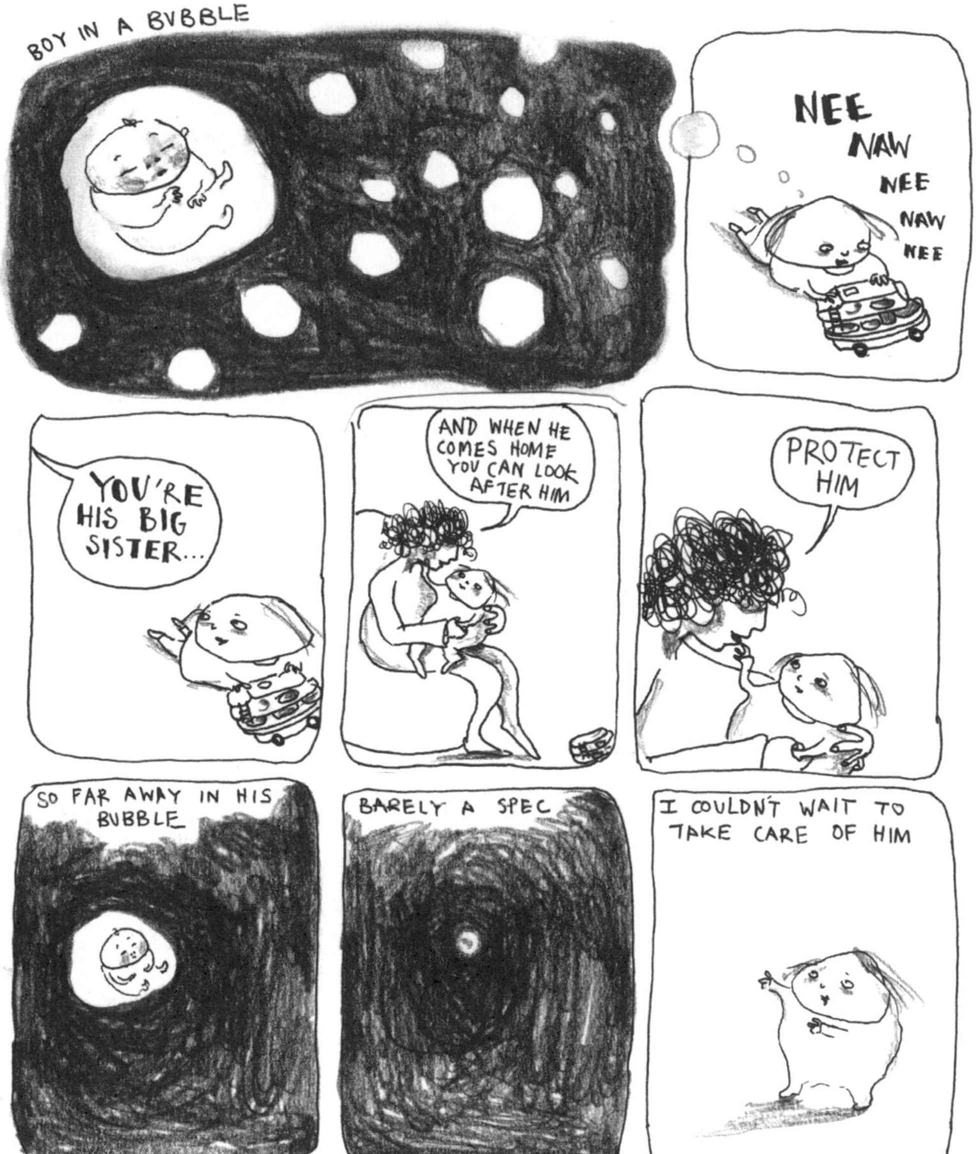
BOY IN A BUBBLE
NEE NAW NEE NAW NEE
YOU'RE HIS BIG SISTER...
AND WHEN HE COMES HOME YOU CAN LOOK AFTER HIM
PROTECT HIM
SO FAR AWAY IN HIS BUBBLE
BARELY A SPEC
I COULDN'T WAIT TO TAKE CARE OF HIM

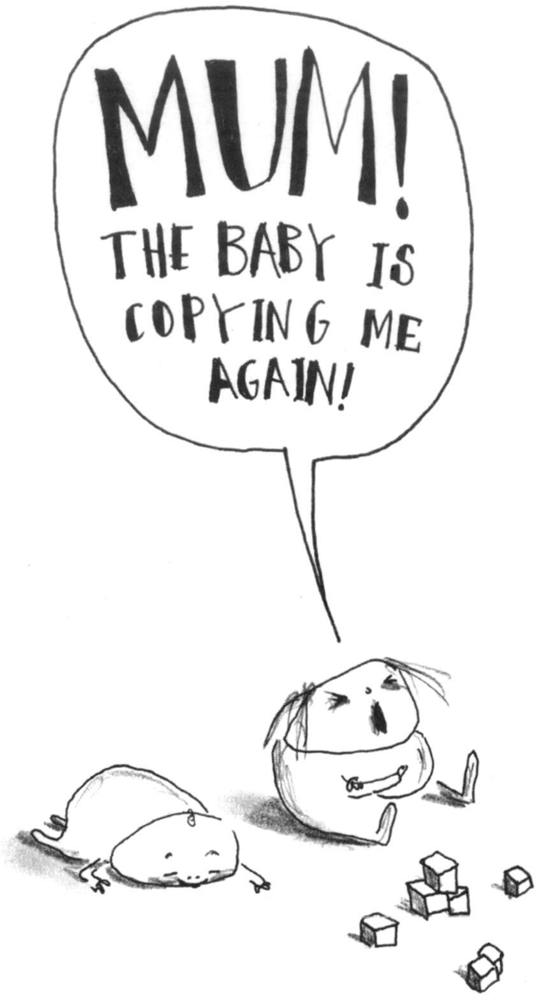
MUM! THE BABY IS COPYING ME AGAIN!

CHAPTER 2
RED HOOPS & GREEN LEMONADE

WHAT'S HE DOING?

DAD WAS A GADGET FREAK

THIS WAY!

HE FILLED OUR HOUSE WITH HOLE PUNCHERS & MACHINES TO CLEAN YOUR TEETH

NO! THE RED ONE!

BUT RECENTLY HE'D BROUGHT HOME SOMETHING QUITE DIFFERENT

LEFT YOU SILLY BUGGER!

TWO SIAMESE FIGHTING FISH

HE'S TRAINING 'EM TO SWIM THROUGH RED & YELLOW HOOPS

WHY?

CAUSE IT'S HIS JOB!

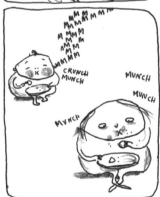

MMM
MMMM
MMMM
MMM
MMM
MMMM
CRUNCH MUNCH

MUNCH

MUNCH

MUNCH

BUT MUM SAYS THE FUNNIEST BIT IS THAT DAD IS COLOUR BLIND HIMSELF!

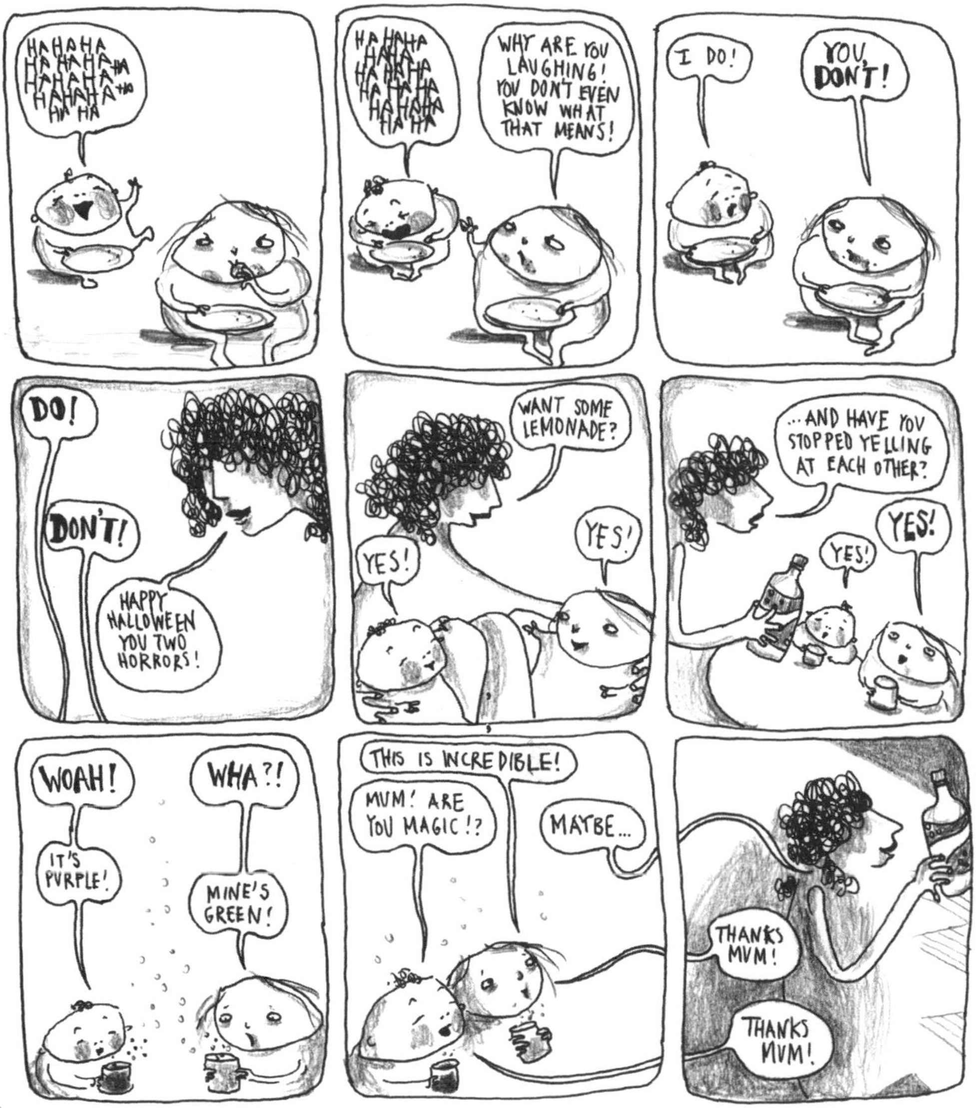
HAHAHA HAHAHAHA HAHAHAHA HAHAHAHA HA HA
HAHAHA HAHA HAHAHA HAHAHA HAHAHA HAHA
WHY ARE YOU LAUGHING! YOU DON'T EVEN KNOW WHAT THAT MEANS!
I DO!
YOU, DON'T!
DO!
DON'T!
HAPPY HALLOWEEN YOU TWO HORRORS!
WANT SOME LEMONADE?
YES!
YES!
...AND HAVE YOU STOPPED YELLING AT EACH OTHER?
YES!
YES!
WOAH!
IT'S PURPLE!
WHA?!
MINE'S GREEN!
THIS IS INCREDIBLE!
MUM! ARE YOU MAGIC!?
MAYBE...
THANKS MUM!
THANKS MUM!

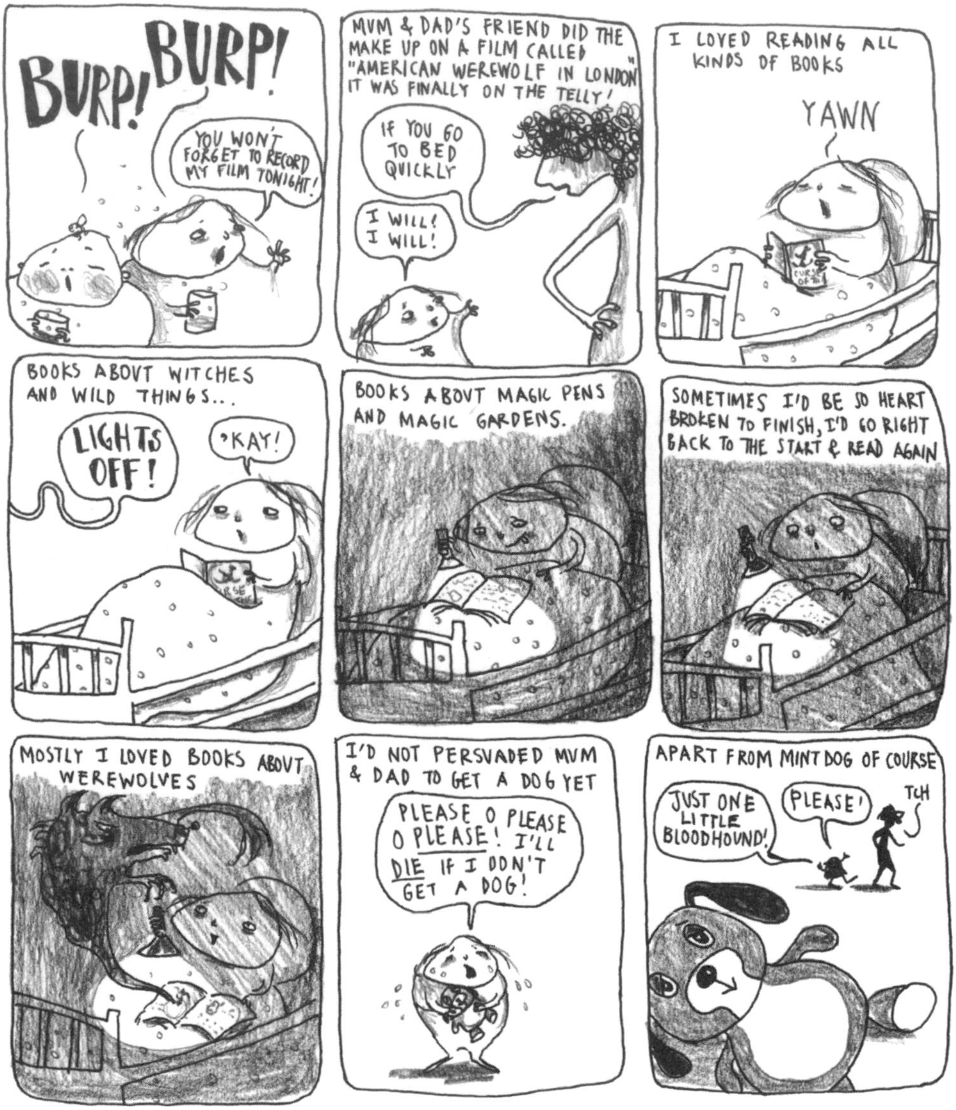

BURP!
BURP!
YOU WON'T FORGET TO RECORD MY FILM TONIGHT!
MUM & DAD'S FRIEND DID THE MAKE UP ON A FILM CALLED "AMERICAN WEREWOLF IN LONDON" IT WAS FINALLY ON THE TELLY!
IF YOU GO TO BED QUICKLY
I WILL! I WILL!
I LOVED READING ALL KINDS OF BOOKS
YAWN
BOOKS ABOUT WITCHES AND WILD THINGS...
LIGHTS OFF!
'KAY!
BOOKS ABOUT MAGIC PENS AND MAGIC GARDENS.
SOMETIMES I'D BE SO HEART BROKEN TO FINISH, I'D GO RIGHT BACK TO THE START & READ AGAIN
MOSTLY I LOVED BOOKS ABOUT WEREWOLVES
I'D NOT PERSUADED MUM & DAD TO GET A DOG YET
PLEASE O PLEASE O PLEASE! I'LL DIE IF I DON'T GET A DOG!
APART FROM MINT DOG OF COURSE
JUST ONE LITTLE BLOODHOUND!
PLEASE!
TCH

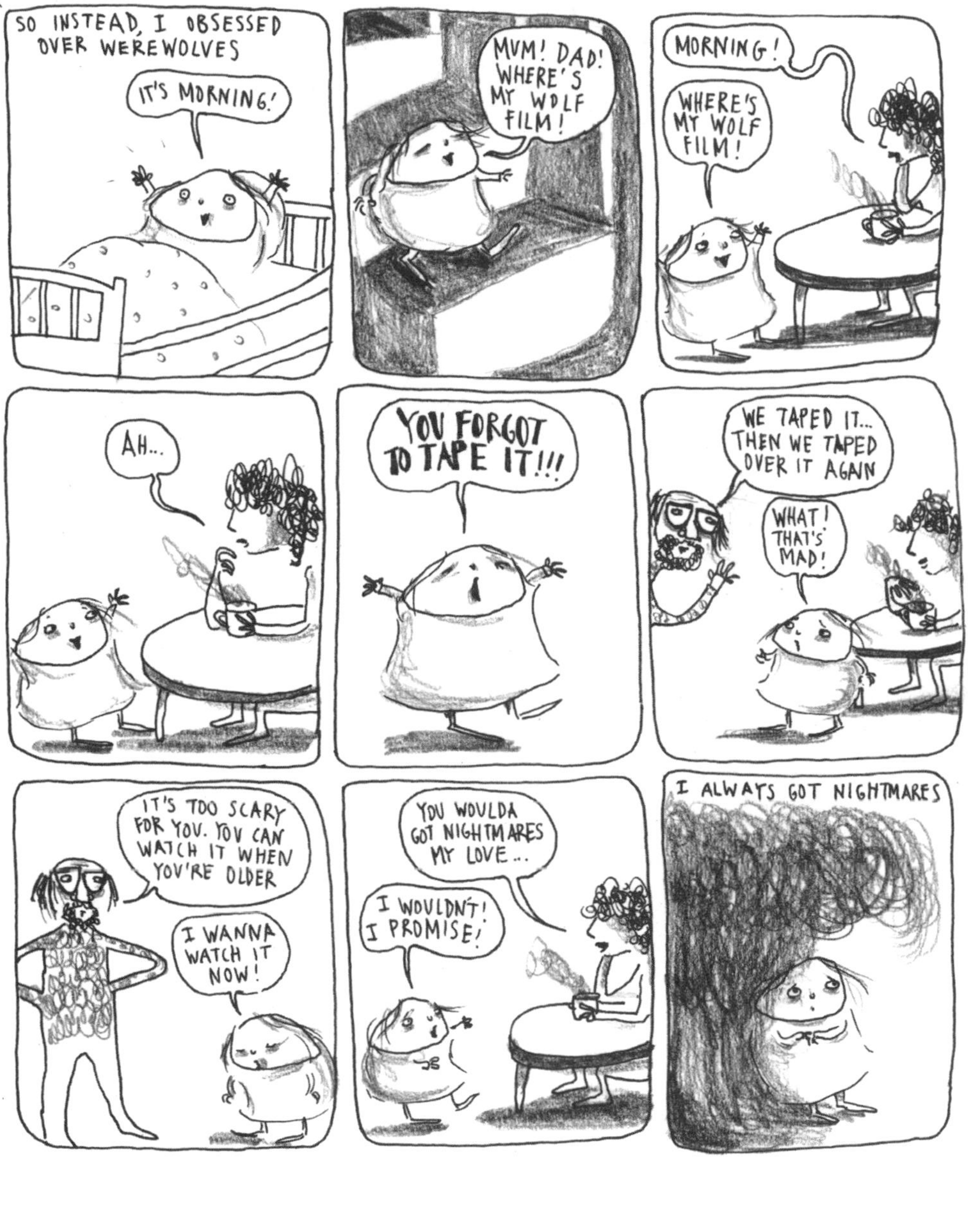
SO INSTEAD, I OBSESSED OVER WEREWOLVES
IT'S MORNING!
MUM! DAD! WHERE'S MY WOLF FILM!
MORNING!
WHERE'S MY WOLF FILM!
AH...
YOU FORGOT TO TAPE IT!!!
WE TAPED IT... THEN WE TAPED OVER IT AGAIN
WHAT! THAT'S MAD!
IT'S TOO SCARY FOR YOU. YOU CAN WATCH IT WHEN YOU'RE OLDER
I WANNA WATCH IT NOW!
YOU WOULDA GOT NIGHTMARES MY LOVE...
I WOULDN'T! I PROMISE!
I ALWAYS GOT NIGHTMARES

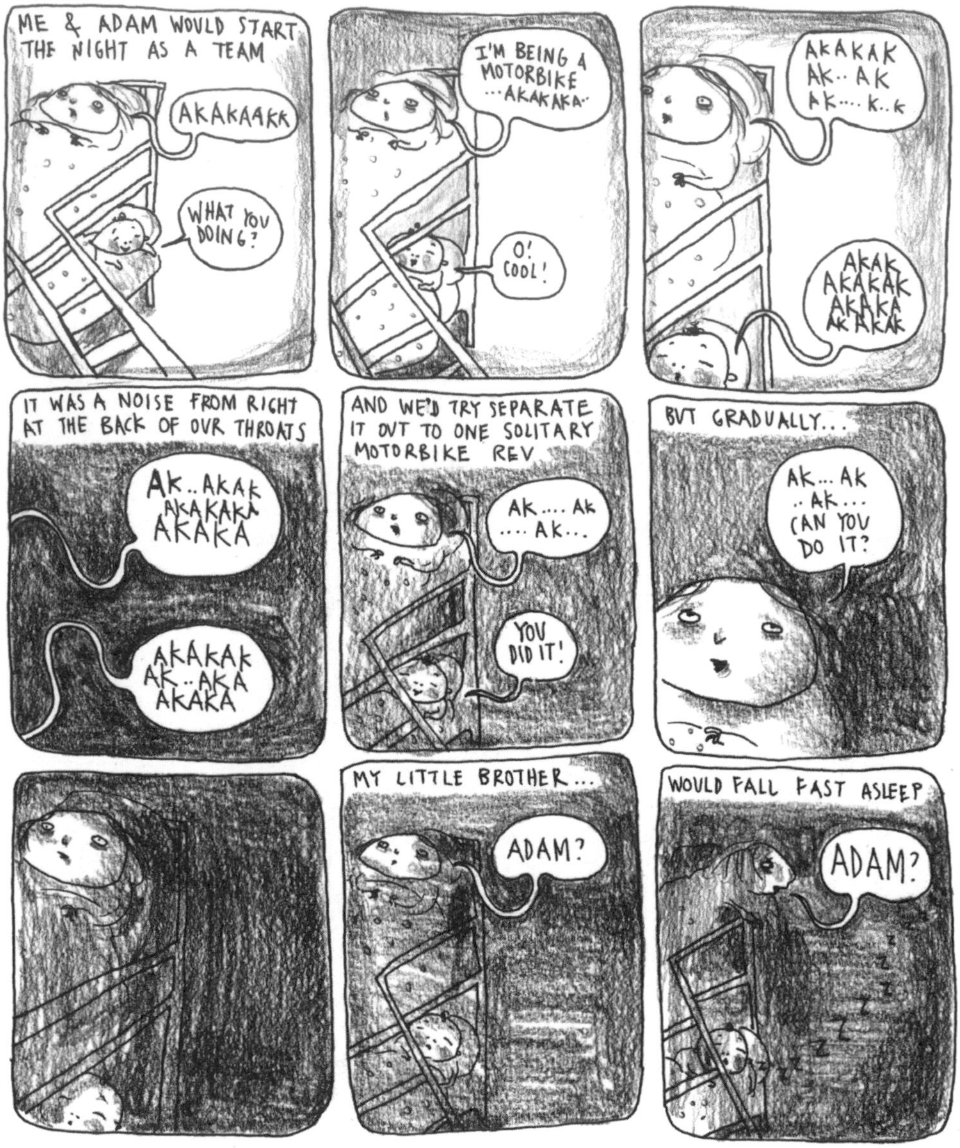
ME & ADAM WOULD START THE NIGHT AS A TEAM
AKAKAAKK
WHAT YOU DOING?
I'M BEING A MOTORBIKE ...AKAKAKA..
O! COOL!
AKAKAK AK.. AK AK.... K..K
AKAK AKAKAK AKAKA AKAKAK
IT WAS A NOISE FROM RIGHT AT THE BACK OF OUR THROATS
AK..AKAK AKAKAKA AKAKA
AKAKAK AK..AKA AKAKA
AND WE'D TRY SEPARATE IT OUT TO ONE SOLITARY MOTORBIKE REV
AK.... AK .... AK...
YOU DID IT!
BUT GRADUALLY...
AK... AK .. AK... CAN YOU DO IT?
MY LITTLE BROTHER...
ADAM?
WOULD FALL FAST ASLEEP
ADAM?

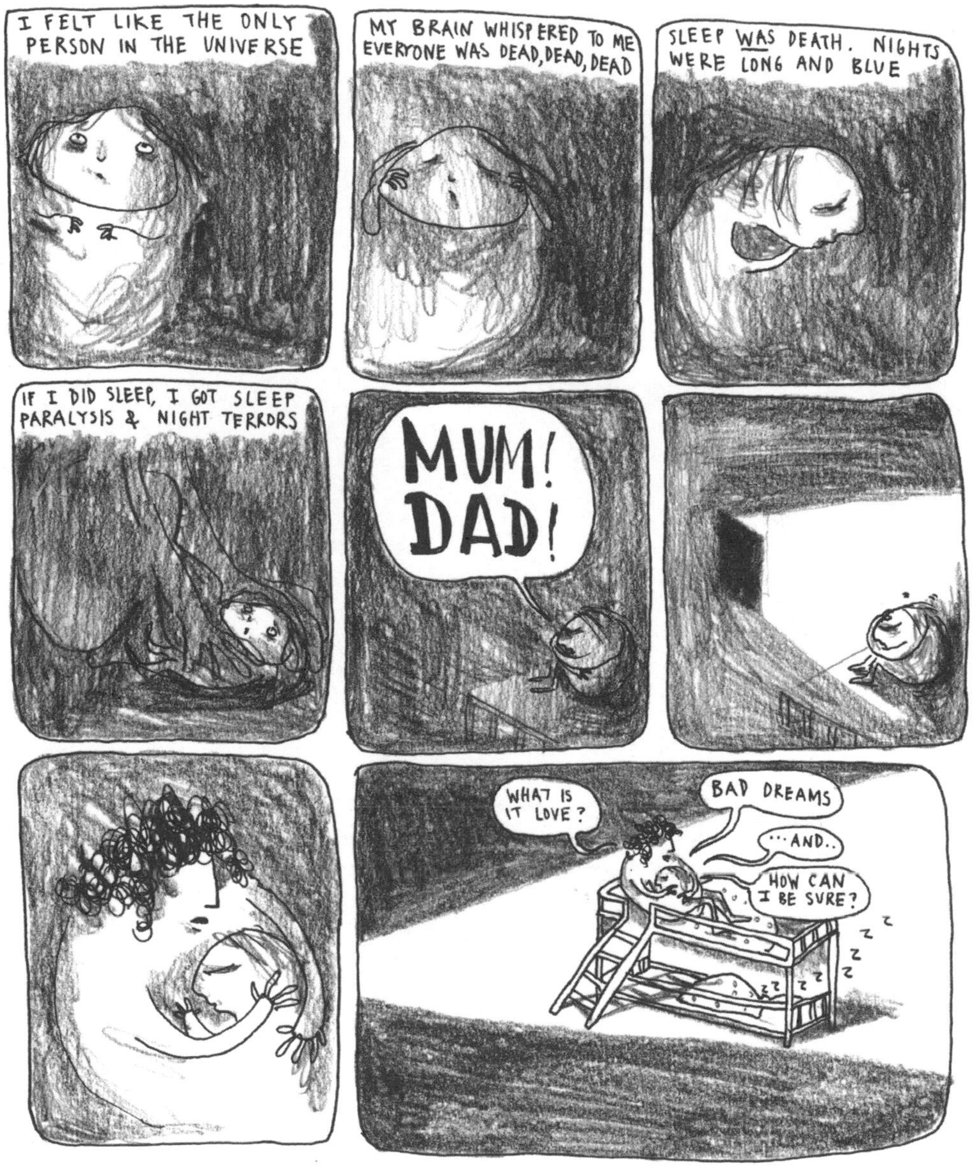
I FELT LIKE THE ONLY PERSON IN THE UNIVERSE
MY BRAIN WHISPERED TO ME EVERYONE WAS DEAD, DEAD, DEAD
SLEEP WAS DEATH. NIGHTS WERE LONG AND BLUE
IF I DID SLEEP, I GOT SLEEP PARALYSIS & NIGHT TERRORS
MUM! DAD!
WHAT IS IT LOVE?
BAD DREAMS
...AND..
HOW CAN I BE SURE?
Z Z Z
Z Z Z Z

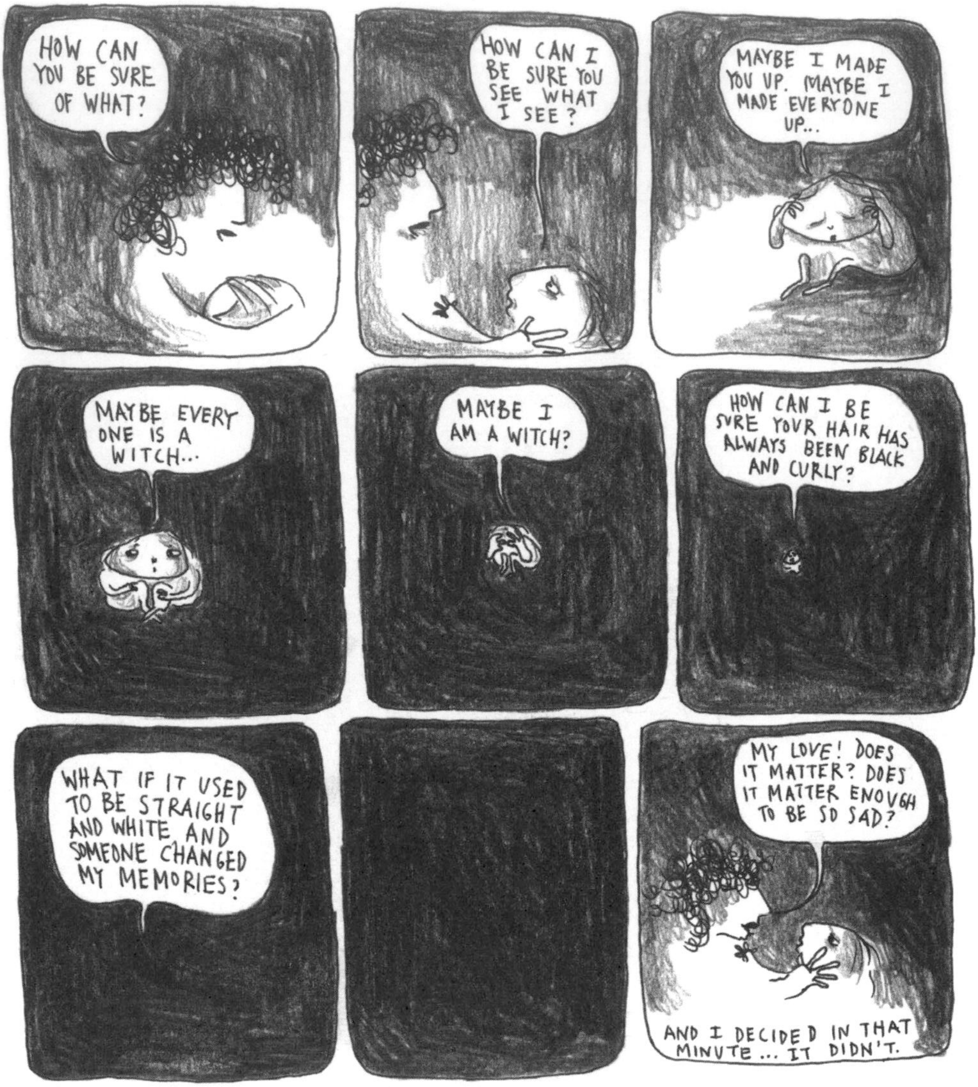
HOW CAN YOU BE SURE OF WHAT?
HOW CAN I BE SURE YOU SEE WHAT I SEE?
MAYBE I MADE YOU UP. MAYBE I MADE EVERYONE UP...
MAYBE EVERY ONE IS A WITCH...
MAYBE I AM A WITCH?
HOW CAN I BE SURE YOUR HAIR HAS ALWAYS BEEN BLACK AND CURLY?
WHAT IF IT USED TO BE STRAIGHT AND WHITE AND SOMEONE CHANGED MY MEMORIES?
MY LOVE! DOES IT MATTER? DOES IT MATTER ENOUGH TO BE SO SAD?
AND I DECIDED IN THAT MINUTE ... IT DIDN'T.

CHAPTER 3
CINNAMON CIGARETTES

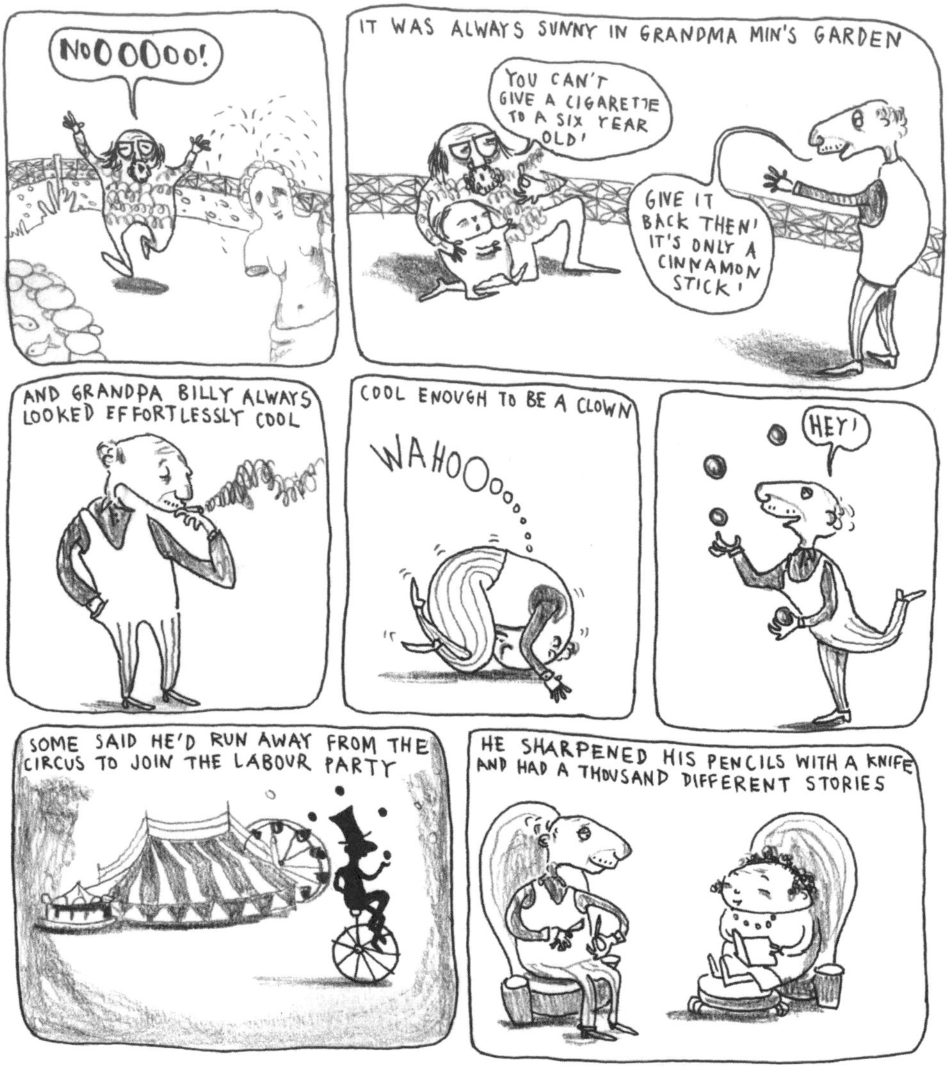
NoOOOoo!
IT WAS ALWAYS SUNNY IN GRANDMA MIN'S GARDEN
YOU CAN'T GIVE A CIGARETTE TO A SIX YEAR OLD!
GIVE IT BACK THEN! IT'S ONLY A CINNAMON STICK!
AND GRANDPA BILLY ALWAYS LOOKED EFFORTLESSLY COOL
COOL ENOUGH TO BE A CLOWN
WAHOOOooooo
HEY!
SOME SAID HE'D RUN AWAY FROM THE CIRCUS TO JOIN THE LABOUR PARTY
HE SHARPENED HIS PENCILS WITH A KNIFE AND HAD A THOUSAND DIFFERENT STORIES

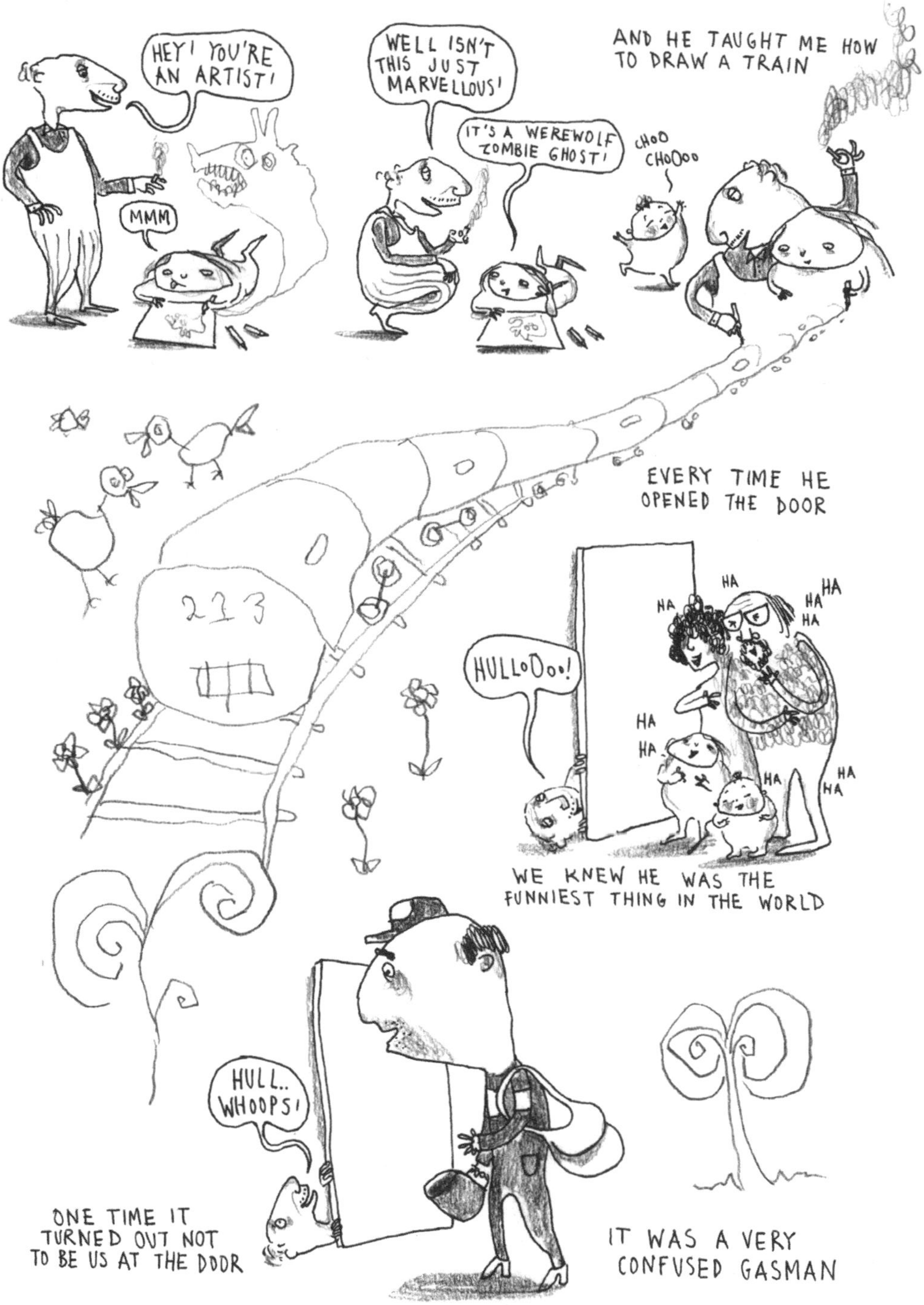
HEY! YOU'RE AN ARTIST!
MMM
WELL ISN'T THIS JUST MARVELLOUS!
IT'S A WEREWOLF ZOMBIE GHOST!
AND HE TAUGHT ME HOW TO DRAW A TRAIN
CHOO CHOOoo
223
EVERY TIME HE OPENED THE DOOR
HULLOOoo!
HA HA HA HA HA
HA HA
HA HA HA
WE KNEW HE WAS THE FUNNIEST THING IN THE WORLD
HULL.. WHOOPS!
ONE TIME IT TURNED OUT NOT TO BE US AT THE DOOR
IT WAS A VERY CONFUSED GASMAN

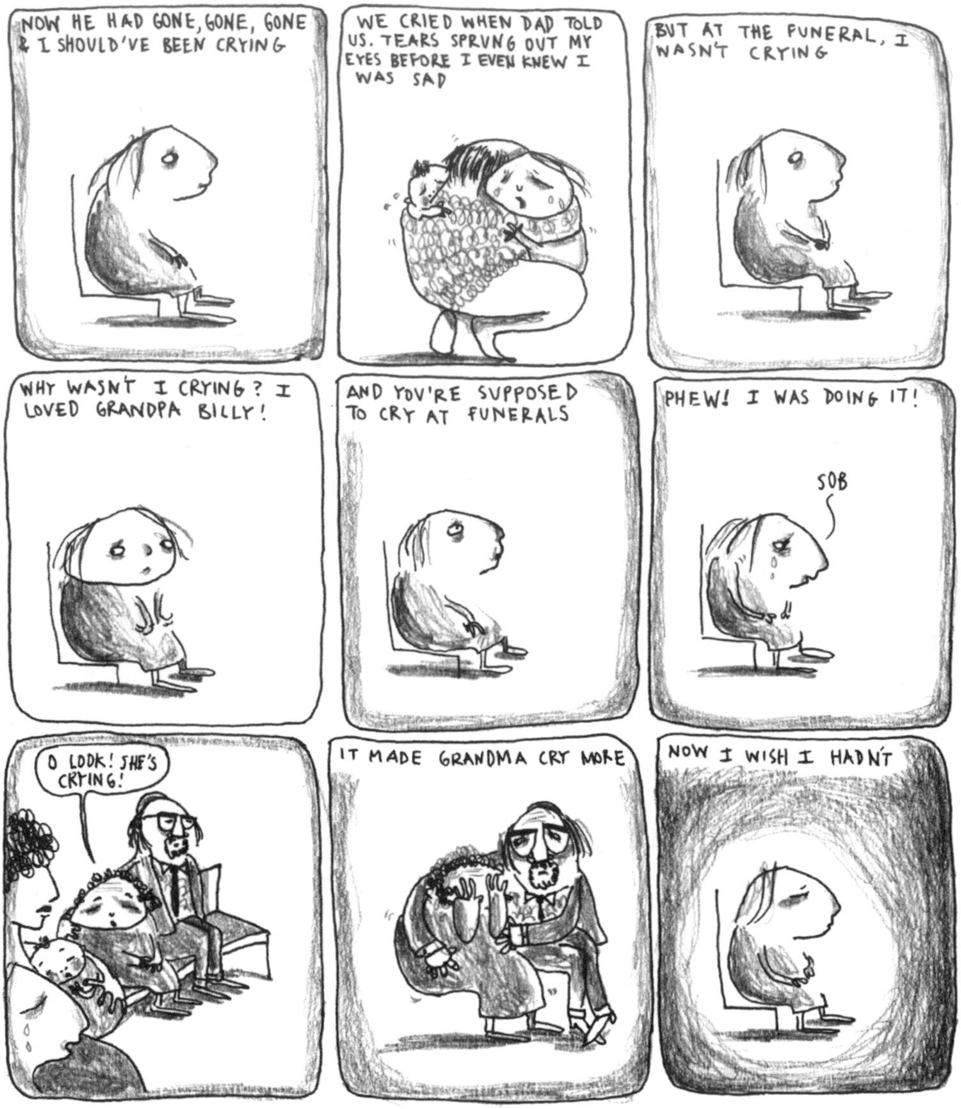
NOW HE HAD GONE, GONE, GONE & I SHOULD'VE BEEN CRYING
WE CRIED WHEN DAD TOLD US. TEARS SPRUNG OUT MY EYES BEFORE I EVEN KNEW I WAS SAD
BUT AT THE FUNERAL, I WASN'T CRYING
WHY WASN'T I CRYING? I LOVED GRANDPA BILLY!
AND YOU'RE SUPPOSED TO CRY AT FUNERALS
PHEW! I WAS DOING IT!
SOB
O LOOK! SHE'S CRYING!
IT MADE GRANDMA CRY MORE
NOW I WISH I HADN'T

AFTER THE FUNERAL WE WENT BACK TO GRANDMA MIN'S TO EAT FRIED GEFILTE FISH & GET HUGGED BY GREAT AUNTS WITH LARGE GLASSES

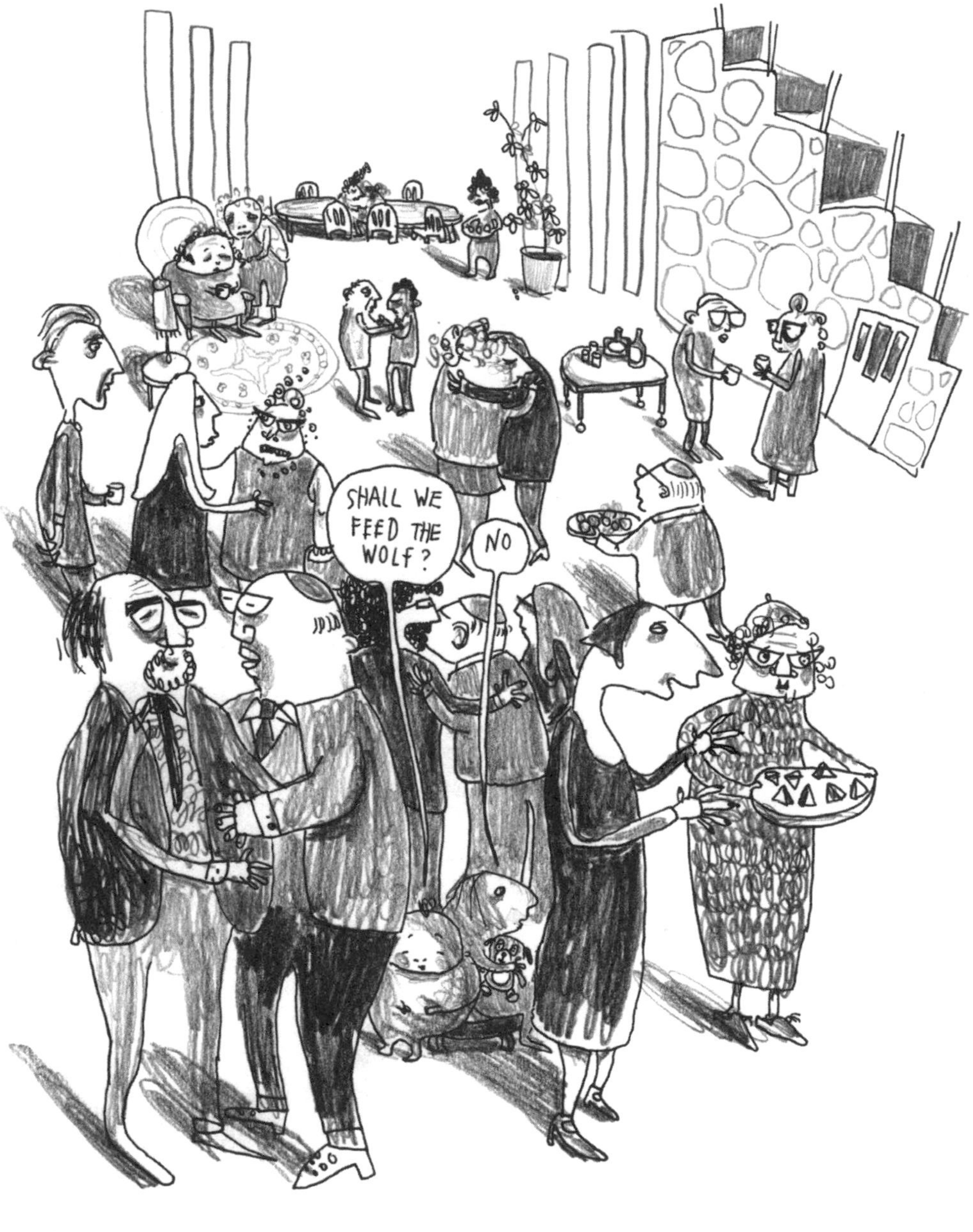
SHALL WE FEED THE WOLF?
NO

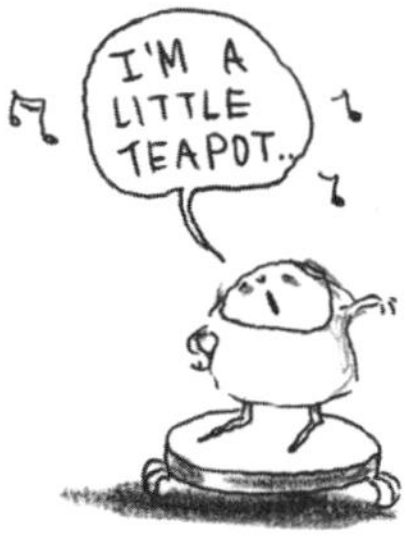
I'M A LITTLE TEAPOT..

CHAPTER 4
THE PERFORMING STOOL

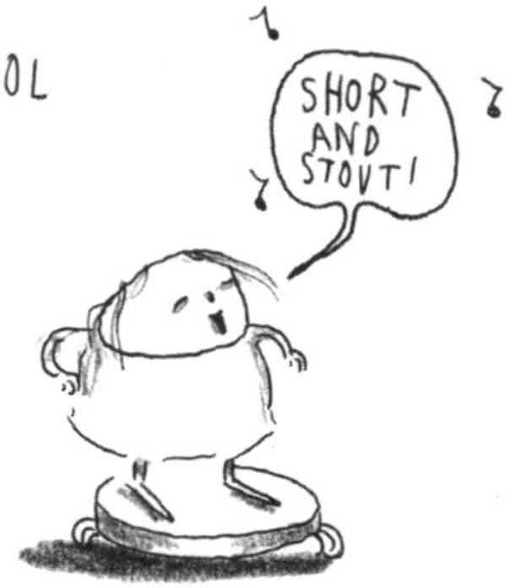
SHORT AND STOUT!

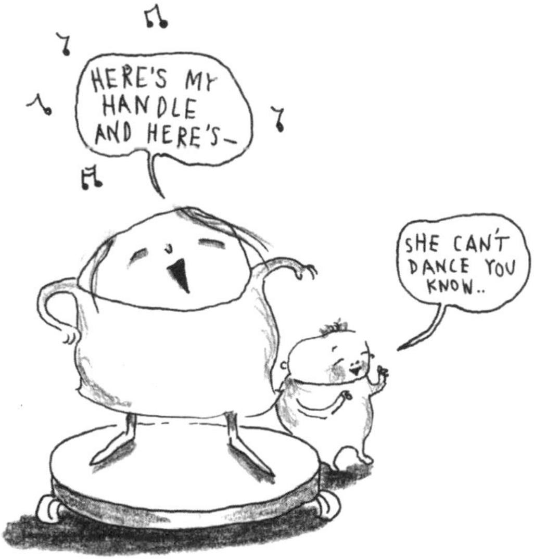
HERE'S MY HANDLE AND HERE'S—
SHE CAN'T DANCE YOU KNOW..

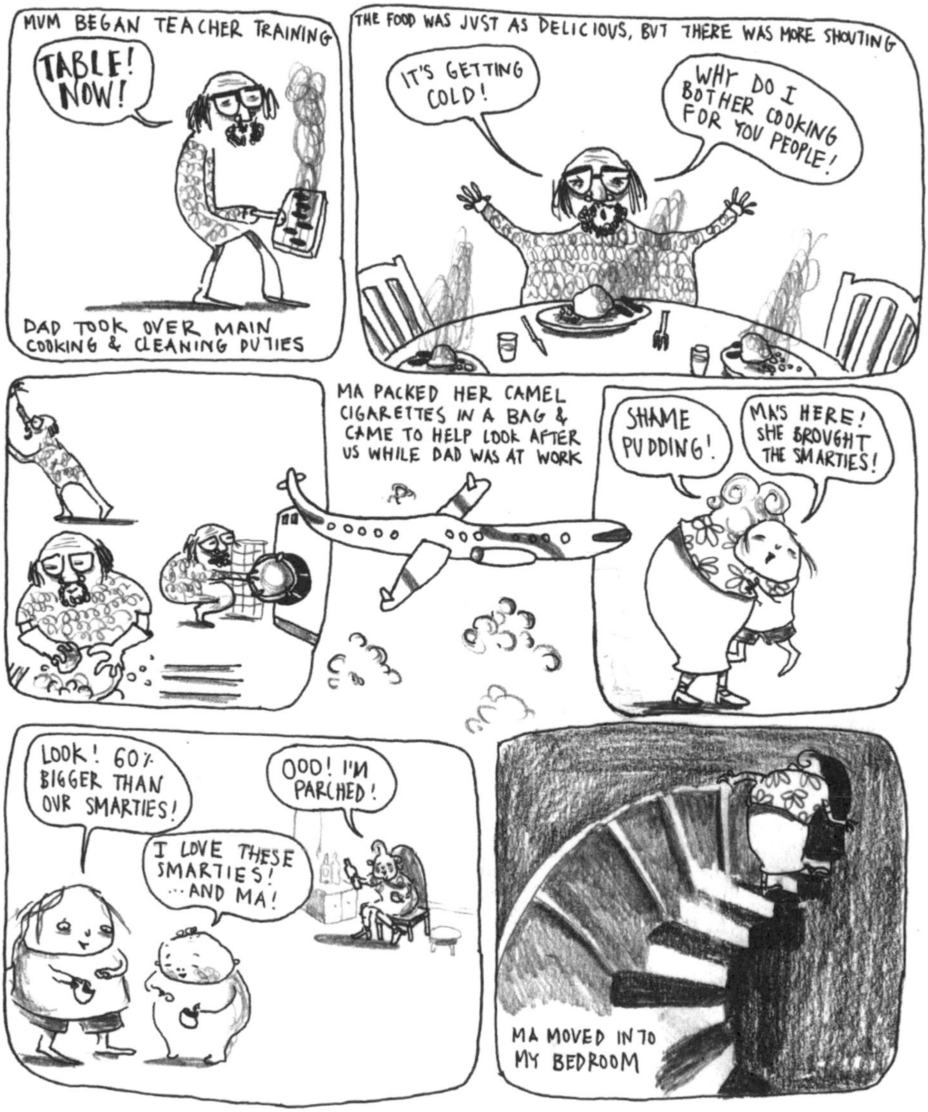
MUM BEGAN TEACHER TRAINING
TABLE! NOW!
DAD TOOK OVER MAIN COOKING & CLEANING DUTIES
THE FOOD WAS JUST AS DELICIOUS, BUT THERE WAS MORE SHOUTING
IT'S GETTING COLD!
WHY DO I BOTHER COOKING FOR YOU PEOPLE!
MA PACKED HER CAMEL CIGARETTES IN A BAG & CAME TO HELP LOOK AFTER US WHILE DAD WAS AT WORK
SHAME PUDDING!
MA'S HERE! SHE BROUGHT THE SMARTIES!
LOOK! 60% BIGGER THAN OUR SMARTIES!
OOO! I'M PARCHED!
I LOVE THESE SMARTIES! ...AND MA!
MA MOVED INTO MY BEDROOM

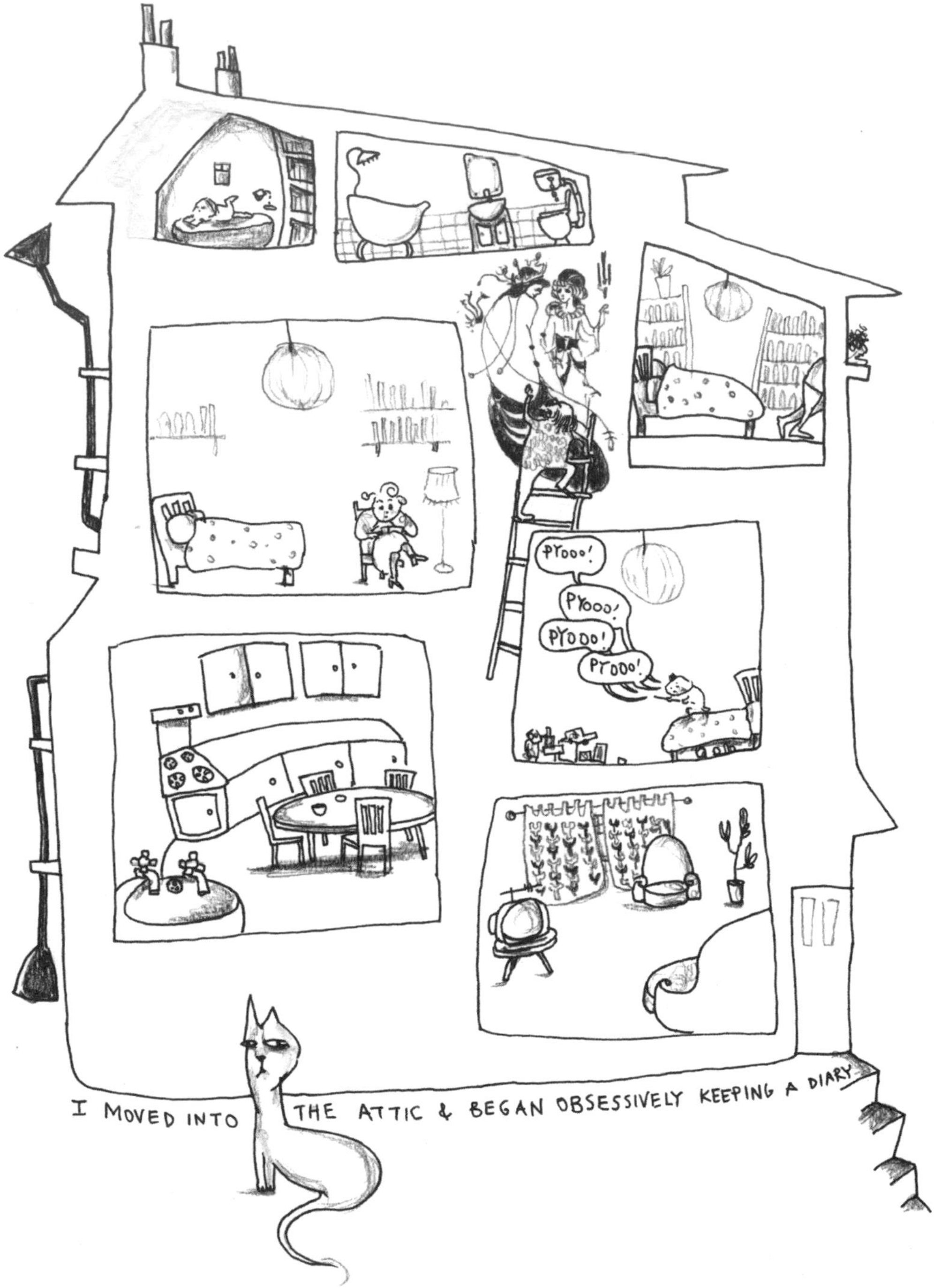
PYOOO!
PYOOO!
PYOOO!
PYOOO!
I MOVED INTO THE ATTIC & BEGAN OBSESSIVELY KEEPING A DIARY

I TOLD THAT DIARY EVERYTHING

I NEVER QUITE FELT LIKE TELLING MY FRIENDS EVERYTHING

BLA BLA BLA BLA BLA BLA BLA BLA

I WAS THE LISTENER

BLA BLA BLA BLA BLA BLA BLA BLA BLA

MY FIRST BEST FRIEND, PAUL WILEY...

HA HA HA HA HA HA HA HA HA HA HA HA

MISREAD AN INSTRUCTION & DREW A HEN WITH TEN LEGS

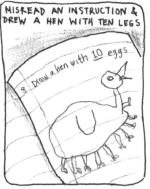

8 Draw a hen with 10 eggs

IT WAS THE FIRST TIME I GOT TOLD OFF AT SCHOOL

GO STAND IN THE CORNER! ... LAUGHING AT PEOPLE'S WORK!

I STILL THINK A HEN WITH TEN LEGS IS FUNNY...

PSST! WANT TO SEE MY PIRATE SHIP AT LUNCH TIME?

OK

..AND PAUL WILEY DIDN'T CARE

MY NEXT BEST FRIEND WAS JULIE, A MORMON WITH ECZEMA

ARRRGH!!

WE PLAYED A GAME CALLED "IMPOSSIBLE DEER"

ARRAUGHH!

RA!

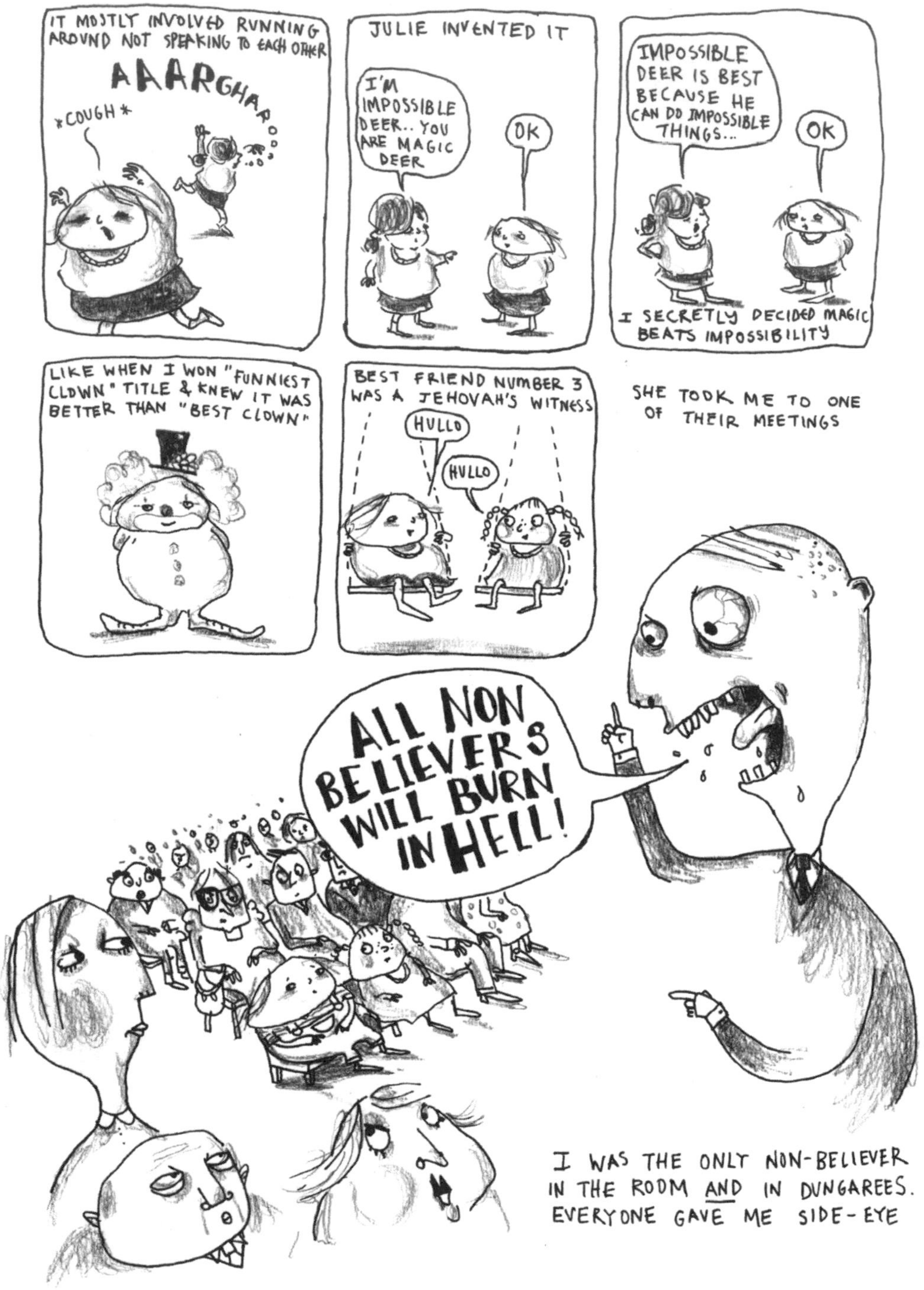
IT MOSTLY INVOLVED RUNNING AROUND NOT SPEAKING TO EACH OTHER
AAARGHAR
COUGH
JULIE INVENTED IT
I'M IMPOSSIBLE DEER.. YOU ARE MAGIC DEER
OK
IMPOSSIBLE DEER IS BEST BECAUSE HE CAN DO IMPOSSIBLE THINGS...
OK
I SECRETLY DECIDED MAGIC BEATS IMPOSSIBILITY
LIKE WHEN I WON "FUNNIEST CLOWN" TITLE & KNEW IT WAS BETTER THAN "BEST CLOWN"
BEST FRIEND NUMBER 3 WAS A JEHOVAH'S WITNESS
HULLO
HULLO
SHE TOOK ME TO ONE OF THEIR MEETINGS
ALL NON BELIEVERS WILL BURN IN HELL!
I WAS THE ONLY NON-BELIEVER IN THE ROOM AND IN DUNGAREES. EVERYONE GAVE ME SIDE-EYE

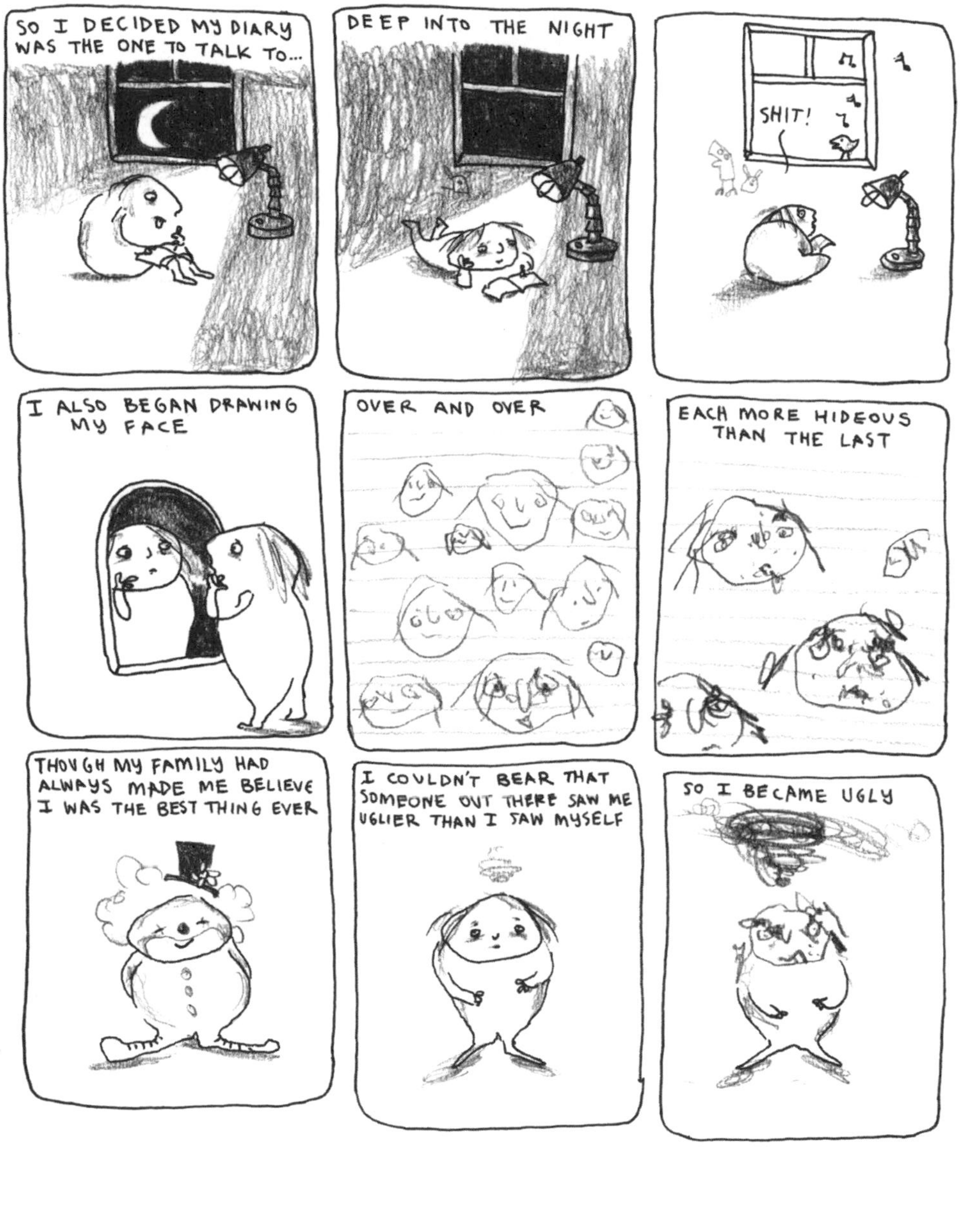
SO I DECIDED MY DIARY WAS THE ONE TO TALK TO...
DEEP INTO THE NIGHT
SHIT!
I ALSO BEGAN DRAWING MY FACE
OVER AND OVER
EACH MORE HIDEOUS THAN THE LAST
THOUGH MY FAMILY HAD ALWAYS MADE ME BELIEVE I WAS THE BEST THING EVER
I COULDN'T BEAR THAT SOMEONE OUT THERE SAW ME UGLIER THAN I SAW MYSELF
SO I BECAME UGLY

Panel 1: ALTHOUGH I KEPT TO MYSELF
WHAT YOU DOING IN THERE?
NOTHING!

Panel 2: I WAS DRAWN TO MORE OPEN PEOPLE
COME DOWN!

Panel 3: I LOVED IT WHEN PEOPLE TOLD EMBARRASSING STORIES
I JUST WEED MY PANTS IN FRONT OF HAMISH BROWN!

Panel 4: MAYBE I WASN'T THE ONLY FREAK
DON'T THINK HE SAW...

Panel 5: I ESPECIALLY LOVED GIRLS WITH GRUBBY STORIES
IT SMELT OF FISHFINGERS!

Panel 6: GIRLS WEREN'T MEANT TO BE GRUBBY & BOYS WOULDN'T LIKE GRUBBY GIRLS.
SO CAN I BORROW SOME PANTS OR WHAT?

Panel 7: ABOUT THIS TIME I DISCOVERED MY JEHOVAH'S WITNESS GOT OUT OF ASSEMBLY
WHERE ARE YOU GOING?
THE SPECIAL ROOM

Panel 8: SHE WAS ALLOWED TO SIT OUT BECAUSE OF HER FAITH
WHUT!

Panel 9: I HAD A PLAN TO GET INTO THAT MYSTERY ROOM
I'LL TELL MISS COX I'M JEWISH & I'M PROBABLY NOT ALLOWED IN ASSEMBLY

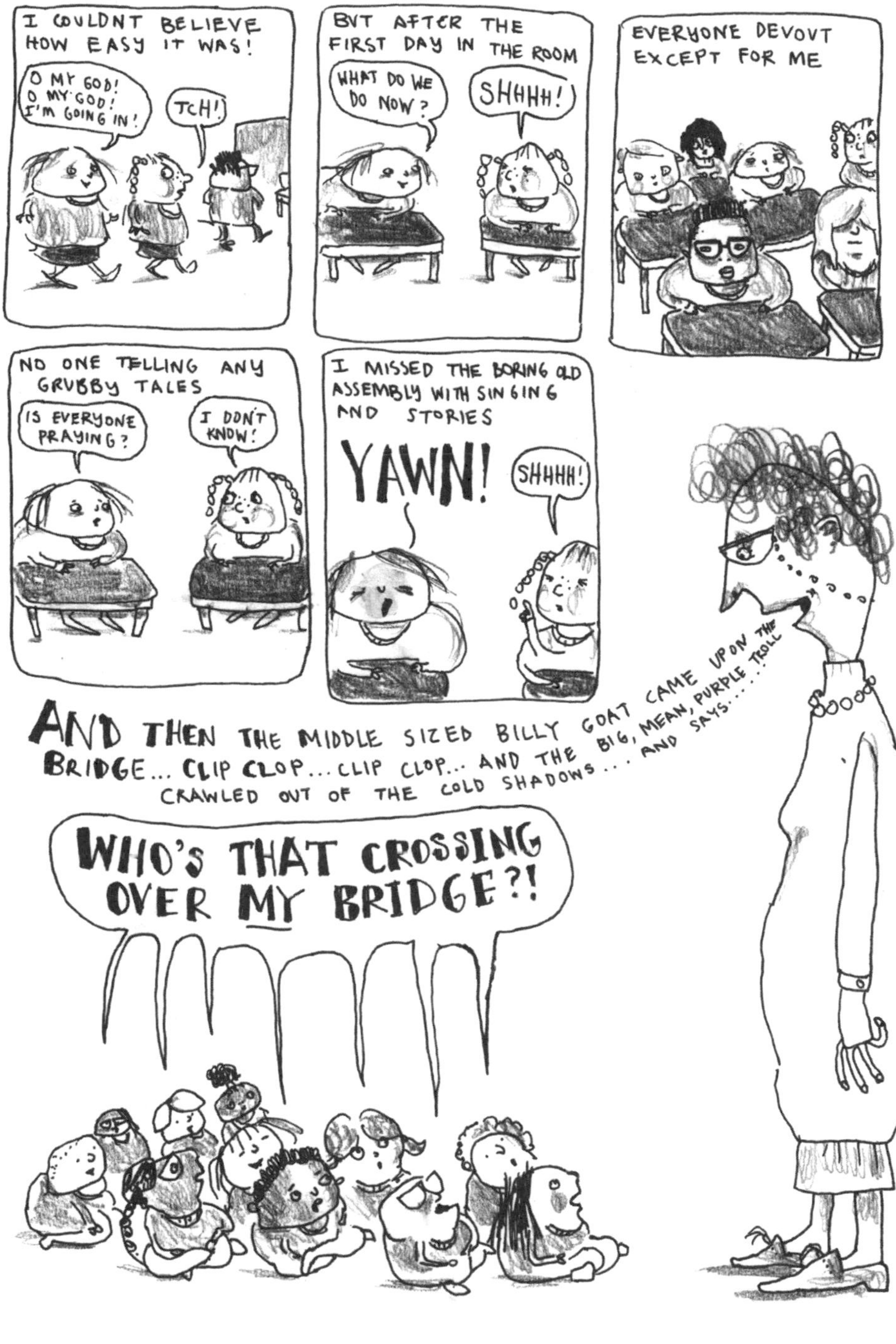
I COULDNT BELIEVE HOW EASY IT WAS!
O MY GOD! O MY GOD! I'M GOING IN!
TCH!
BUT AFTER THE FIRST DAY IN THE ROOM
WHAT DO WE DO NOW?
SHHHH!
EVERYONE DEVOUT EXCEPT FOR ME
NO ONE TELLING ANY GRUBBY TALES
IS EVERYONE PRAYING?
I DON'T KNOW!
I MISSED THE BORING OLD ASSEMBLY WITH SINGING AND STORIES
YAWN!
SHHHH!
AND THEN THE MIDDLE SIZED BILLY GOAT CAME UPON THE BRIDGE... CLIP CLOP... CLIP CLOP... AND THE BIG, MEAN, PURPLE TROLL CRAWLED OUT OF THE COLD SHADOWS... AND SAYS.....
WHO'S THAT CROSSING OVER MY BRIDGE?!

SPRING WAS FOR PESACH... PASSOVER... AND FULL OF GREAT AUNTS AND UNCLES WITH MASSIVE EARS AND INCREDIBLE NOISE...

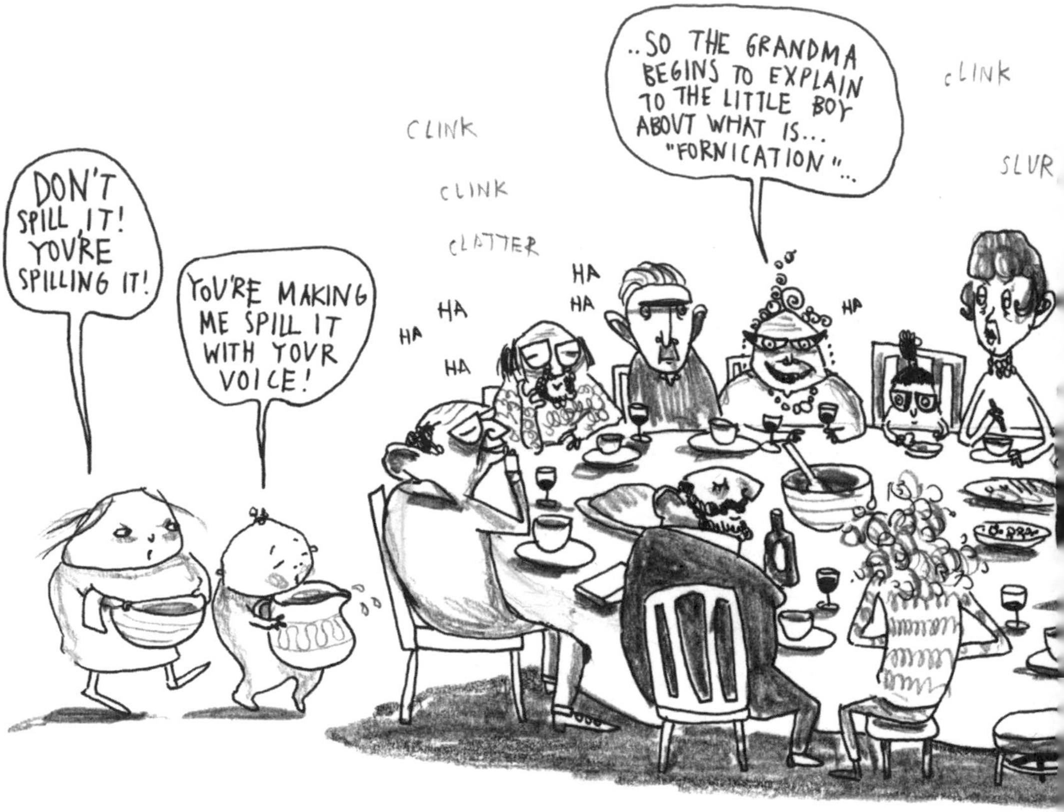
DON'T SPILL IT! YOU'RE SPILLING IT!
YOU'RE MAKING ME SPILL IT WITH YOUR VOICE!
CLINK
CLINK
CLATTER
HA
HA
HA
HA
HA
HA
HA
..SO THE GRANDMA BEGINS TO EXPLAIN TO THE LITTLE BOY ABOUT WHAT IS... "FORNICATION"...
CLINK
SLUR

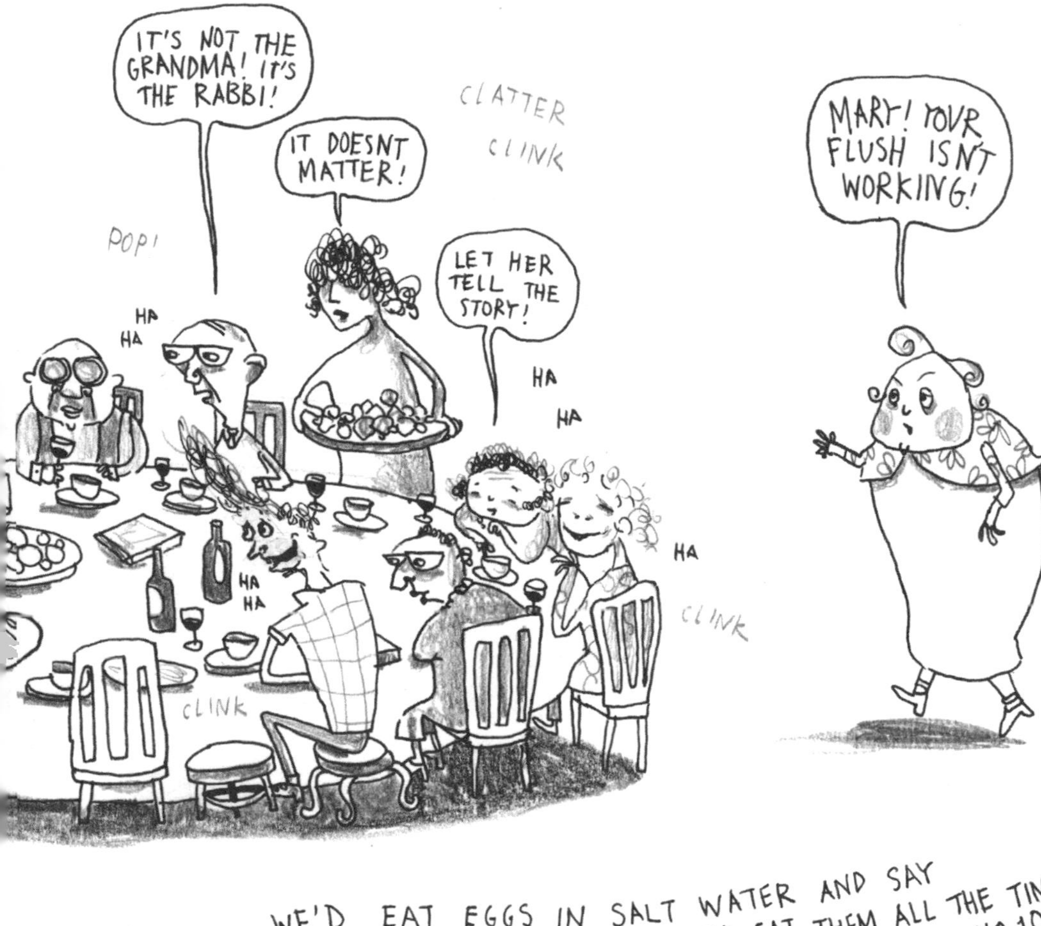

POP!
IT'S NOT THE GRANDMA! IT'S THE RABBI!
IT DOESNT MATTER!
CLATTER
CLINK
LET HER TELL THE STORY!
HA HA
HA
HA
HA HA
HA
CLINK
CLINK
MARY! YOUR FLUSH ISN'T WORKING!

WE'D EAT EGGS IN SALT WATER AND SAY
"O! THESE TASTE SO GOOD! WE SHOULD EAT THEM ALL THE TIME!"
BUT WE NEVER DID. AND WE DRANK PALWINS NO.10
UNTIL OUR TEETH WENT BLUE.

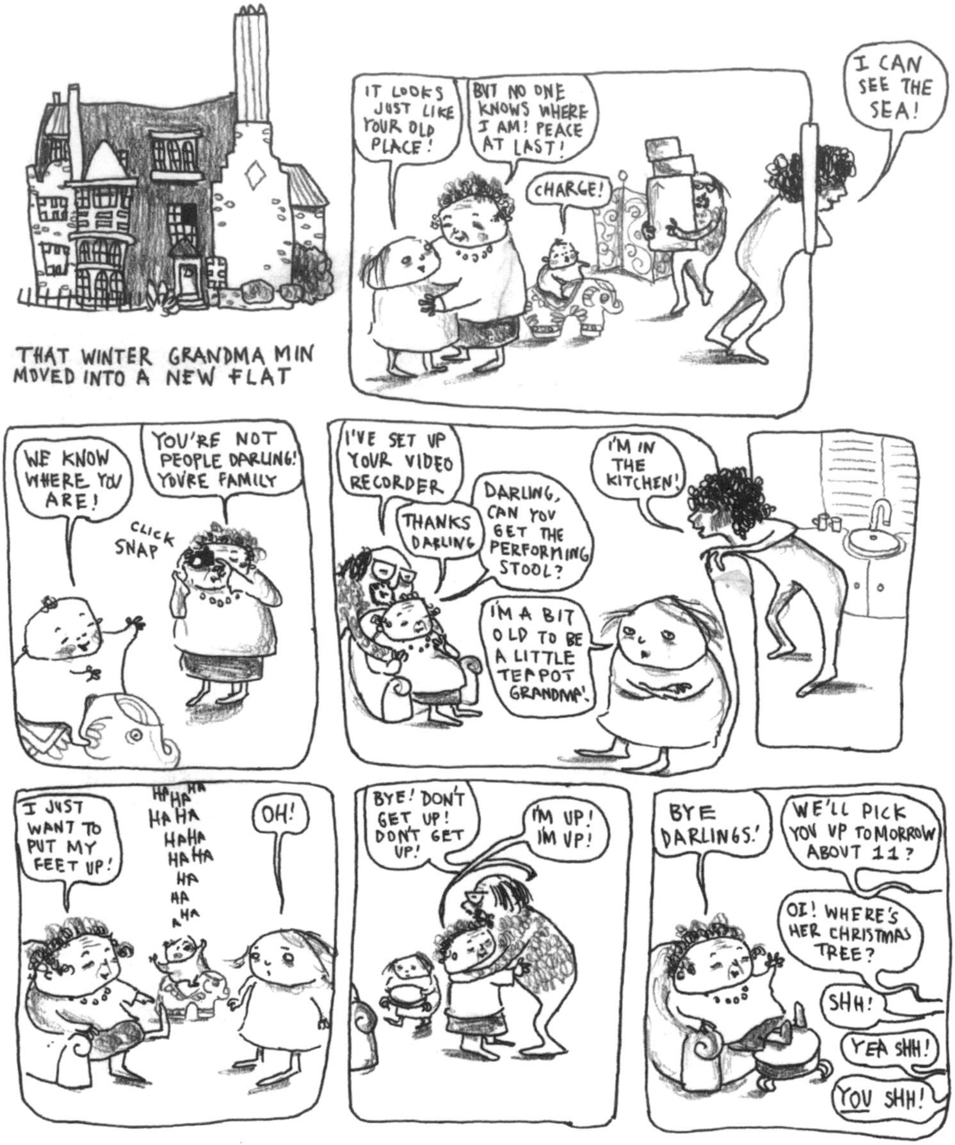
THAT WINTER GRANDMA MIN MOVED INTO A NEW FLAT
IT LOOKS JUST LIKE YOUR OLD PLACE!
BUT NO ONE KNOWS WHERE I AM! PEACE AT LAST!
CHARGE!
I CAN SEE THE SEA!
WE KNOW WHERE YOU ARE!
YOU'RE NOT PEOPLE DARLING! YOU'RE FAMILY
CLICK
SNAP
I'VE SET UP YOUR VIDEO RECORDER
THANKS DARLING
DARLING, CAN YOU GET THE PERFORMING STOOL?
I'M IN THE KITCHEN!
I'M A BIT OLD TO BE A LITTLE TEAPOT GRANDMA!
I JUST WANT TO PUT MY FEET UP!
HA HA HA HA HA HA HA HA HA HA HA HA
OH!
BYE! DON'T GET UP! DON'T GET UP!
I'M UP! I'M UP!
BYE DARLINGS!
WE'LL PICK YOU UP TOMORROW ABOUT 11?
OI! WHERE'S HER CHRISTMAS TREE?
SHH!
YEA SHH!
YOU SHH!

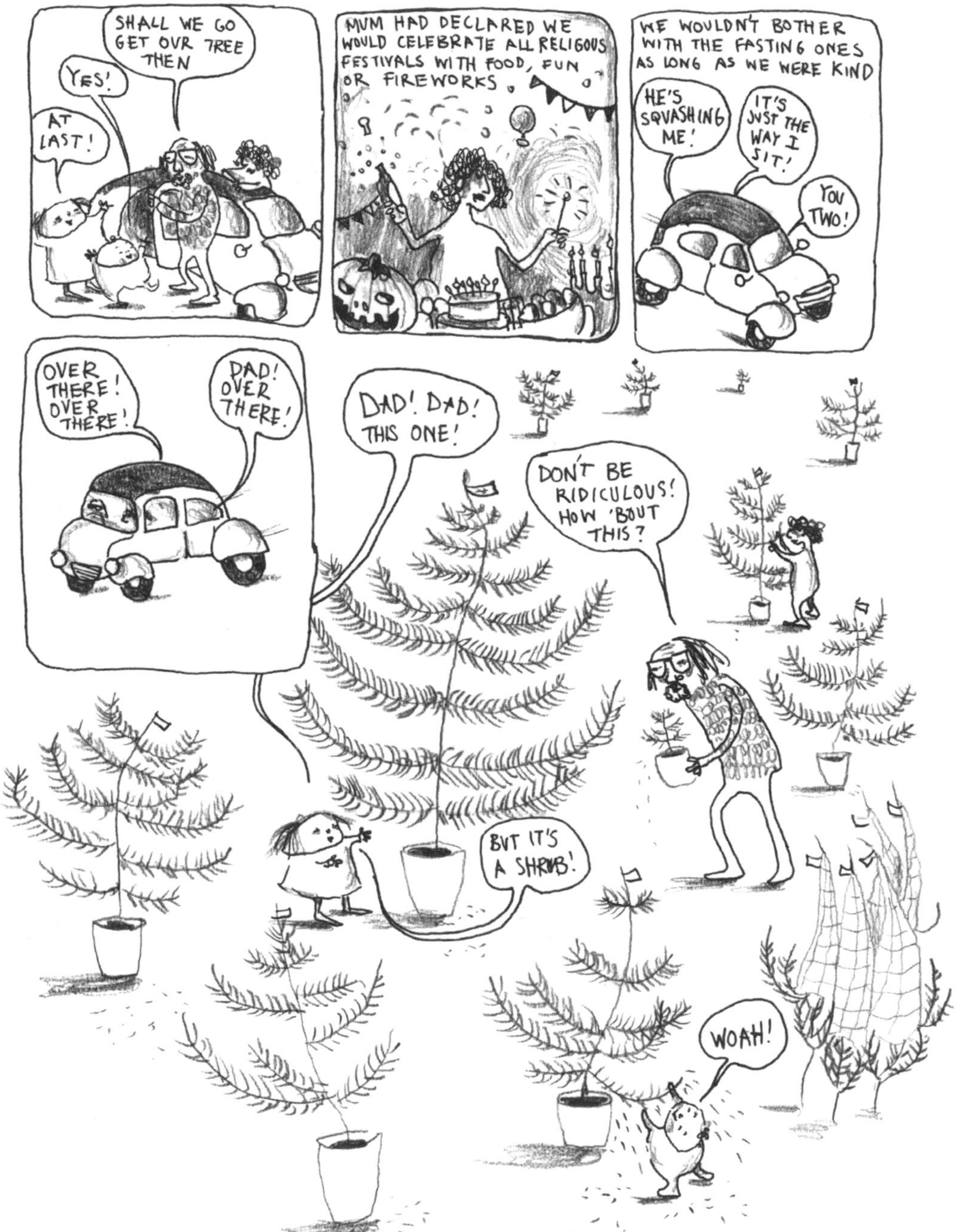
SHALL WE GO GET OUR TREE THEN
YES!
AT LAST!
MUM HAD DECLARED WE WOULD CELEBRATE ALL RELIGOUS FESTIVALS WITH FOOD, FUN OR FIREWORKS
WE WOULDN'T BOTHER WITH THE FASTING ONES AS LONG AS WE WERE KIND
HE'S SQUASHING ME!
IT'S JUST THE WAY I SIT!
YOU TWO!
OVER THERE! OVER THERE!
DAD! OVER THERE!
DAD! DAD! THIS ONE!
DON'T BE RIDICULOUS! HOW 'BOUT THIS?
BUT IT'S A SHRUB!
WOAH!

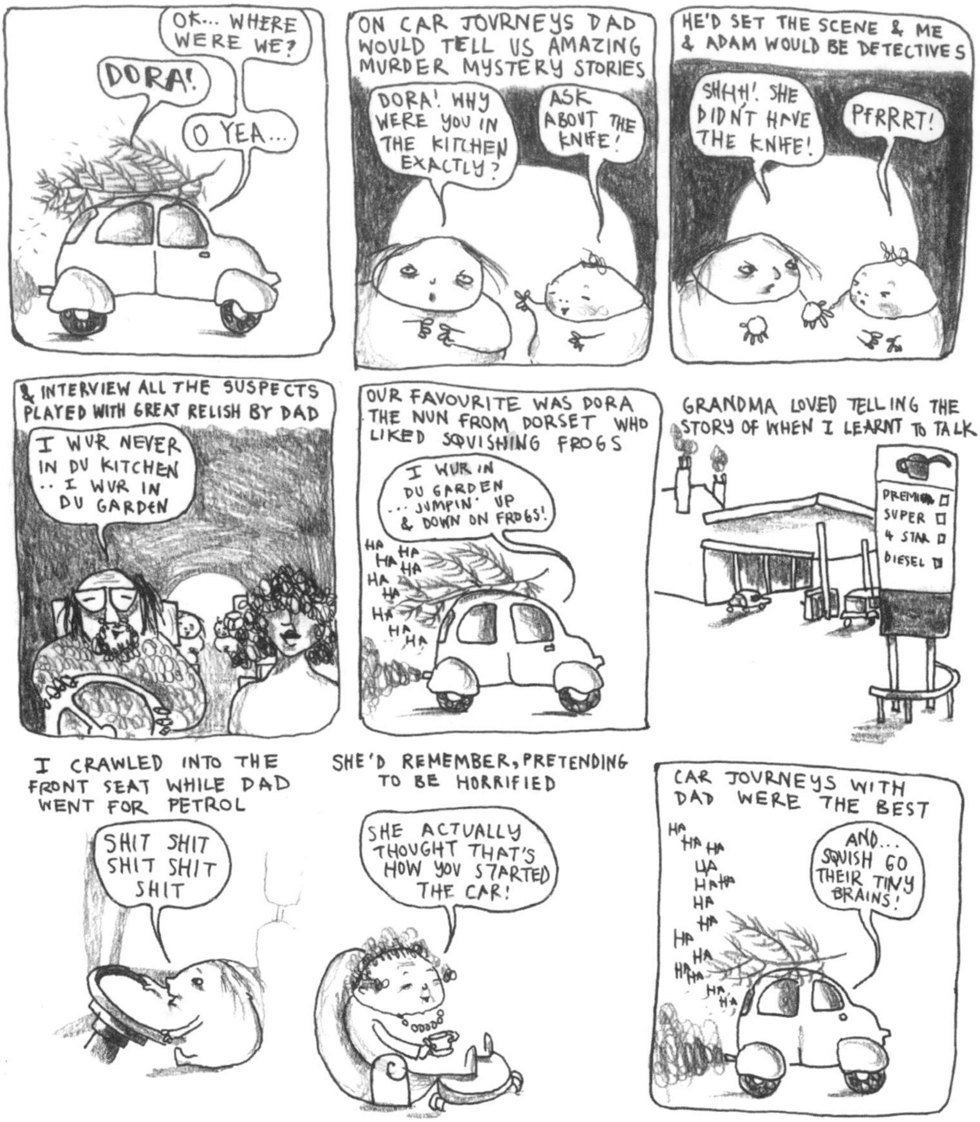
OK... WHERE WERE WE?
DORA!
O YEA...
ON CAR JOURNEYS DAD WOULD TELL US AMAZING MURDER MYSTERY STORIES
DORA! WHY WERE YOU IN THE KITCHEN EXACTLY?
ASK ABOUT THE KNIFE!
HE'D SET THE SCENE & ME & ADAM WOULD BE DETECTIVES
SHHH! SHE DIDN'T HAVE THE KNIFE!
PFRRRT!
& INTERVIEW ALL THE SUSPECTS PLAYED WITH GREAT RELISH BY DAD
I WUR NEVER IN DU KITCHEN .. I WUR IN DU GARDEN
OUR FAVOURITE WAS DORA THE NUN FROM DORSET WHO LIKED SQUISHING FROGS
I WUR IN DU GARDEN ... JUMPIN' UP & DOWN ON FROGS!
HA HA HA HA HA HA HA HA HA HA
GRANDMA LOVED TELLING THE STORY OF WHEN I LEARNT TO TALK
SUPER
4 STAR
DIESEL
I CRAWLED INTO THE FRONT SEAT WHILE DAD WENT FOR PETROL
SHIT SHIT SHIT SHIT SHIT
SHE'D REMEMBER, PRETENDING TO BE HORRIFIED
SHE ACTUALLY THOUGHT THAT'S HOW YOU STARTED THE CAR!
CAR JOURNEYS WITH DAD WERE THE BEST
AND... SQUISH GO THEIR TINY BRAINS!
HA HA HA HA HA HA HA HA HA HA HA HA HA HA

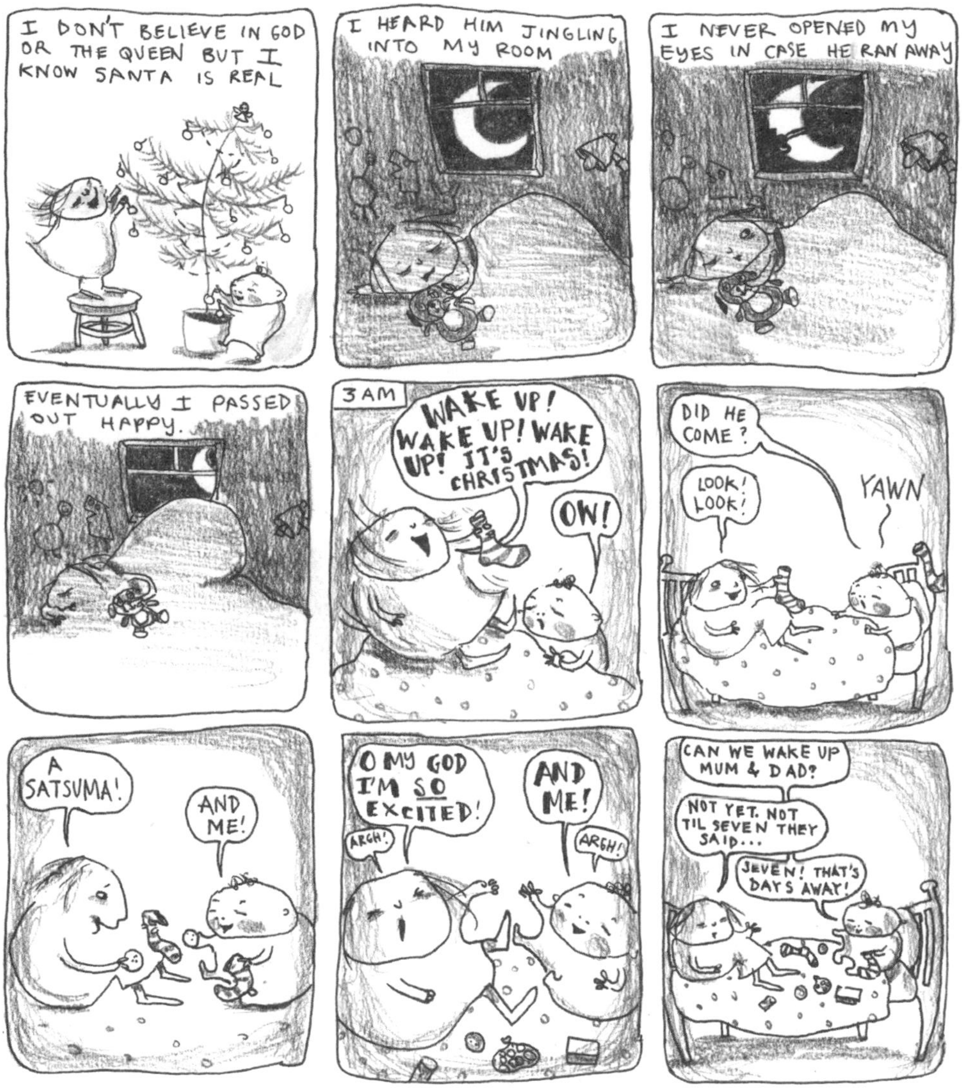
I DON'T BELIEVE IN GOD OR THE QUEEN BUT I KNOW SANTA IS REAL
I HEARD HIM JINGLING INTO MY ROOM
I NEVER OPENED MY EYES IN CASE HE RAN AWAY
EVENTUALLY I PASSED OUT HAPPY.
3AM
WAKE UP! WAKE UP! WAKE UP! IT'S CHRISTMAS!
OW!
DID HE COME?
LOOK! LOOK!
YAWN
A SATSUMA!
AND ME!
O MY GOD I'M SO EXCITED!
ARGH!
AND ME!
ARGH!
CAN WE WAKE UP MUM & DAD?
NOT YET. NOT TIL SEVEN THEY SAID...
SEVEN! THAT'S DAYS AWAY!

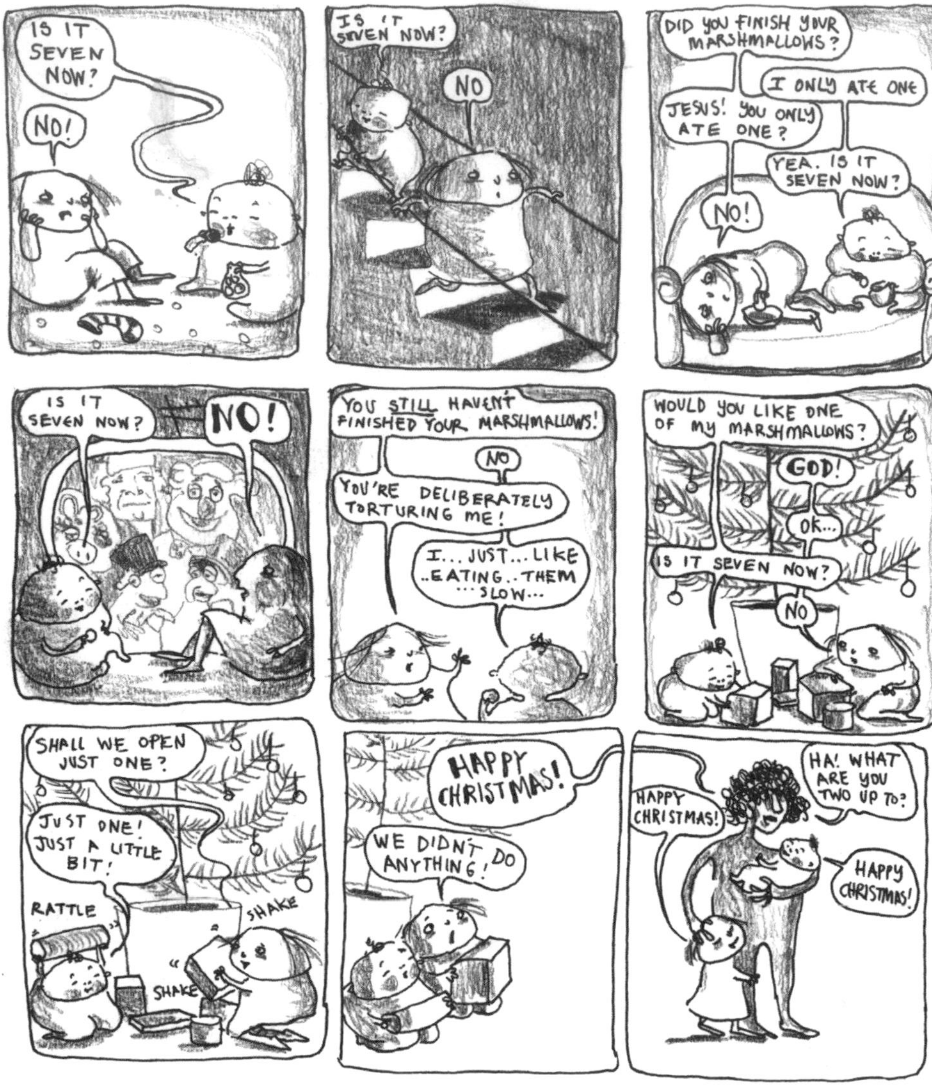

IS IT SEVEN NOW?
NO!
IS IT SEVEN NOW?
NO
DID YOU FINISH YOUR MARSHMALLOWS?
I ONLY ATE ONE
JESUS! YOU ONLY ATE ONE?
YEA. IS IT SEVEN NOW?
NO!
IS IT SEVEN NOW?
NO!
YOU STILL HAVEN'T FINISHED YOUR MARSHMALLOWS!
NO
YOU'RE DELIBERATELY TORTURING ME!
I... JUST... LIKE ..EATING.. THEM ...SLOW...
WOULD YOU LIKE ONE OF MY MARSHMALLOWS?
GOD!
OK...
IS IT SEVEN NOW?
NO
SHALL WE OPEN JUST ONE?
JUST ONE! JUST A LITTLE BIT!
RATTLE
SHAKE
SHAKE
HAPPY CHRISTMAS!
WE DIDN'T DO ANYTHING!
HA! WHAT ARE YOU TWO UP TO?
HAPPY CHRISTMAS!
HAPPY CHRISTMAS!

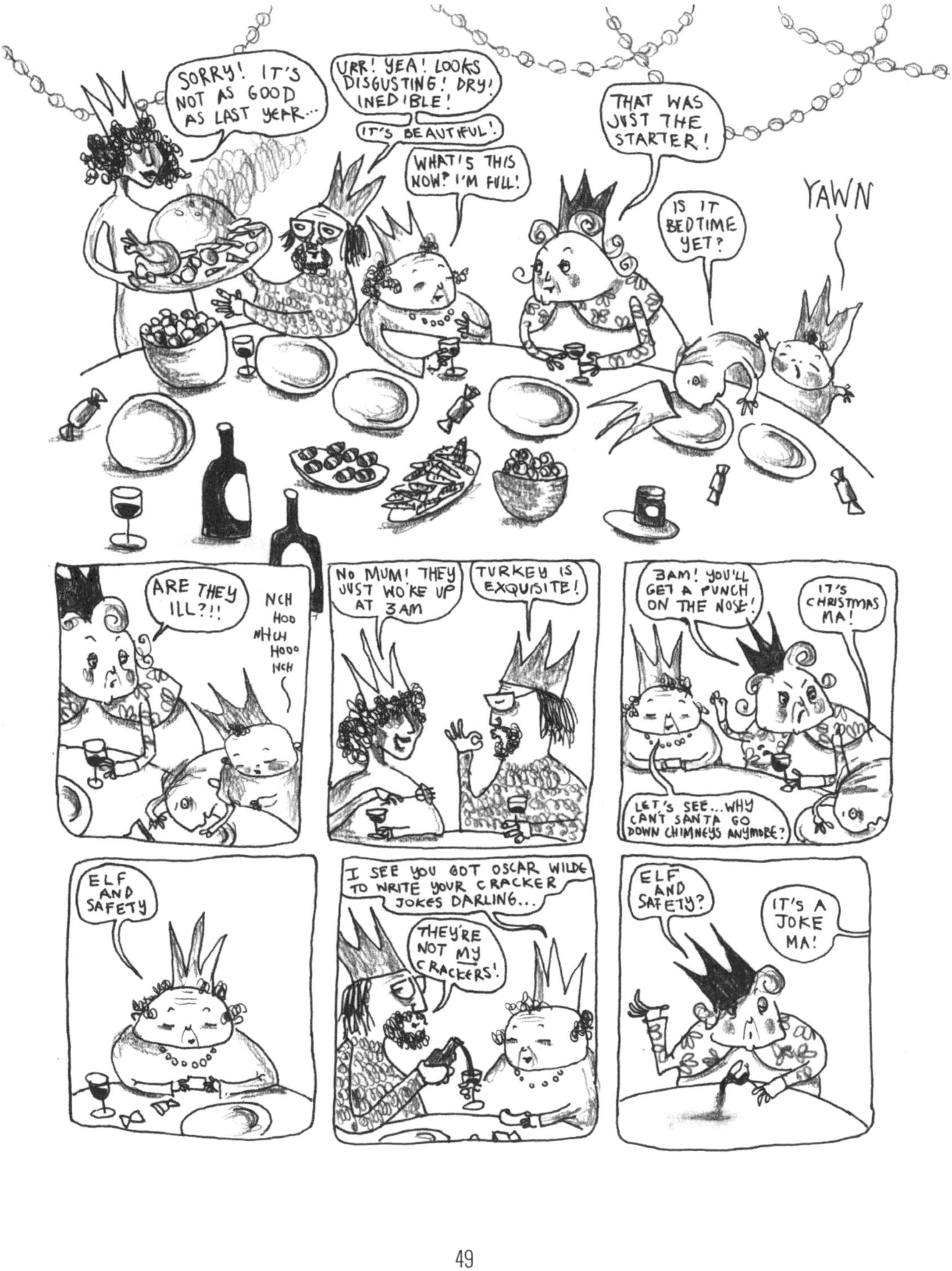
SORRY! IT'S NOT AS GOOD AS LAST YEAR...
URR! YEA! LOOKS DISGUSTING! DRY! INEDIBLE!
IT'S BEAUTIFUL!
WHAT'S THIS NOW? I'M FULL!
THAT WAS JUST THE STARTER!
IS IT BEDTIME YET?
YAWN
ARE THEY ILL?!!
NCH HOO NHCH HOOO NCH
NO MUM! THEY JUST WOKE UP AT 3AM
TURKEY IS EXQUISITE!
3AM! YOU'LL GET A PUNCH ON THE NOSE!
IT'S CHRISTMAS MA!
LET'S SEE... WHY CAN'T SANTA GO DOWN CHIMNEYS ANYMORE?
ELF AND SAFETY
I SEE YOU GOT OSCAR WILDE TO WRITE YOUR CRACKER JOKES DARLING...
THEY'RE NOT MY CRACKERS!
ELF AND SAFETY?
IT'S A JOKE MA!

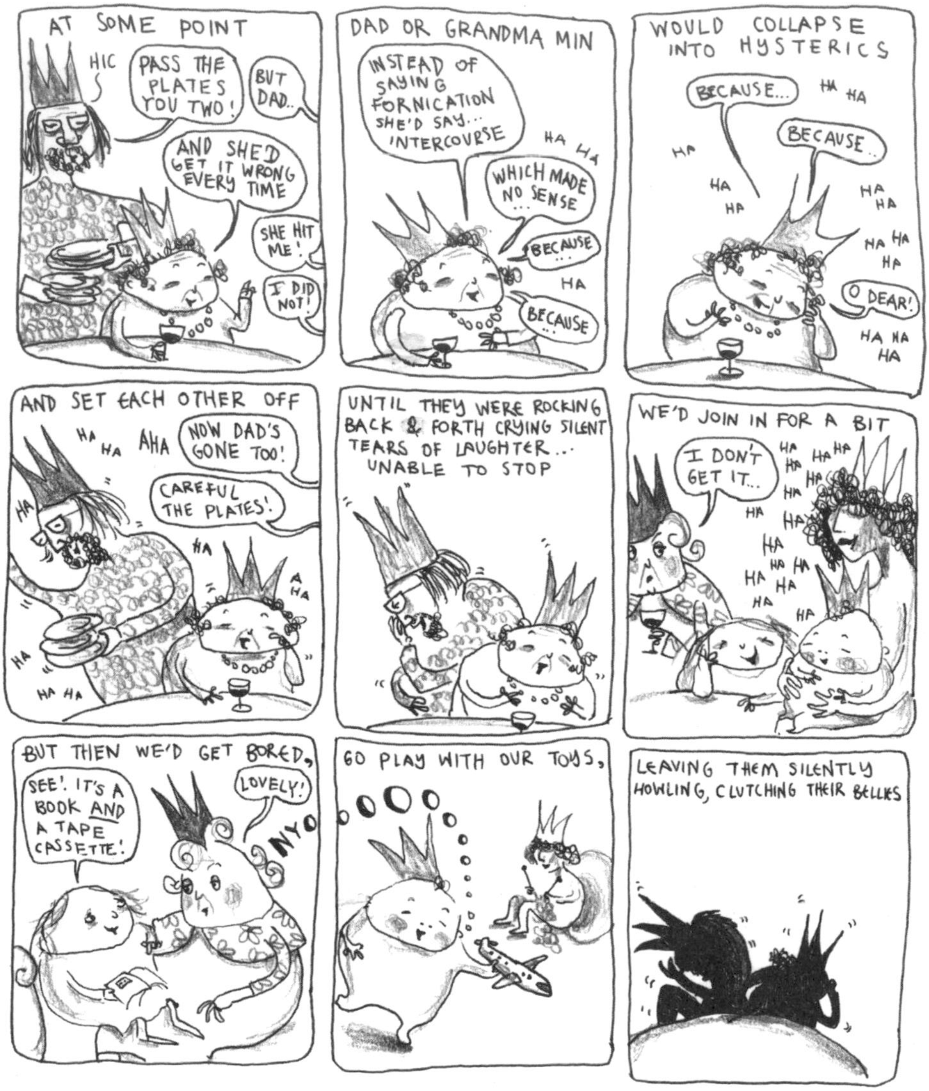
AT SOME POINT
HIC
PASS THE PLATES YOU TWO!
BUT DAD..
AND SHE'D GET IT WRONG EVERY TIME
SHE HIT ME!
I DID NOT!
DAD OR GRANDMA MIN
INSTEAD OF SAYING FORNICATION SHE'D SAY... INTERCOURSE
HA HA
WHICH MADE NO SENSE ...
BECAUSE ...
HA
BECAUSE ...
WOULD COLLAPSE INTO HYSTERICS
BECAUSE...
HA HA
BECAUSE..
HA HA HA HA HA HA HA HA
O DEAR!
HA HA HA
AND SET EACH OTHER OFF
HA HA AHA
NOW DAD'S GONE TOO!
CAREFUL THE PLATES!
HA HA HA AHA HA HA HA
UNTIL THEY WERE ROCKING BACK & FORTH CRYING SILENT TEARS OF LAUGHTER... UNABLE TO STOP
WE'D JOIN IN FOR A BIT
I DON'T GET IT...
BUT THEN WE'D GET BORED,
SEE! IT'S A BOOK AND A TAPE CASSETTE!
LOVELY!
NYO
GO PLAY WITH OUR TOYS,
LEAVING THEM SILENTLY HOWLING, CLUTCHING THEIR BELLIES

CHAPTER 5
DISCO ON A FERRY TO FRANCE

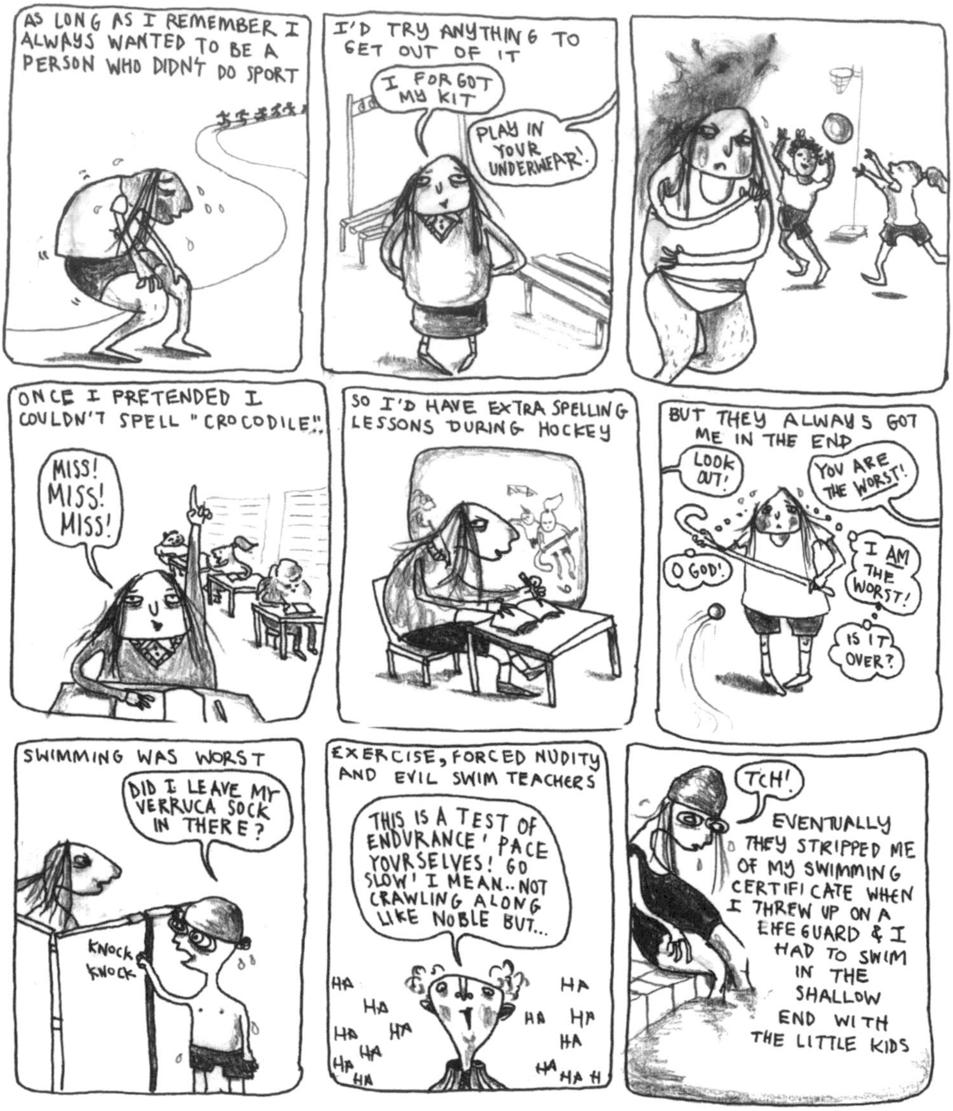
AS LONG AS I REMEMBER I ALWAYS WANTED TO BE A PERSON WHO DIDN'T DO SPORT
I'D TRY ANYTHING TO GET OUT OF IT
I FORGOT MY KIT
PLAY IN YOUR UNDERWEAR!
ONCE I PRETENDED I COULDN'T SPELL "CROCODILE"
MISS! MISS! MISS!
SO I'D HAVE EXTRA SPELLING LESSONS DURING HOCKEY
BUT THEY ALWAYS GOT ME IN THE END
LOOK OUT!
YOU ARE THE WORST!
O GOD!
I AM THE WORST!
IS IT OVER?
SWIMMING WAS WORST
DID I LEAVE MY VERRUCA SOCK IN THERE?
KNOCK KNOCK
EXERCISE, FORCED NUDITY AND EVIL SWIM TEACHERS
THIS IS A TEST OF ENDURANCE! PACE YOURSELVES! GO SLOW! I MEAN.. NOT CRAWLING ALONG LIKE NOBLE BUT...
HA HA HA HA HA HA HA HA HA HA HA HA HA H
TCH!
EVENTUALLY THEY STRIPPED ME OF MY SWIMMING CERTIFICATE WHEN I THREW UP ON A LIFEGUARD & I HAD TO SWIM IN THE SHALLOW END WITH THE LITTLE KIDS

THOUGH STILL A NATURAL ENEMY OF SPORT, I SOMEHOW BECAME A JUNIOR SEAGULL... A FERVENT SUPPORTER OF MY LOCAL FOOTBALL TEAM

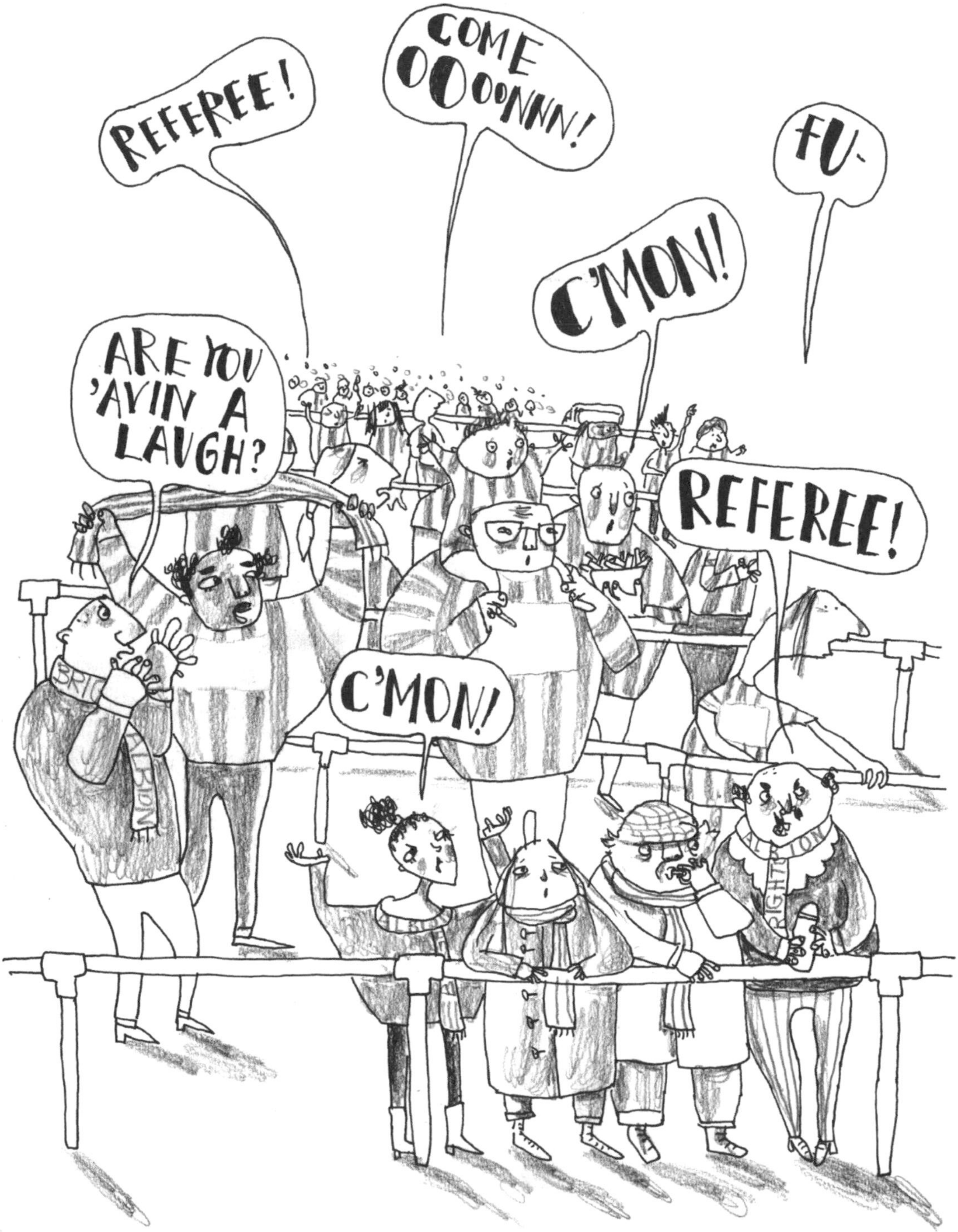
REFEREE!
COME OOOOONNN!
FU-
C'MON!
ARE YOU 'AVIN A LAUGH?
REFEREE!
C'MON!
BRIG
ALBION
ALBION
BRIGHTON

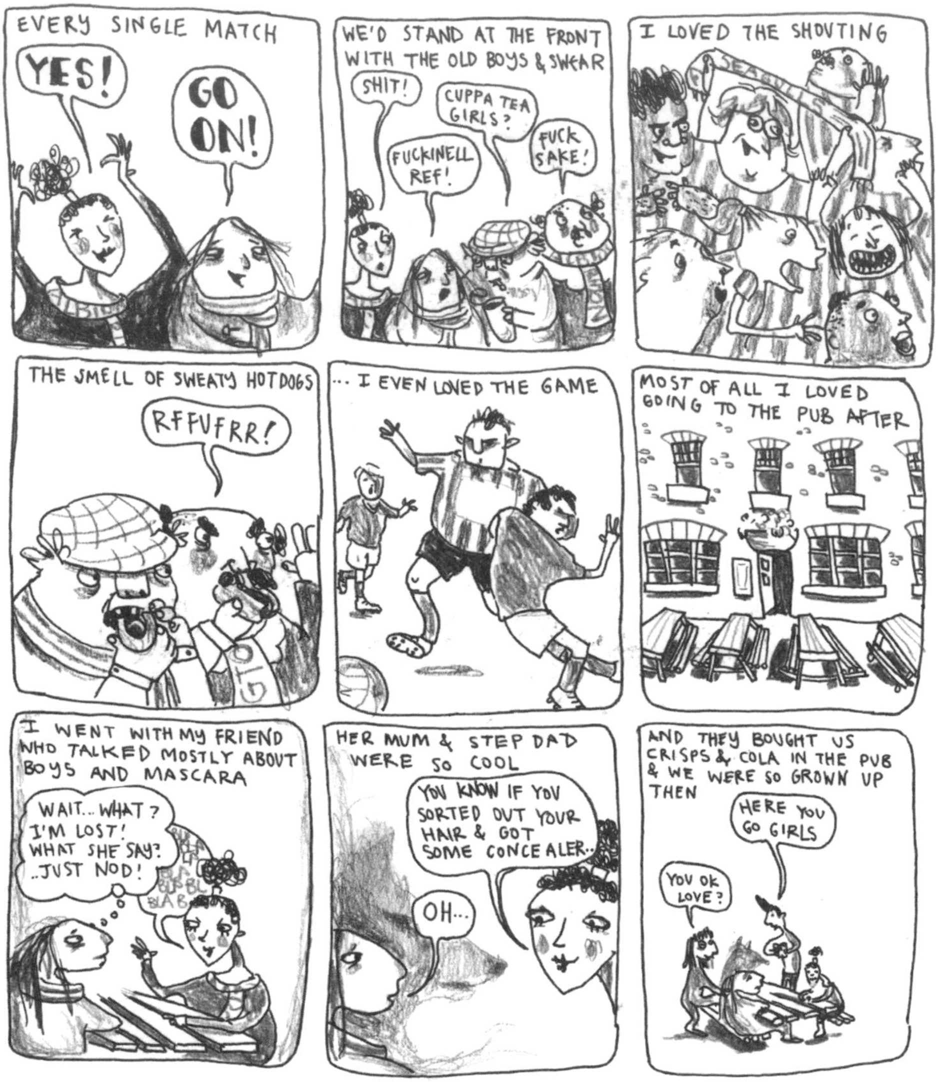
EVERY SINGLE MATCH
YES!
GO ON!
WE'D STAND AT THE FRONT WITH THE OLD BOYS & SWEAR
SHIT!
CUPPA TEA GIRLS?
FUCKINELL REF!
FUCK SAKE!
I LOVED THE SHOUTING
THE SMELL OF SWEATY HOTDOGS
RFFUFRR!
... I EVEN LOVED THE GAME
MOST OF ALL I LOVED GOING TO THE PUB AFTER
I WENT WITH MY FRIEND WHO TALKED MOSTLY ABOUT BOYS AND MASCARA
WAIT... WHAT? I'M LOST! WHAT SHE SAY? ..JUST NOD!
HER MUM & STEP DAD WERE SO COOL
YOU KNOW IF YOU SORTED OUT YOUR HAIR & GOT SOME CONCEALER..
OH...
AND THEY BOUGHT US CRISPS & COLA IN THE PUB & WE WERE SO GROWN UP THEN
HERE YOU GO GIRLS
YOU OK LOVE?

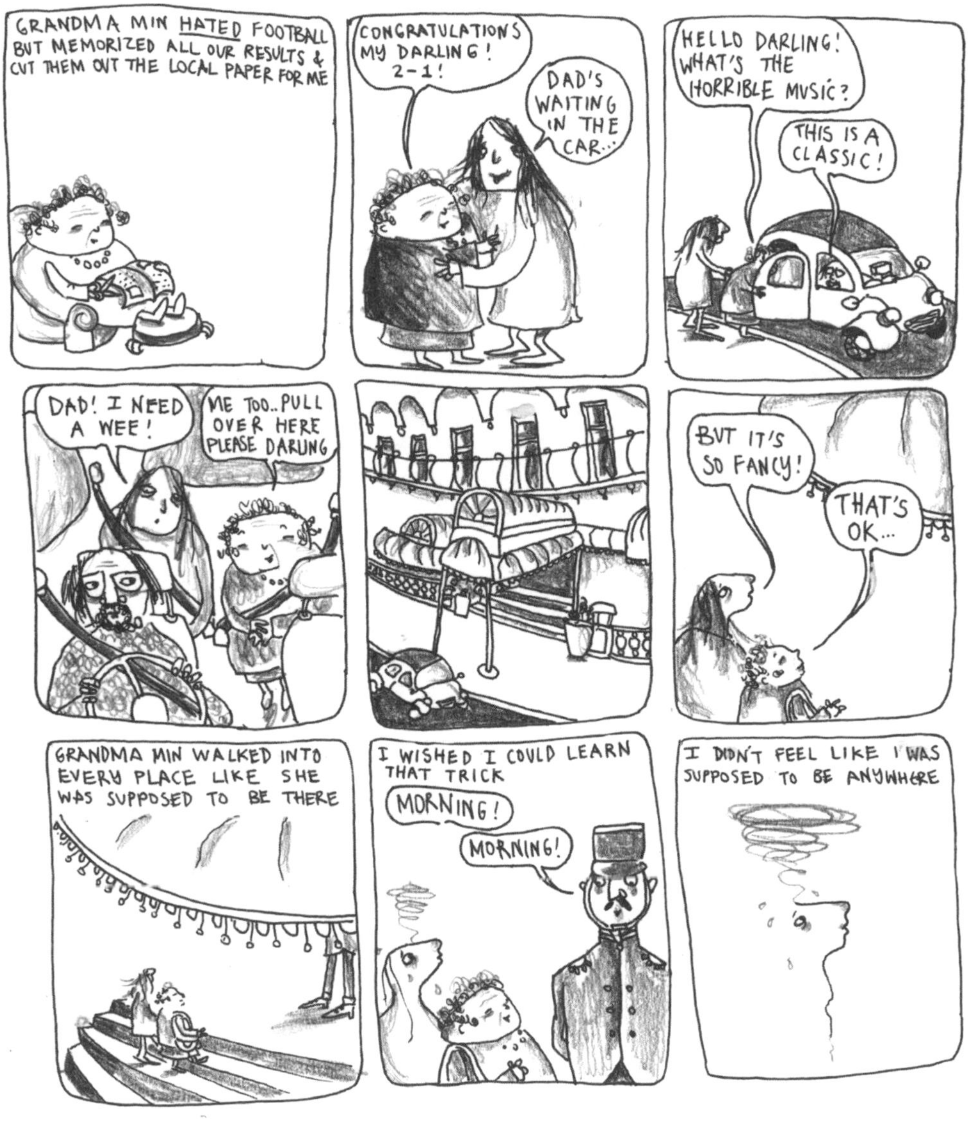
GRANDMA MIN HATED FOOTBALL BUT MEMORIZED ALL OUR RESULTS & CUT THEM OUT THE LOCAL PAPER FOR ME
CONGRATULATIONS MY DARLING! 2-1!
DAD'S WAITING IN THE CAR...
HELLO DARLING! WHAT'S THE HORRIBLE MUSIC?
THIS IS A CLASSIC!
DAD! I NEED A WEE!
ME TOO.. PULL OVER HERE PLEASE DARLING
BUT IT'S SO FANCY!
THAT'S OK...
GRANDMA MIN WALKED INTO EVERY PLACE LIKE SHE WAS SUPPOSED TO BE THERE
I WISHED I COULD LEARN THAT TRICK
MORNING!
MORNING!
I DIDN'T FEEL LIKE I WAS SUPPOSED TO BE ANYWHERE

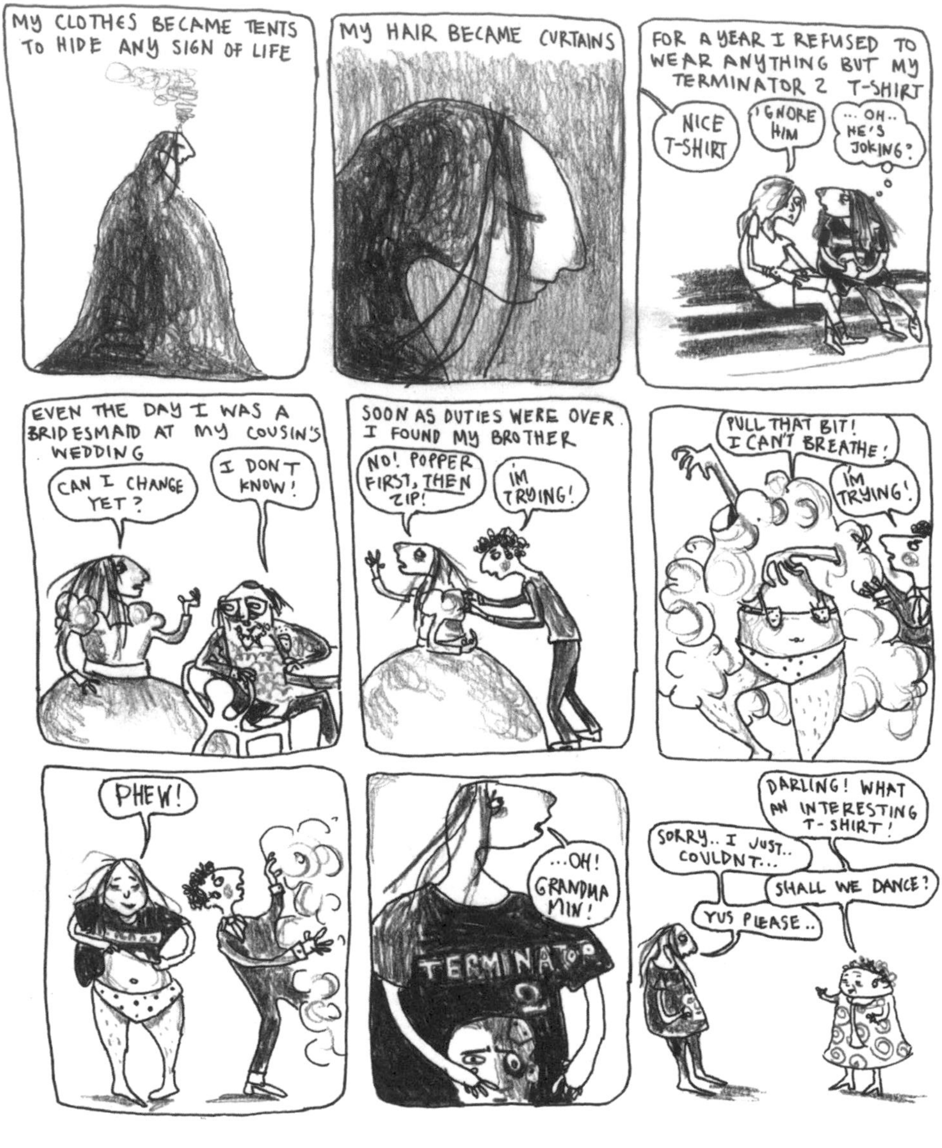
MY CLOTHES BECAME TENTS TO HIDE ANY SIGN OF LIFE
MY HAIR BECAME CURTAINS
FOR A YEAR I REFUSED TO WEAR ANYTHING BUT MY TERMINATOR 2 T-SHIRT
NICE T-SHIRT
IGNORE HIM
... OH.. HE'S JOKING?
EVEN THE DAY I WAS A BRIDESMAID AT MY COUSIN'S WEDDING
CAN I CHANGE YET?
I DON'T KNOW!
SOON AS DUTIES WERE OVER I FOUND MY BROTHER
NO! POPPER FIRST, THEN ZIP!
I'M TRYING!
PULL THAT BIT! I CAN'T BREATHE!
I'M TRYING!
PHEW!
...OH! GRANDMA MIN!
TERMINATOR
DARLING! WHAT AN INTERESTING T-SHIRT!
SORRY.. I JUST.. COULDN'T...
SHALL WE DANCE?
YUS PLEASE..

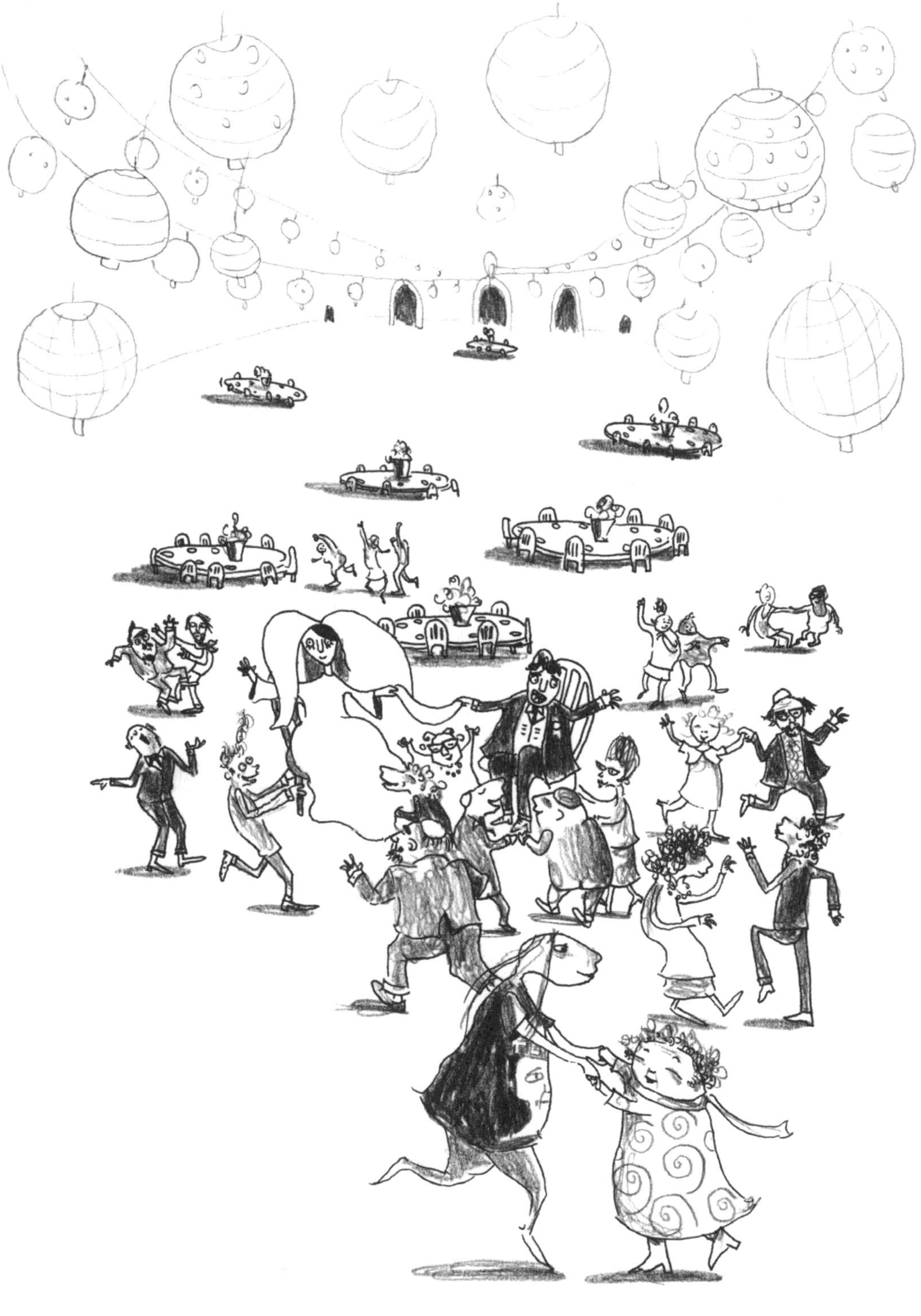

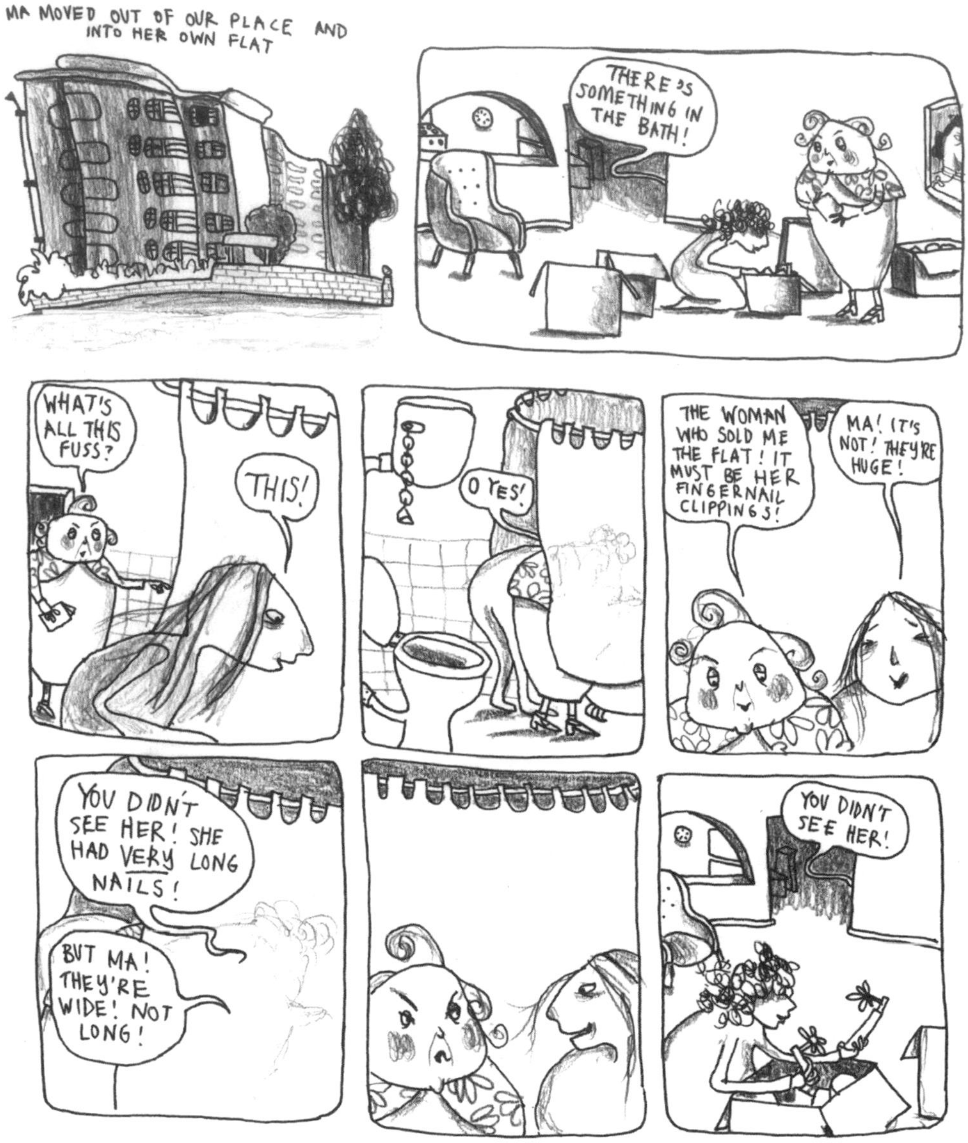
MA MOVED OUT OF OUR PLACE AND INTO HER OWN FLAT
THERE'S SOMETHING IN THE BATH!
WHAT'S ALL THIS FUSS?
THIS!
O YES!
THE WOMAN WHO SOLD ME THE FLAT! IT MUST BE HER FINGERNAIL CLIPPINGS!
MA! IT'S NOT! THEY'RE HUGE!
YOU DIDN'T SEE HER! SHE HAD VERY LONG NAILS!
BUT MA! THEY'RE WIDE! NOT LONG!
YOU DIDN'T SEE HER!

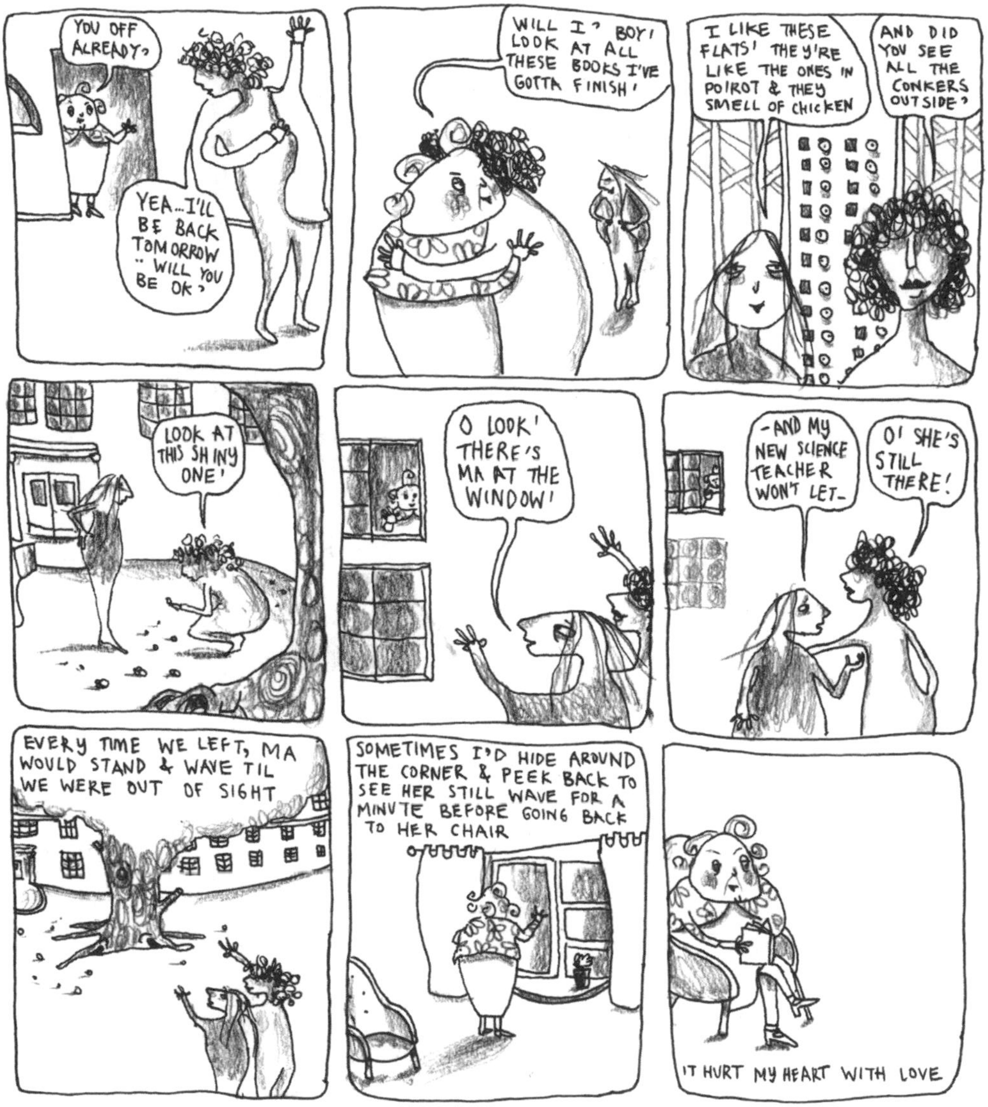
YOU OFF ALREADY?
YEA...I'LL BE BACK TOMORROW .. WILL YOU BE OK?
WILL I? BOY! LOOK AT ALL THESE BOOKS I'VE GOTTA FINISH!
I LIKE THESE FLATS! THEY'RE LIKE THE ONES IN POIROT & THEY SMELL OF CHICKEN
AND DID YOU SEE ALL THE CONKERS OUTSIDE?
LOOK AT THIS SHINY ONE!
O LOOK! THERE'S MA AT THE WINDOW!
-AND MY NEW SCIENCE TEACHER WON'T LET-
O! SHE'S STILL THERE!
EVERY TIME WE LEFT, MA WOULD STAND & WAVE TIL WE WERE OUT OF SIGHT
SOMETIMES I'D HIDE AROUND THE CORNER & PEEK BACK TO SEE HER STILL WAVE FOR A MINUTE BEFORE GOING BACK TO HER CHAIR
IT HURT MY HEART WITH LOVE

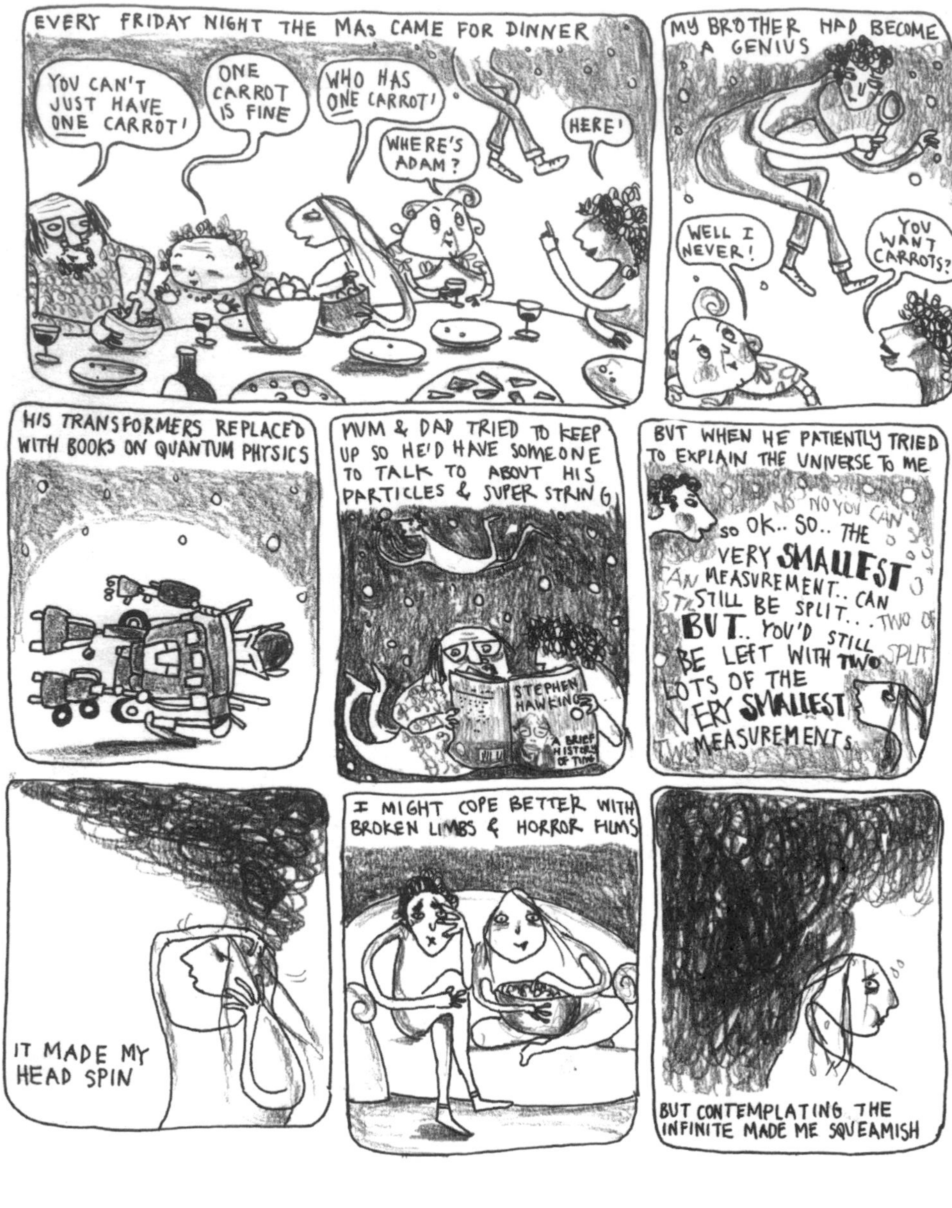
EVERY FRIDAY NIGHT THE MAs CAME FOR DINNER
YOU CAN'T JUST HAVE ONE CARROT!
ONE CARROT IS FINE
WHO HAS ONE CARROT!
WHERE'S ADAM?
HERE!
MY BROTHER HAD BECOME A GENIUS
WELL I NEVER!
YOU WANT CARROTS?
HIS TRANSFORMERS REPLACED WITH BOOKS ON QUANTUM PHYSICS
MUM & DAD TRIED TO KEEP UP SO HE'D HAVE SOMEONE TO TALK TO ABOUT HIS PARTICLES & SUPER STRING
STEPHEN HAWKING
A BRIEF HISTORY OF TIME
BUT WHEN HE PATIENTLY TRIED TO EXPLAIN THE UNIVERSE TO ME
NO YOU CAN
SO OK.. SO.. THE VERY SMALLEST MEASUREMENT.. CAN STILL BE SPLIT... BUT.. YOU'D STILL BE LEFT WITH TWO LOTS OF THE VERY SMALLEST MEASUREMENTS
TWO OF
SPLIT
IT MADE MY HEAD SPIN
I MIGHT COPE BETTER WITH BROKEN LIMBS & HORROR FILMS
BUT CONTEMPLATING THE INFINITE MADE ME SQUEAMISH

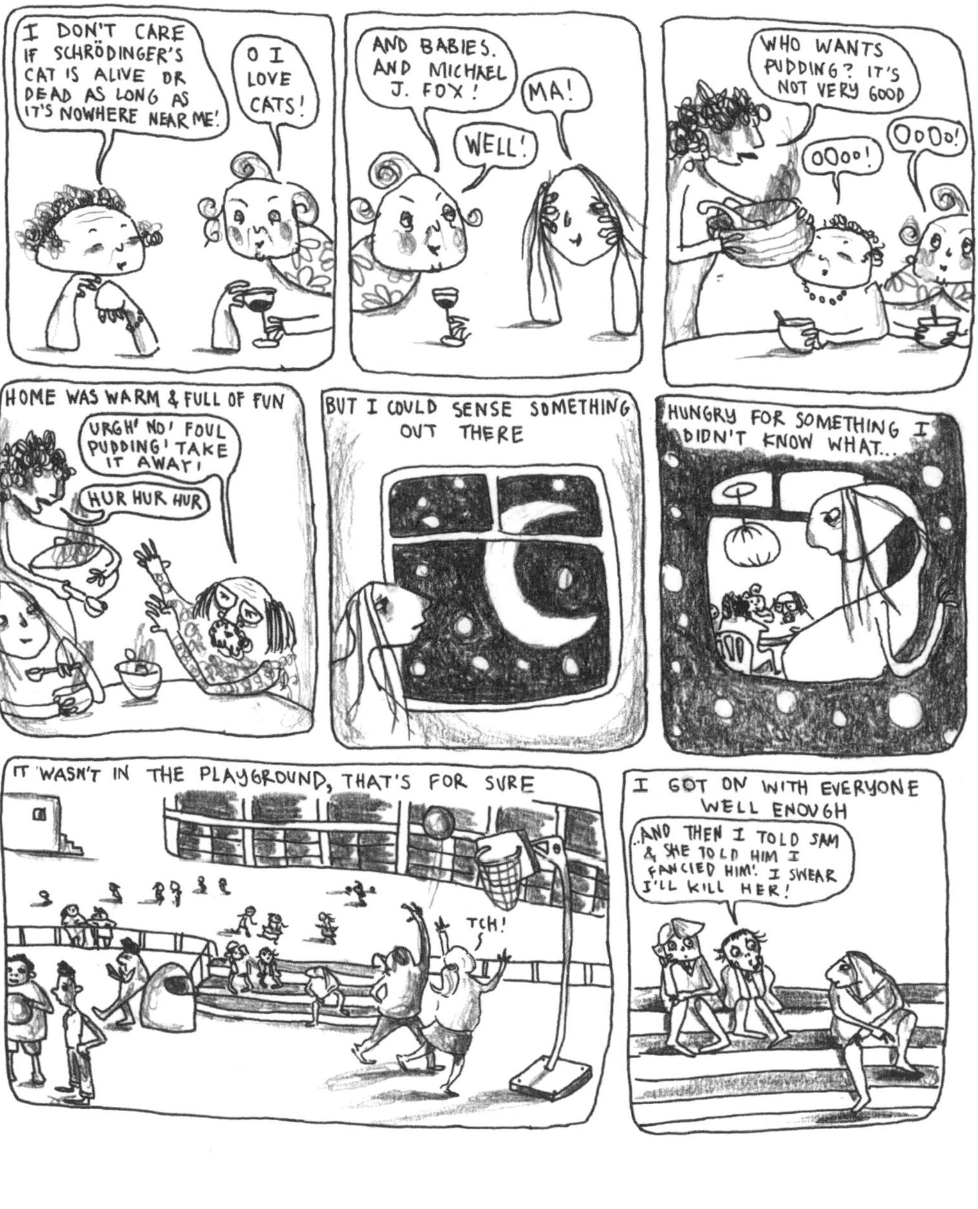
I DON'T CARE IF SCHRÖDINGER'S CAT IS ALIVE OR DEAD AS LONG AS IT'S NOWHERE NEAR ME!
O I LOVE CATS!
AND BABIES. AND MICHAEL J. FOX!
WELL!
MA!
WHO WANTS PUDDING? IT'S NOT VERY GOOD
OOoo!
OoOo!
HOME WAS WARM & FULL OF FUN
URGH! NO! FOUL PUDDING! TAKE IT AWAY!
HUR HUR HUR
BUT I COULD SENSE SOMETHING OUT THERE
HUNGRY FOR SOMETHING I DIDN'T KNOW WHAT...
IT WASN'T IN THE PLAYGROUND, THAT'S FOR SURE
TCH!
I GOT ON WITH EVERYONE WELL ENOUGH
..AND THEN I TOLD SAM & SHE TOLD HIM I FANCIED HIM! I SWEAR I'LL KILL HER!

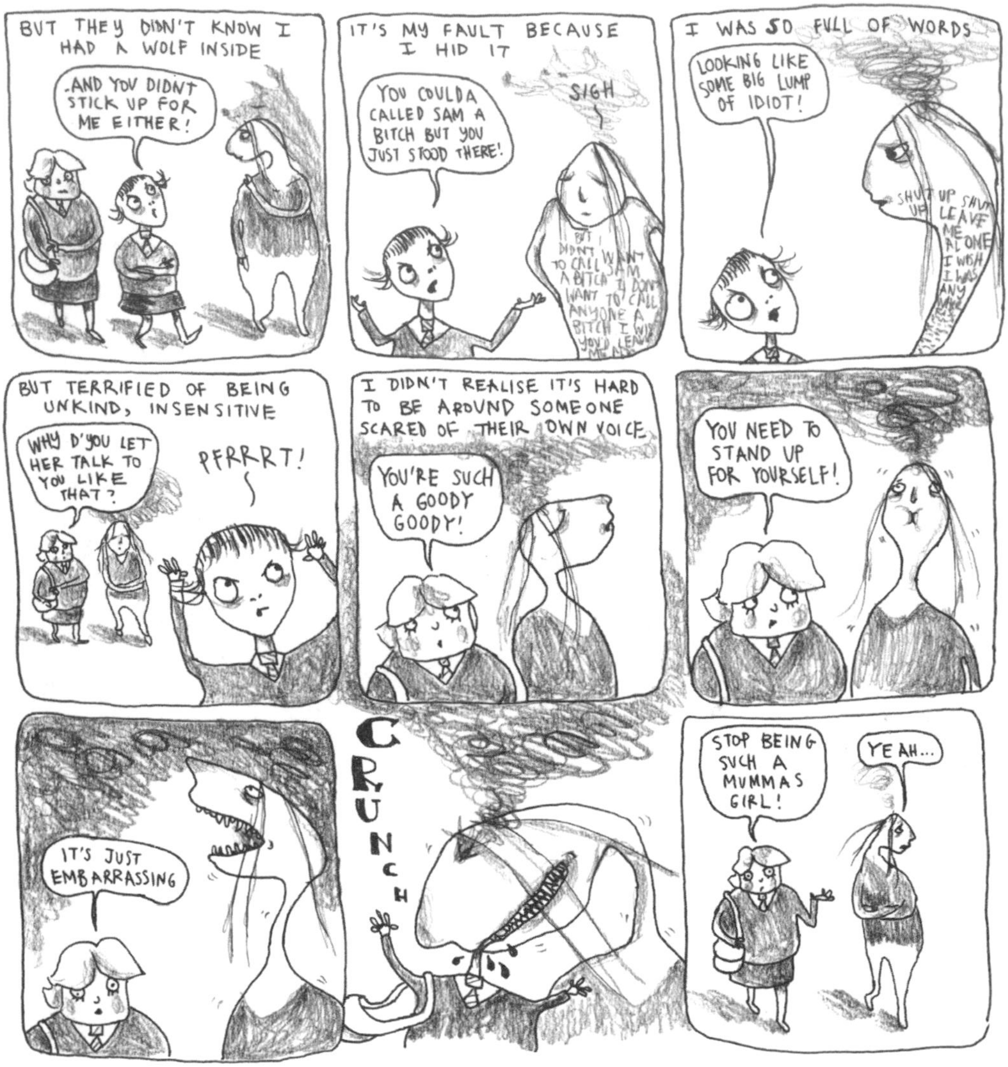
BUT THEY DIDN'T KNOW I HAD A WOLF INSIDE
-AND YOU DIDN'T STICK UP FOR ME EITHER!
IT'S MY FAULT BECAUSE I HID IT
YOU COULDA CALLED SAM A BITCH BUT YOU JUST STOOD THERE!
SIGH
BUT I DIDN'T WANT TO CALL SAM A BITCH I DON'T WANT TO CALL ANYONE A BITCH
I WAS SO FULL OF WORDS
LOOKING LIKE SOME BIG LUMP OF IDIOT!
SHUT UP SHUT UP LEAVE ME ALONE I WISH I WAS
BUT TERRIFIED OF BEING UNKIND, INSENSITIVE
WHY D'YOU LET HER TALK TO YOU LIKE THAT?
PFRRRT!
I DIDN'T REALISE IT'S HARD TO BE AROUND SOMEONE SCARED OF THEIR OWN VOICE
YOU'RE SUCH A GOODY GOODY!
YOU NEED TO STAND UP FOR YOURSELF!
IT'S JUST EMBARRASSING
CRUNCH
STOP BEING SUCH A MUMMAS GIRL!
YEAH...

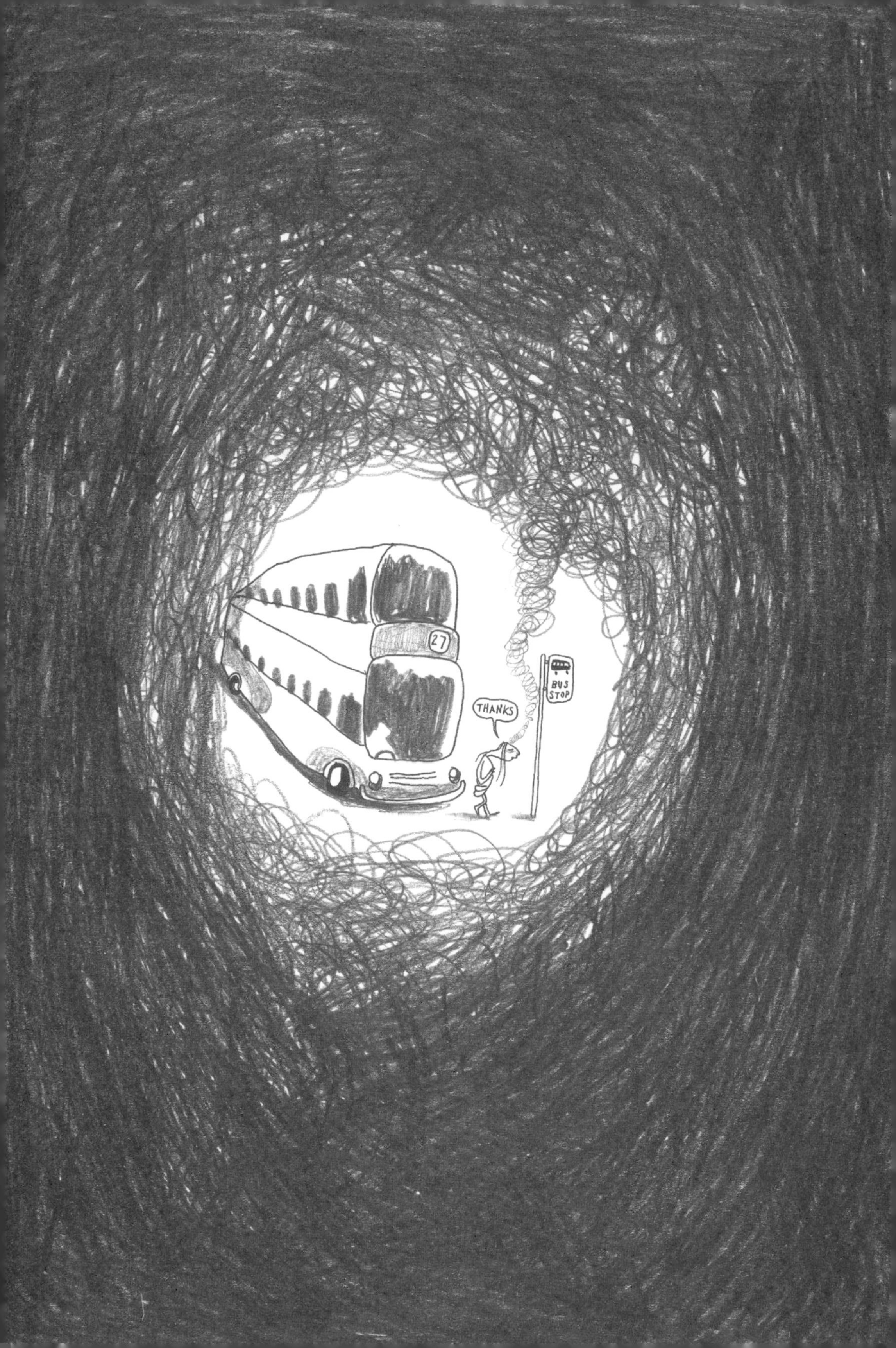
27
THANKS
BUS
STOP

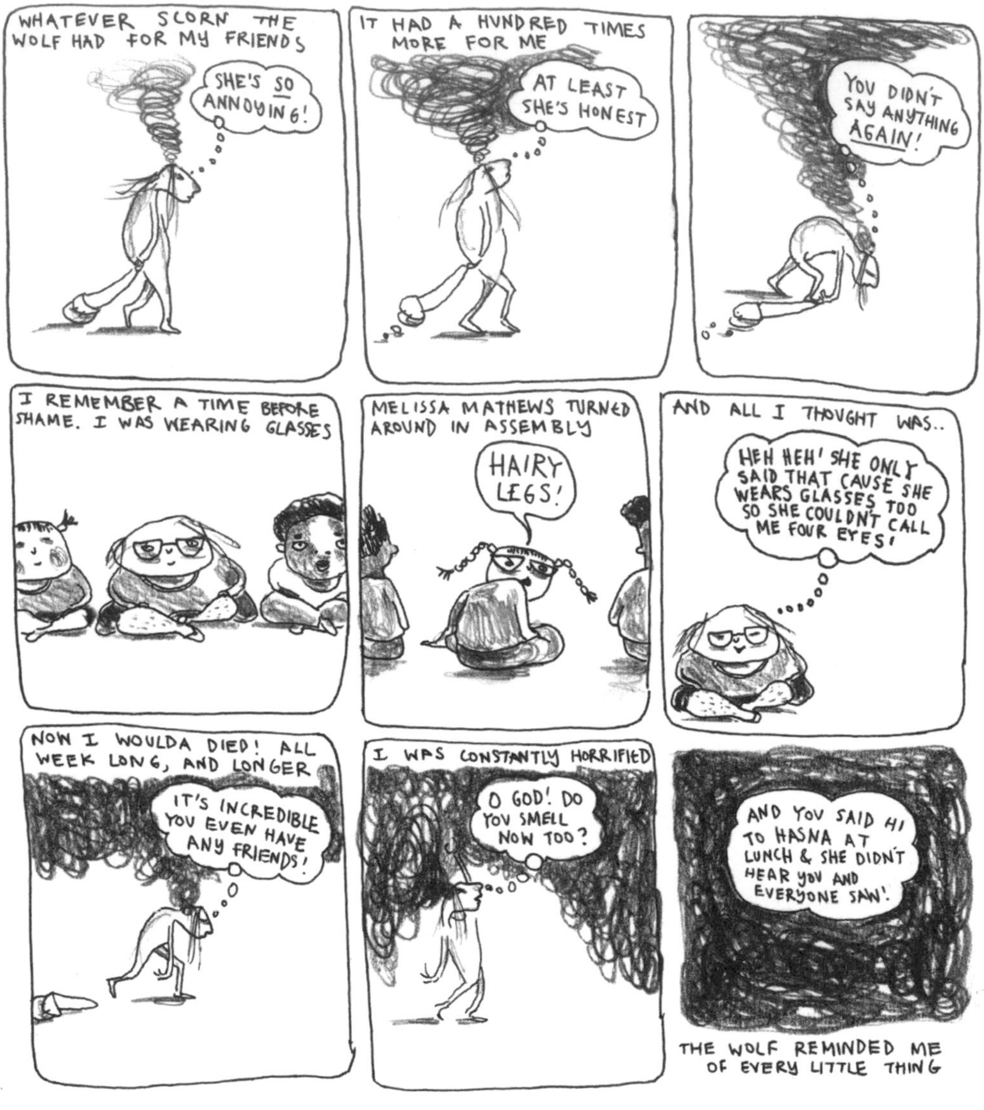
WHATEVER SCORN THE WOLF HAD FOR MY FRIENDS
SHE'S SO ANNOYING!
IT HAD A HUNDRED TIMES MORE FOR ME
AT LEAST SHE'S HONEST
YOU DIDN'T SAY ANYTHING AGAIN!
I REMEMBER A TIME BEFORE SHAME. I WAS WEARING GLASSES
MELISSA MATHEWS TURNED AROUND IN ASSEMBLY
HAIRY LEGS!
AND ALL I THOUGHT WAS..
HEH HEH! SHE ONLY SAID THAT CAUSE SHE WEARS GLASSES TOO SO SHE COULDN'T CALL ME FOUR EYES!
NOW I WOULDA DIED! ALL WEEK LONG, AND LONGER
IT'S INCREDIBLE YOU EVEN HAVE ANY FRIENDS!
I WAS CONSTANTLY HORRIFIED
O GOD! DO YOU SMELL NOW TOO?
AND YOU SAID HI TO HASNA AT LUNCH & SHE DIDN'T HEAR YOU AND EVERYONE SAW!
THE WOLF REMINDED ME OF EVERY LITTLE THING

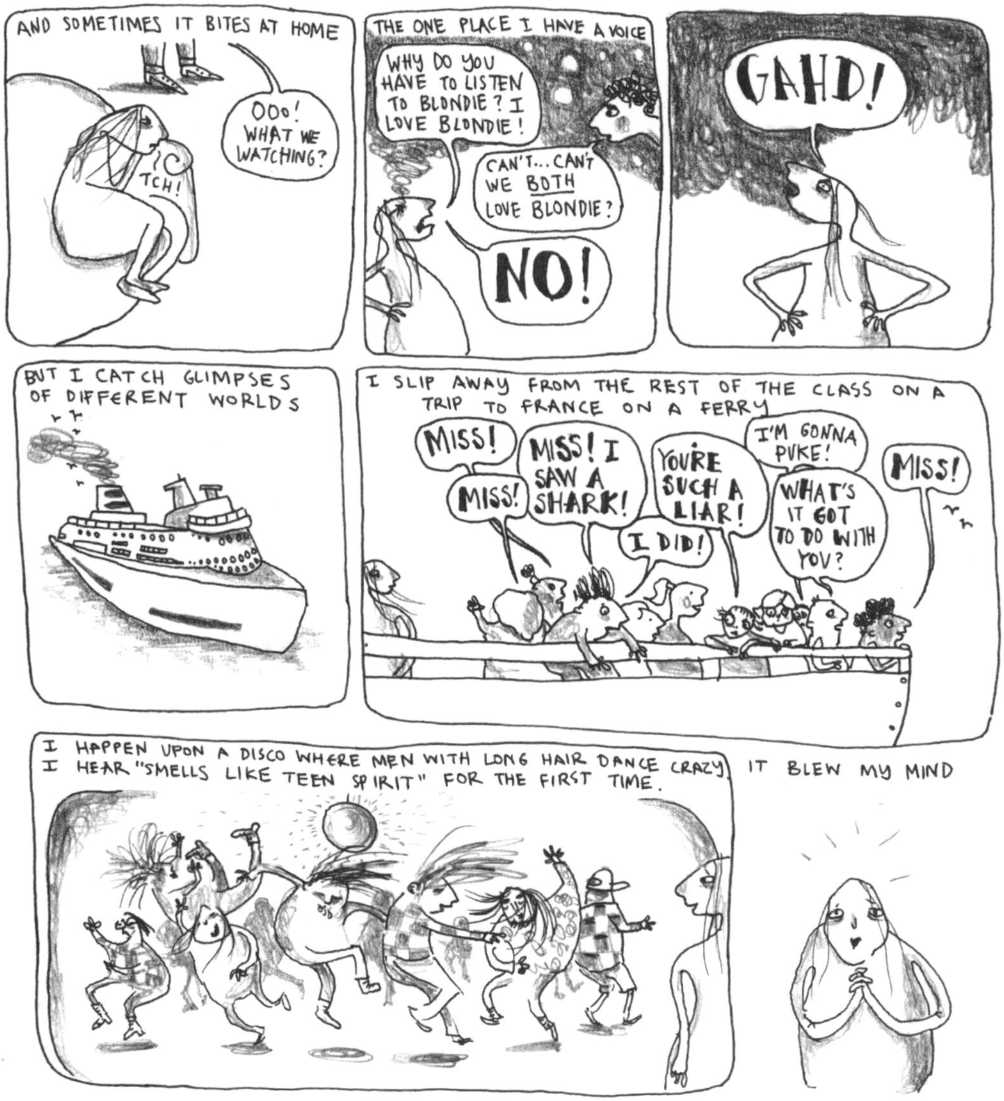

AND SOMETIMES IT BITES AT HOME
OOO! WHAT WE WATCHING?
TCH!
THE ONE PLACE I HAVE A VOICE
WHY DO YOU HAVE TO LISTEN TO BLONDIE? I LOVE BLONDIE!
CAN'T... CAN'T WE BOTH LOVE BLONDIE?
NO!
GAHD!
BUT I CATCH GLIMPSES OF DIFFERENT WORLDS
I SLIP AWAY FROM THE REST OF THE CLASS ON A TRIP TO FRANCE ON A FERRY
MISS!
MISS!
MISS! I SAW A SHARK!
YOU'RE SUCH A LIAR!
I DID!
I'M GONNA PUKE!
WHAT'S IT GOT TO DO WITH YOU?
MISS!
I HAPPEN UPON A DISCO WHERE MEN WITH LONG HAIR DANCE CRAZY
I HEAR "SMELLS LIKE TEEN SPIRIT" FOR THE FIRST TIME.
IT BLEW MY MIND

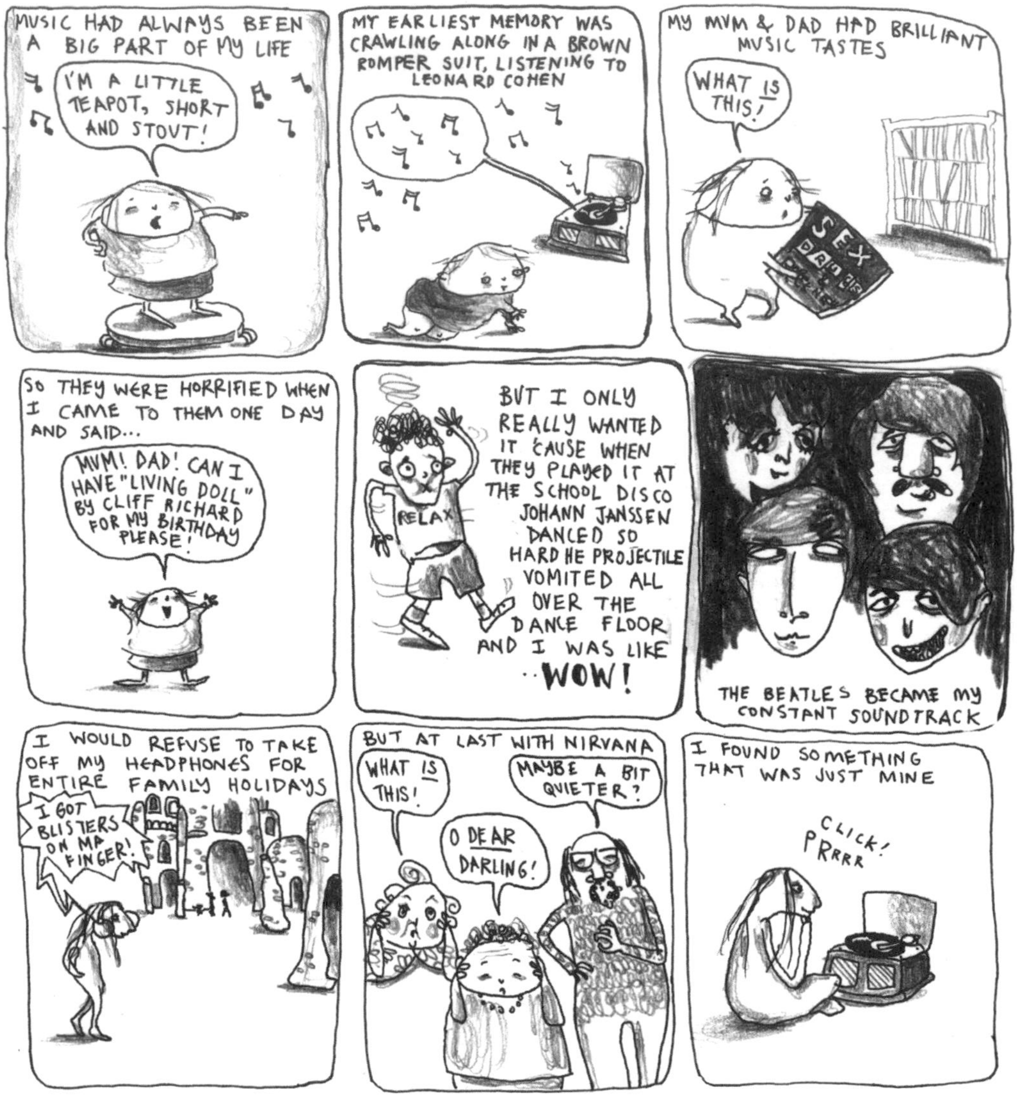
MUSIC HAD ALWAYS BEEN A BIG PART OF MY LIFE
I'M A LITTLE TEAPOT, SHORT AND STOUT!
MY EARLIEST MEMORY WAS CRAWLING ALONG IN A BROWN ROMPER SUIT, LISTENING TO LEONARD COHEN
MY MUM & DAD HAD BRILLIANT MUSIC TASTES
WHAT IS THIS!
SEX
SO THEY WERE HORRIFIED WHEN I CAME TO THEM ONE DAY AND SAID...
MUM! DAD! CAN I HAVE "LIVING DOLL" BY CLIFF RICHARD FOR MY BIRTHDAY PLEASE!
BUT I ONLY REALLY WANTED IT 'CAUSE WHEN THEY PLAYED IT AT THE SCHOOL DISCO JOHANN JANSSEN DANCED SO HARD HE PROJECTILE VOMITED ALL OVER THE DANCE FLOOR AND I WAS LIKE ..WOW!
RELAX
THE BEATLES BECAME MY CONSTANT SOUNDTRACK
I WOULD REFUSE TO TAKE OFF MY HEADPHONES FOR ENTIRE FAMILY HOLIDAYS
I GOT BLISTERS ON MA FINGER!
BUT AT LAST WITH NIRVANA
WHAT IS THIS!
O DEAR DARLING!
MAYBE A BIT QUIETER?
I FOUND SOMETHING THAT WAS JUST MINE
CLICK!
PRRRR

CHAPTER 6
FLYPOSTING WITH BERNIE KATZ

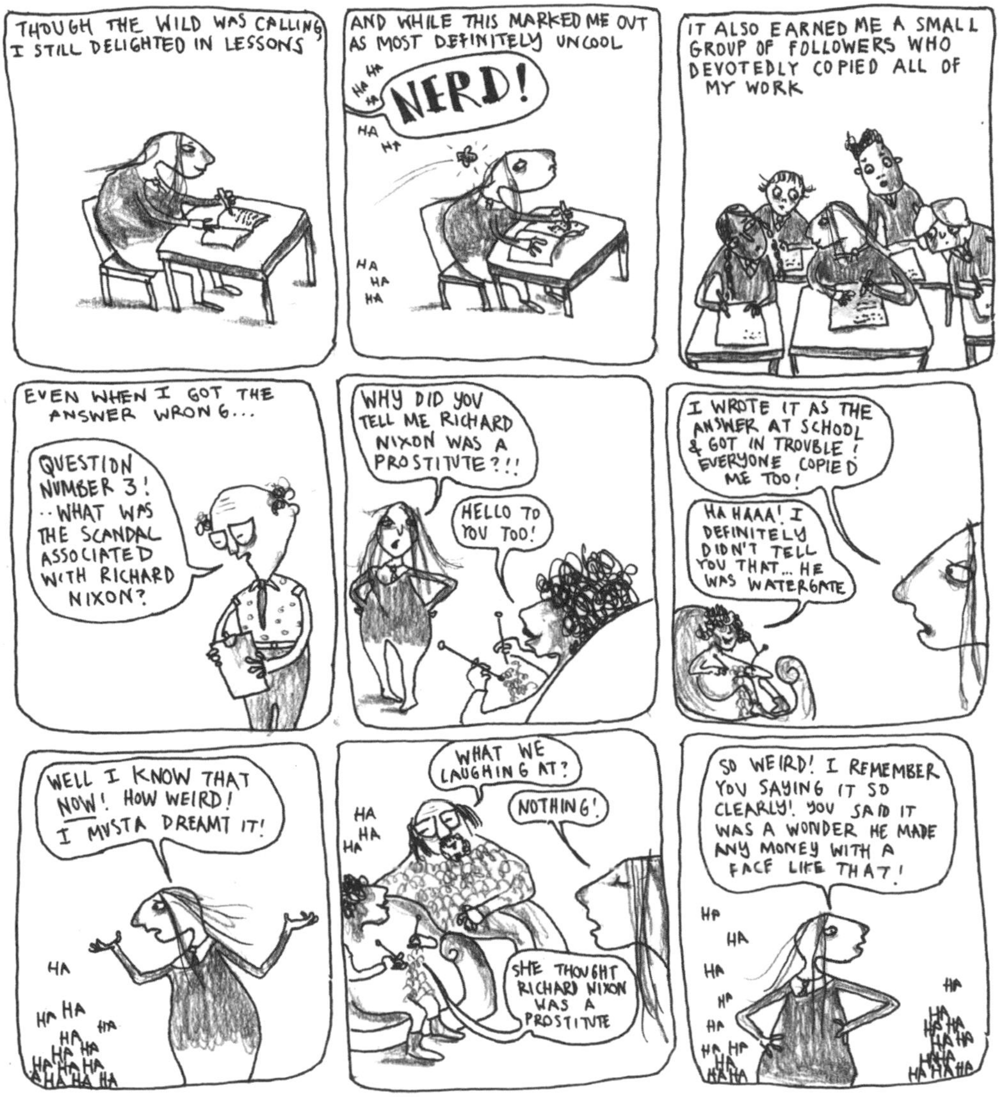
THOUGH THE WILD WAS CALLING I STILL DELIGHTED IN LESSONS
AND WHILE THIS MARKED ME OUT AS MOST DEFINITELY UNCOOL
HA HA HA
NERD!
HA HA
HA HA HA
IT ALSO EARNED ME A SMALL GROUP OF FOLLOWERS WHO DEVOTEDLY COPIED ALL OF MY WORK
EVEN WHEN I GOT THE ANSWER WRONG...
QUESTION NUMBER 3! ..WHAT WAS THE SCANDAL ASSOCIATED WITH RICHARD NIXON?
WHY DID YOU TELL ME RICHARD NIXON WAS A PROSTITUTE?!!
HELLO TO YOU TOO!
I WROTE IT AS THE ANSWER AT SCHOOL & GOT IN TROUBLE! EVERYONE COPIED ME TOO!
HA HAAA! I DEFINITELY DIDN'T TELL YOU THAT... HE WAS WATERGATE
WELL I KNOW THAT NOW! HOW WEIRD! I MUSTA DREAMT IT!
HA HA HA HA HA HA HA HA HA HA HA HA
WHAT WE LAUGHING AT?
NOTHING!
HA HA HA
SHE THOUGHT RICHARD NIXON WAS A PROSTITUTE
SO WEIRD! I REMEMBER YOU SAYING IT SO CLEARLY! YOU SAID IT WAS A WONDER HE MADE ANY MONEY WITH A FACE LIFE THAT!
HA HA HA HA HA HA HA HA HA HA HA HA HA HA HA HA HA HA HA

WHEN MY JEHOVAH'S WITNESS LEFT ME FOR A QUIET GIRL WITH A BOB...

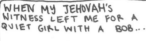

WHISPER WHISPER WHISPER

I ENDED UP ACCIDENTAL BEST FRIENDS WITH THE QUIET GIRL'S REJECTED FRIEND, PAM.

AFTER A WEEK MY JEHOVAH'S WITNESS & THE QUIET GIRL REALISED THEY HAD NOTHING IN COMMON

BUT BY THAT TIME ME AND PAM WERE STUCK WITH EACH OTHER

AND HE KEPT MAKING THIS SUCH ANNOYING NOISE & SO I WENT & HIT HIM IN THE HEAD... AND THEN HE HIT ME & I ENDED UP CRYING SO I PRETENDED HE HURT MY EAR INFECTION BUT I...

IT WASN'T AN EASY FRIENDSHIP

ARE YOU EVEN LISTENING!

KEEP UP!

BUT WE BOTH LOVED MAKING UP STORIES...

WITH AN EAR PIERCING HOWL IT...

STUCK ITS CLAWS IN HER EYEBALLS LIKE TWO FRIED EGGS!

YES! FRIED EGGS!

AND WE BOTH WENT INTO MOURNING WHEN FREDDIE MERCURY DIED

PAM HIT ALL THE BOYS WHO MADE AIDS JOKES

WHAT THE FU-

RA!

AND WE BOTH HAD ROWS WITH ANYONE WHO MADE GAY JOKES.

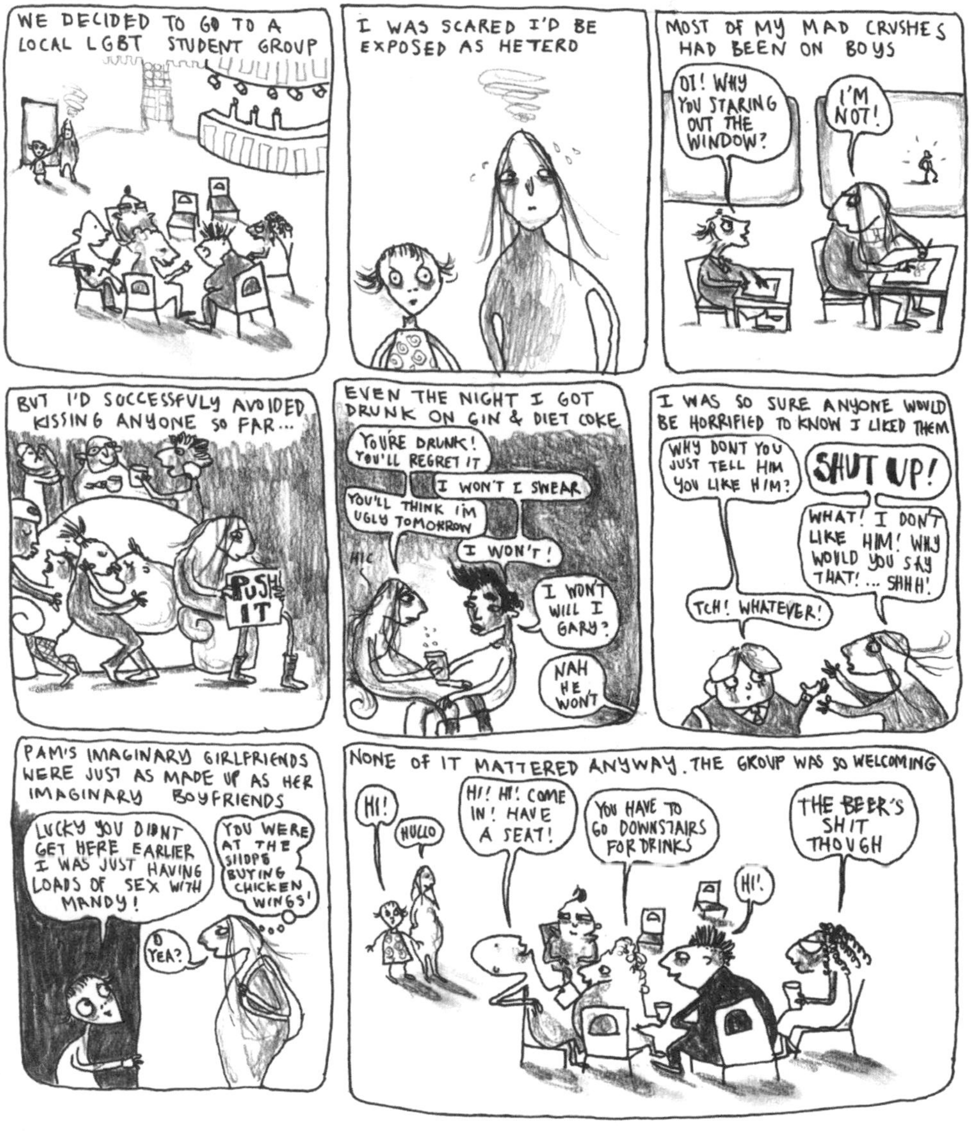
WE DECIDED TO GO TO A LOCAL LGBT STUDENT GROUP
I WAS SCARED I'D BE EXPOSED AS HETERO
MOST OF MY MAD CRUSHES HAD BEEN ON BOYS
OI! WHY YOU STARING OUT THE WINDOW?
I'M NOT!
BUT I'D SUCCESSFULY AVOIDED KISSING ANYONE SO FAR...
PUSH IT
EVEN THE NIGHT I GOT DRUNK ON GIN & DIET COKE
YOU'RE DRUNK! YOU'LL REGRET IT
I WON'T I SWEAR
YOU'LL THINK I'M UGLY TOMORROW
I WON'T!
HIC
I WON'T WILL I GARY?
NAH HE WON'T
I WAS SO SURE ANYONE WOULD BE HORRIFIED TO KNOW I LIKED THEM
WHY DONT YOU JUST TELL HIM YOU LIKE HIM?
SHUT UP!
WHAT! I DON'T LIKE HIM! WHY WOULD YOU SAY THAT! ... SHHH!
TCH! WHATEVER!
PAM'S IMAGINARY GIRLFRIENDS WERE JUST AS MADE UP AS HER IMAGINARY BOYFRIENDS
LUCKY YOU DIDNT GET HERE EARLIER I WAS JUST HAVING LOADS OF SEX WITH MANDY!
YOU WERE AT THE SHOPS BUYING CHICKEN WINGS!
O YEA?
NONE OF IT MATTERED ANYWAY. THE GROUP WAS SO WELCOMING
HI!
HULLO
HI! HI! COME IN! HAVE A SEAT!
YOU HAVE TO GO DOWNSTAIRS FOR DRINKS
HI!
THE BEER'S SHIT THOUGH

IN BETWEEN THE PINTS AND THE JOKES AND THE BORING CLERICAL BUSINESS

WHO'S TAKING THE FLYERS TO THE PRINTERS?

WE STILL NEED TO VOTE ON THE FONT

JESUS! WHO GIVES A FVCK ABOUT THE FONT!

HA!

WE LEARNT ABOUT STONEWALL, ABOUT DIFFERENT KINDS OF ACTIVISM

WE JOINED LEFT WING ORGANISATIONS

LOOK AT THIS! SMASH THE TORIES!

WE HATE THE TORIES!

SMASH THE TORIES

BEGAN DEVOURING NEWSPAPERS

GIRLS! THIS IS A SCIENCE LESSON!

CUTS CUTS CUTS

POLICE BRUTAL

HANDED OUT LEAFLETS

SUPPORT THE FIRE FIGHTERS...

HIPPY!

WE STOOD ON RAINY PICKET LINES

OFFICIAL PICKET

SAFETY AT WORK

NO MORE UNPAID OVER TIME

SAFETY THE WORK PLACE

CONSTANTLY HIGH ON NERVOUS ENERGY, THE WOLF WAS ACTUALLY HELPING ME SPEAK

SAVE THE WOMEN'S REFUGE?

SCROUNGERS!

SCUMBAG!

SAVE OUR REFUGE

SIGN THE PLAN

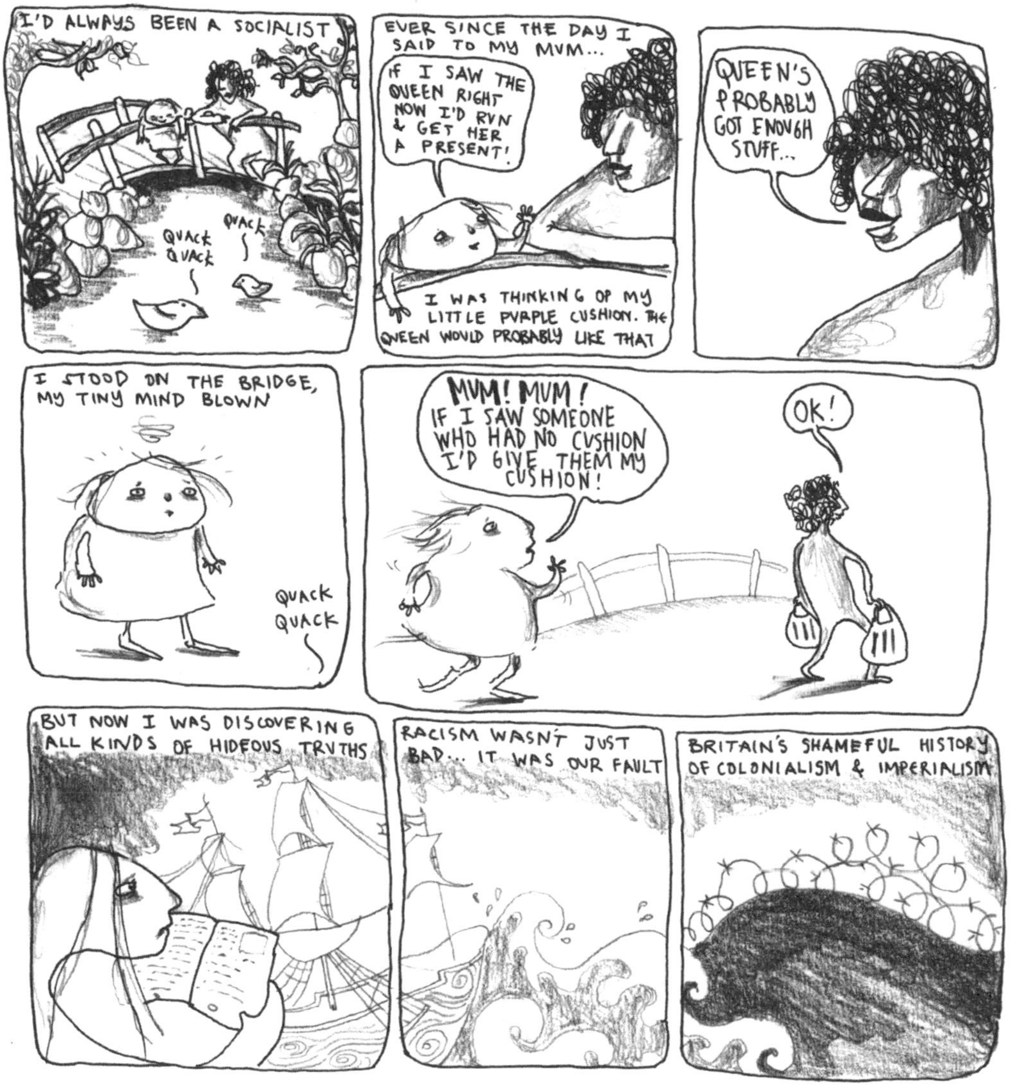
I'D ALWAYS BEEN A SOCIALIST
QUACK QUACK
QUACK
EVER SINCE THE DAY I SAID TO MY MUM...
IF I SAW THE QUEEN RIGHT NOW I'D RUN & GET HER A PRESENT!
I WAS THINKING OF MY LITTLE PURPLE CUSHION. THE QUEEN WOULD PROBABLY LIKE THAT
QUEEN'S PROBABLY GOT ENOUGH STUFF...
I STOOD ON THE BRIDGE, MY TINY MIND BLOWN
QUACK QUACK
MUM! MUM! IF I SAW SOMEONE WHO HAD NO CUSHION I'D GIVE THEM MY CUSHION!
OK!
BUT NOW I WAS DISCOVERING ALL KINDS OF HIDEOUS TRUTHS
RACISM WASN'T JUST BAD... IT WAS OUR FAULT
BRITAIN'S SHAMEFUL HISTORY OF COLONIALISM & IMPERIALISM

WE WENT ON MARCHES & DISCOVERED THE POLICE
WERE NOT OUR FRIENDS...

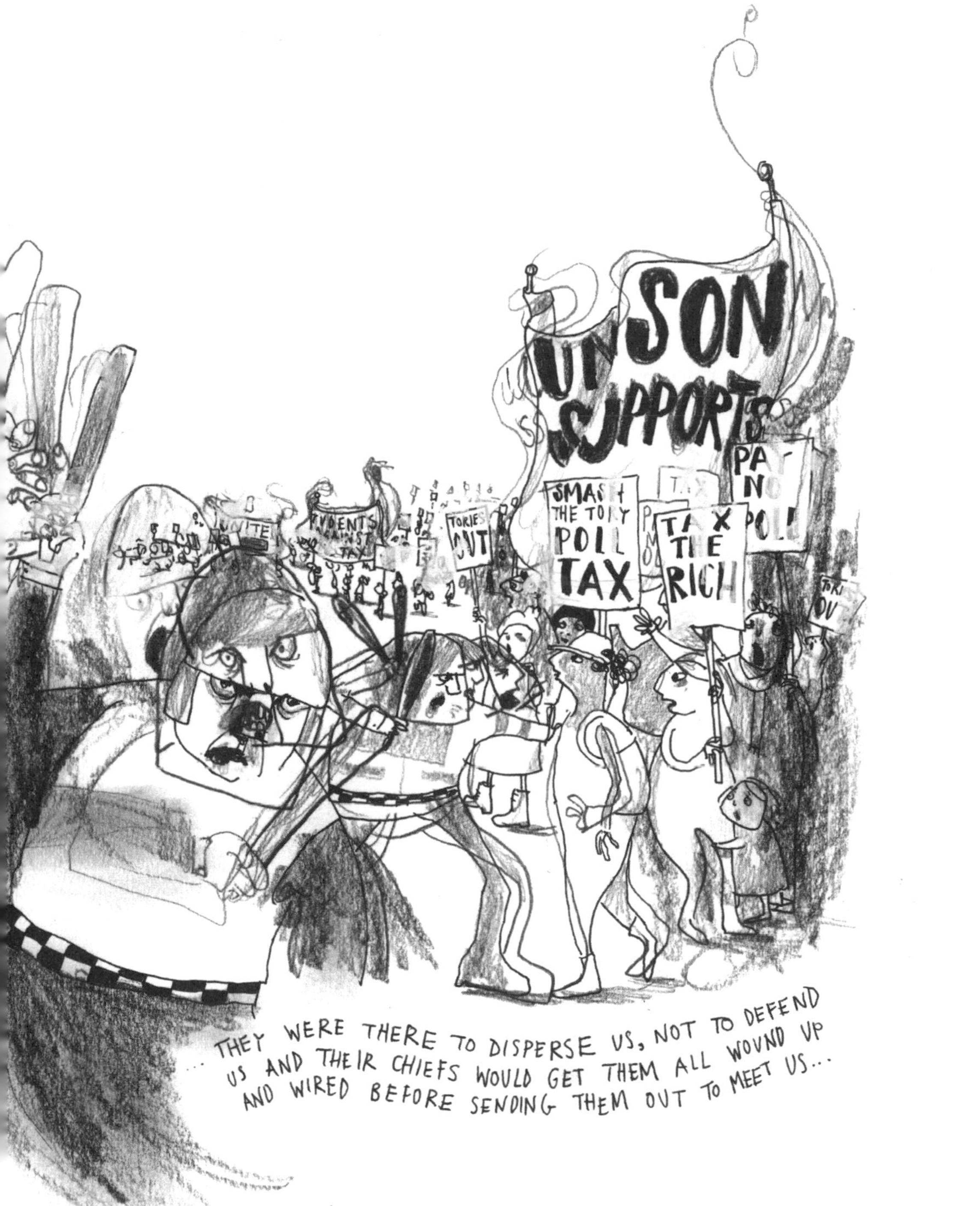
STUDENTS AGAINST TAX
TORIES OUT
SMASH THE TORY POLL TAX
TAX THE RICH
...THEY WERE THERE TO DISPERSE US, NOT TO DEFEND US AND THEIR CHIEFS WOULD GET THEM ALL WOUND UP AND WIRED BEFORE SENDING THEM OUT TO MEET US...

WE NOTICED THE PAPERS DIDN'T REPORT THE MARCHES HOW WE SAW IT

PROTESTERS ATTACK POLICE ON THIRD DAY OF VIOLENT... WAIT... ..WHAT?!

THUGS

...REALISED OTHER PEOPLE'S STORIES MAY HAVE BEEN MISTOLD

WANTED BY THE FBI
ANGELA YVONNE DAVIS

DESCRIPTION
AGE.... 26 BORN JANUARY 24 1944 BIRTH
HEIGHT..-5'8   EYES: BRN

WE BEGAN TO HEAR VOICES FROM ALL OVER THE WORLD

OUR NEXT SPEAKER WAS 11 YEARS OLD WHEN SHE WAS TAKEN TO AUSCHWITZ..

GRANDMA MIN STOPPED COLLECTING FOOTBALL RESULTS & BEGAN TO CUT OUT ARTICLES 'BOUT STRIKING BIN MEN

THREE WEEKS THEY'VE BEEN OUT!

THOUGH SHE WAS PROBABLY HORRIFIED WITH MY NEW RADICALISM

WELL DONE DARLING!

WELL... I DIDN'T REALLY DO ANYTHING

MA, ON THE OTHER HAND, WAS A LEFTY LIKE ME. WE WERE ROUGHER WITH EACH OTHER

WHAT DO YOU MEAN?

WHAT DO YOU MEAN "WHAT DO I MEAN"?!

WE'D HAVE ARGUMENTS LONG INTO THE NIGHT

HOW CAN YOU BE A SOCIALIST AND A ZIONIST!!

HOW CAN YOU SUPPORT A GOVERNMENT THAT —

I DON'T SUPPORT... YOU'RE RIGHT THOUGH... I KNOW YOU'RE RIGHT

AND IGNORE ALL THE BRUTAL—

I KNOW...

I WASN'T VERY GOOD AT LISTENING

AND MA WOULD ALWAYS END UP SAYING...

I CAN'T EXPLAIN IT COOKIE .. IT'S AN EMOTIONAL THING

ME AND PAM WENT TO SOCIALIST MEETINGS, BOTH SUPREMELY EXCITING AND INCREDIBLY DULL

WE HAD CRUSHES ON <u>EVERYONE</u>...

AND I FOUGHT MY TERROR OF PUBLIC SPEAKING

ANY QUESTIONS FOR OUR SPEAKERS?

CAUSE IT SEEMED TOO IMPORTANT TO STAY QUIET

BUT I WAS CONSTANTLY TERRIFIED

BLABLABLA BLABLA BLABLA...

SOMEONE WOULD NOTICE I HAD NO IDEA WHAT I WAS TALKING ABOUT

IMPOSTER!
FRAUD!
FAKE!
JOKE!
IDIOT!

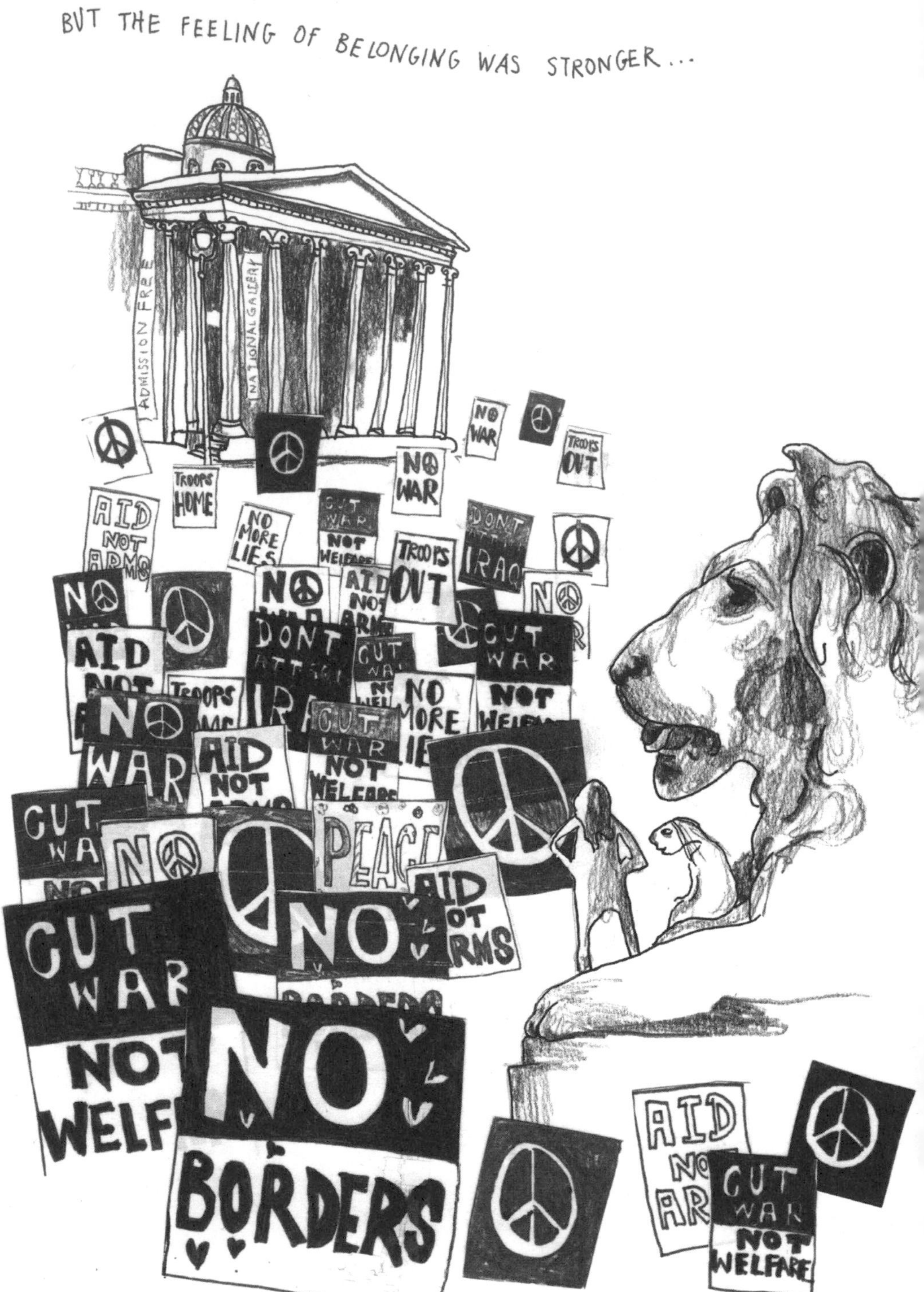
BUT THE FEELING OF BELONGING WAS STRONGER...
ADMISSION FREE
NATIONAL GALLERY
NO WAR
TROOPS OUT
TROOPS HOME
AID NOT ARMS
NO MORE LIES
CUT WAR NOT WELFARE
DONT ATTACK IRAQ
PEACE
NO BORDERS

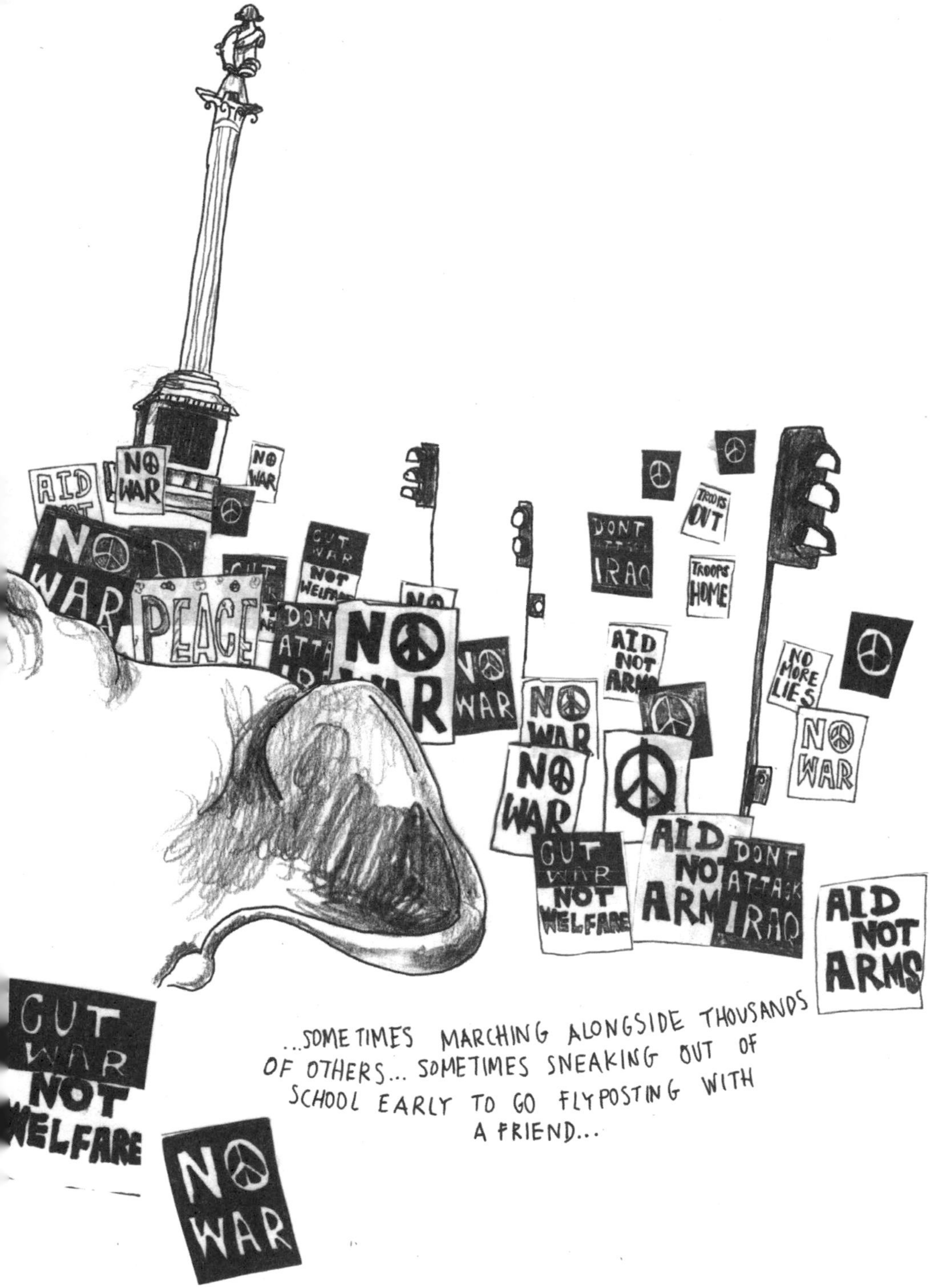
NO WAR
NO WAR
NO WAR
PEACE
CUT WAR NOT WELFARE
NO WAR
NO WAR
DONT ATTACK IRAQ
TROOPS OUT
TROOPS HOME
AID NOT ARMS
NO MORE LIES
NO WAR
NO WAR
NO WAR
CUT WAR NOT WELFARE
AID NOT ARMS
DONT ATTACK IRAQ
AID NOT ARMS
CUT WAR NOT WELFARE
NO WAR
...SOMETIMES MARCHING ALONGSIDE THOUSANDS OF OTHERS... SOMETIMES SNEAKING OUT OF SCHOOL EARLY TO GO FLYPOSTING WITH A FRIEND...

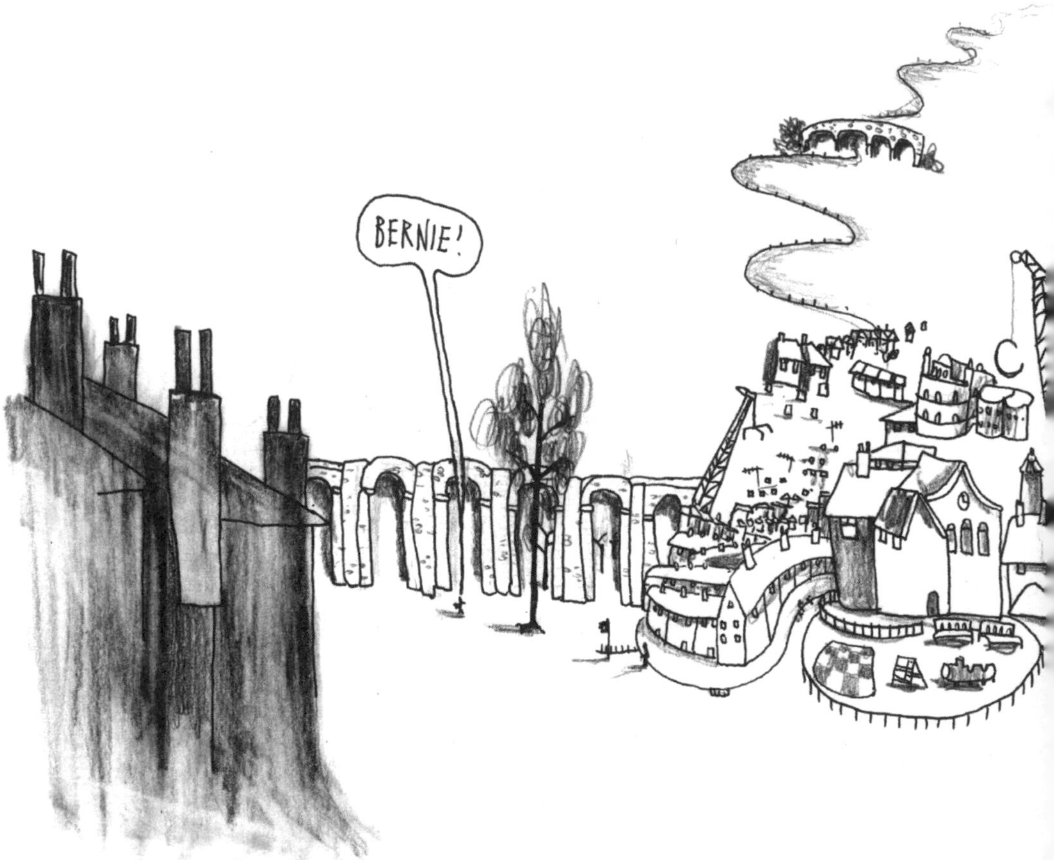
BERNIE!

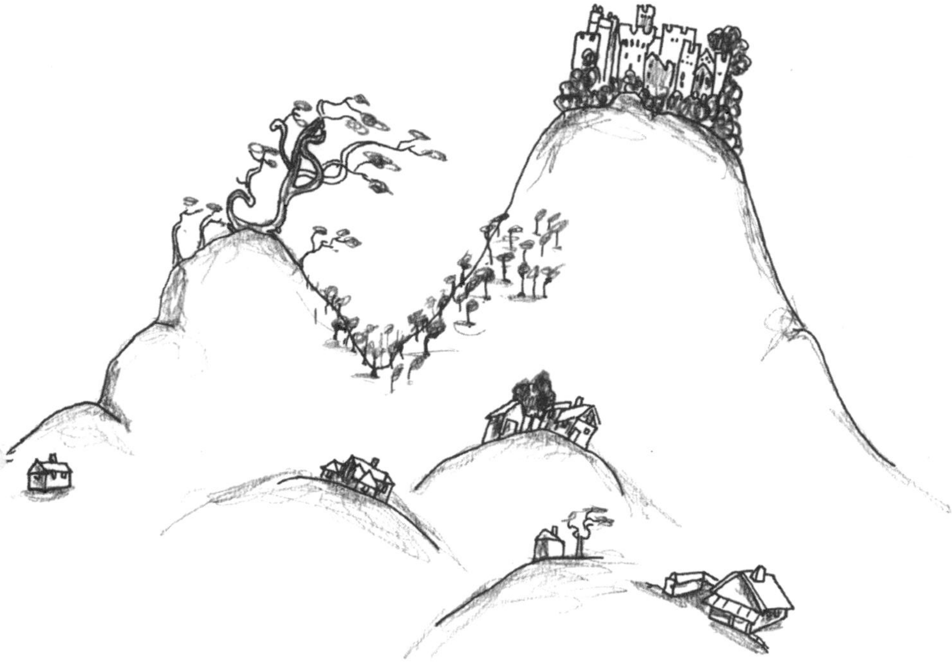

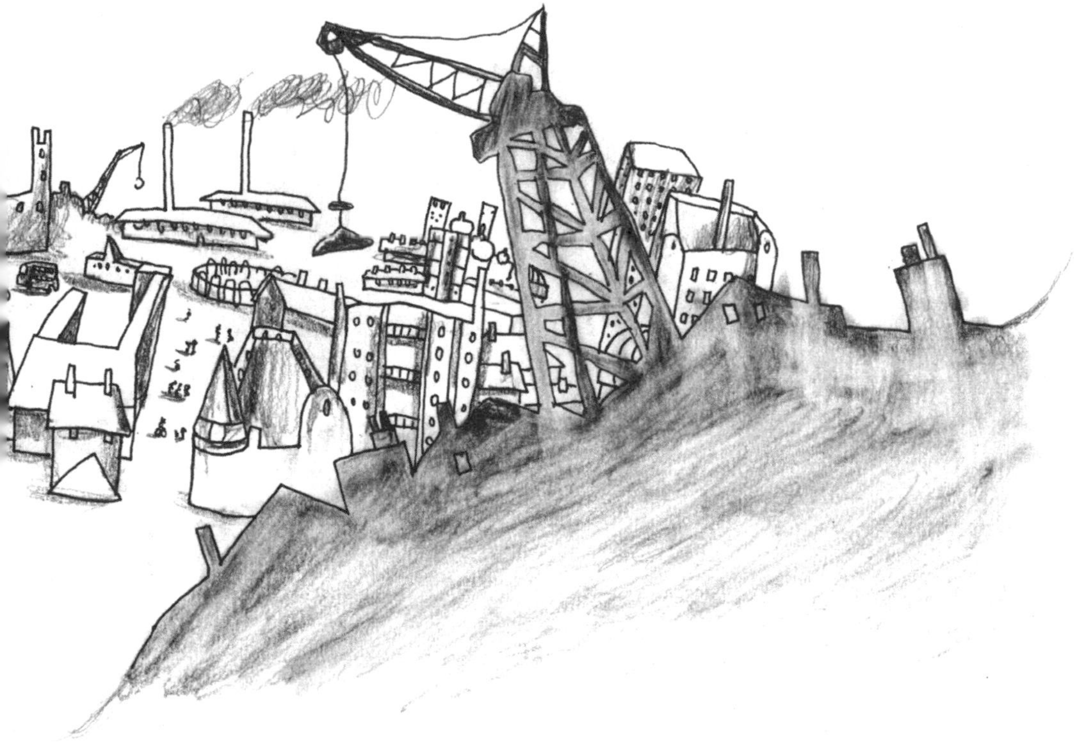

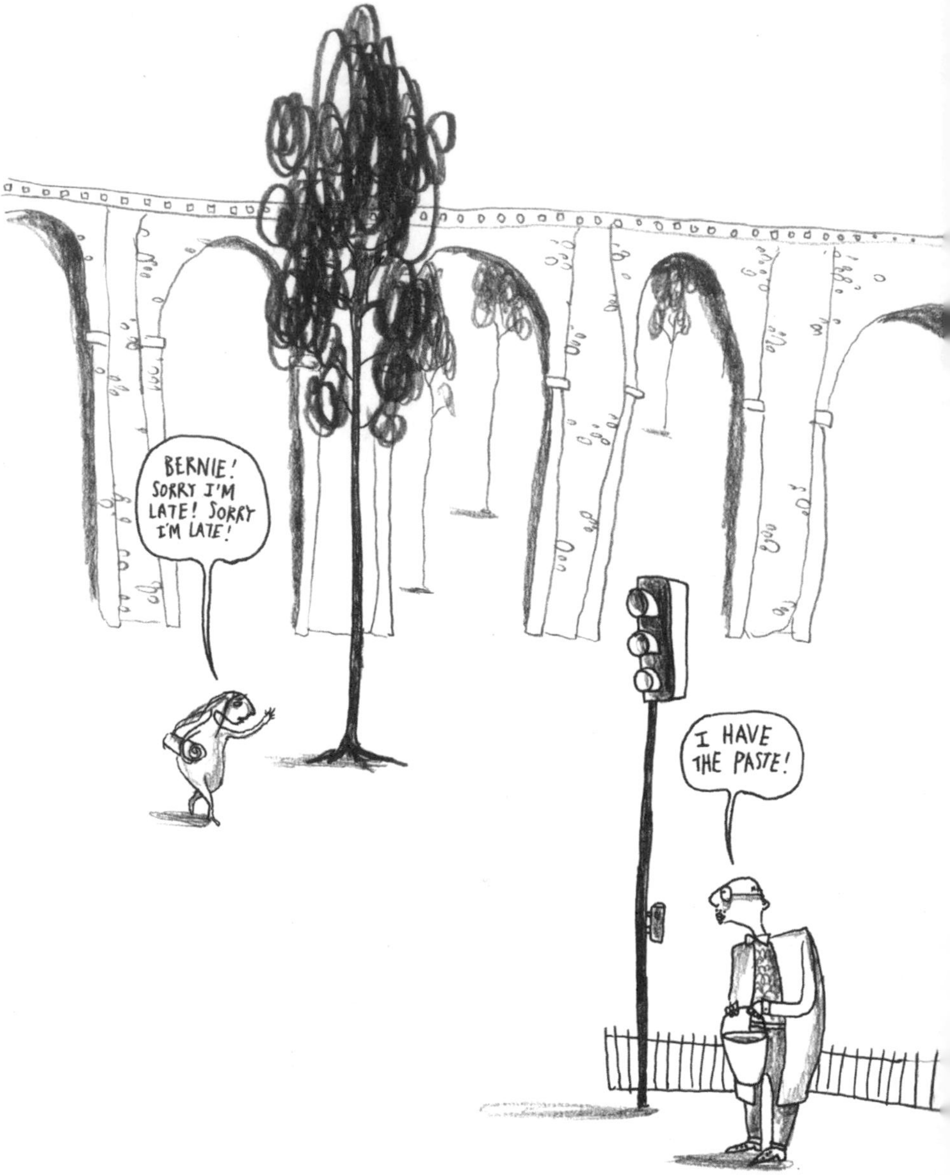
BERNIE! SORRY I'M LATE! SORRY I'M LATE!
I HAVE THE PASTE!

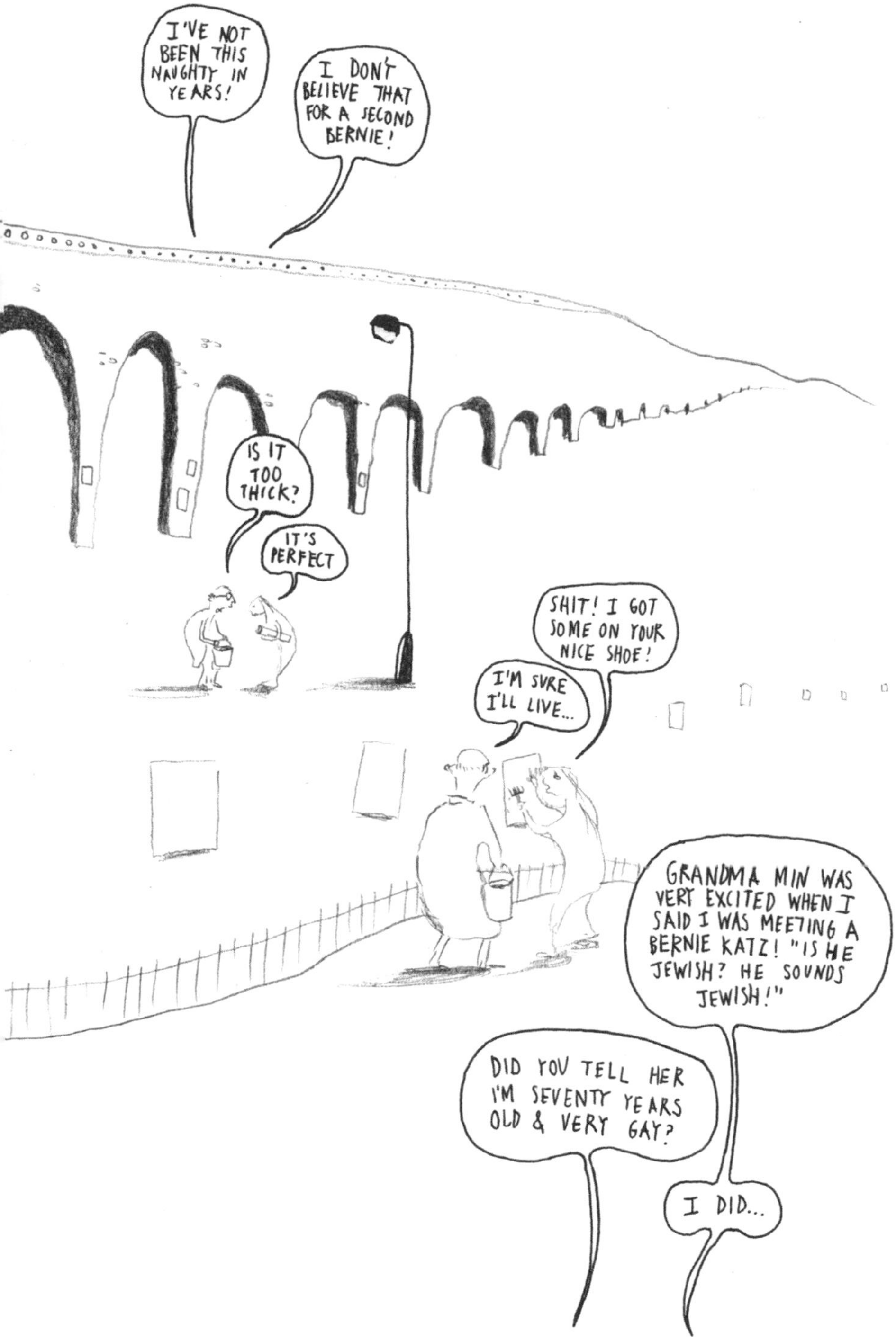
I'VE NOT BEEN THIS NAUGHTY IN YEARS!
I DON'T BELIEVE THAT FOR A SECOND BERNIE!
IS IT TOO THICK?
IT'S PERFECT
SHIT! I GOT SOME ON YOUR NICE SHOE!
I'M SURE I'LL LIVE...
GRANDMA MIN WAS VERY EXCITED WHEN I SAID I WAS MEETING A BERNIE KATZ! "IS HE JEWISH? HE SOUNDS JEWISH!"
DID YOU TELL HER I'M SEVENTY YEARS OLD & VERY GAY?
I DID...

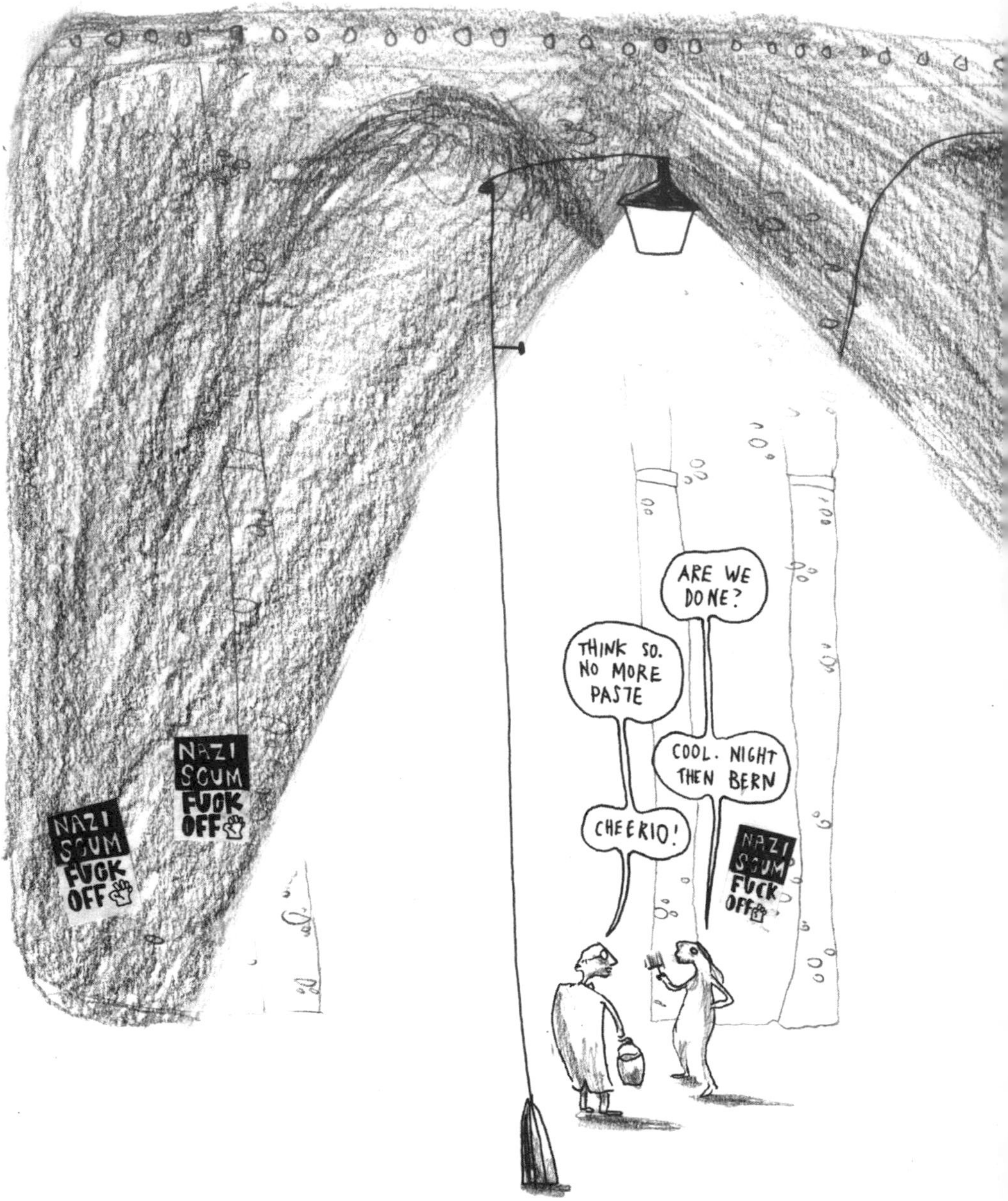
NAZI SCUM FUCK OFF
NAZI SCUM FUCK OFF
ARE WE DONE?
THINK SO. NO MORE PASTE
COOL. NIGHT THEN BERN
CHEERIO!
NAZI SCUM FUCK OFF

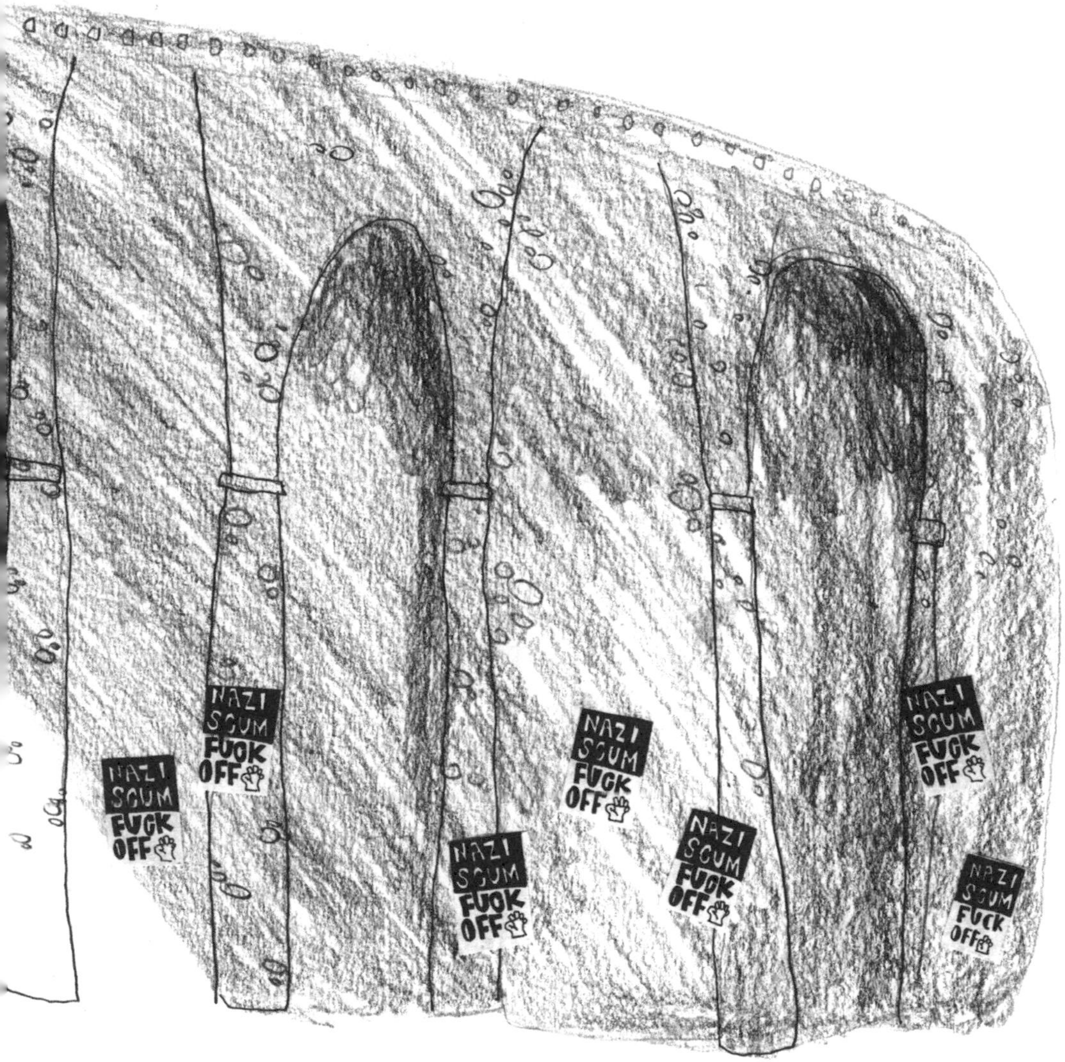
NAZI SCUM FUCK OFF
NAZI SCUM FUCK OFF
NAZI SCUM FUCK OFF
NAZI SCUM FUCK OFF
NAZI SCUM FUCK OFF
NAZI SCUM FUCK OFF
NAZI SCUM FUCK OFF

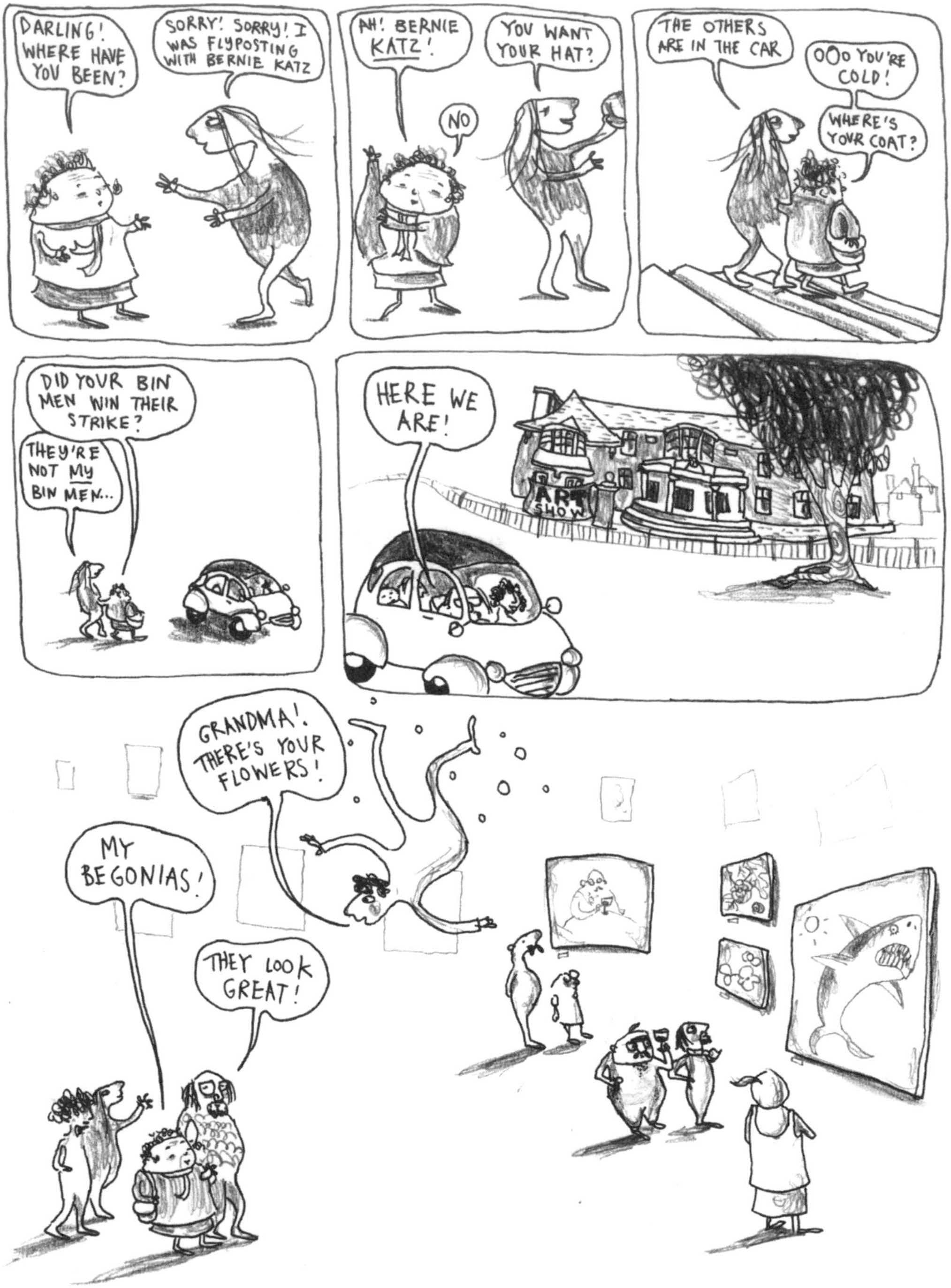

DARLING! WHERE HAVE YOU BEEN?
SORRY! SORRY! I WAS FLYPOSTING WITH BERNIE KATZ
AH! BERNIE KATZ!
YOU WANT YOUR HAT?
NO
THE OTHERS ARE IN THE CAR
OOO YOU'RE COLD!
WHERE'S YOUR COAT?
DID YOUR BIN MEN WIN THEIR STRIKE?
THEY'RE NOT MY BIN MEN...
HERE WE ARE!
ART SHOW
GRANDMA! THERE'S YOUR FLOWERS!
MY BEGONIAS!
THEY LOOK GREAT!

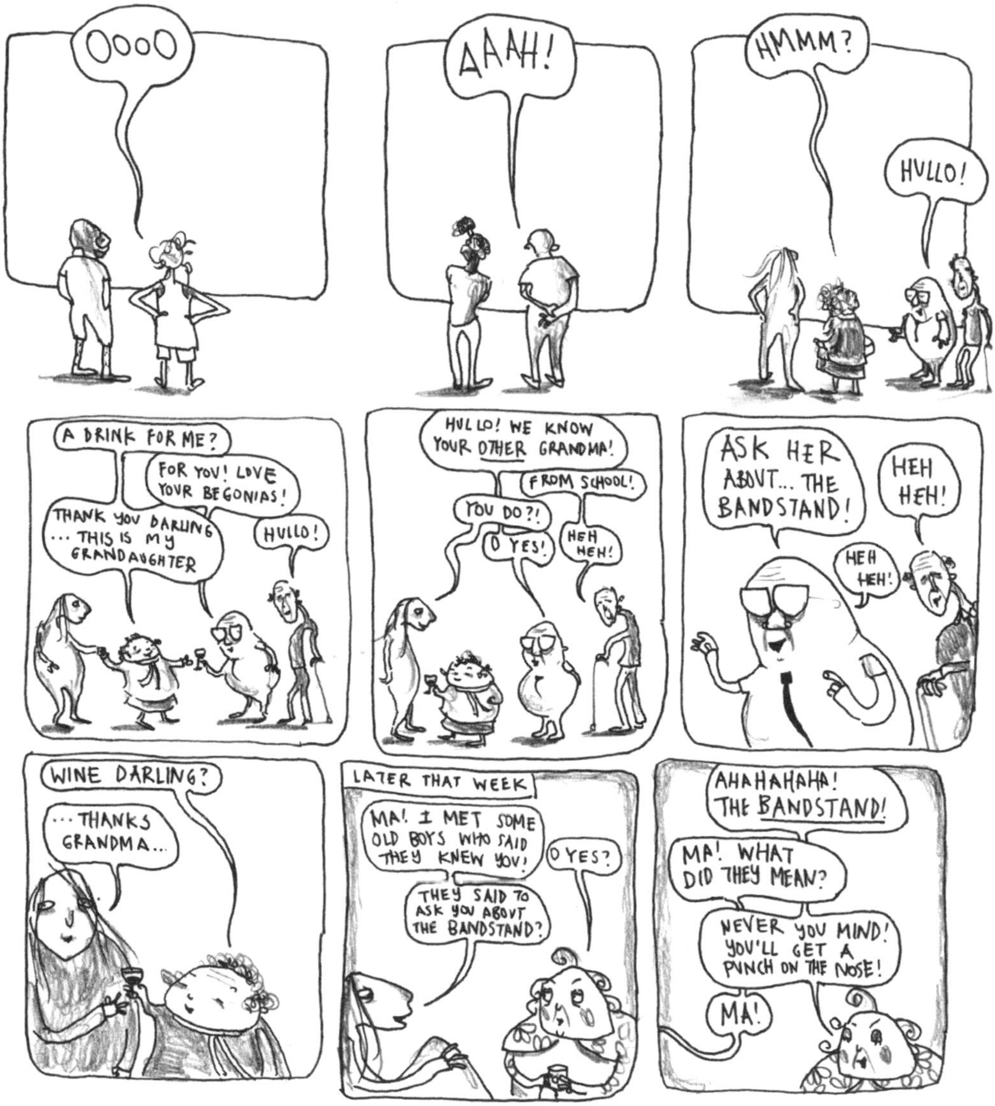
OOOO
AAAH!
HMMM?
HULLO!
A DRINK FOR ME?
FOR YOU! LOVE YOUR BEGONIAS!
THANK YOU DARLING ... THIS IS MY GRANDAUGHTER
HULLO!
HULLO! WE KNOW YOUR OTHER GRANDMA!
FROM SCHOOL!
YOU DO?!
O YES!
HEH HEH!
ASK HER ABOUT... THE BANDSTAND!
HEH HEH!
HEH HEH!
WINE DARLING?
... THANKS GRANDMA...
LATER THAT WEEK
MA! I MET SOME OLD BOYS WHO SAID THEY KNEW YOU!
O YES?
THEY SAID TO ASK YOU ABOUT THE BANDSTAND?
AHAHAHAHA! THE BANDSTAND!
MA! WHAT DID THEY MEAN?
NEVER YOU MIND! YOU'LL GET A PUNCH ON THE NOSE!
MA!

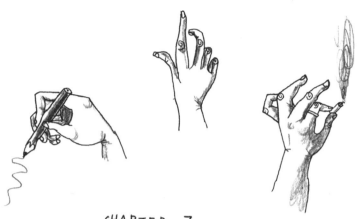

CHAPTER 7

THINGS TO DO WITH YOUR HANDS SO NO ONE
NOTICES YOU'RE TERRIFIED

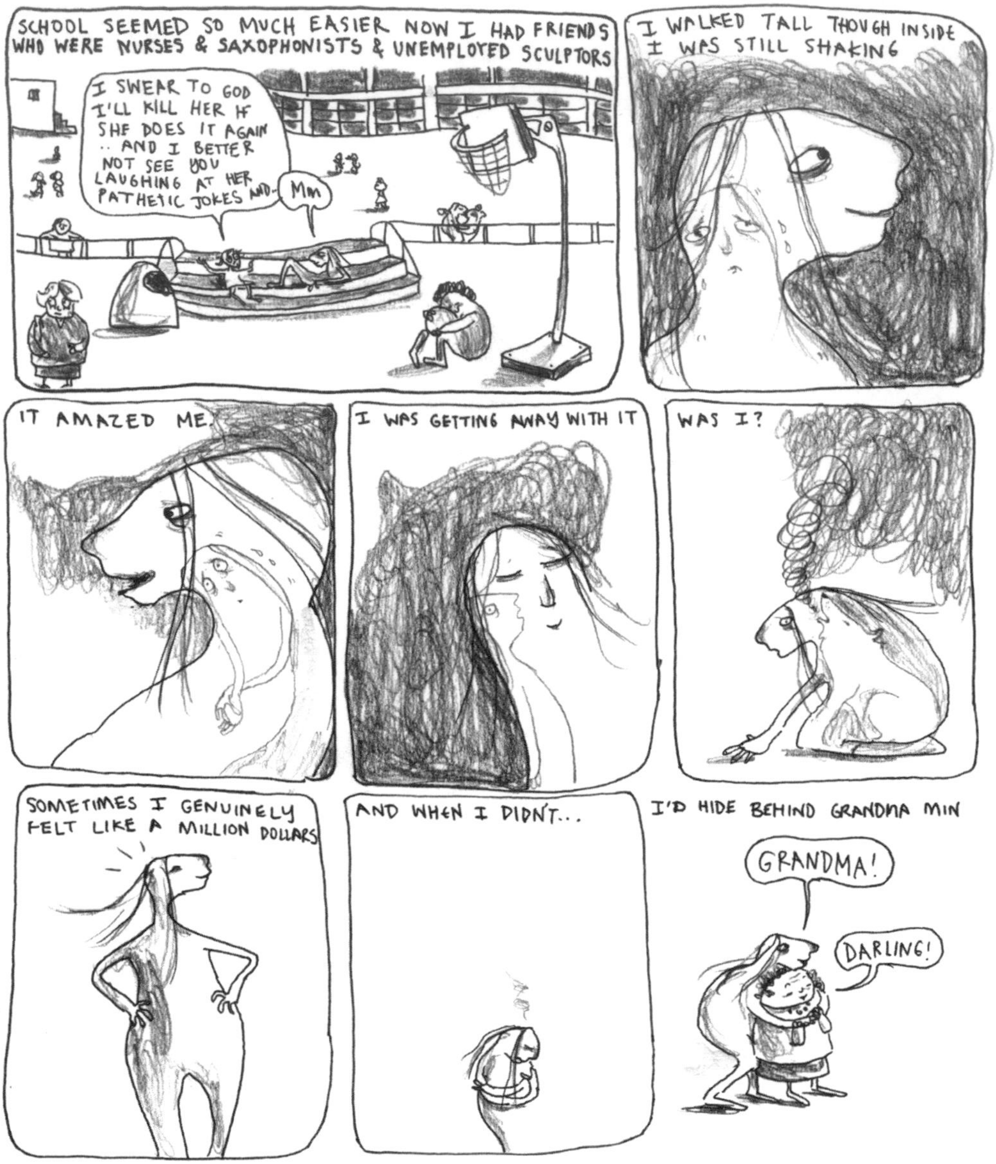
SCHOOL SEEMED SO MUCH EASIER NOW I HAD FRIENDS WHO WERE NURSES & SAXOPHONISTS & UNEMPLOYED SCULPTORS
I SWEAR TO GOD I'LL KILL HER IF SHE DOES IT AGAIN .. AND I BETTER NOT SEE YOU LAUGHING AT HER PATHETIC JOKES AND-
Mm
I WALKED TALL THOUGH INSIDE I WAS STILL SHAKING
IT AMAZED ME.
I WAS GETTING AWAY WITH IT
WAS I?
SOMETIMES I GENUINELY FELT LIKE A MILLION DOLLARS
AND WHEN I DIDN'T...
I'D HIDE BEHIND GRANDMA MIN
GRANDMA!
DARLING!

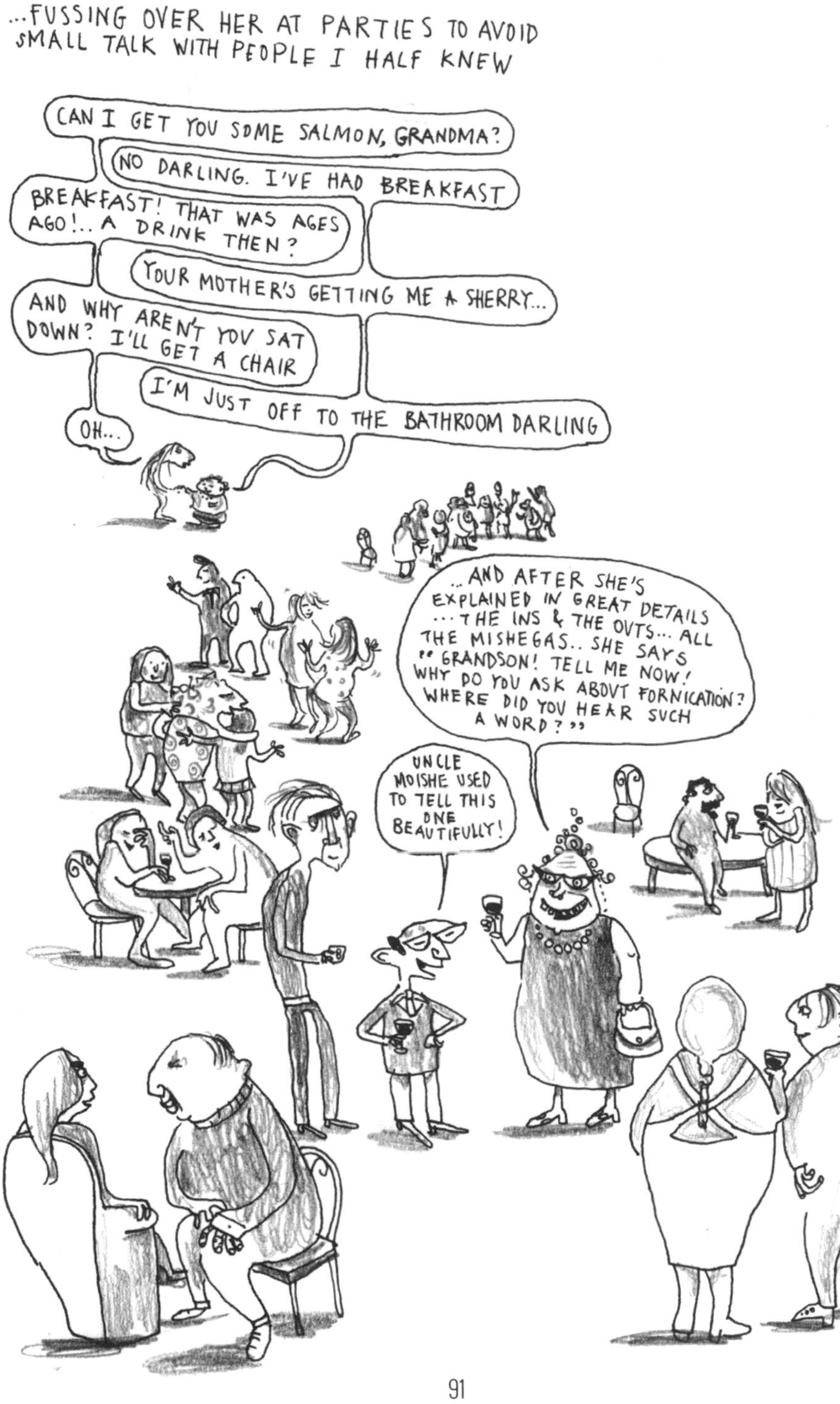
...FUSSING OVER HER AT PARTIES TO AVOID SMALL TALK WITH PEOPLE I HALF KNEW
CAN I GET YOU SOME SALMON, GRANDMA?
NO DARLING. I'VE HAD BREAKFAST
BREAKFAST! THAT WAS AGES AGO!.. A DRINK THEN?
YOUR MOTHER'S GETTING ME A SHERRY...
AND WHY AREN'T YOU SAT DOWN? I'LL GET A CHAIR
I'M JUST OFF TO THE BATHROOM DARLING
OH...
...AND AFTER SHE'S EXPLAINED IN GREAT DETAILS ...THE INS & THE OUTS... ALL THE MISHEGAS.. SHE SAYS "GRANDSON! TELL ME NOW! WHY DO YOU ASK ABOUT FORNICATION? WHERE DID YOU HEAR SUCH A WORD?"
UNCLE MOISHE USED TO TELL THIS ONE BEAUTIFULLY!

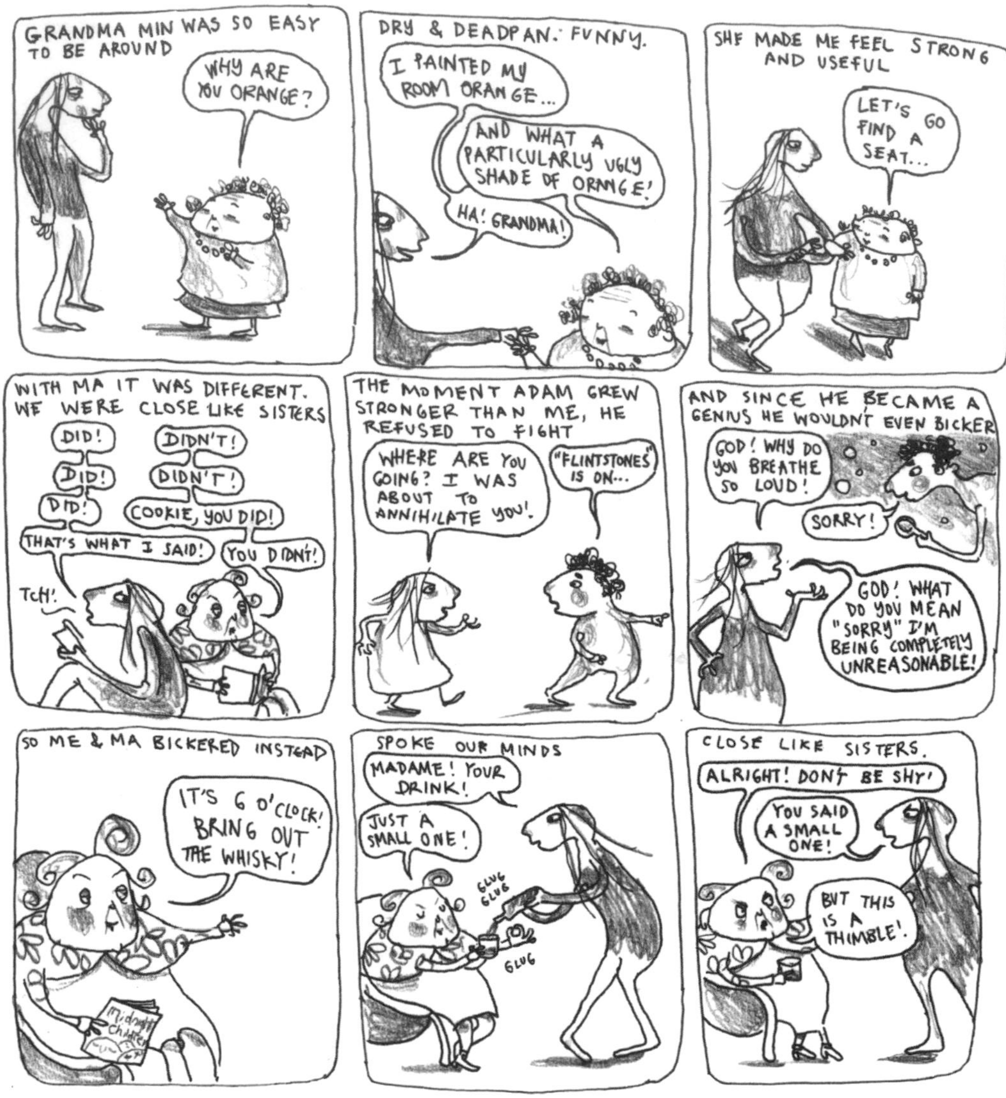
GRANDMA MIN WAS SO EASY TO BE AROUND
WHY ARE YOU ORANGE?
DRY & DEADPAN. FUNNY.
I PAINTED MY ROOM ORANGE...
AND WHAT A PARTICULARLY UGLY SHADE OF ORANGE!
HA! GRANDMA!
SHE MADE ME FEEL STRONG AND USEFUL
LET'S GO FIND A SEAT...
WITH MA IT WAS DIFFERENT. WE WERE CLOSE LIKE SISTERS
DID!
DIDN'T!
DID!
DIDN'T!
DID!
COOKIE, YOU DID!
THAT'S WHAT I SAID!
YOU DIDN'T!
TCH!
THE MOMENT ADAM GREW STRONGER THAN ME, HE REFUSED TO FIGHT
WHERE ARE YOU GOING? I WAS ABOUT TO ANNIHILATE YOU!
"FLINTSTONES" IS ON...
AND SINCE HE BECAME A GENIUS HE WOULDN'T EVEN BICKER
GOD! WHY DO YOU BREATHE SO LOUD!
SORRY!
GOD! WHAT DO YOU MEAN "SORRY" I'M BEING COMPLETELY UNREASONABLE!
SO ME & MA BICKERED INSTEAD
IT'S 6 O'CLOCK! BRING OUT THE WHISKY!
SPOKE OUR MINDS
MADAME! YOUR DRINK!
JUST A SMALL ONE!
GLUG GLUG
GLUG
CLOSE LIKE SISTERS.
ALRIGHT! DON'T BE SHY!
YOU SAID A SMALL ONE!
BUT THIS IS A THIMBLE!

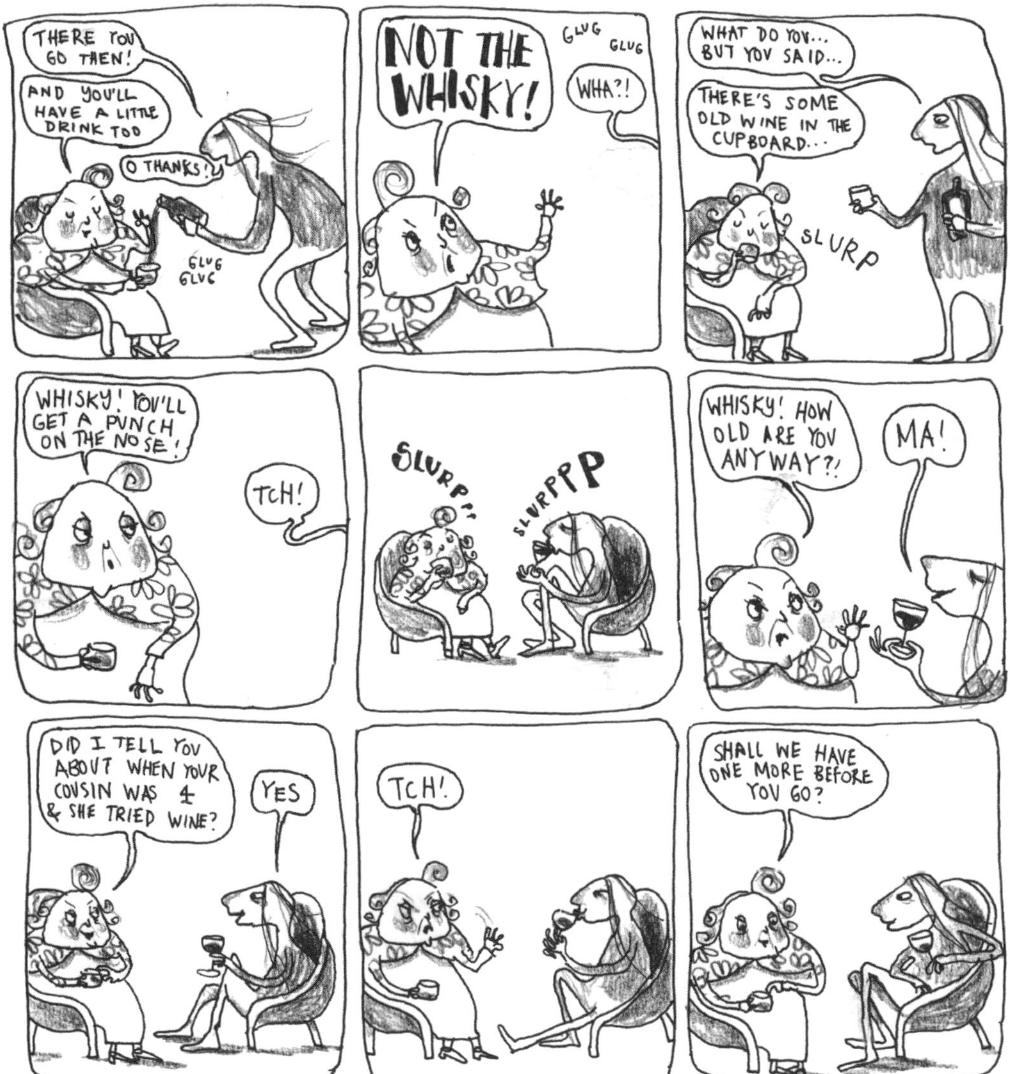
THERE YOU GO THEN!
AND YOU'LL HAVE A LITTLE DRINK TOO
O THANKS!
GLUG GLUG
NOT THE WHISKY!
GLUG GLUG
WHA?!
WHAT DO YOU... BUT YOU SAID...
THERE'S SOME OLD WINE IN THE CUPBOARD...
SLURP
WHISKY! YOU'LL GET A PUNCH ON THE NOSE!
TCH!
SLURPPP
SLURPPP
WHISKY! HOW OLD ARE YOU ANYWAY?!
MA!
DID I TELL YOU ABOUT WHEN YOUR COUSIN WAS 4 & SHE TRIED WINE?
YES
TCH!
SHALL WE HAVE ONE MORE BEFORE YOU GO?

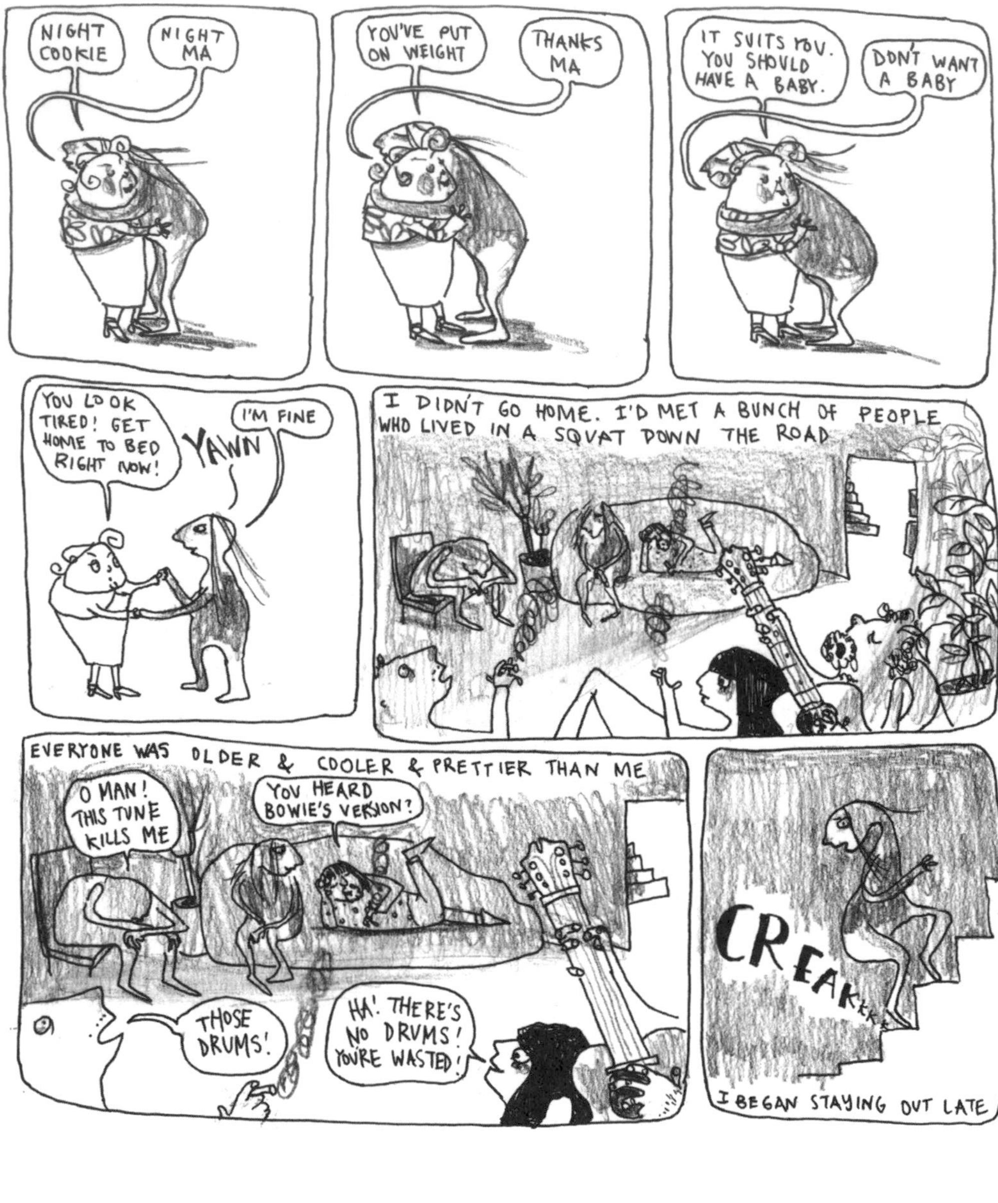
NIGHT COOKIE
NIGHT MA
YOU'VE PUT ON WEIGHT
THANKS MA
IT SUITS YOU. YOU SHOULD HAVE A BABY.
DON'T WANT A BABY
YOU LOOK TIRED! GET HOME TO BED RIGHT NOW!
YAWN
I'M FINE
I DIDN'T GO HOME. I'D MET A BUNCH OF PEOPLE WHO LIVED IN A SQUAT DOWN THE ROAD
EVERYONE WAS OLDER & COOLER & PRETTIER THAN ME
O MAN! THIS TUNE KILLS ME
YOU HEARD BOWIE'S VERSION?
THOSE DRUMS!
HA! THERE'S NO DRUMS! YOU'RE WASTED!
CREAKKKK
I BEGAN STAYING OUT LATE

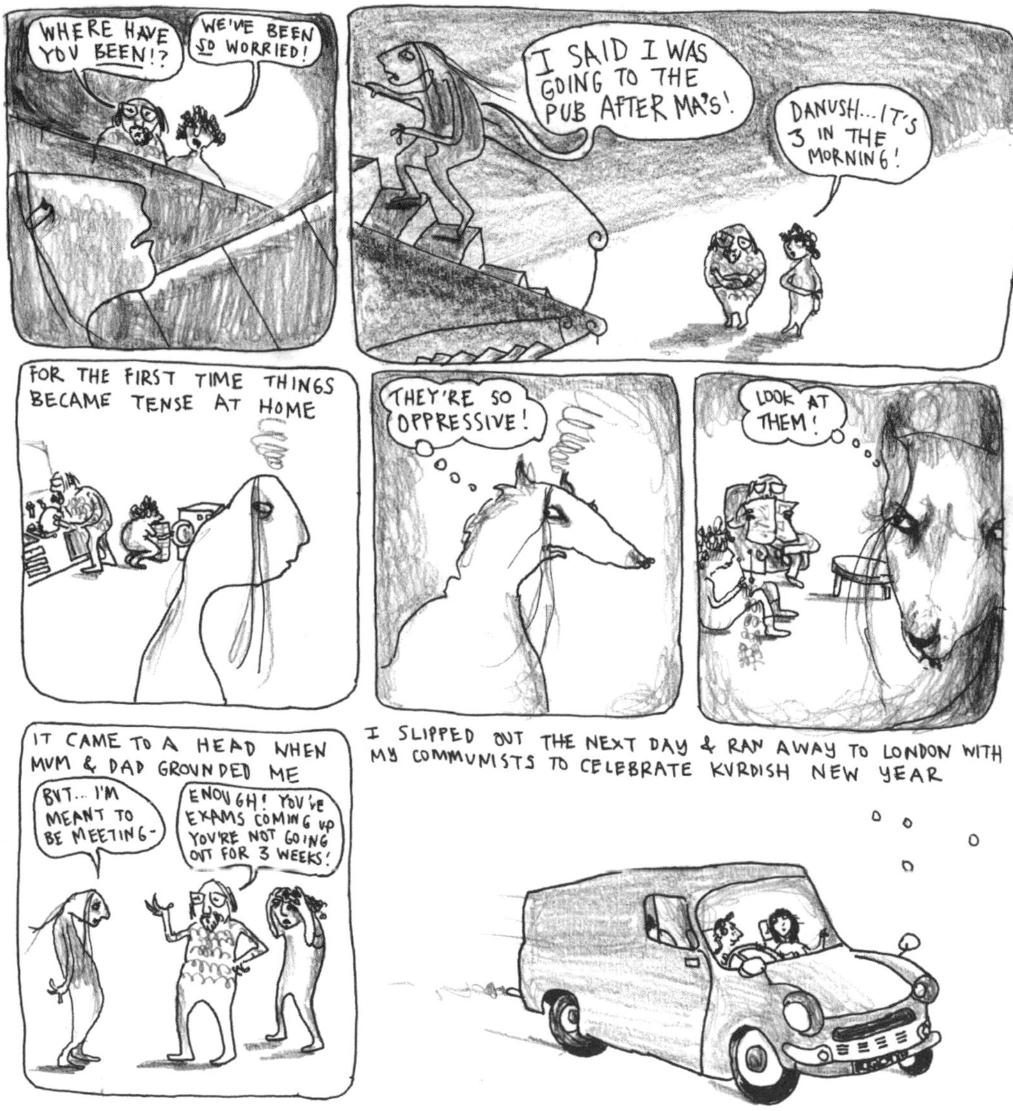
WHERE HAVE YOU BEEN!?
WE'VE BEEN SO WORRIED!
I SAID I WAS GOING TO THE PUB AFTER MA'S!
DANUSH... IT'S 3 IN THE MORNING!
FOR THE FIRST TIME THINGS BECAME TENSE AT HOME
THEY'RE SO OPPRESSIVE!
LOOK AT THEM!
IT CAME TO A HEAD WHEN MUM & DAD GROUNDED ME
BUT... I'M MEANT TO BE MEETING-
ENOUGH! YOU'VE EXAMS COMING UP YOU'RE NOT GOING OUT FOR 3 WEEKS!
I SLIPPED OUT THE NEXT DAY & RAN AWAY TO LONDON WITH MY COMMUNISTS TO CELEBRATE KURDISH NEW YEAR

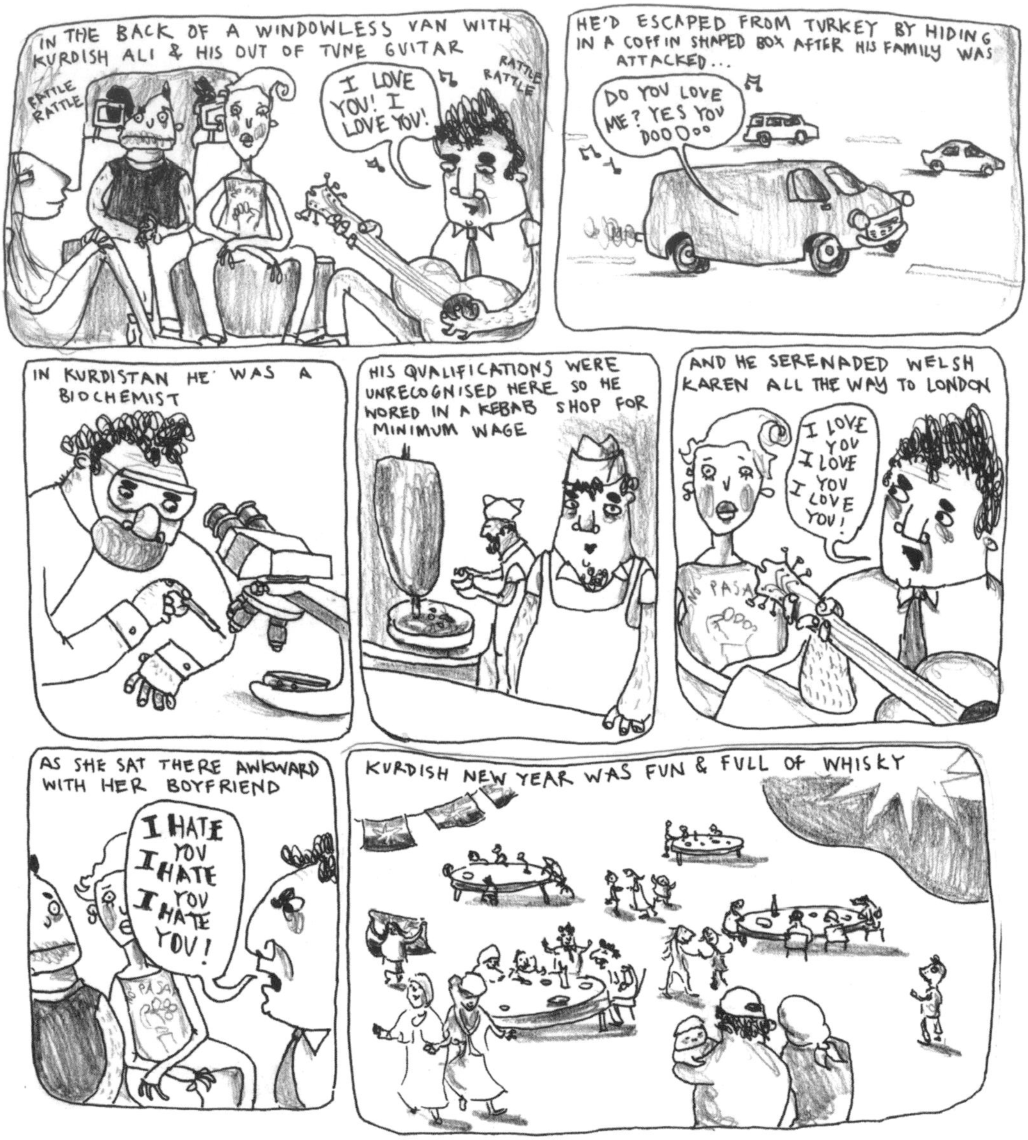
IN THE BACK OF A WINDOWLESS VAN WITH KURDISH ALI & HIS OUT OF TUNE GUITAR
RATTLE RATTLE
I LOVE YOU! I LOVE YOU!
RATTLE RATTLE
HE'D ESCAPED FROM TURKEY BY HIDING IN A COFFIN SHAPED BOX AFTER HIS FAMILY WAS ATTACKED...
DO YOU LOVE ME? YES YOU DOOOoo
IN KURDISTAN HE WAS A BIOCHEMIST
HIS QUALIFICATIONS WERE UNRECOGNISED HERE SO HE WORED IN A KEBAB SHOP FOR MINIMUM WAGE
AND HE SERENADED WELSH KAREN ALL THE WAY TO LONDON
I LOVE YOU I LOVE YOU I LOVE YOU!
AS SHE SAT THERE AWKWARD WITH HER BOYFRIEND
I HATE YOU I HATE YOU I HATE YOU!
KURDISH NEW YEAR WAS FUN & FULL OF WHISKY

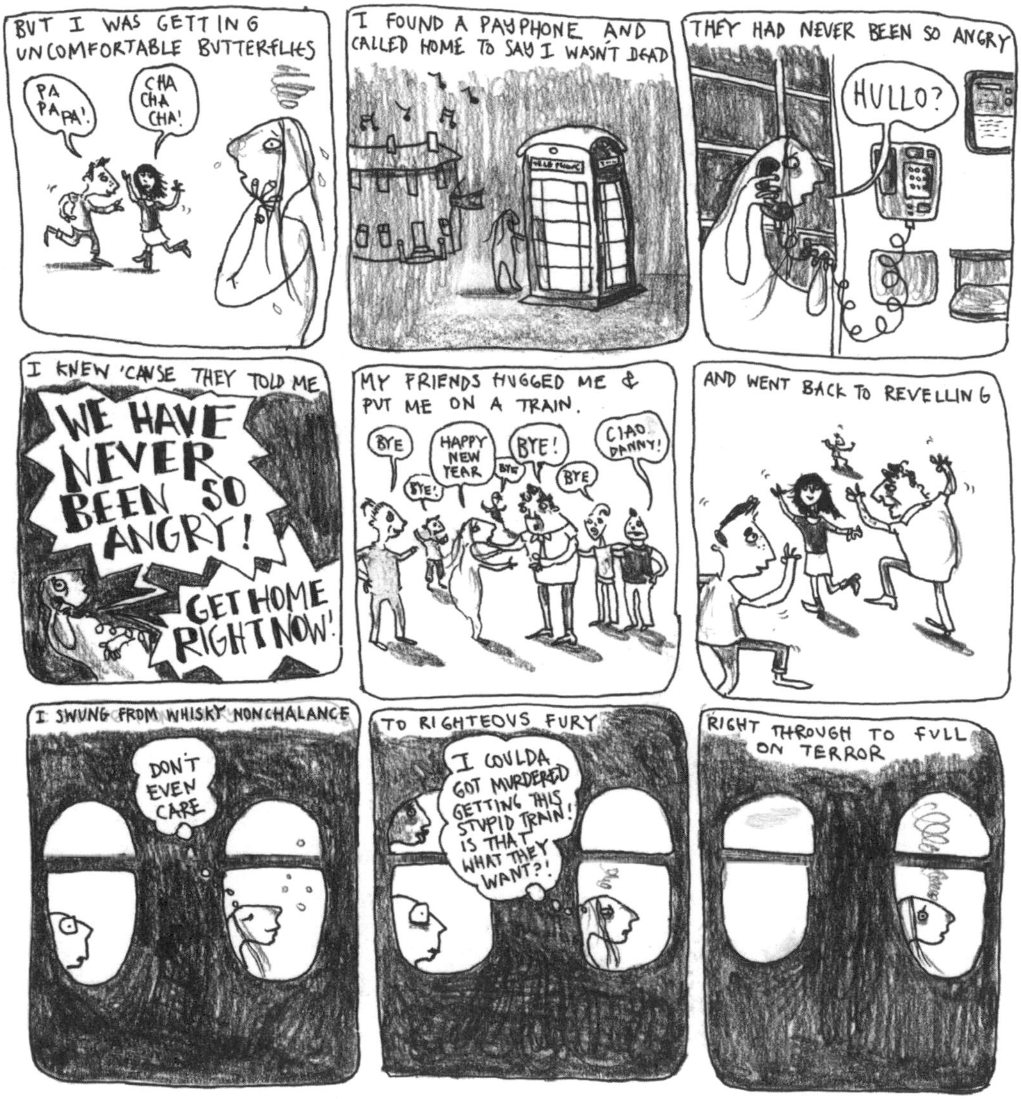
BUT I WAS GETTING UNCOMFORTABLE BUTTERFLIES
PA PA PA!
CHA CHA CHA!
I FOUND A PAYPHONE AND CALLED HOME TO SAY I WASN'T DEAD
THEY HAD NEVER BEEN SO ANGRY
HULLO?
I KNEW 'CAUSE THEY TOLD ME
WE HAVE NEVER BEEN SO ANGRY!
GET HOME RIGHT NOW!
MY FRIENDS HUGGED ME & PUT ME ON A TRAIN.
BYE
BYE!
HAPPY NEW YEAR
BYE
BYE!
BYE
CIAO DANNY!
AND WENT BACK TO REVELLING
I SWUNG FROM WHISKY NONCHALANCE
DON'T EVEN CARE
TO RIGHTEOUS FURY
I COULDA GOT MURDERED GETTING THIS STUPID TRAIN! IS THAT WHAT THEY WANT?!
RIGHT THROUGH TO FULL ON TERROR

WE'LL TALK TOMORROW!

Z Z z z z

THE NEXT DAY I TOOK MY TELLING OFF

WEEKS LATER WHEN I WAS ALLOWED BACK OUT

I RAN STRAIGHT BACK TO THE SQUAT

SO UNREASONABLE! WHY ARE THEY SO SMOTHERING?!

FACISTS!

YEA YEA MAN

I DON'T KNOW DUDE. I ALWAYS LET MY FLATMATE KNOW WHERE I AM SO SHE KNOWS I'M SAFE. IT'S NOT A BIG DEAL...

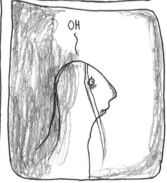

OH

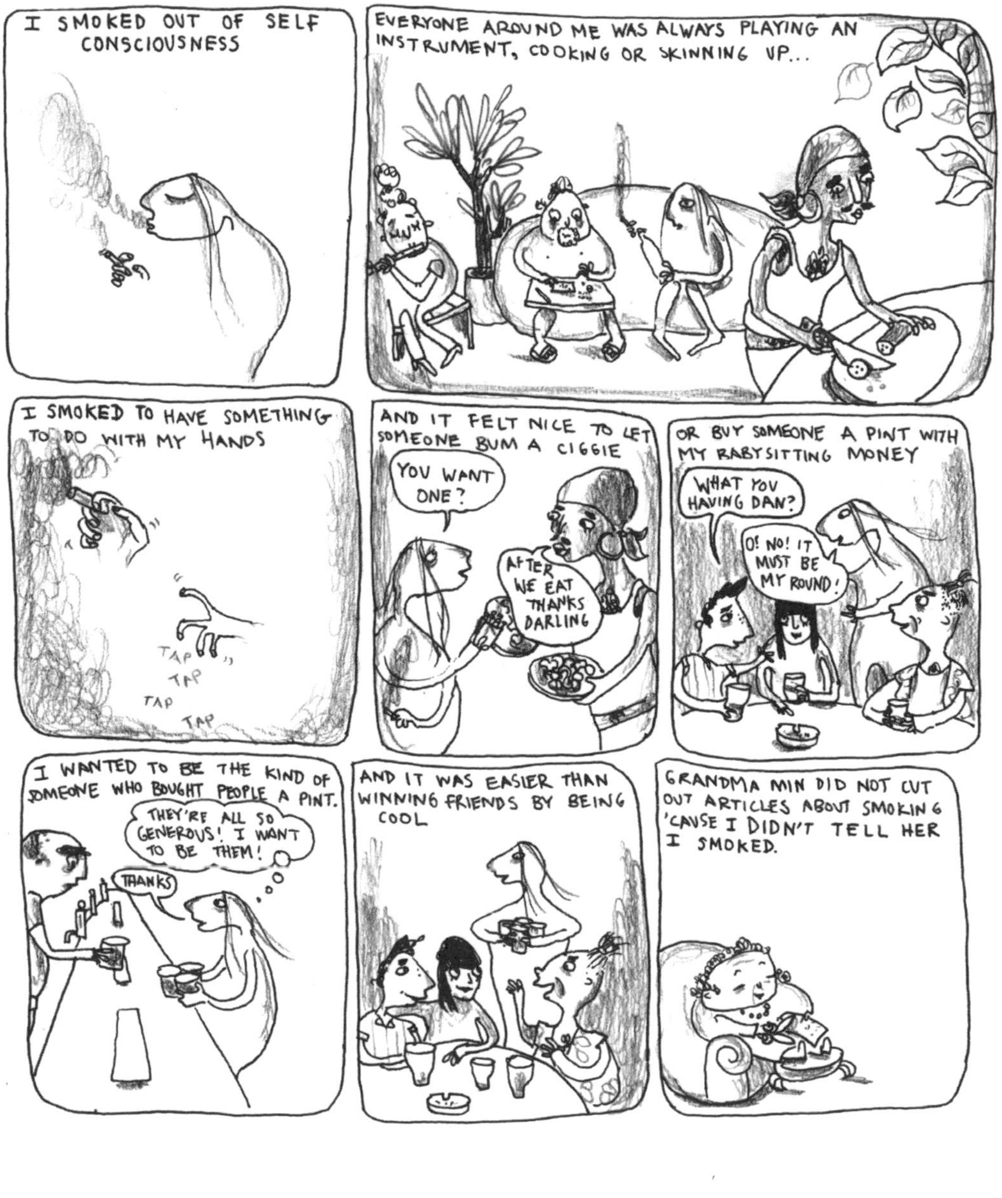
I SMOKED OUT OF SELF CONSCIOUSNESS
EVERYONE AROUND ME WAS ALWAYS PLAYING AN INSTRUMENT, COOKING OR SKINNING UP...
I SMOKED TO HAVE SOMETHING TO DO WITH MY HANDS
TAP TAP TAP TAP
AND IT FELT NICE TO LET SOMEONE BUM A CIGGIE
YOU WANT ONE?
AFTER WE EAT THANKS DARLING
OR BUY SOMEONE A PINT WITH MY BABYSITTING MONEY
WHAT YOU HAVING DAN?
O! NO! IT MUST BE MY ROUND!
I WANTED TO BE THE KIND OF SOMEONE WHO BOUGHT PEOPLE A PINT.
THEY'RE ALL SO GENEROUS! I WANT TO BE THEM!
THANKS
AND IT WAS EASIER THAN WINNING FRIENDS BY BEING COOL
GRANDMA MIN DID NOT CUT OUT ARTICLES ABOUT SMOKING 'CAUSE I DIDN'T TELL HER I SMOKED.

CHAPTER 8
A FLOATING GLACIAL DEPOSIT

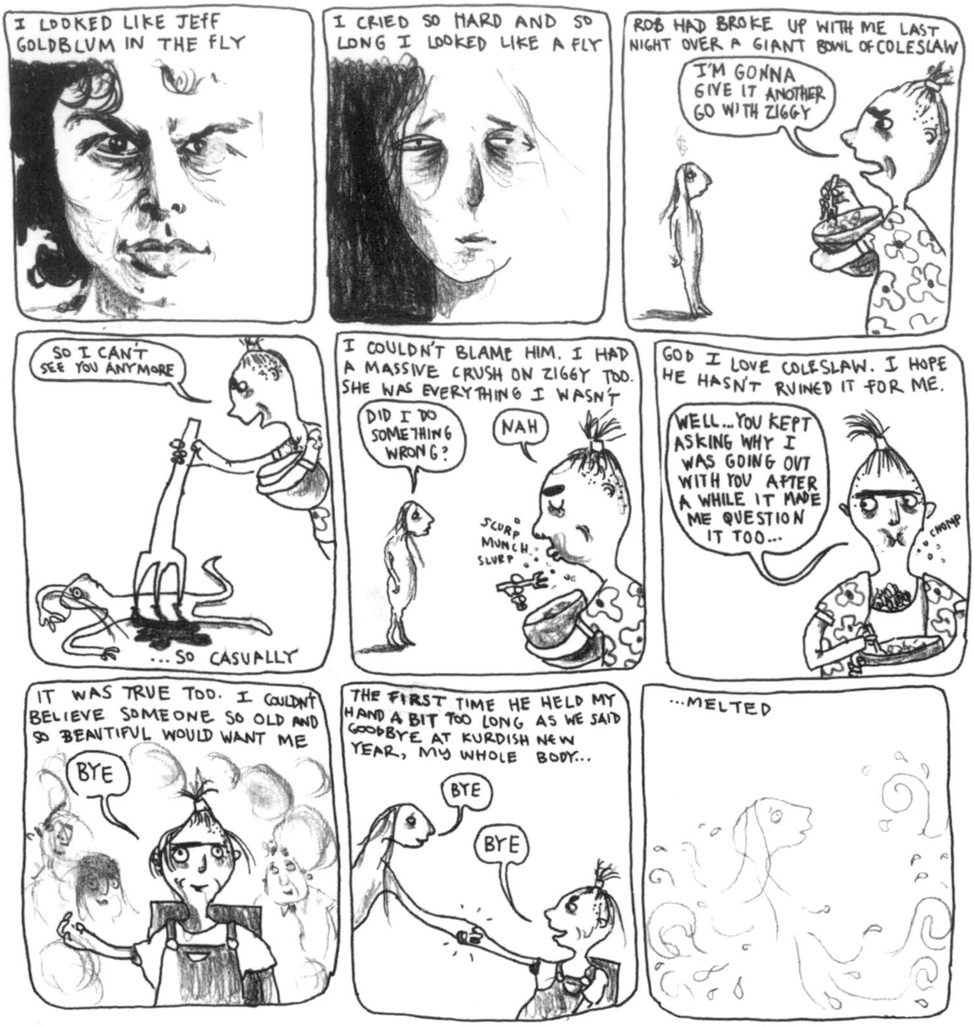
I LOOKED LIKE JEFF GOLDBLUM IN THE FLY
I CRIED SO HARD AND SO LONG I LOOKED LIKE A FLY
ROB HAD BROKE UP WITH ME LAST NIGHT OVER A GIANT BOWL OF COLESLAW
I'M GONNA GIVE IT ANOTHER GO WITH ZIGGY
SO I CAN'T SEE YOU ANYMORE
...SO CASUALLY
I COULDN'T BLAME HIM. I HAD A MASSIVE CRUSH ON ZIGGY TOO. SHE WAS EVERYTHING I WASN'T
DID I DO SOMETHING WRONG?
NAH
SCURP
MUNCH
SLURP
GOD I LOVE COLESLAW. I HOPE HE HASN'T RUINED IT FOR ME.
WELL... YOU KEPT ASKING WHY I WAS GOING OUT WITH YOU AFTER A WHILE IT MADE ME QUESTION IT TOO...
CHOMP
IT WAS TRUE TOO. I COULDN'T BELIEVE SOMEONE SO OLD AND SO BEAUTIFUL WOULD WANT ME
BYE
THE FIRST TIME HE HELD MY HAND A BIT TOO LONG AS WE SAID GOODBYE AT KURDISH NEW YEAR, MY WHOLE BODY...
BYE
BYE
...MELTED

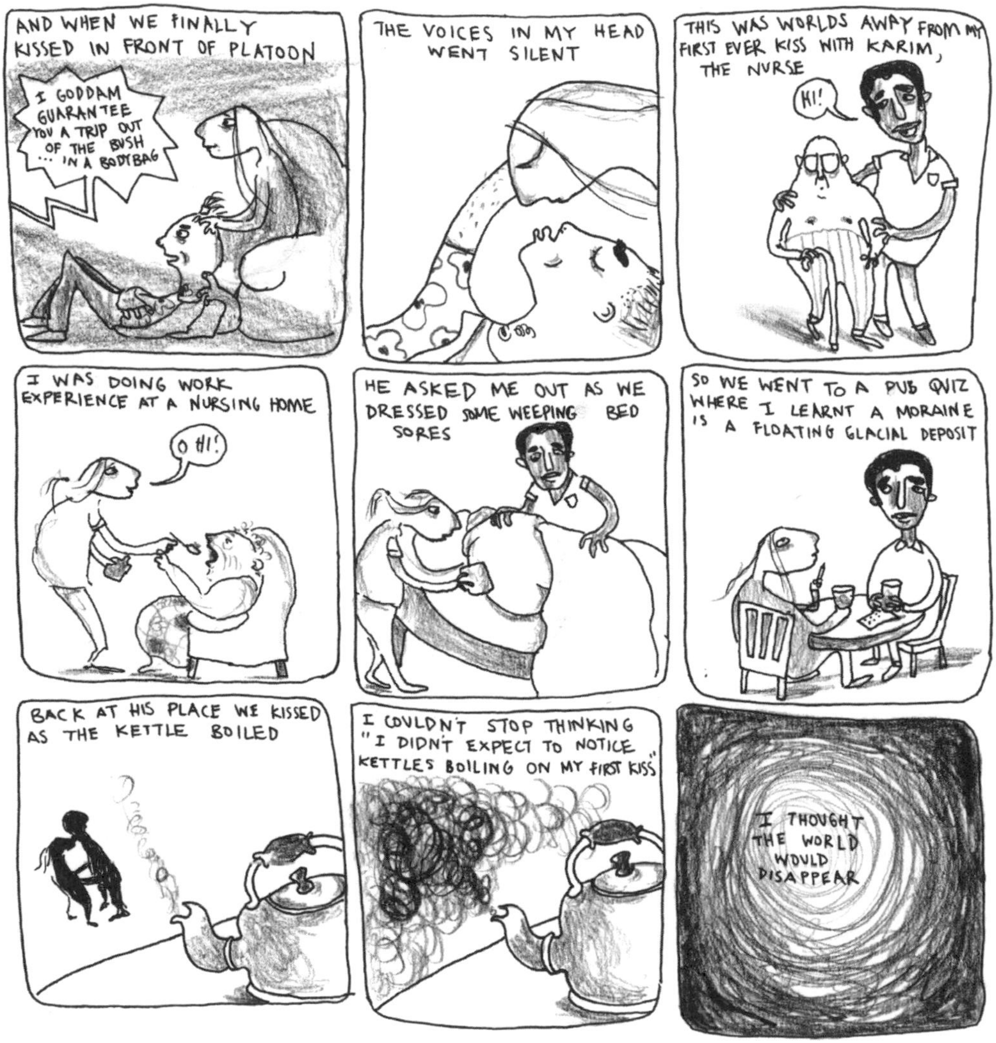
AND WHEN WE FINALLY KISSED IN FRONT OF PLATOON
I GODDAM GUARANTEE YOU A TRIP OUT OF THE BUSH ... IN A BODYBAG
THE VOICES IN MY HEAD WENT SILENT
THIS WAS WORLDS AWAY FROM MY FIRST EVER KISS WITH KARIM, THE NURSE
HI!
I WAS DOING WORK EXPERIENCE AT A NURSING HOME
O HI!
HE ASKED ME OUT AS WE DRESSED SOME WEEPING BED SORES
SO WE WENT TO A PUB QUIZ WHERE I LEARNT A MORAINE IS A FLOATING GLACIAL DEPOSIT
BACK AT HIS PLACE WE KISSED AS THE KETTLE BOILED
I COULDN'T STOP THINKING "I DIDN'T EXPECT TO NOTICE KETTLES BOILING ON MY FIRST KISS"
I THOUGHT THE WORLD WOULD DISAPPEAR

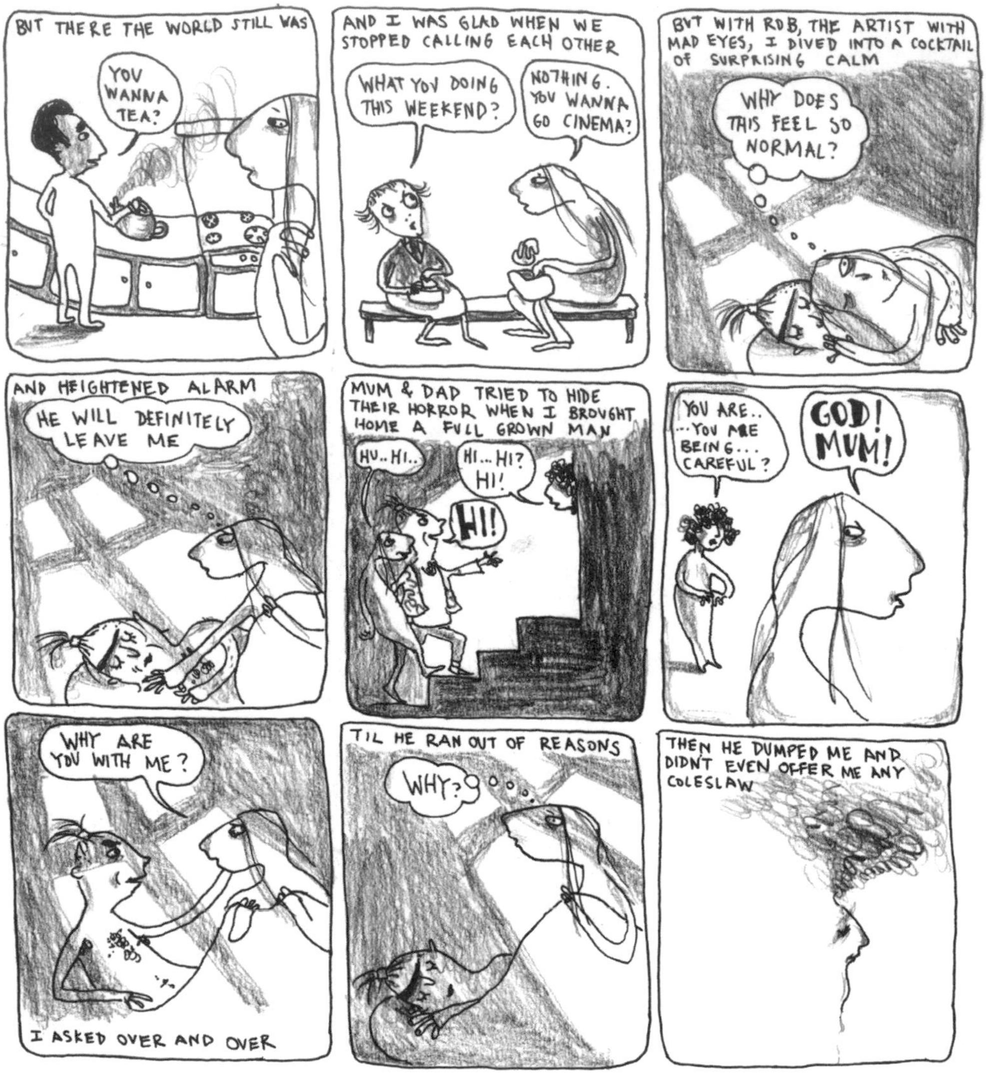
BUT THERE THE WORLD STILL WAS
YOU WANNA TEA?
AND I WAS GLAD WHEN WE STOPPED CALLING EACH OTHER
WHAT YOU DOING THIS WEEKEND?
NOTHING. YOU WANNA GO CINEMA?
BUT WITH ROB, THE ARTIST WITH MAD EYES, I DIVED INTO A COCKTAIL OF SURPRISING CALM
WHY DOES THIS FEEL SO NORMAL?
AND HEIGHTENED ALARM
HE WILL DEFINITELY LEAVE ME
MUM & DAD TRIED TO HIDE THEIR HORROR WHEN I BROUGHT HOME A FULL GROWN MAN
HU.. HI..
HI... HI? HI!
HI!
YOU ARE.. ...YOU ARE BEING... CAREFUL?
GOD! MUM!
WHY ARE YOU WITH ME?
I ASKED OVER AND OVER
TIL HE RAN OUT OF REASONS
WHY?
THEN HE DUMPED ME AND DIDN'T EVEN OFFER ME ANY COLESLAW

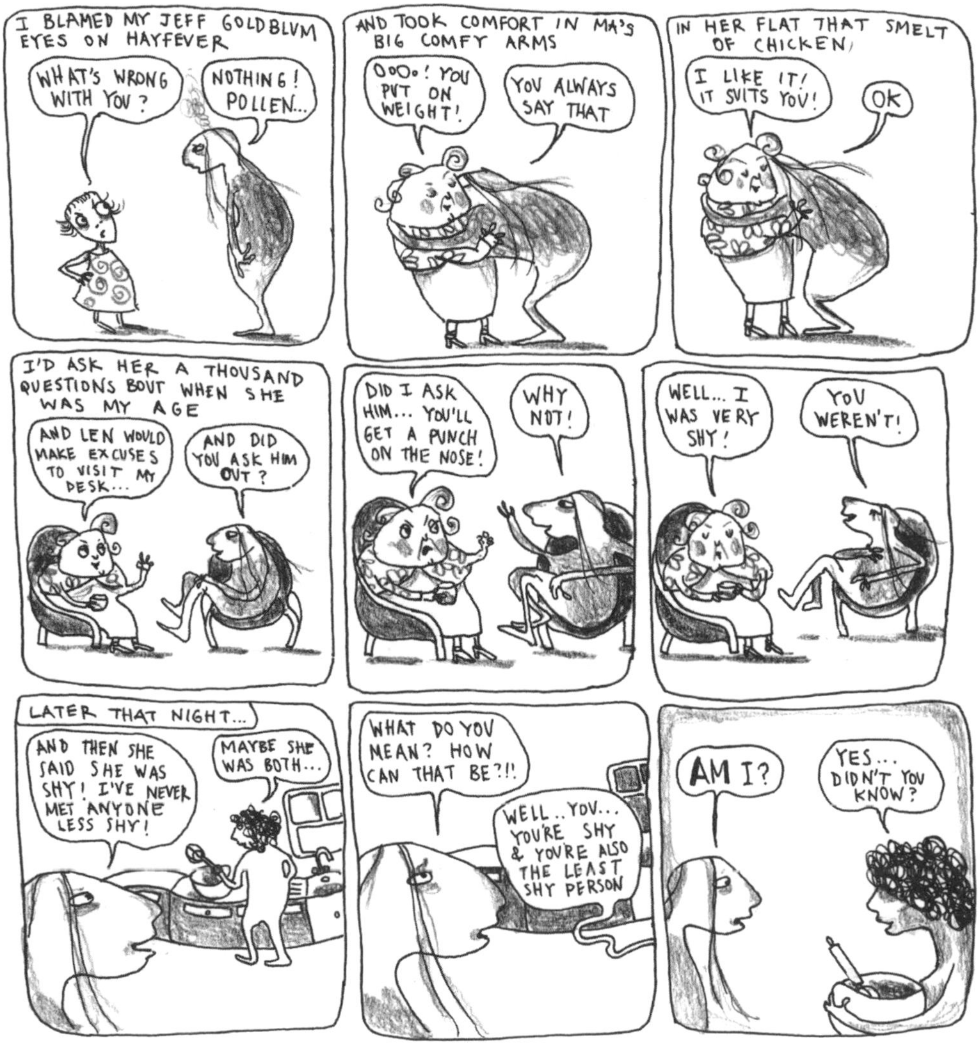
I BLAMED MY JEFF GOLDBLUM EYES ON HAYFEVER
WHAT'S WRONG WITH YOU?
NOTHING! POLLEN...
AND TOOK COMFORT IN MA'S BIG COMFY ARMS
OOOo! YOU PUT ON WEIGHT!
YOU ALWAYS SAY THAT
IN HER FLAT THAT SMELT OF CHICKEN,
I LIKE IT! IT SUITS YOU!
OK
I'D ASK HER A THOUSAND QUESTIONS BOUT WHEN SHE WAS MY AGE
AND LEN WOULD MAKE EXCUSES TO VISIT MY DESK...
AND DID YOU ASK HIM OUT?
DID I ASK HIM... YOU'LL GET A PUNCH ON THE NOSE!
WHY NOT!
WELL... I WAS VERY SHY!
YOU WEREN'T!
LATER THAT NIGHT...
AND THEN SHE SAID SHE WAS SHY! I'VE NEVER MET ANYONE LESS SHY!
MAYBE SHE WAS BOTH...
WHAT DO YOU MEAN? HOW CAN THAT BE?!!
WELL.. YOU... YOU'RE SHY & YOU'RE ALSO THE LEAST SHY PERSON
AM I?
YES... DIDN'T YOU KNOW?

I'D WATCH THE MAS ON OUR SOFA EVERY FRIDAY NIGHT
AND WISH FOR A TIME MACHINE SO I COULD GO BACK AND
SPY ON WHAT MISCHIEF THEY GOT UP TO WHEN THEY WERE YOUNG

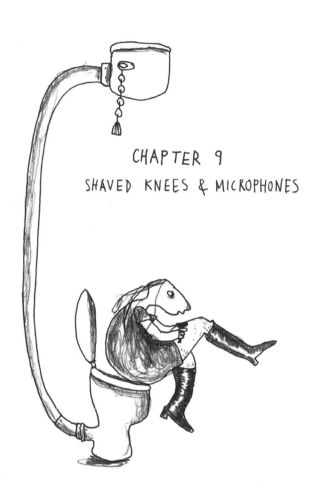

CHAPTER 9
SHAVED KNEES & MICROPHONES

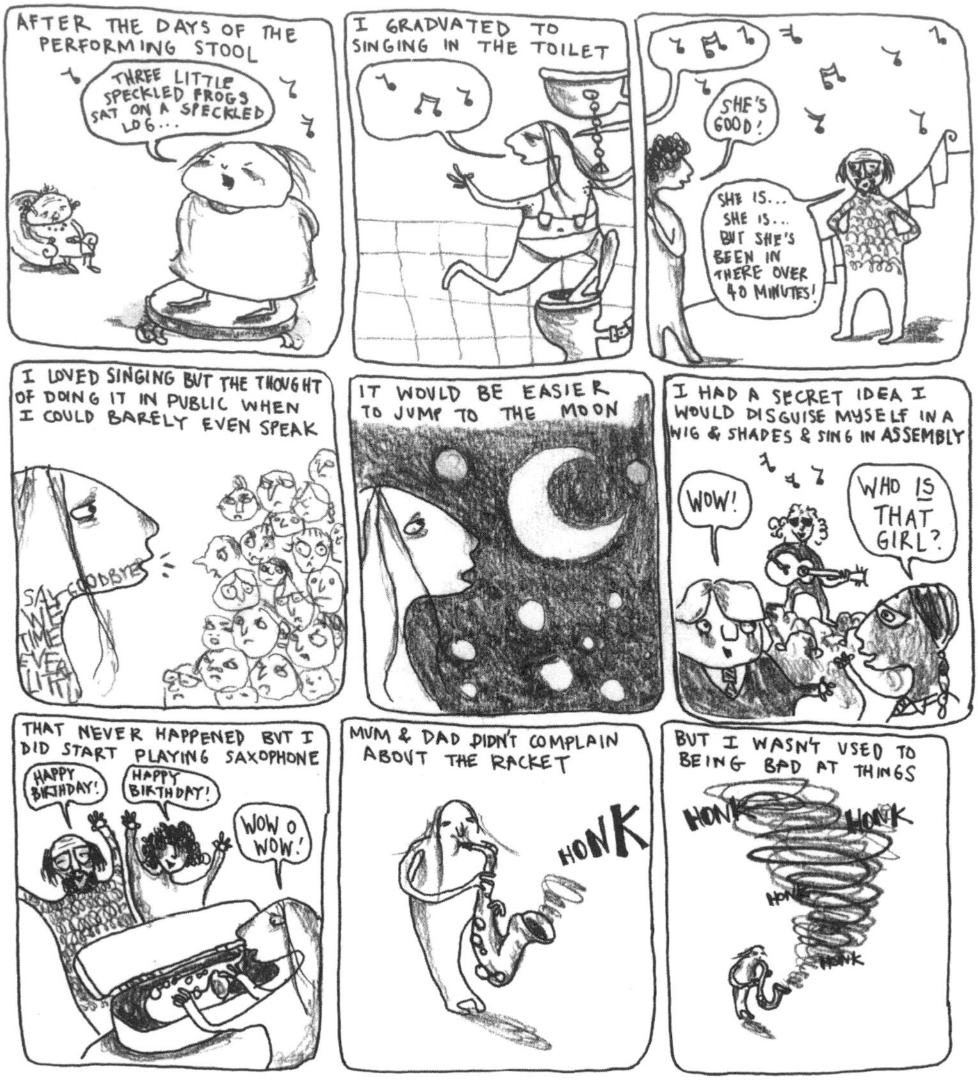
AFTER THE DAYS OF THE PERFORMING STOOL
THREE LITTLE SPECKLED FROGS SAT ON A SPECKLED LOG...
I GRADUATED TO SINGING IN THE TOILET
SHE'S GOOD!
SHE IS... SHE IS... BUT SHE'S BEEN IN THERE OVER 40 MINUTES!
I LOVED SINGING BUT THE THOUGHT OF DOING IT IN PUBLIC WHEN I COULD BARELY EVEN SPEAK
GOODBYE
IT WOULD BE EASIER TO JUMP TO THE MOON
I HAD A SECRET IDEA I WOULD DISGUISE MYSELF IN A WIG & SHADES & SING IN ASSEMBLY
WOW!
WHO IS THAT GIRL?
THAT NEVER HAPPENED BUT I DID START PLAYING SAXOPHONE
HAPPY BIRTHDAY!
HAPPY BIRTHDAY!
WOW O WOW!
MUM & DAD DIDN'T COMPLAIN ABOUT THE RACKET
HONK
BUT I WASN'T USED TO BEING BAD AT THINGS
HONK
HONK
HONK
HONK

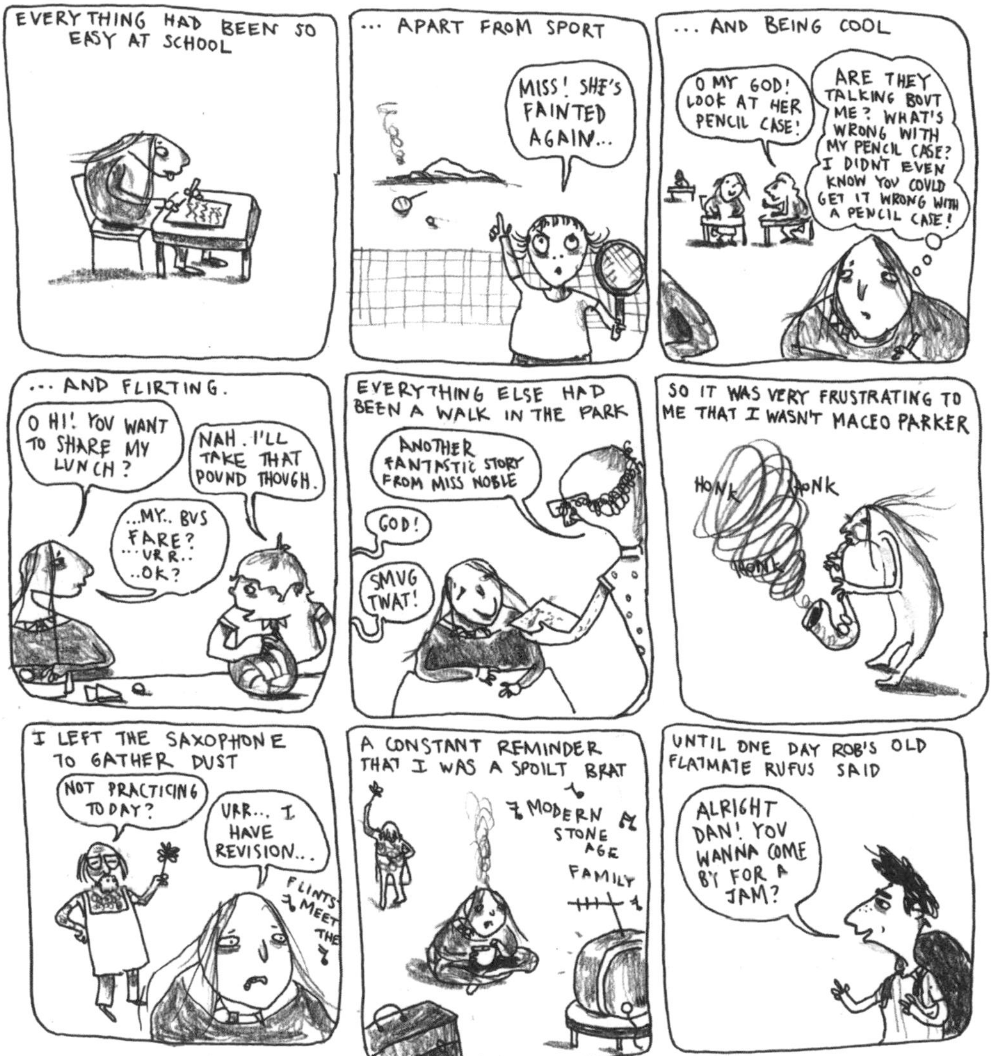
EVERYTHING HAD BEEN SO EASY AT SCHOOL
... APART FROM SPORT
MISS! SHE'S FAINTED AGAIN...
... AND BEING COOL
O MY GOD! LOOK AT HER PENCIL CASE!
ARE THEY TALKING BOUT ME? WHAT'S WRONG WITH MY PENCIL CASE? I DIDN'T EVEN KNOW YOU COULD GET IT WRONG WITH A PENCIL CASE!
... AND FLIRTING.
O HI! YOU WANT TO SHARE MY LUNCH?
NAH. I'LL TAKE THAT POUND THOUGH.
...MY.. BUS FARE? ... URR.. ..OK?
EVERYTHING ELSE HAD BEEN A WALK IN THE PARK
ANOTHER FANTASTIC STORY FROM MISS NOBLE
GOD!
SMUG TWAT!
SO IT WAS VERY FRUSTRATING TO ME THAT I WASN'T MACEO PARKER
HONK HONK
HONK
I LEFT THE SAXOPHONE TO GATHER DUST
NOT PRACTICING TODAY?
URR... I HAVE REVISION...
FLINTS MEET THE
A CONSTANT REMINDER THAT I WAS A SPOILT BRAT
MODERN STONE AGE FAMILY
UNTIL ONE DAY ROB'S OLD FLATMATE RUFUS SAID
ALRIGHT DAN! YOU WANNA COME BY FOR A JAM?

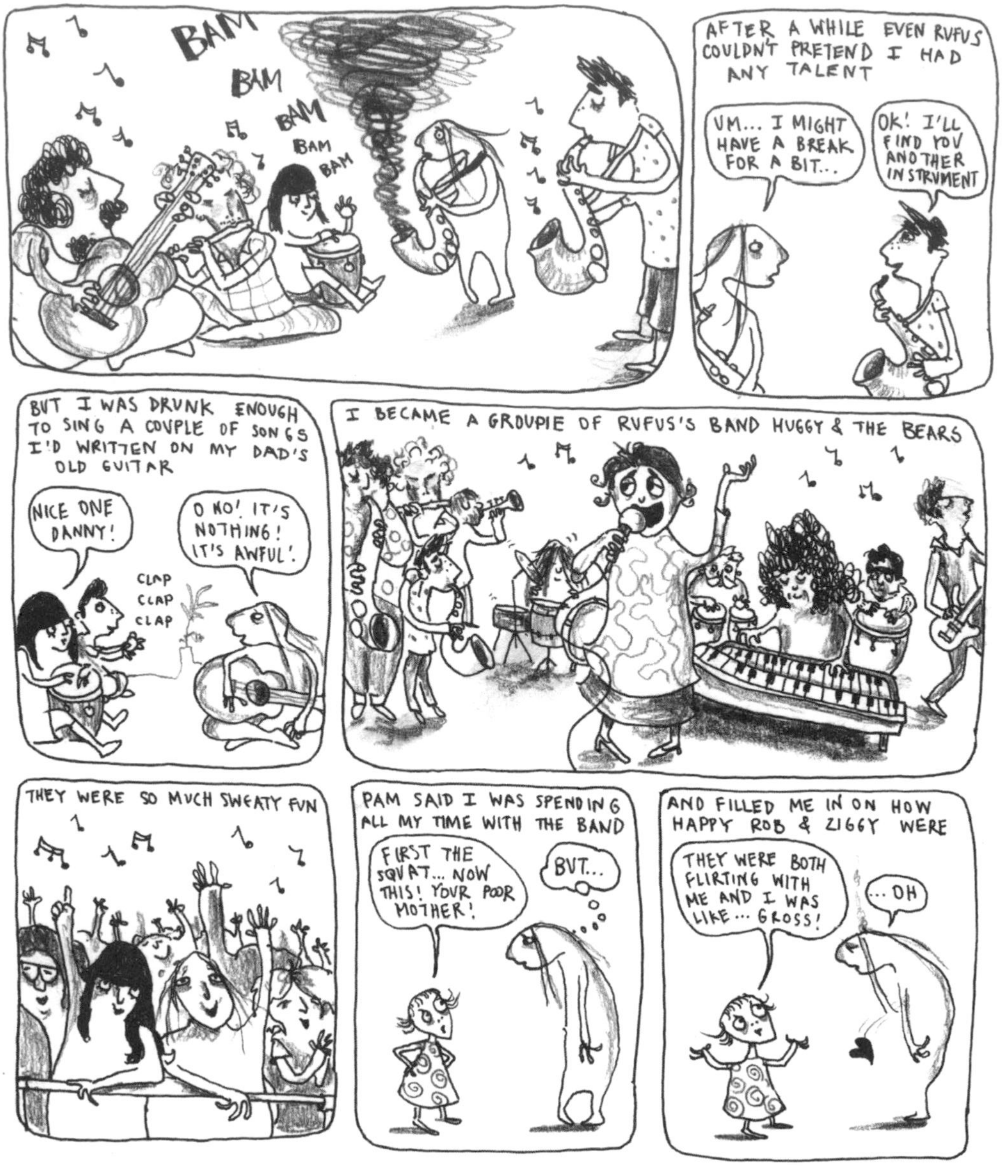
BAM
BAM
BAM
BAM
BAM
AFTER A WHILE EVEN RUFUS COULDN'T PRETEND I HAD ANY TALENT
UM... I MIGHT HAVE A BREAK FOR A BIT...
OK! I'LL FIND YOU ANOTHER INSTRUMENT
BUT I WAS DRUNK ENOUGH TO SING A COUPLE OF SONGS I'D WRITTEN ON MY DAD'S OLD GUITAR
NICE ONE DANNY!
CLAP
CLAP
CLAP
O NO! IT'S NOTHING! IT'S AWFUL!
I BECAME A GROUPIE OF RUFUS'S BAND HUGGY & THE BEARS
THEY WERE SO MUCH SWEATY FUN
PAM SAID I WAS SPENDING ALL MY TIME WITH THE BAND
FIRST THE SQUAT... NOW THIS! YOUR POOR MOTHER!
BUT...
AND FILLED ME IN ON HOW HAPPY ROB & ZIGGY WERE
THEY WERE BOTH FLIRTING WITH ME AND I WAS LIKE... GROSS!
...OH

I REALISED MY NEW FRIENDS SEEMED ACTUALLY TO LIKE ME...

Cheers

DAN!

DAN!

DAN!

DAN!

NORM!

I DIDN'T GET A KNOT IN MY STOMACH WITH THEM

HA

HA

HAHA

HA

HA

OR SWALLOW DOWN MY WORDS

BLA BLA BLA BLA BLA BLA BLA RUB BLA BLA BLA BLA BLA BLA BLA BLA BLA BLA

SO I LET ME AND PAM FLOAT APART

I LET THESE NEW FRIENDS BUILD ME UP

LET RUFUS TALK ME UP WHEN I COULD NOT

YOU GOTTA HEAR DAN SING!

O.. NO NO.. NO! .. NO!

HIS GIRLFRIEND MAZ WAS MY HERO & MY MUSICAL WINGMAN

IT'S TRUE! SHE MADE ME CRY!

O NO! I WAS DRUNK! .. I.. COULDN'T!

UNTIL ONE DAY CRAIG, THE KEYBOARDIST, PUSHED HIS 6 TRACK RECORDER MY WAY

YOU JUST SING INTO THIS BIT...

111

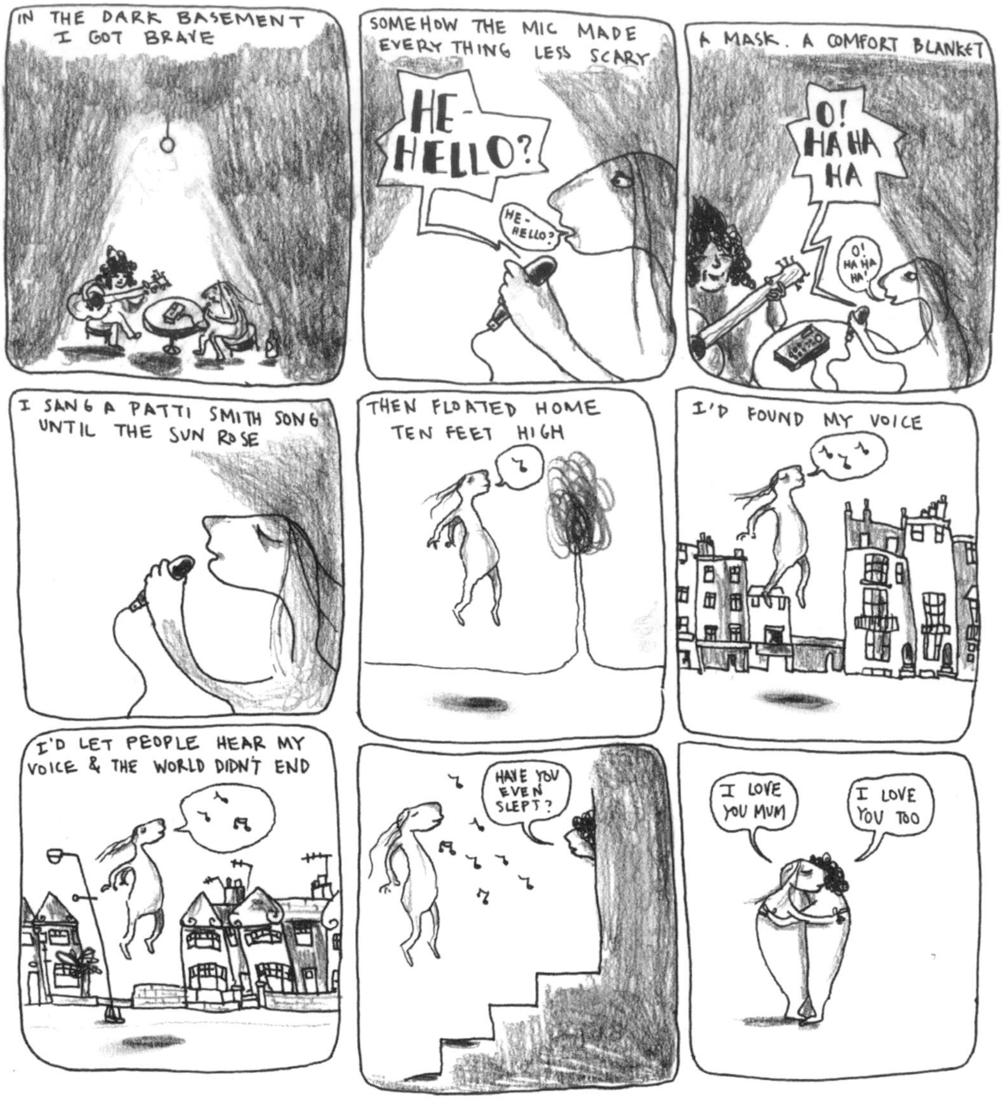
IN THE DARK BASEMENT I GOT BRAVE
SOMEHOW THE MIC MADE EVERYTHING LESS SCARY
HE-HELLO?
HE-HELLO?
A MASK. A COMFORT BLANKET
O! HA HA HA
O! HA HA HA!
I SANG A PATTI SMITH SONG UNTIL THE SUN ROSE
THEN FLOATED HOME TEN FEET HIGH
I'D FOUND MY VOICE
I'D LET PEOPLE HEAR MY VOICE & THE WORLD DIDN'T END
HAVE YOU EVEN SLEPT?
I LOVE YOU MUM
I LOVE YOU TOO

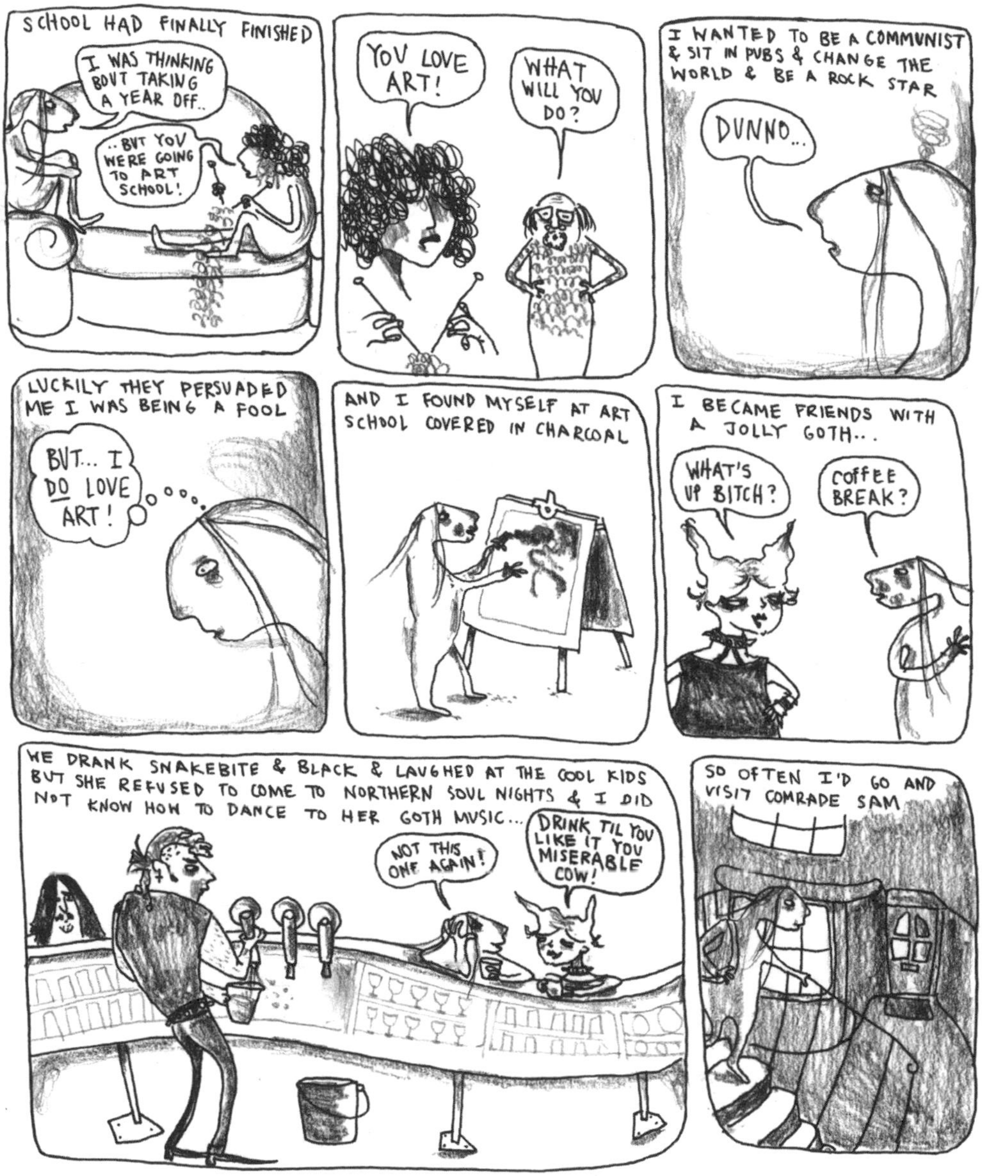
SCHOOL HAD FINALLY FINISHED
I WAS THINKING BOUT TAKING A YEAR OFF..
..BUT YOU WERE GOING TO ART SCHOOL!
YOU LOVE ART!
WHAT WILL YOU DO?
I WANTED TO BE A COMMUNIST & SIT IN PUBS & CHANGE THE WORLD & BE A ROCK STAR
DUNNO...
LUCKILY THEY PERSUADED ME I WAS BEING A FOOL
BUT... I DO LOVE ART!
AND I FOUND MYSELF AT ART SCHOOL COVERED IN CHARCOAL
I BECAME FRIENDS WITH A JOLLY GOTH...
WHAT'S UP BITCH?
COFFEE BREAK?
WE DRANK SNAKEBITE & BLACK & LAUGHED AT THE COOL KIDS BUT SHE REFUSED TO COME TO NORTHERN SOUL NIGHTS & I DID NOT KNOW HOW TO DANCE TO HER GOTH MUSIC...
NOT THIS ONE AGAIN!
DRINK TIL YOU LIKE IT YOU MISERABLE COW!
SO OFTEN I'D GO AND VISIT COMRADE SAM

HE HAD THE BEST SKA & SOUL COLLECTION IN TOWN

HI!

COME IN! COME IN! WE'RE JUST STARTING!

SAM DIDN'T DRINK BUT WE'D GET STONED & EAT CHOCOLATE CAKE THE SIZE OF OUR HEADS, LISTEN TO NORA DEAN & OTIS REDDING.

WORKERS

RESISTANCE

star

ARE MAZ & RU HERE YET?

GET CARTER

YEA!.. AND BERNIE KATZ

SOMETIMES WE'D PLAY SUBBUTEO, EVER SO SERIOUSLY

HEY BERNIE!

SALUTATIONS!

SOMETIMES WE'D WATCH OLD COMEDY SHOWS

WHATEVER WE DID, WE'D ALWAYS LAUGH UNTIL OUR BELLIES ACHED

SICK OF THE MODERN MUSIC SCENE, SAM DECIDED TO PUT TOGETHER A BAND TO PLAY HIS FAVOURITE SONGS

I CAN'T PLAY ANYTHING, SO I'LL BE THE NEFARIOUS MANAGER

HEY! DAN CAN PLAY SAX TOO!

AND SING!

HAHA! BLESS YOU! I CAN'T!

114

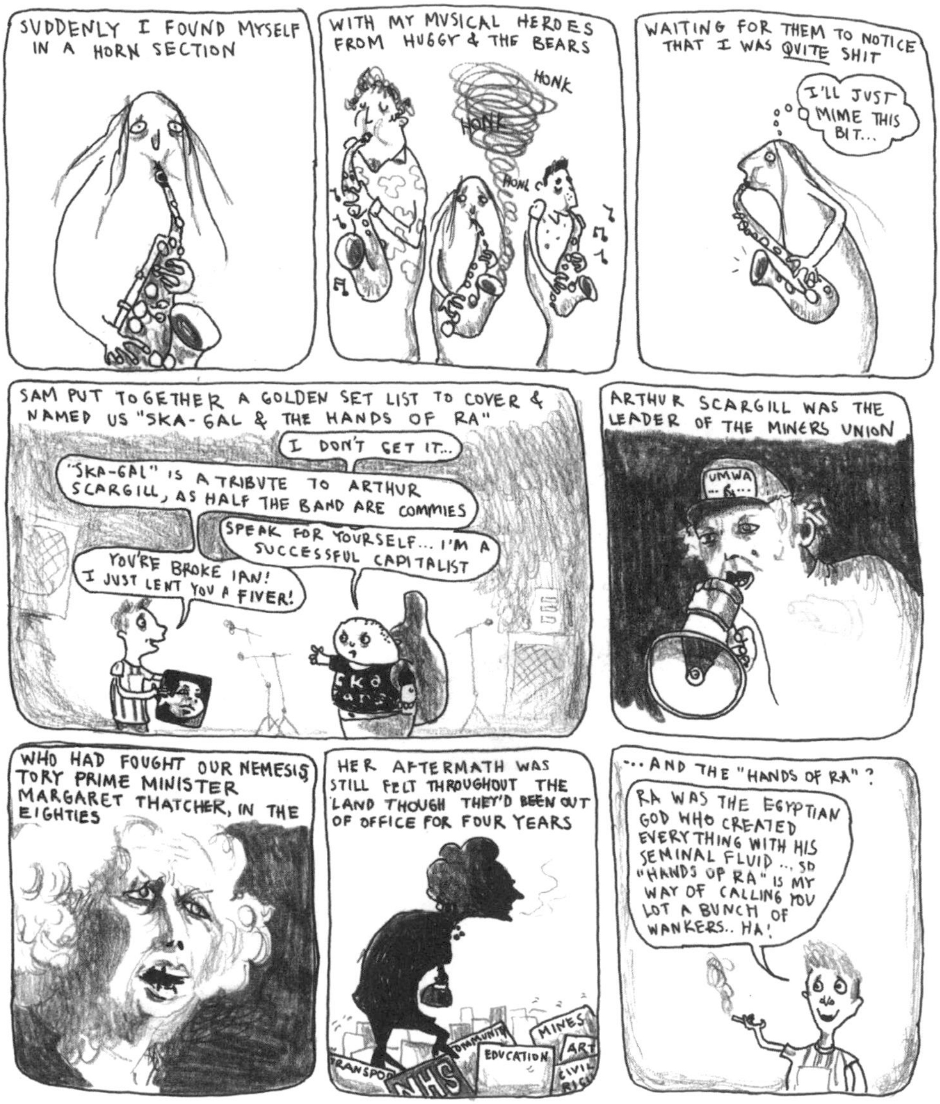
SUDDENLY I FOUND MYSELF IN A HORN SECTION
WITH MY MUSICAL HEROES FROM HUGGY & THE BEARS
HONK
HONK
HONK
WAITING FOR THEM TO NOTICE THAT I WAS QUITE SHIT
I'LL JUST MIME THIS BIT...
SAM PUT TOGETHER A GOLDEN SET LIST TO COVER & NAMED US "SKA-GAL & THE HANDS OF RA"
I DON'T GET IT...
"SKA-GAL" IS A TRIBUTE TO ARTHUR SCARGILL, AS HALF THE BAND ARE COMMIES
SPEAK FOR YOURSELF... I'M A SUCCESSFUL CAPITALIST
YOU'RE BROKE IAN! I JUST LENT YOU A FIVER!
ARTHUR SCARGILL WAS THE LEADER OF THE MINERS UNION
UMWA
WHO HAD FOUGHT OUR NEMESIS, TORY PRIME MINISTER MARGARET THATCHER, IN THE EIGHTIES
HER AFTERMATH WAS STILL FELT THROUGHOUT THE LAND THOUGH THEY'D BEEN OUT OF OFFICE FOR FOUR YEARS
NHS
EDUCATION
MINES
ART
...AND THE "HANDS OF RA"?
RA WAS THE EGYPTIAN GOD WHO CREATED EVERYTHING WITH HIS SEMINAL FLUID... SO "HANDS OF RA" IS MY WAY OF CALLING YOU LOT A BUNCH OF WANKERS.. HA!

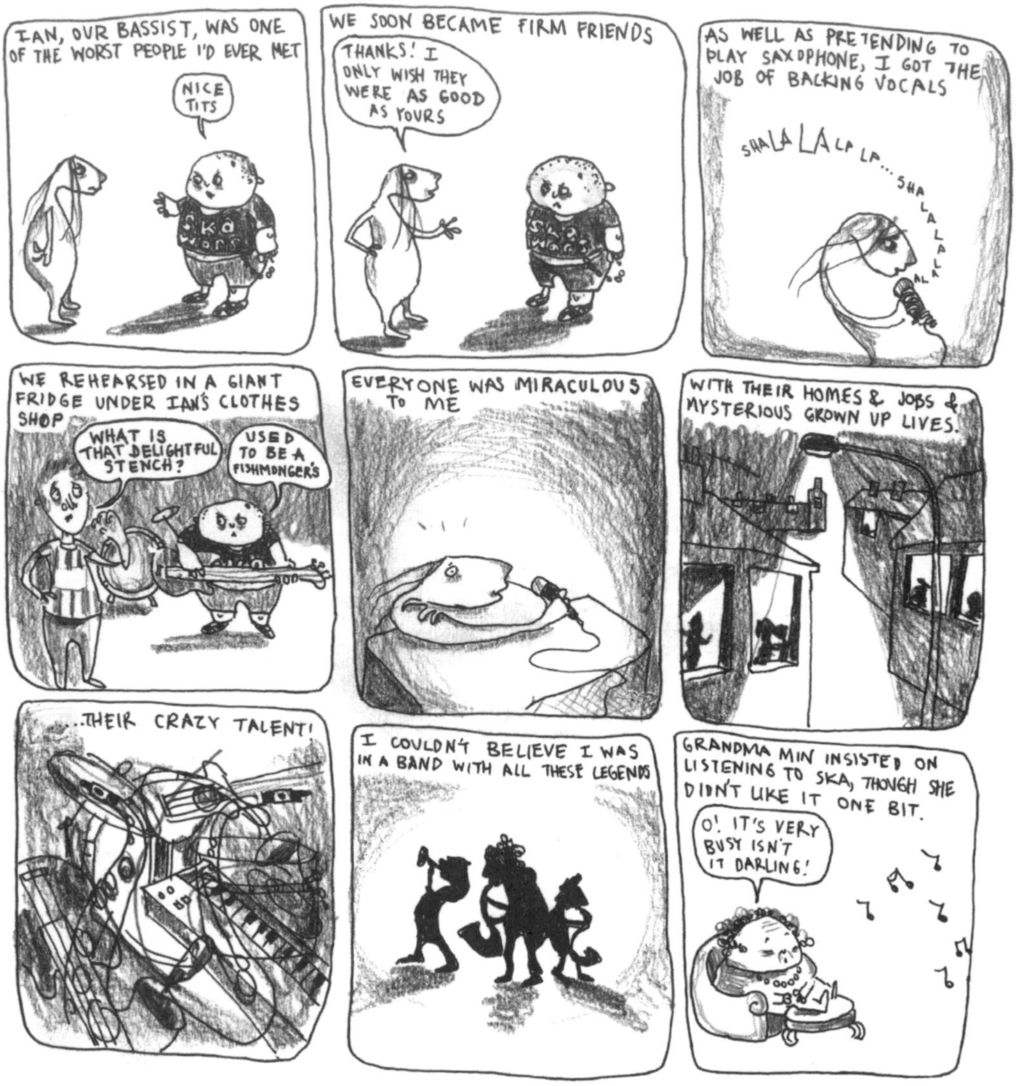
IAN, OUR BASSIST, WAS ONE OF THE WORST PEOPLE I'D EVER MET
NICE TITS
WE SOON BECAME FIRM FRIENDS
THANKS! I ONLY WISH THEY WERE AS GOOD AS YOURS
AS WELL AS PRETENDING TO PLAY SAXOPHONE, I GOT THE JOB OF BACKING VOCALS
SHALALALALA LA... SHA LA LA LA LA LA
WE REHEARSED IN A GIANT FRIDGE UNDER IAN'S CLOTHES SHOP
WHAT IS THAT DELIGHTFUL STENCH?
USED TO BE A FISHMONGER'S
EVERYONE WAS MIRACULOUS TO ME
WITH THEIR HOMES & JOBS & MYSTERIOUS GROWN UP LIVES.
...THEIR CRAZY TALENT!
I COULDN'T BELIEVE I WAS IN A BAND WITH ALL THESE LEGENDS
GRANDMA MIN INSISTED ON LISTENING TO SKA, THOUGH SHE DIDN'T LIKE IT ONE BIT.
O! IT'S VERY BUSY ISN'T IT DARLING!

FOR SOUL YOU NEED A GREAT BIG BOOMING BARRY WHITE VOICE

BOO OO OO AA OO OO AHHH AAOO OFF...

BUT SKA CALLS FOR SOMETHING HIGH AND CHILDLIKE

DAN.. YOU SHOULD SING LEAD ON THIS ONE..

I WAS SO DELIGHTED I FORGOT TO COME UP WITH A HUNDRED REASONS WHY I SHOULDN'T

O! I'LL GIVE IT A GO!

BEFORE WE KNEW IT, IT WAS THE DAY OF THE GIG

O GOD! I'M GONNA THROW UP...

I SQUEEZED INTO A PURPLE DRESS & KNEE HIGH BOOTS

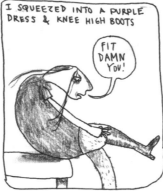

FIT DAMN YOU!

AND TO MARK THIS MOMENTOUS OCCASION, I EVEN SHAVED MY LEGS

BUT ONLY ON MY KNEES, CAUSE THAT'S THE ONLY BIT YOU COULD SEE

THAT'LL DO...

AND RAN DOWN TO THE FREE BUTT INN

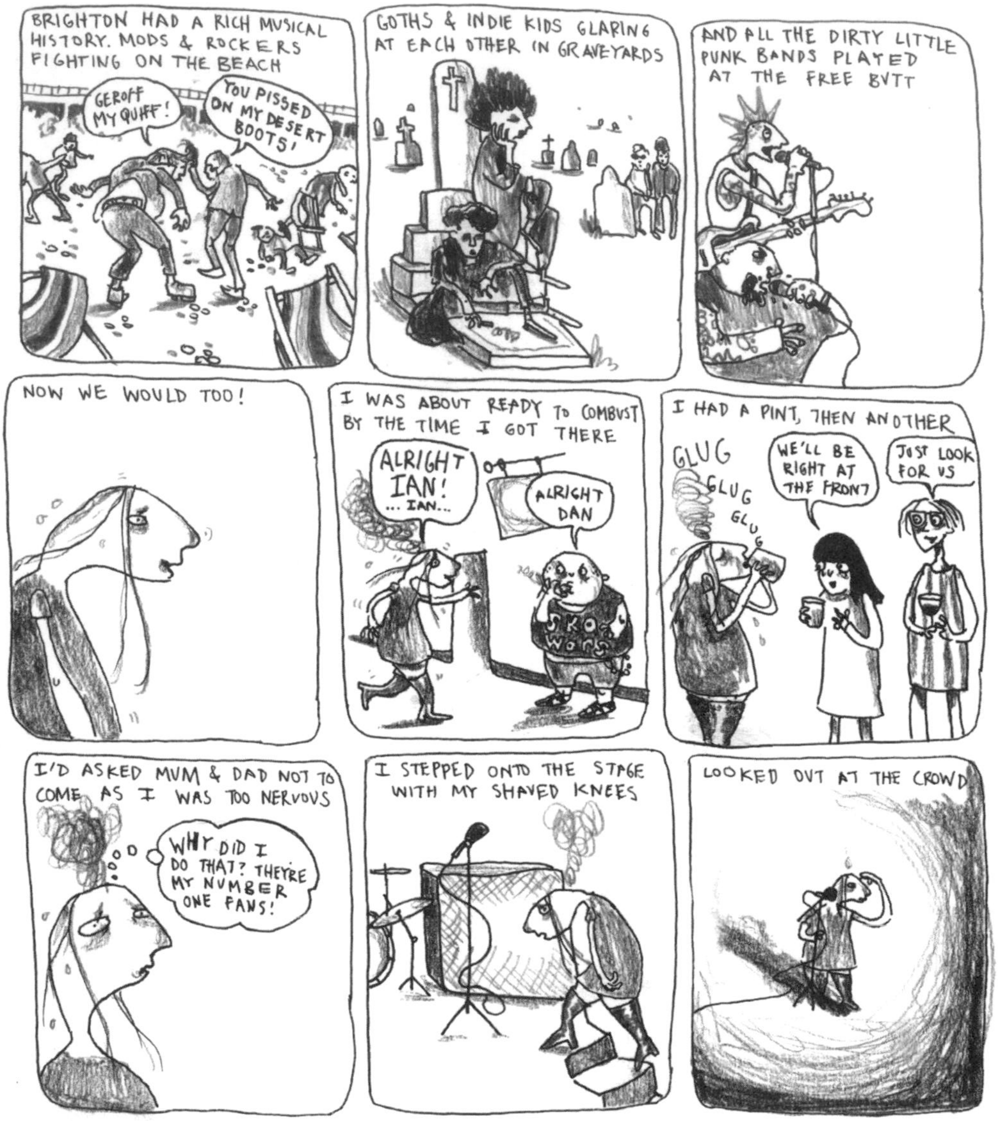
BRIGHTON HAD A RICH MUSICAL HISTORY. MODS & ROCKERS FIGHTING ON THE BEACH
GEROFF MY QUIFF!
YOU PISSED ON MY DESERT BOOTS!
GOTHS & INDIE KIDS GLARING AT EACH OTHER IN GRAVEYARDS
AND ALL THE DIRTY LITTLE PUNK BANDS PLAYED AT THE FREE BUTT
NOW WE WOULD TOO!
I WAS ABOUT READY TO COMBUST BY THE TIME I GOT THERE
ALRIGHT IAN! ... IAN...
ALRIGHT DAN
I HAD A PINT, THEN ANOTHER
GLUG GLUG GLUG
WE'LL BE RIGHT AT THE FRONT
JUST LOOK FOR US
I'D ASKED MUM & DAD NOT TO COME AS I WAS TOO NERVOUS
WHY DID I DO THAT? THEY'RE MY NUMBER ONE FANS!
I STEPPED ONTO THE STAGE WITH MY SHAVED KNEES
LOOKED OUT AT THE CROWD

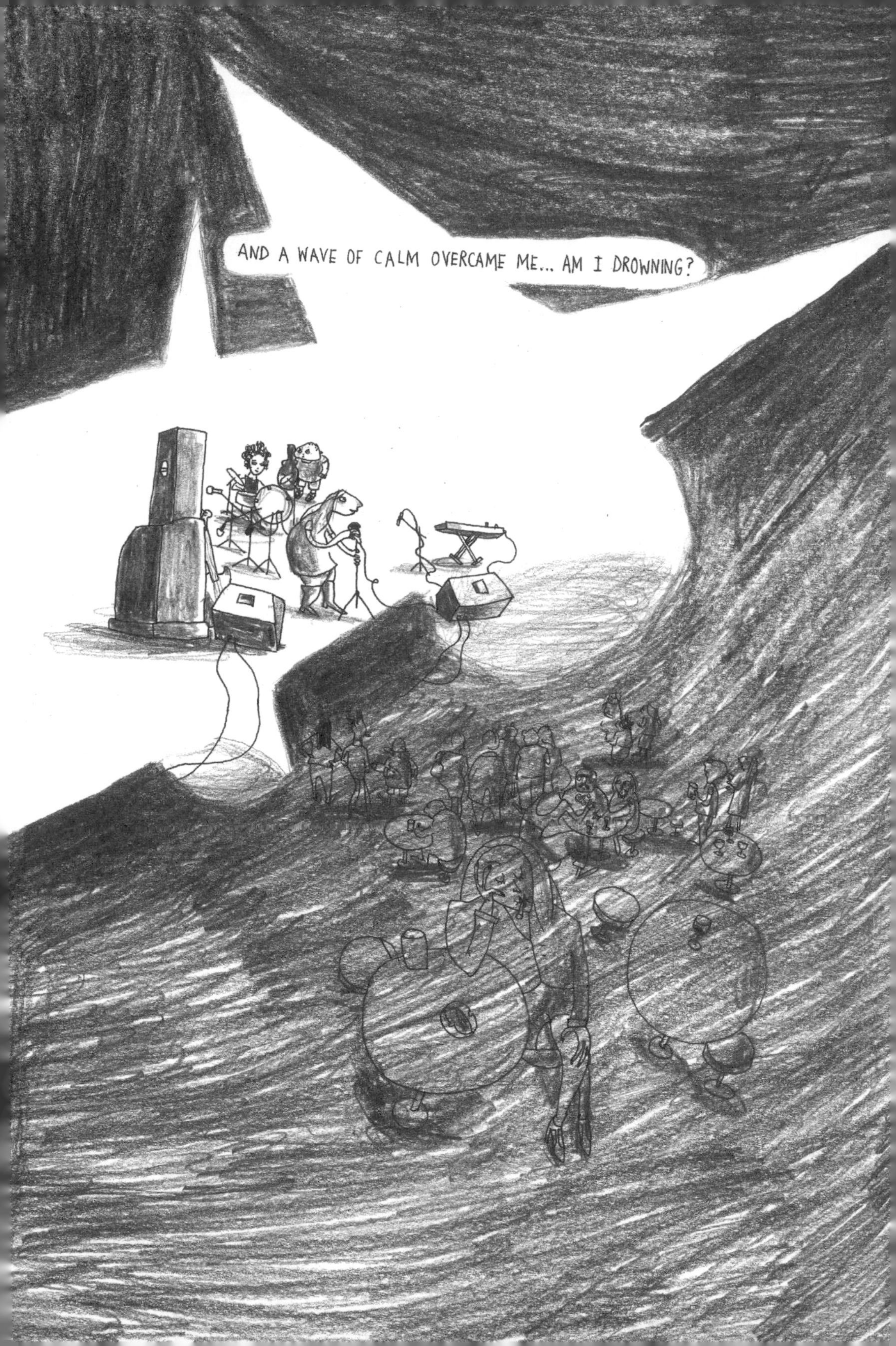
AND A WAVE OF CALM OVERCAME ME... AM I DROWNING?

ADRENALINE KICKED IN JUST IN TIME TO REMIND ME OF LYRICS

THERE WERE NO MOUNTAINS ... TO KEEP US FAR APART

I EVEN CHOKED OUT A FEW NOTES ON THE SAXOPHONE

HONK
HONK
HONK

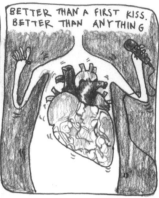

BETTER THAN A FIRST KISS. BETTER THAN ANYTHING

TWO GIRLS APPROACHED ME AFTER THE GIG

HI!
HI!
WE'RE GOING TO BE YOUR GROUPIES
JUST SO YOU KNOW...
YES HI!

CIDER EVERYWHERE & SO MUCH FUN...

I'VE LOST MY BLOODY PILL!
IT'S STUCK TO YOUR LIP
I'VE LOOKED EVERYWHERE!
IT'S ON YOUR LIP!
WHERE CAN IT BE?

SHINY, SWEATY FACES. OLD AND NEW

BUT THE NIGHT OF THE FIRST GIG... I WAS ON MY OWN ... 3 MILES HIGH...

CHAPTER 10

THE RETURN OF THE NIGHT MONSTERS

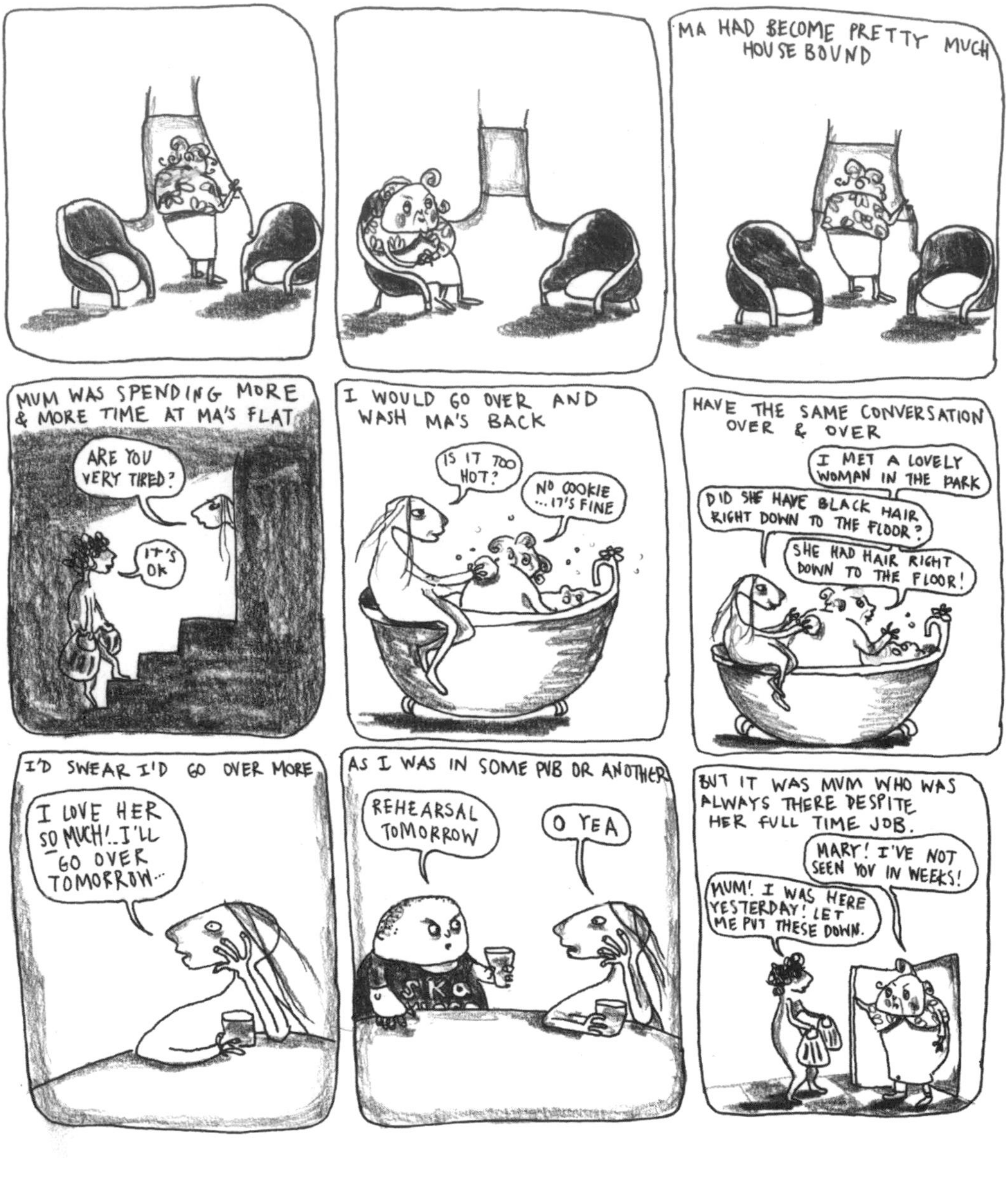

MA HAD BECOME PRETTY MUCH HOUSE BOUND
MUM WAS SPENDING MORE & MORE TIME AT MA'S FLAT
ARE YOU VERY TIRED?
IT'S OK
I WOULD GO OVER AND WASH MA'S BACK
IS IT TOO HOT?
NO COOKIE ...IT'S FINE
HAVE THE SAME CONVERSATION OVER & OVER
I MET A LOVELY WOMAN IN THE PARK
DID SHE HAVE BLACK HAIR RIGHT DOWN TO THE FLOOR?
SHE HAD HAIR RIGHT DOWN TO THE FLOOR!
I'D SWEAR I'D GO OVER MORE
I LOVE HER SO MUCH!..I'LL GO OVER TOMORROW...
AS I WAS IN SOME PUB OR ANOTHER
REHEARSAL TOMORROW
O YEA
SKA
BUT IT WAS MUM WHO WAS ALWAYS THERE DESPITE HER FULL TIME JOB.
MARY! I'VE NOT SEEN YOU IN WEEKS!
MUM! I WAS HERE YESTERDAY! LET ME PUT THESE DOWN.

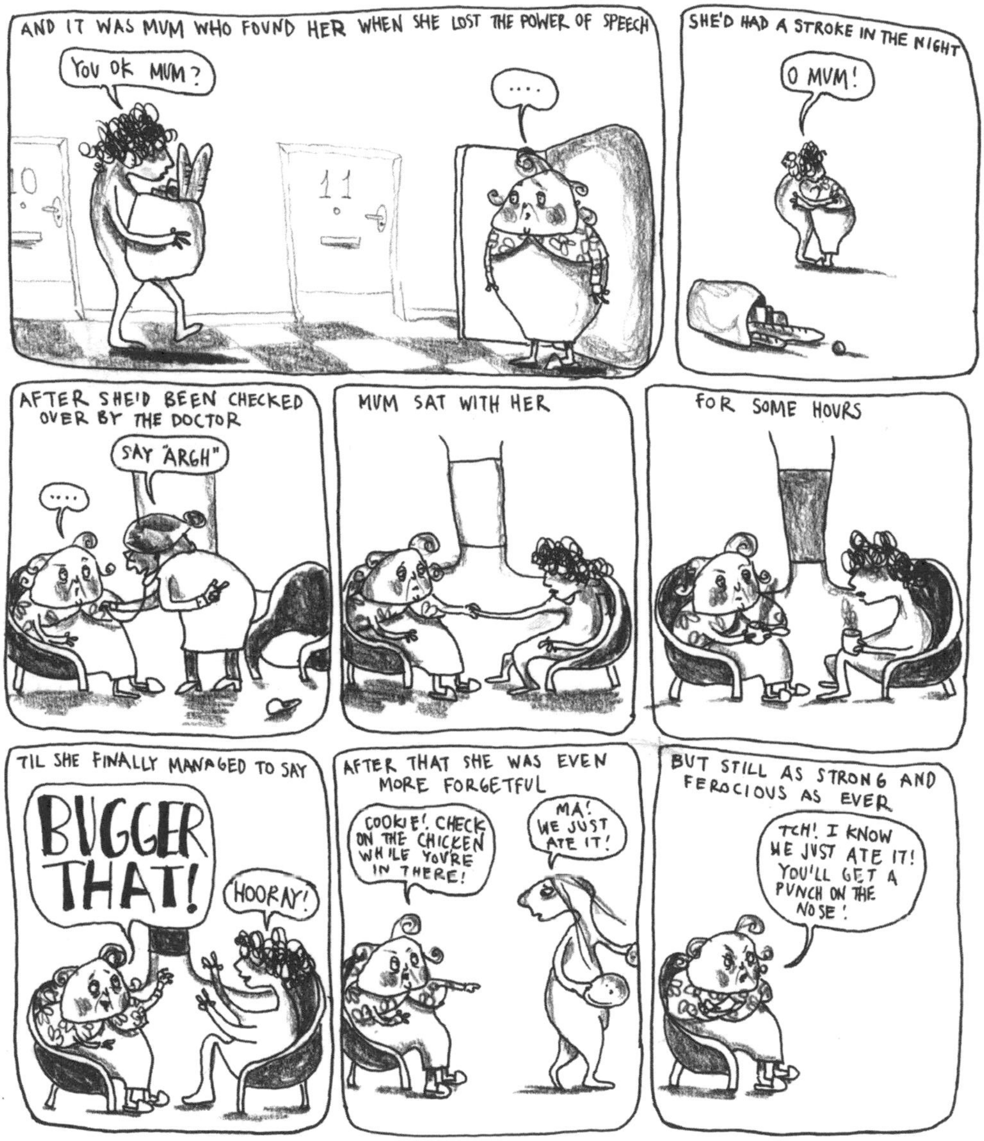
AND IT WAS MUM WHO FOUND HER WHEN SHE LOST THE POWER OF SPEECH
YOU OK MUM?
....
SHE'D HAD A STROKE IN THE NIGHT
O MUM!
AFTER SHE'D BEEN CHECKED OVER BY THE DOCTOR
SAY "ARGH"
....
MUM SAT WITH HER
FOR SOME HOURS
TIL SHE FINALLY MANAGED TO SAY
BUGGER THAT!
HOORAY!
AFTER THAT SHE WAS EVEN MORE FORGETFUL
COOKIE! CHECK ON THE CHICKEN WHILE YOU'RE IN THERE!
MA! WE JUST ATE IT!
BUT STILL AS STRONG AND FEROCIOUS AS EVER
TCH! I KNOW WE JUST ATE IT! YOU'LL GET A PUNCH ON THE NOSE!

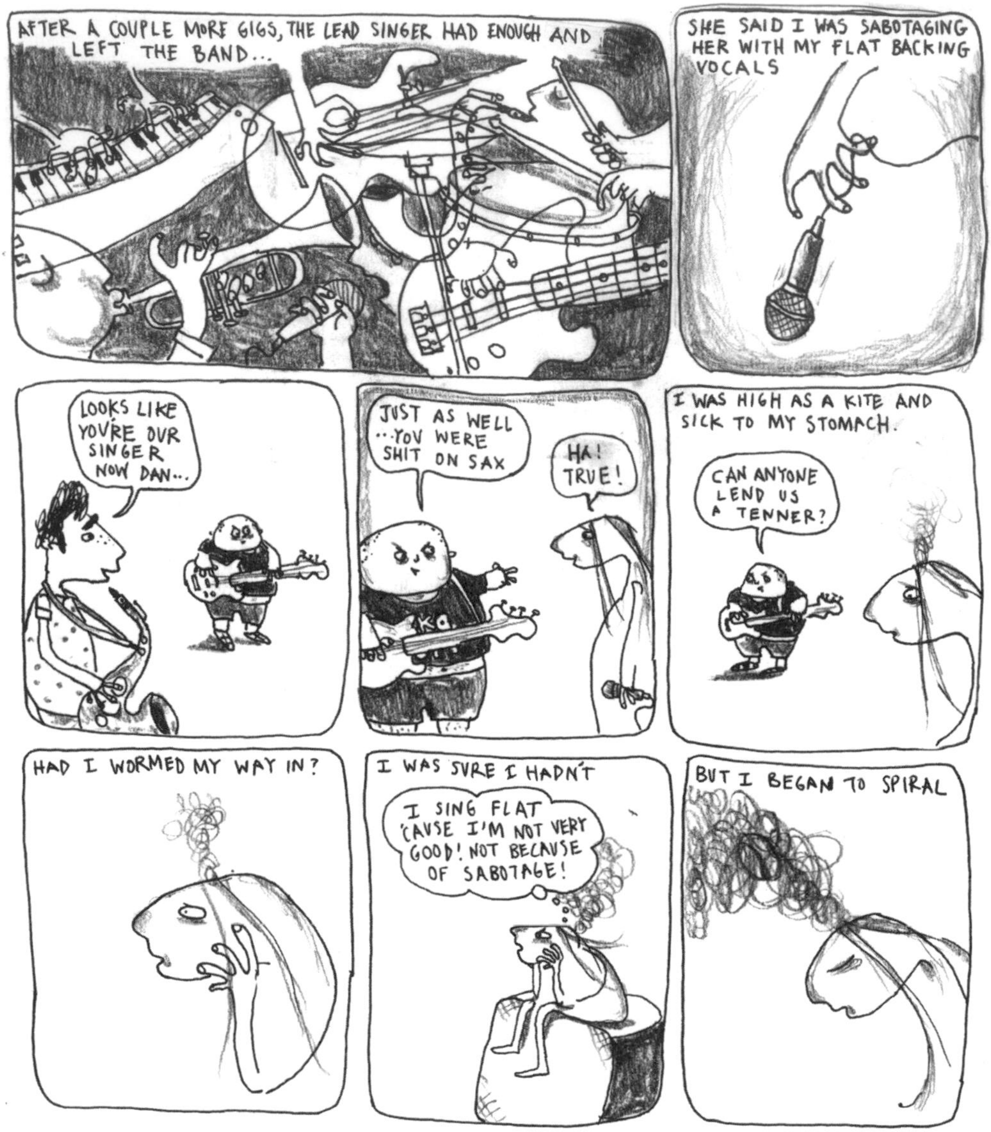
AFTER A COUPLE MORE GIGS, THE LEAD SINGER HAD ENOUGH AND LEFT THE BAND...
SHE SAID I WAS SABOTAGING HER WITH MY FLAT BACKING VOCALS
LOOKS LIKE YOU'RE OUR SINGER NOW DAN...
JUST AS WELL ...YOU WERE SHIT ON SAX
HA! TRUE!
I WAS HIGH AS A KITE AND SICK TO MY STOMACH.
CAN ANYONE LEND US A TENNER?
HAD I WORMED MY WAY IN?
I WAS SURE I HADN'T
I SING FLAT 'CAUSE I'M NOT VERY GOOD! NOT BECAUSE OF SABOTAGE!
BUT I BEGAN TO SPIRAL

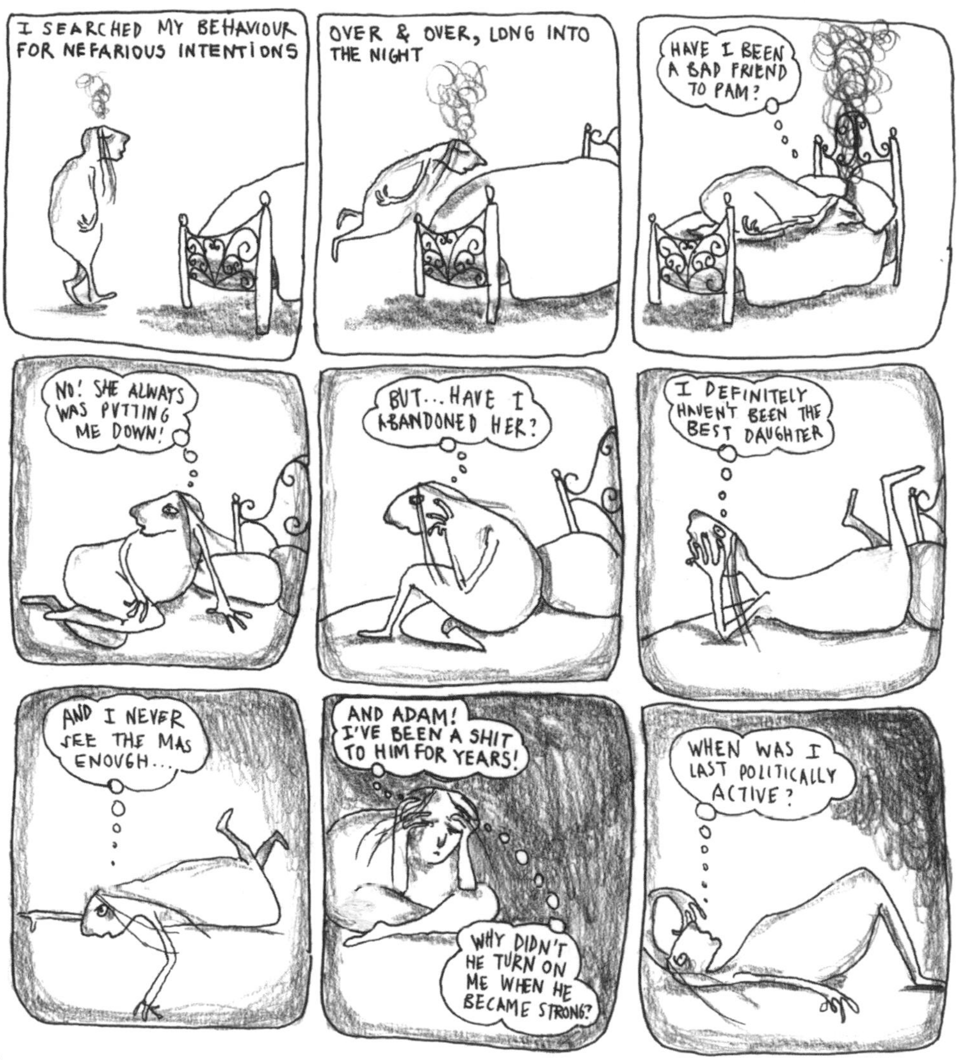
I SEARCHED MY BEHAVIOUR FOR NEFARIOUS INTENTIONS
OVER & OVER, LONG INTO THE NIGHT
HAVE I BEEN A BAD FRIEND TO PAM?
NO! SHE ALWAYS WAS PUTTING ME DOWN!
BUT... HAVE I ABANDONED HER?
I DEFINITELY HAVEN'T BEEN THE BEST DAUGHTER
AND I NEVER SEE THE MAS ENOUGH...
AND ADAM! I'VE BEEN A SHIT TO HIM FOR YEARS!
WHY DIDN'T HE TURN ON ME WHEN HE BECAME STRONG?
WHEN WAS I LAST POLITICALLY ACTIVE?

... THE NIGHT TERRORS WERE JOINED BY THE SHAME MONSTER...

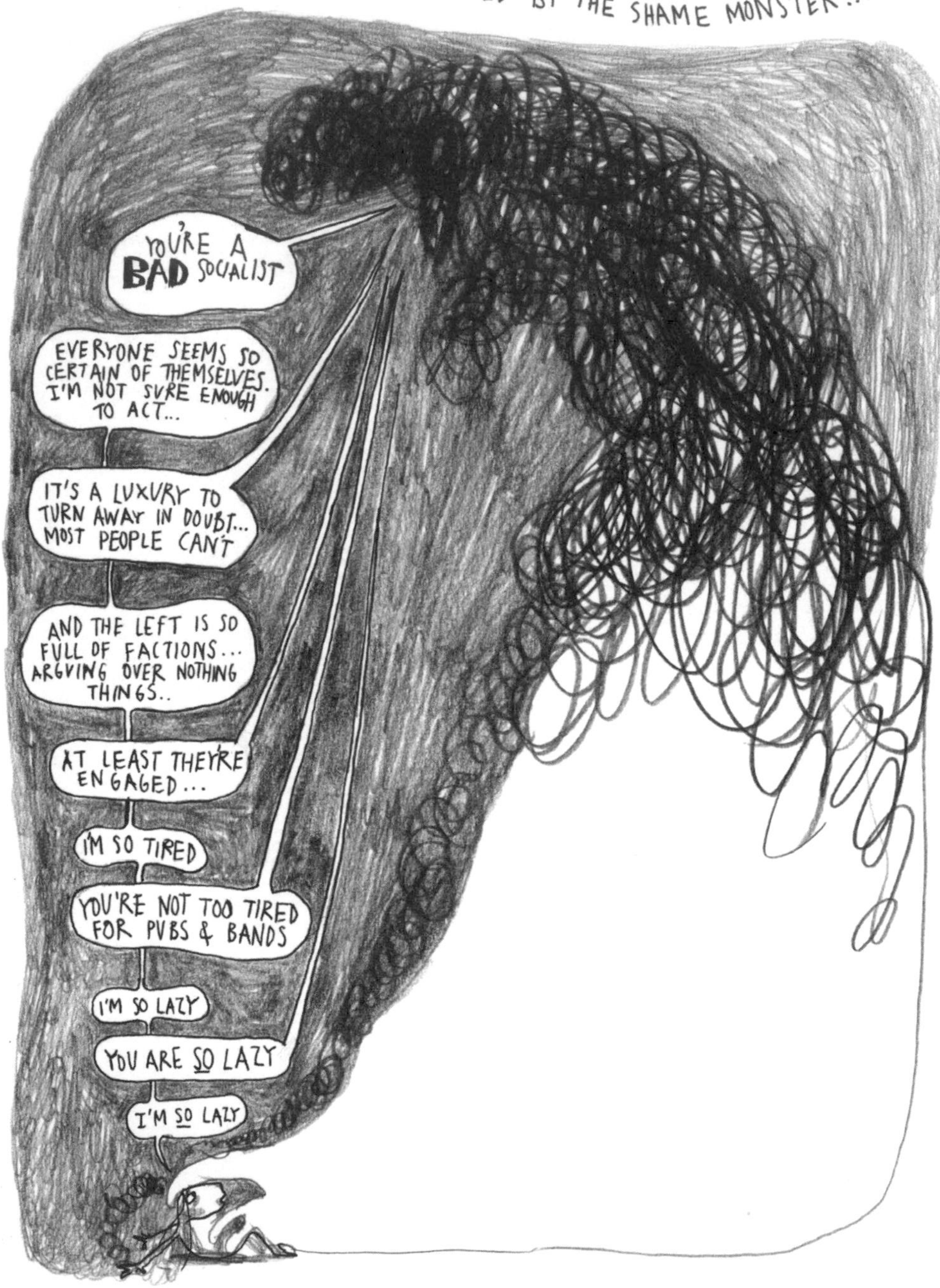
YOU'RE A BAD SOCIALIST
EVERYONE SEEMS SO CERTAIN OF THEMSELVES. I'M NOT SURE ENOUGH TO ACT...
IT'S A LUXURY TO TURN AWAY IN DOUBT... MOST PEOPLE CAN'T
AND THE LEFT IS SO FULL OF FACTIONS... ARGUING OVER NOTHING THINGS..
AT LEAST THEY'RE ENGAGED...
I'M SO TIRED
YOU'RE NOT TOO TIRED FOR PUBS & BANDS
I'M SO LAZY
YOU ARE SO LAZY
I'M SO LAZY

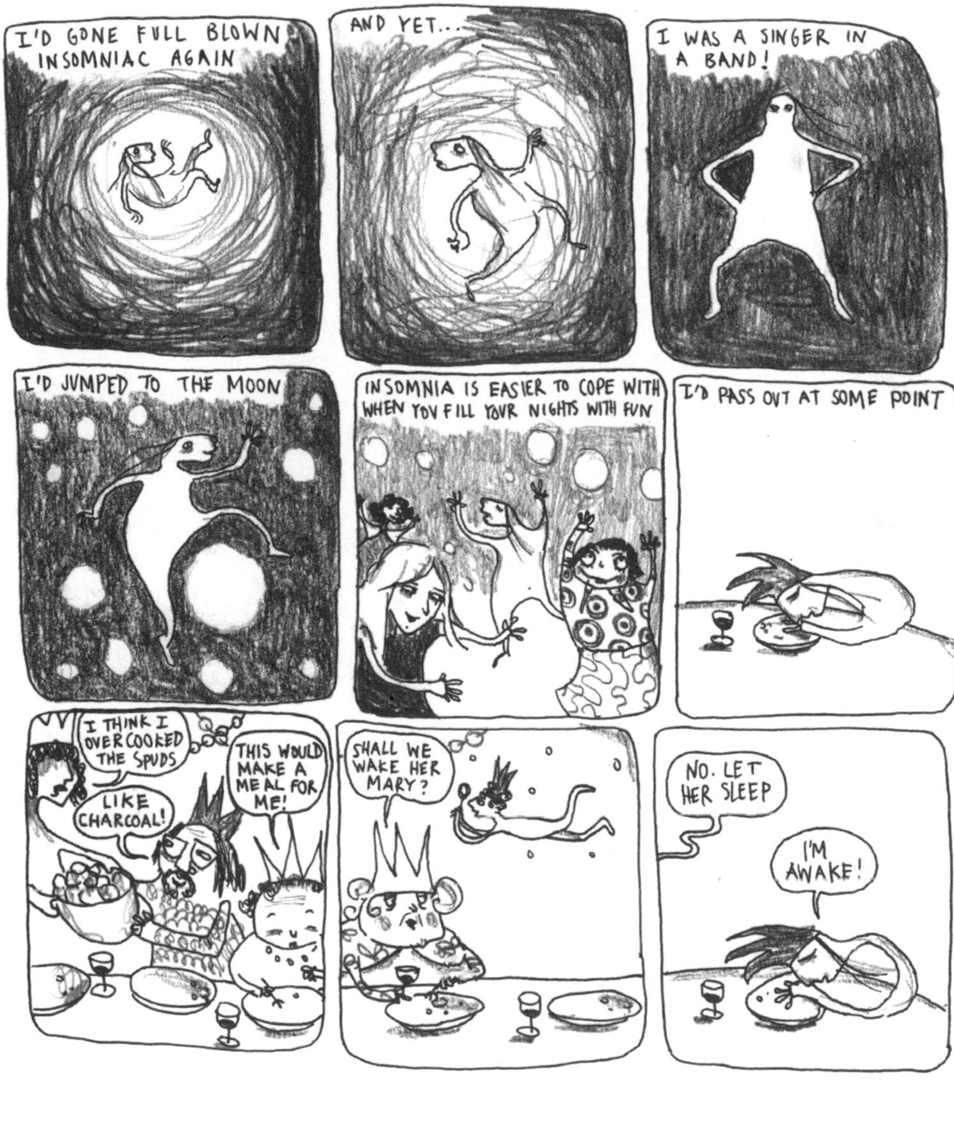
I'D GONE FULL BLOWN INSOMNIAC AGAIN
AND YET...
I WAS A SINGER IN A BAND!
I'D JUMPED TO THE MOON
INSOMNIA IS EASIER TO COPE WITH WHEN YOU FILL YOUR NIGHTS WITH FUN
I'D PASS OUT AT SOME POINT
I THINK I OVERCOOKED THE SPUDS
LIKE CHARCOAL!
THIS WOULD MAKE A MEAL FOR ME!
SHALL WE WAKE HER MARY?
NO. LET HER SLEEP
I'M AWAKE!

CHAPTER 11

STUCK IN A VAN WITH A BAND

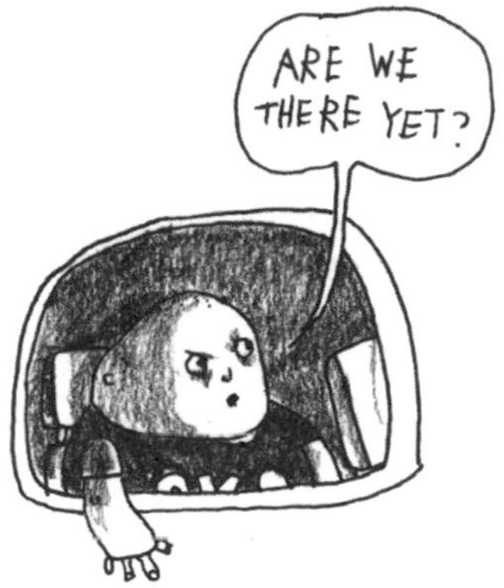
ARE WE THERE YET?

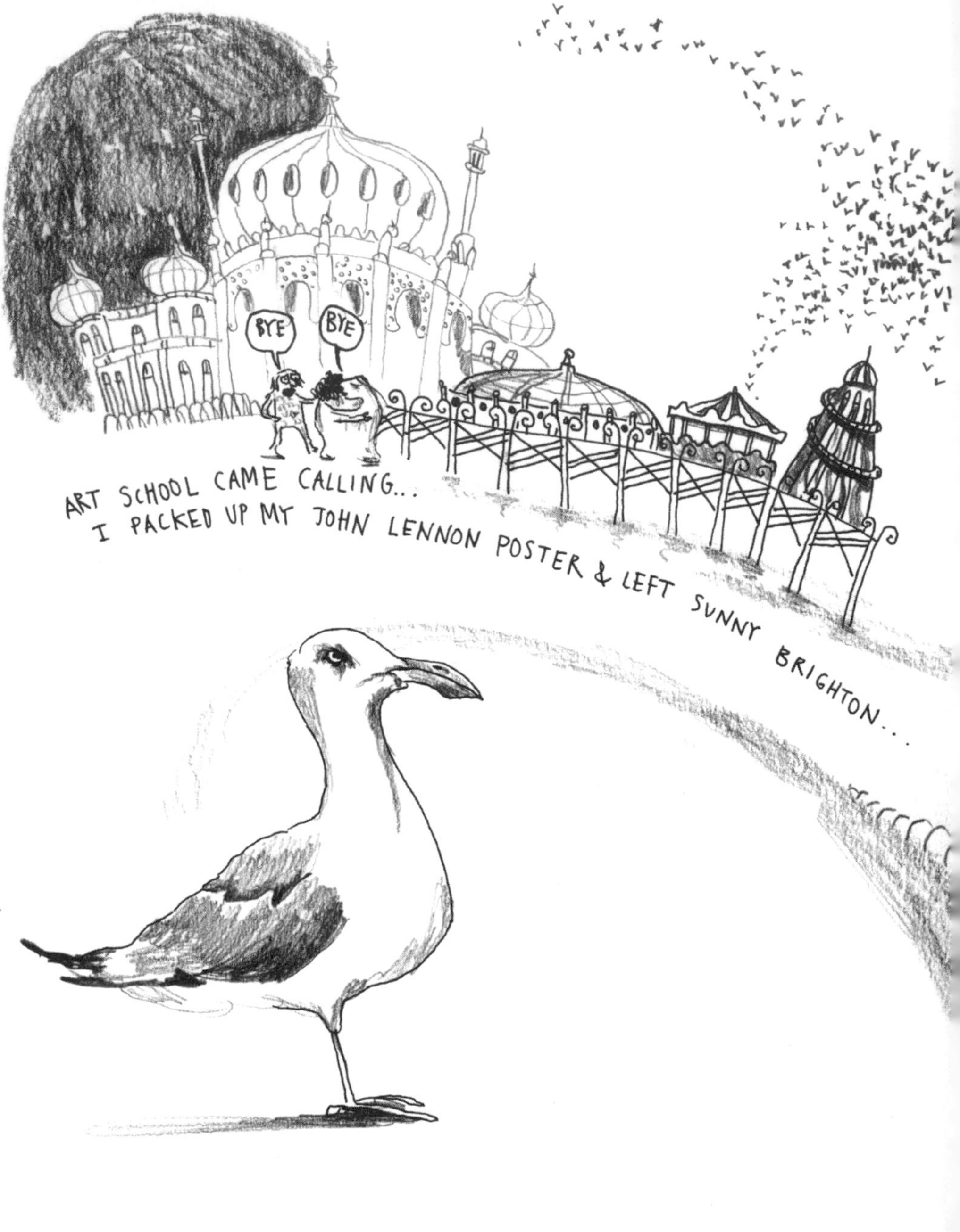
BYE
BYE
ART SCHOOL CAME CALLING...
I PACKED UP MY JOHN LENNON POSTER & LEFT SUNNY BRIGHTON...

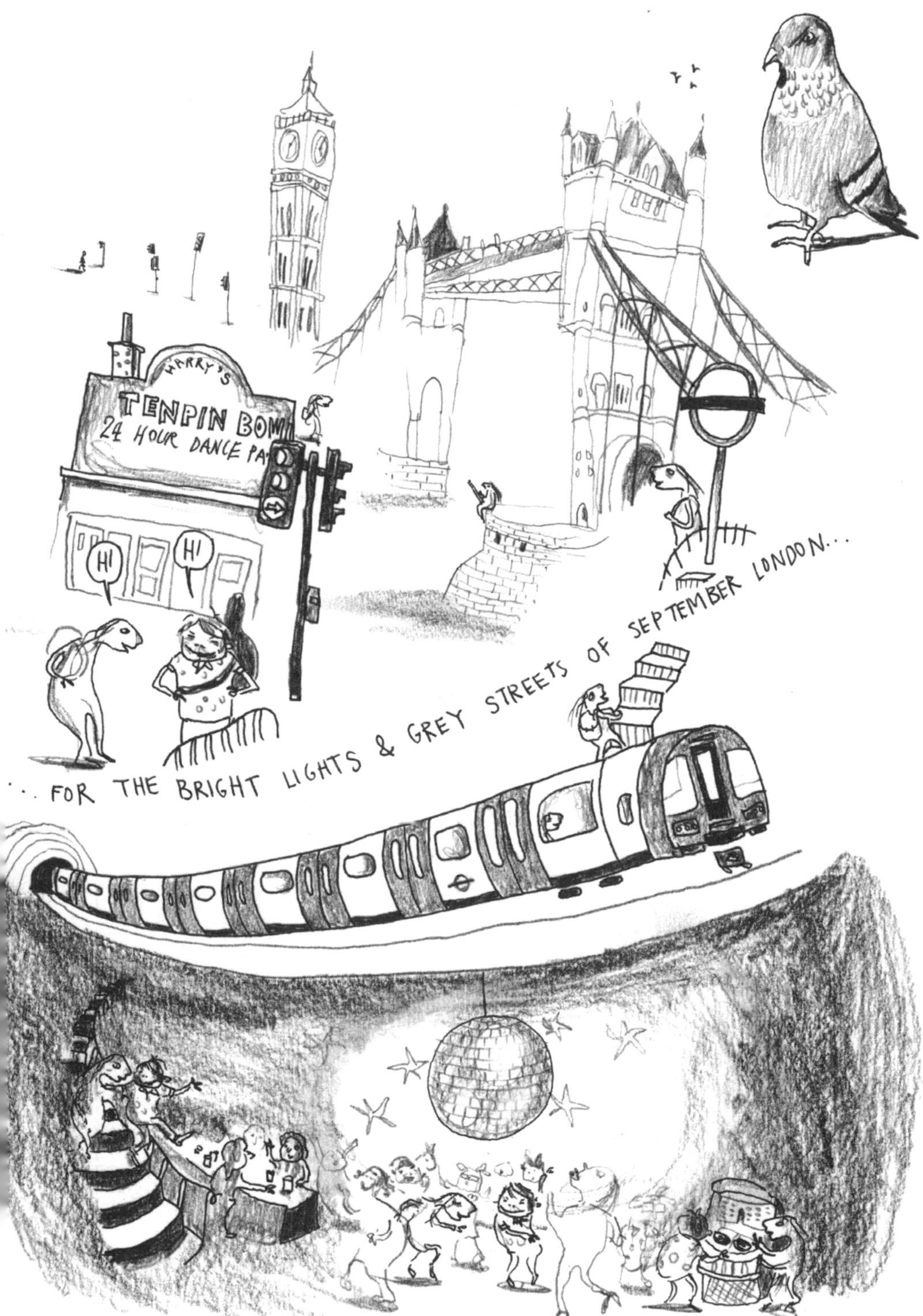
HARRY'S
TENPIN BOW
24 HOUR DANCE PA
HI!
HI!
. . . FOR THE BRIGHT LIGHTS & GREY STREETS OF SEPTEMBER LONDON . . .

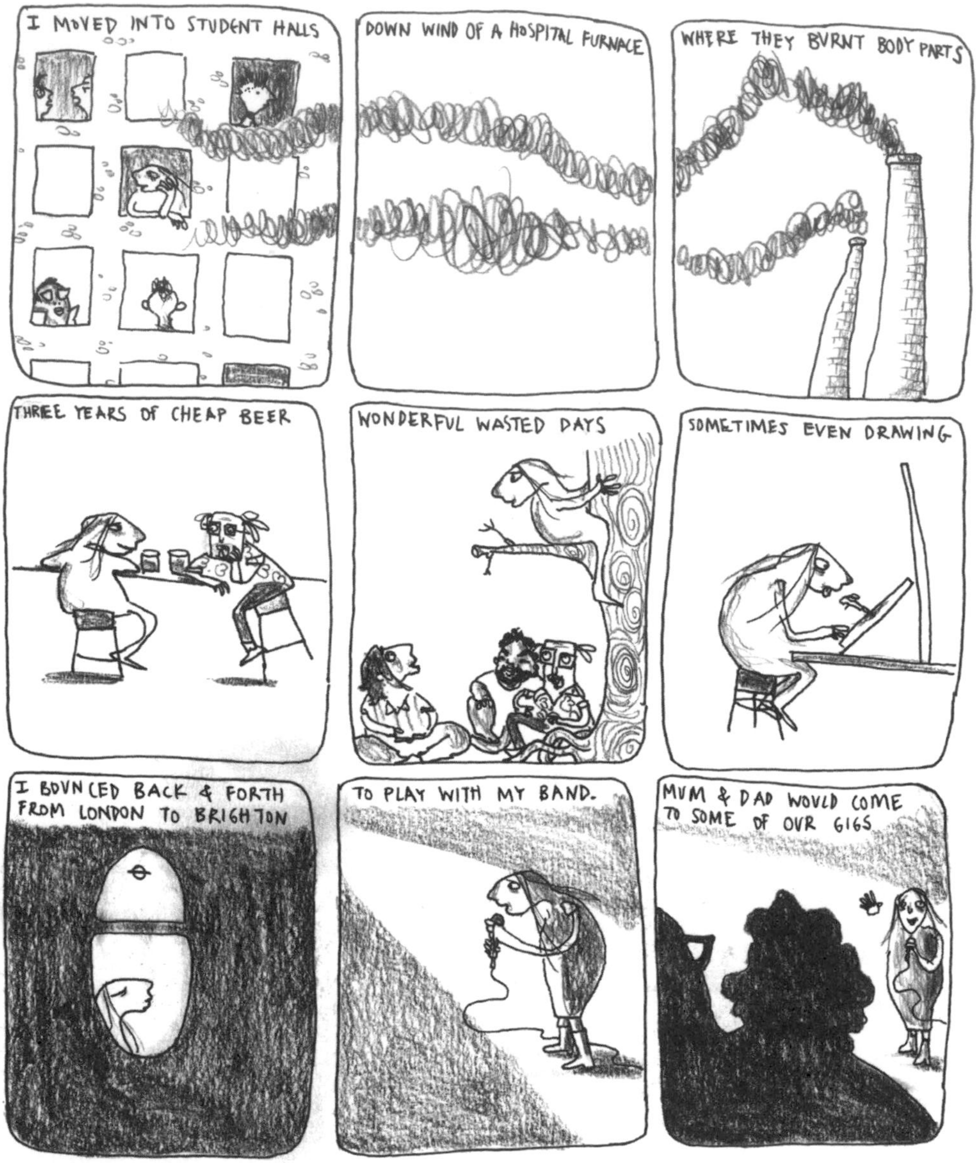
I MOVED INTO STUDENT HALLS
DOWN WIND OF A HOSPITAL FURNACE
WHERE THEY BURNT BODY PARTS
THREE YEARS OF CHEAP BEER
WONDERFUL WASTED DAYS
SOMETIMES EVEN DRAWING
I BOUNCED BACK & FORTH FROM LONDON TO BRIGHTON
TO PLAY WITH MY BAND.
MUM & DAD WOULD COME TO SOME OF OUR GIGS

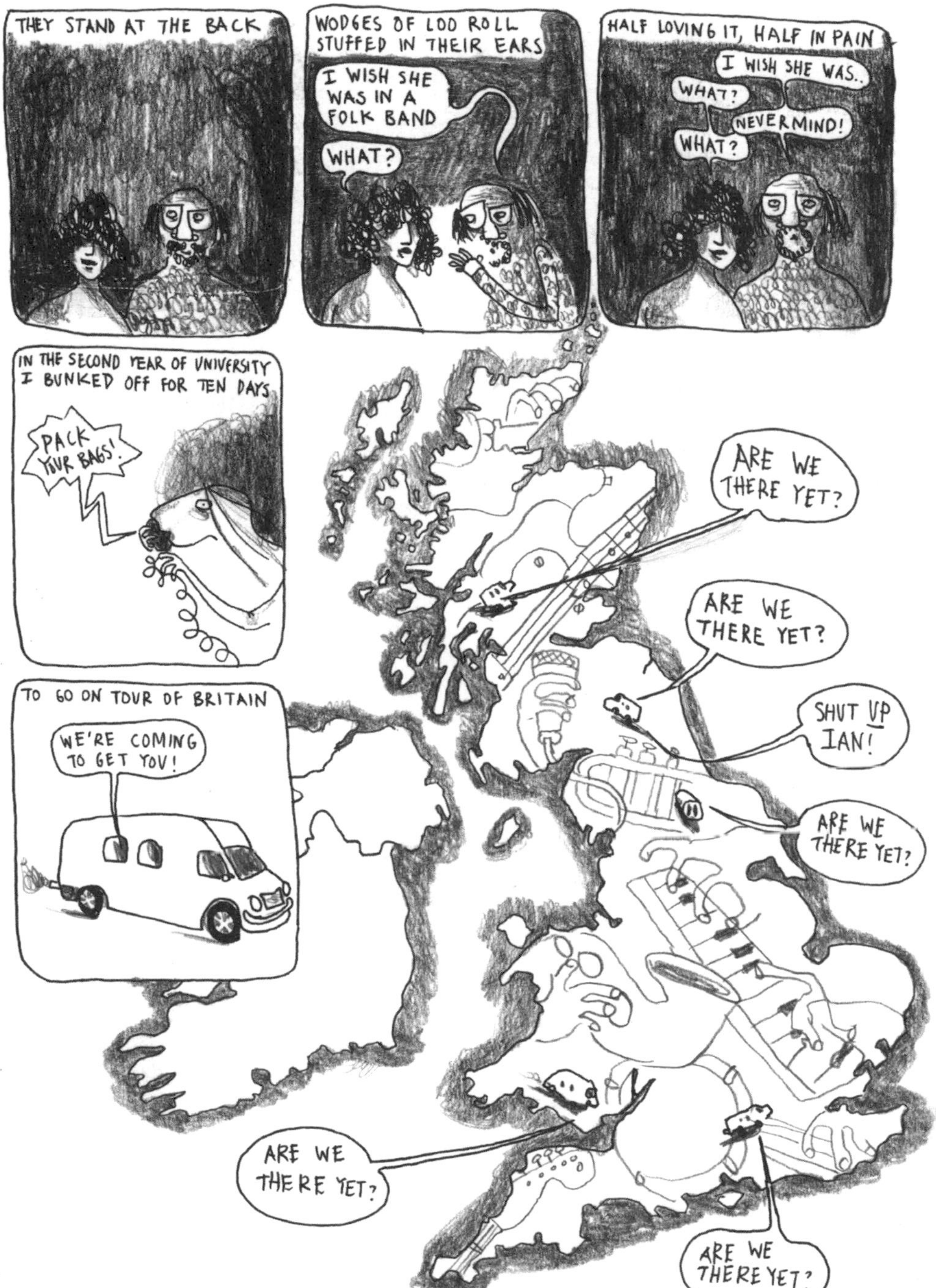
THEY STAND AT THE BACK
WODGES OF LOO ROLL STUFFED IN THEIR EARS
I WISH SHE WAS IN A FOLK BAND
WHAT?
HALF LOVING IT, HALF IN PAIN
I WISH SHE WAS..
WHAT?
NEVERMIND!
WHAT?
IN THE SECOND YEAR OF UNIVERSITY I BUNKED OFF FOR TEN DAYS
PACK YOUR BAGS!
TO GO ON TOUR OF BRITAIN
WE'RE COMING TO GET YOU!
ARE WE THERE YET?
ARE WE THERE YET?
SHUT UP IAN!
ARE WE THERE YET?
ARE WE THERE YET?
ARE WE THERE YET?

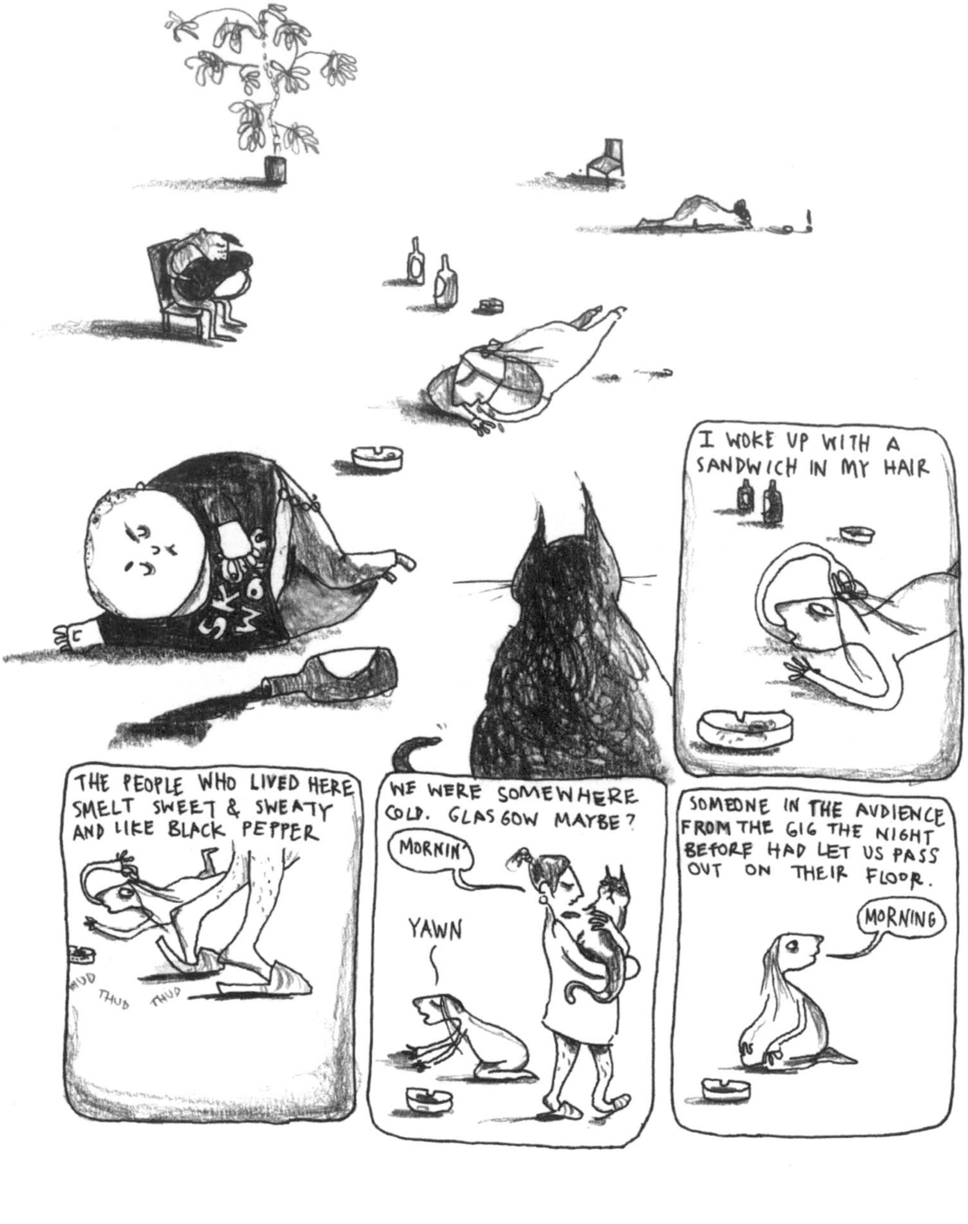
I WOKE UP WITH A SANDWICH IN MY HAIR
THE PEOPLE WHO LIVED HERE SMELT SWEET & SWEATY AND LIKE BLACK PEPPER
THUD THUD THUD
WE WERE SOMEWHERE COLD. GLASGOW MAYBE?
MORNIN'
YAWN
SOMEONE IN THE AUDIENCE FROM THE GIG THE NIGHT BEFORE HAD LET US PASS OUT ON THEIR FLOOR.
MORNING

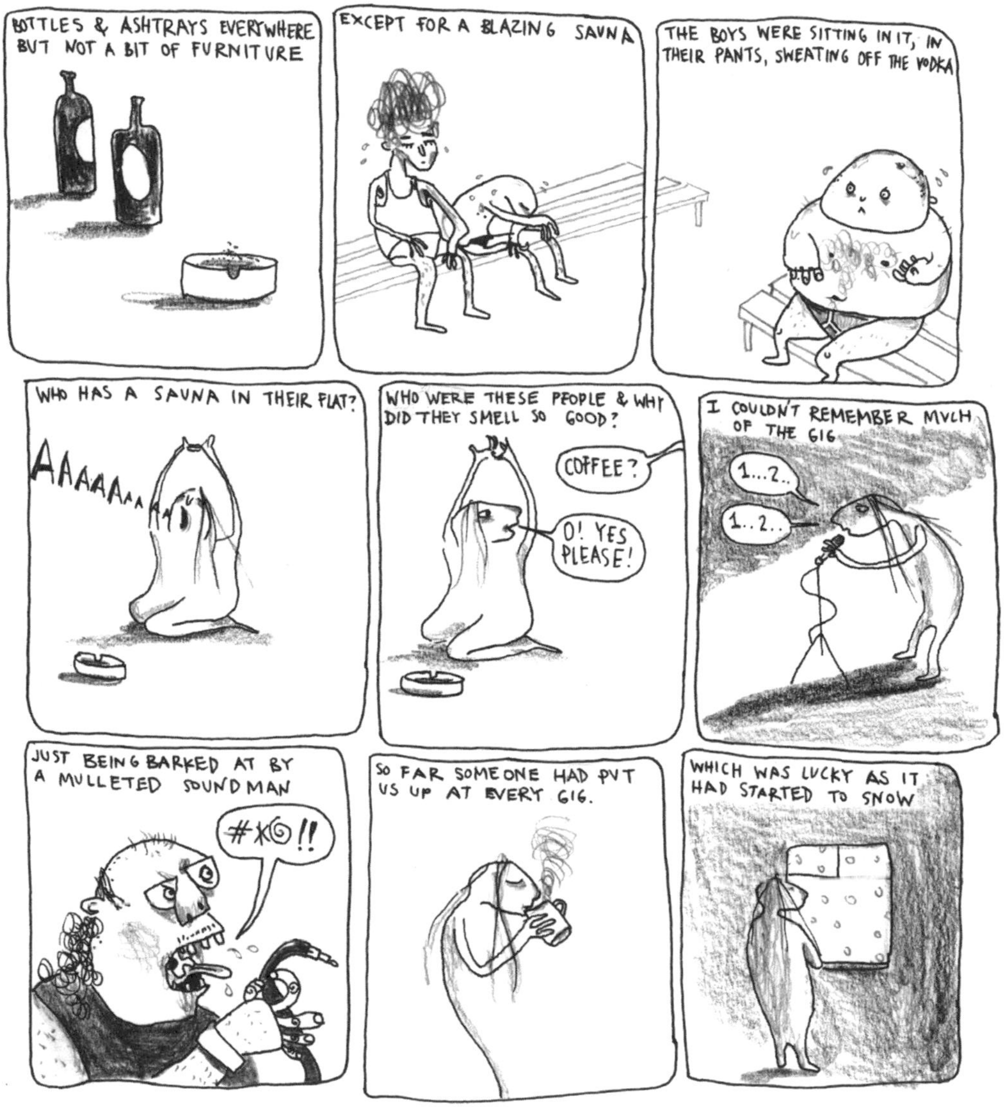
BOTTLES & ASHTRAYS EVERYWHERE BUT NOT A BIT OF FURNITURE
EXCEPT FOR A BLAZING SAUNA
THE BOYS WERE SITTING IN IT, IN THEIR PANTS, SWEATING OFF THE VODKA
WHO HAS A SAUNA IN THEIR FLAT?
AAAAAAA...
WHO WERE THESE PEOPLE & WHY DID THEY SMELL SO GOOD?
COFFEE?
O! YES PLEASE!
I COULDN'T REMEMBER MUCH OF THE GIG
1...2..
1..2..
JUST BEING BARKED AT BY A MULLETED SOUNDMAN
#*@!!
SO FAR SOMEONE HAD PUT US UP AT EVERY GIG.
WHICH WAS LUCKY AS IT HAD STARTED TO SNOW

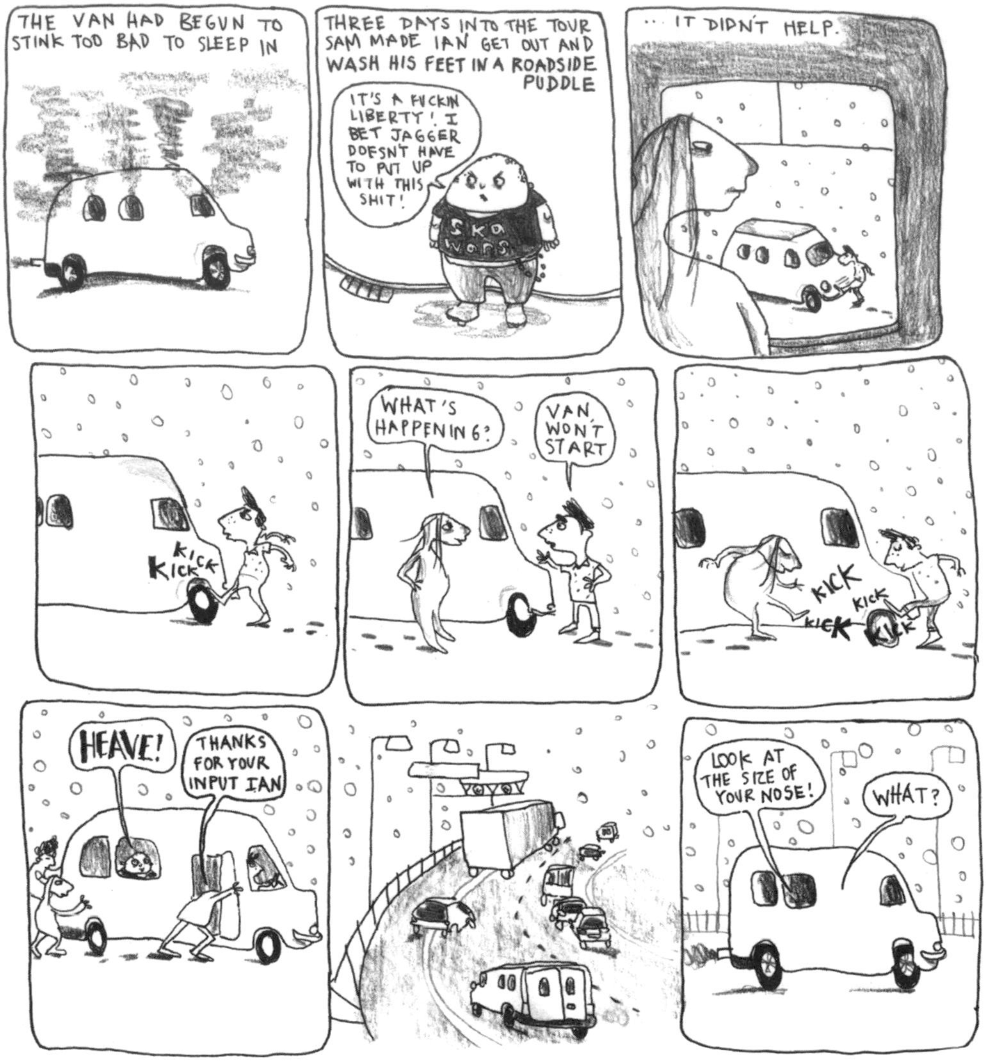
THE VAN HAD BEGUN TO STINK TOO BAD TO SLEEP IN
THREE DAYS INTO THE TOUR SAM MADE IAN GET OUT AND WASH HIS FEET IN A ROADSIDE PUDDLE
IT'S A FUCKIN LIBERTY! I BET JAGGER DOESN'T HAVE TO PUT UP WITH THIS SHIT!
SKA WARS
... IT DIDN'T HELP.
KICK KICK
WHAT'S HAPPENING?
VAN WON'T START
KICK KICK KICK KICK
HEAVE!
THANKS FOR YOUR INPUT IAN
LOOK AT THE SIZE OF YOUR NOSE!
WHAT?

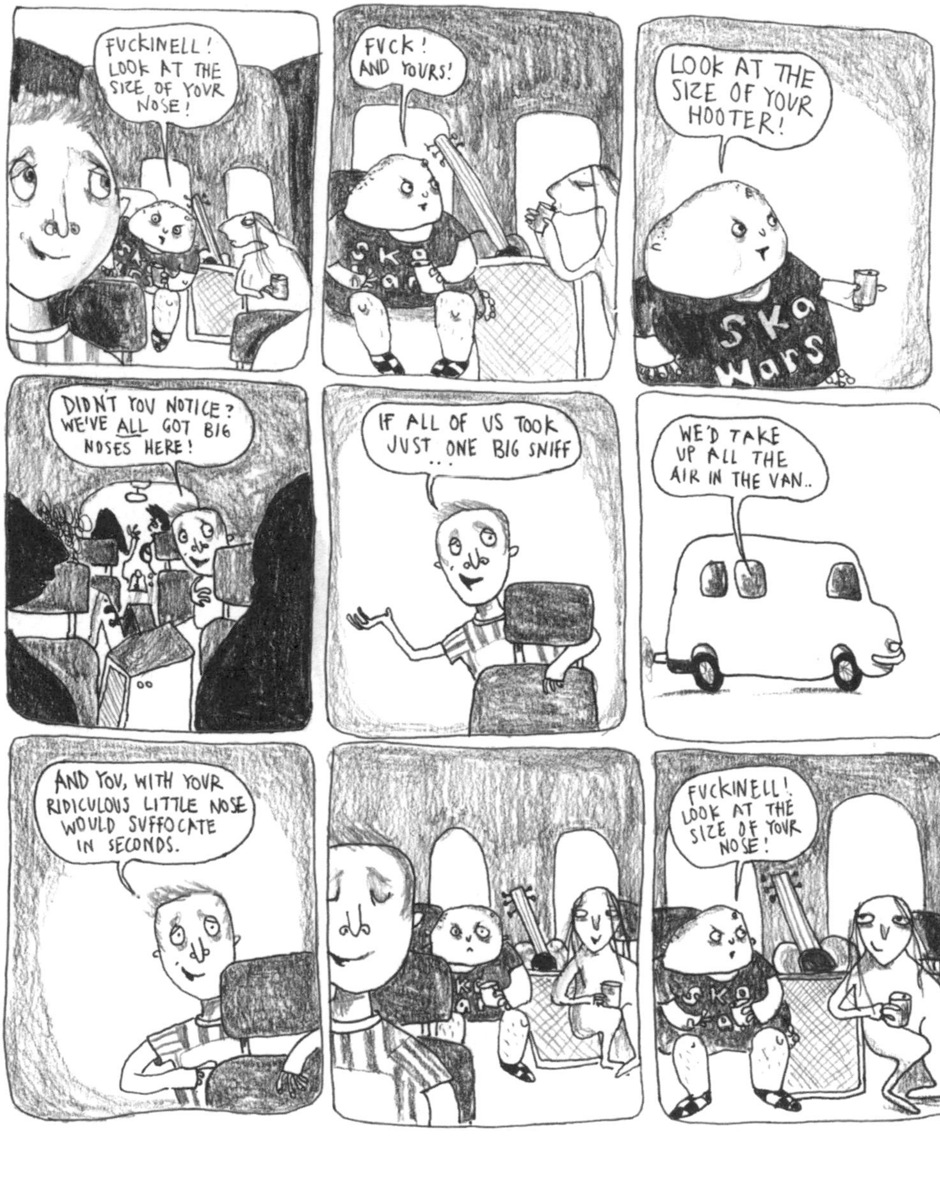
FUCKINELL! LOOK AT THE SIZE OF YOUR NOSE!
FUCK! AND YOURS!
SKA WARS
LOOK AT THE SIZE OF YOUR HOOTER!
SKA WARS
DIDN'T YOU NOTICE? WE'VE ALL GOT BIG NOSES HERE!
IF ALL OF US TOOK JUST ONE BIG SNIFF...
WE'D TAKE UP ALL THE AIR IN THE VAN..
AND YOU, WITH YOUR RIDICULOUS LITTLE NOSE WOULD SUFFOCATE IN SECONDS.
FUCKINELL! LOOK AT THE SIZE OF YOUR NOSE!

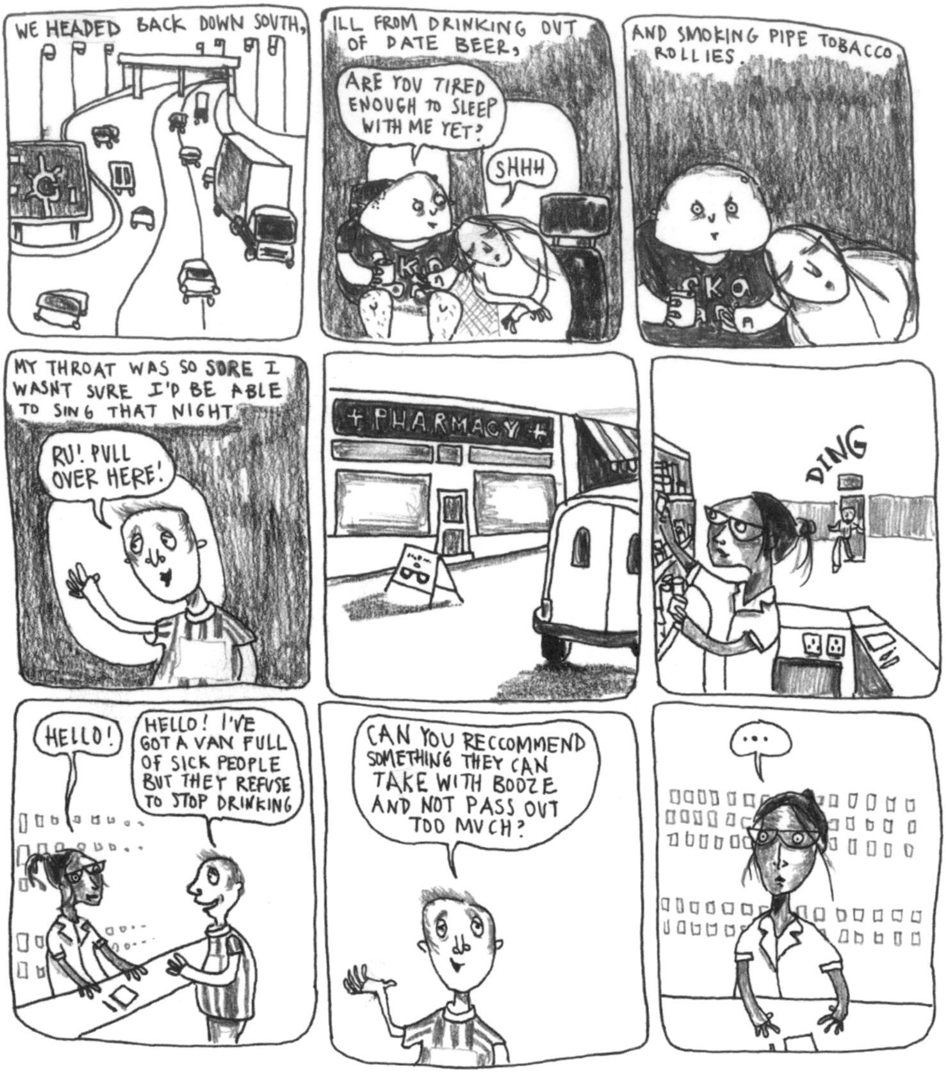
WE HEADED BACK DOWN SOUTH,
ILL FROM DRINKING OUT OF DATE BEER,
ARE YOU TIRED ENOUGH TO SLEEP WITH ME YET?
SHHH
AND SMOKING PIPE TOBACCO ROLLIES.
MY THROAT WAS SO SORE I WASNT SURE I'D BE ABLE TO SING THAT NIGHT
RU! PULL OVER HERE!
PHARMACY
DING
HELLO!
HELLO! I'VE GOT A VAN FULL OF SICK PEOPLE BUT THEY REFUSE TO STOP DRINKING
CAN YOU RECCOMMEND SOMETHING THEY CAN TAKE WITH BOOZE AND NOT PASS OUT TOO MUCH?
...

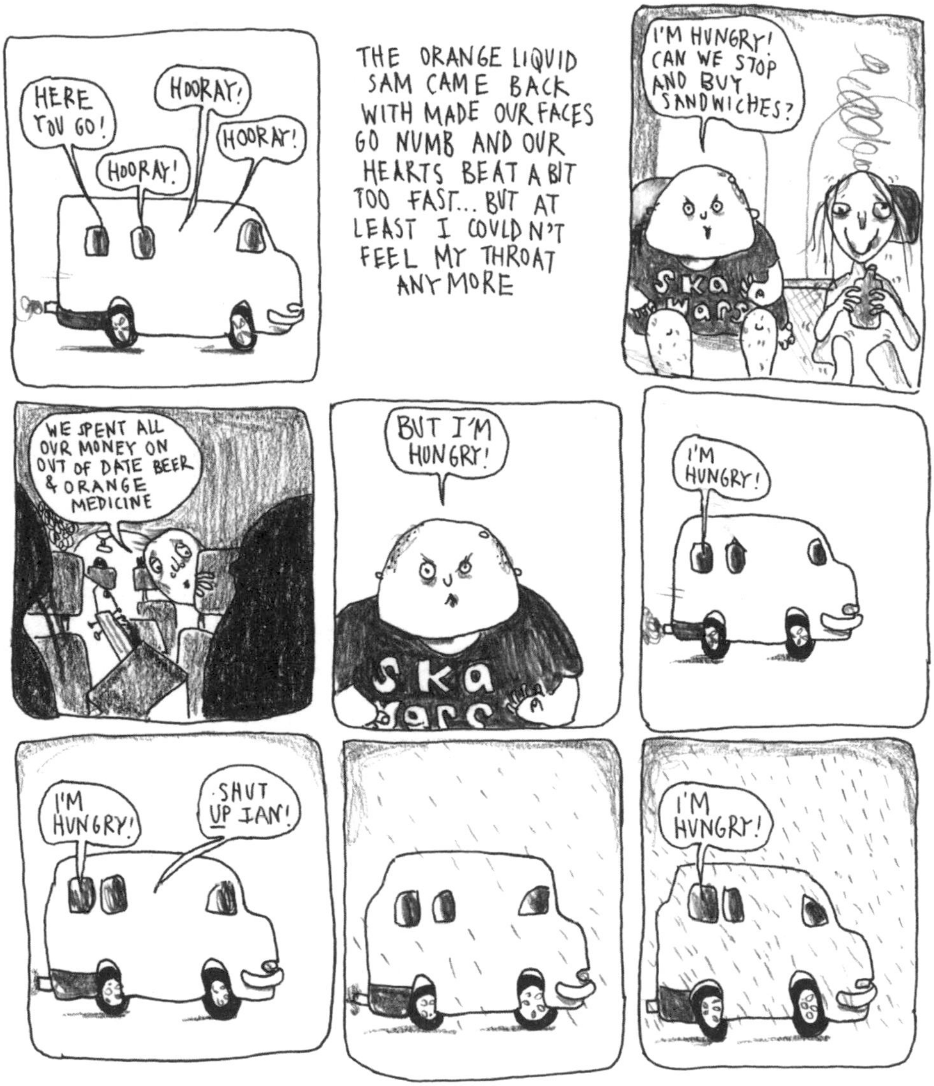
HERE YOU GO!
HOORAY!
HOORAY!
HOORAY!
THE ORANGE LIQUID SAM CAME BACK WITH MADE OUR FACES GO NUMB AND OUR HEARTS BEAT A BIT TOO FAST... BUT AT LEAST I COULDN'T FEEL MY THROAT ANYMORE
I'M HUNGRY! CAN WE STOP AND BUY SANDWICHES?
ska wars
WE SPENT ALL OUR MONEY ON OUT OF DATE BEER & ORANGE MEDICINE
BUT I'M HUNGRY!
I'M HUNGRY!
I'M HUNGRY!
SHUT UP IAN!
I'M HUNGRY!

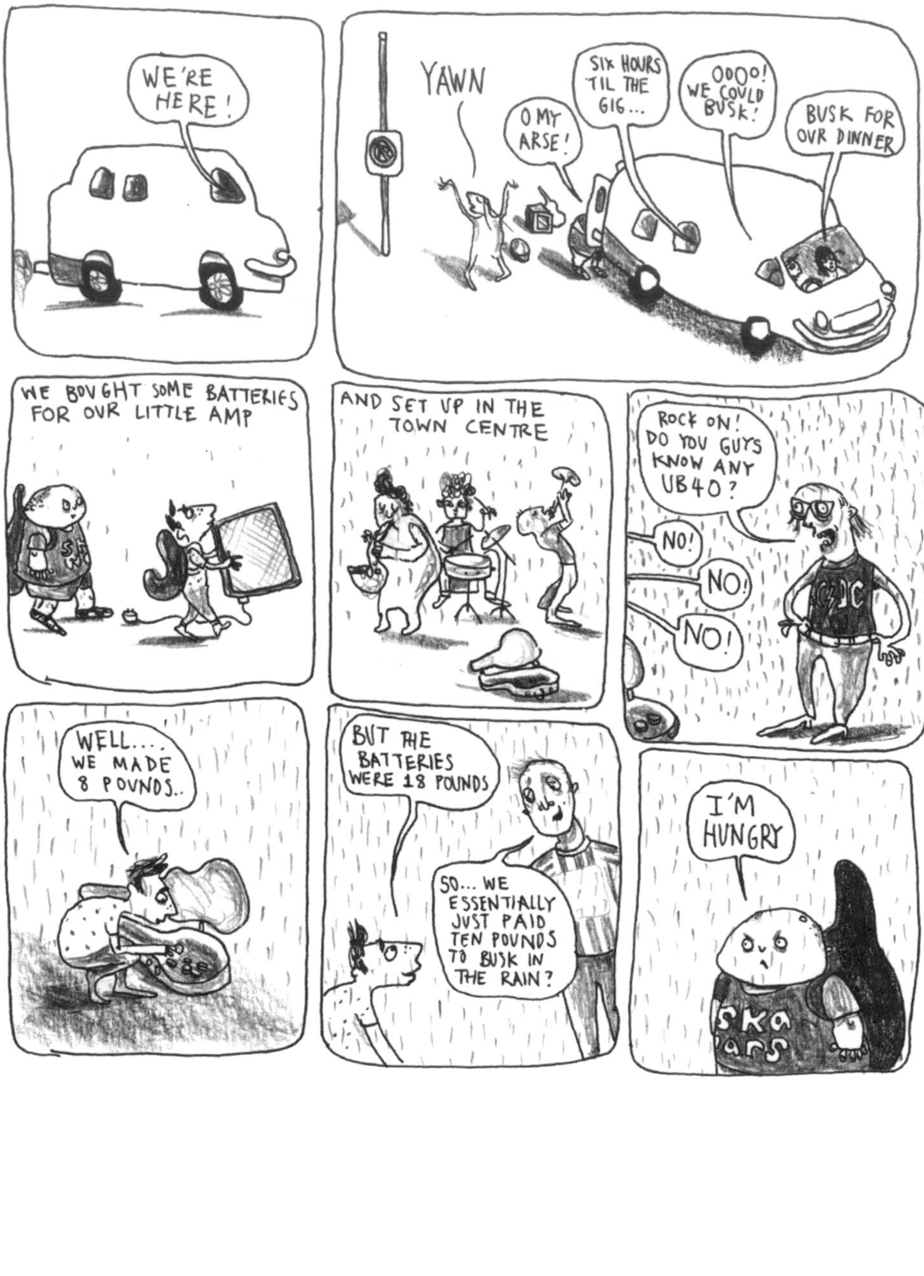
WE'RE HERE!
YAWN
O MY ARSE!
SIX HOURS 'TIL THE GIG...
OOOO! WE COULD BUSK!
BUSK FOR OUR DINNER
WE BOUGHT SOME BATTERIES FOR OUR LITTLE AMP
AND SET UP IN THE TOWN CENTRE
ROCK ON! DO YOU GUYS KNOW ANY UB40?
NO!
NO!
NO!
WELL.... WE MADE 8 POUNDS..
BUT THE BATTERIES WERE 18 POUNDS
SO... WE ESSENTIALLY JUST PAID TEN POUNDS TO BUSK IN THE RAIN?
I'M HUNGRY

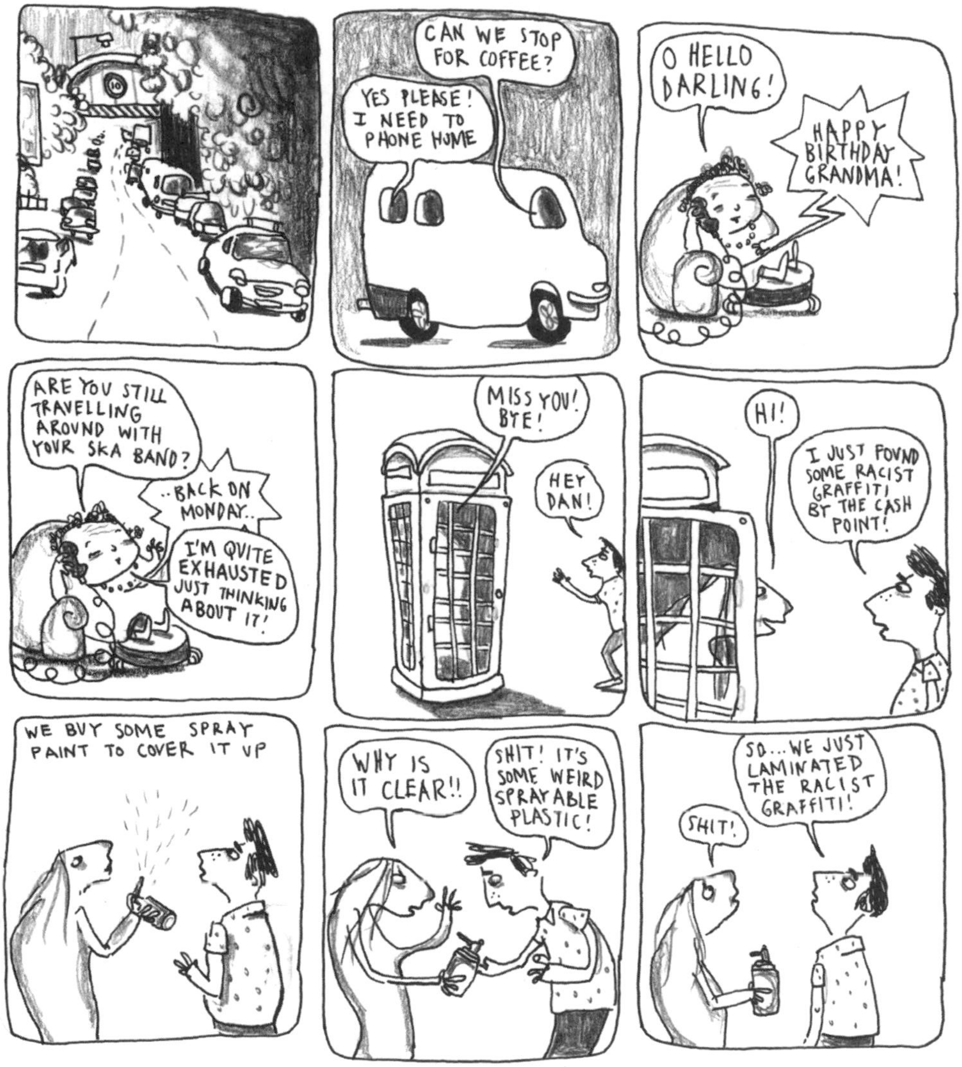
CAN WE STOP FOR COFFEE?
YES PLEASE! I NEED TO PHONE HOME
O HELLO DARLING!
HAPPY BIRTHDAY GRANDMA!
ARE YOU STILL TRAVELLING AROUND WITH YOUR SKA BAND?
..BACK ON MONDAY..
I'M QUITE EXHAUSTED JUST THINKING ABOUT IT!
MISS YOU! BYE!
HEY DAN!
HI!
I JUST FOUND SOME RACIST GRAFFITI BY THE CASH POINT!
WE BUY SOME SPRAY PAINT TO COVER IT UP
WHY IS IT CLEAR!!
SHIT! IT'S SOME WEIRD SPRAYABLE PLASTIC!
SO...WE JUST LAMINATED THE RACIST GRAFFITI!
SHIT!

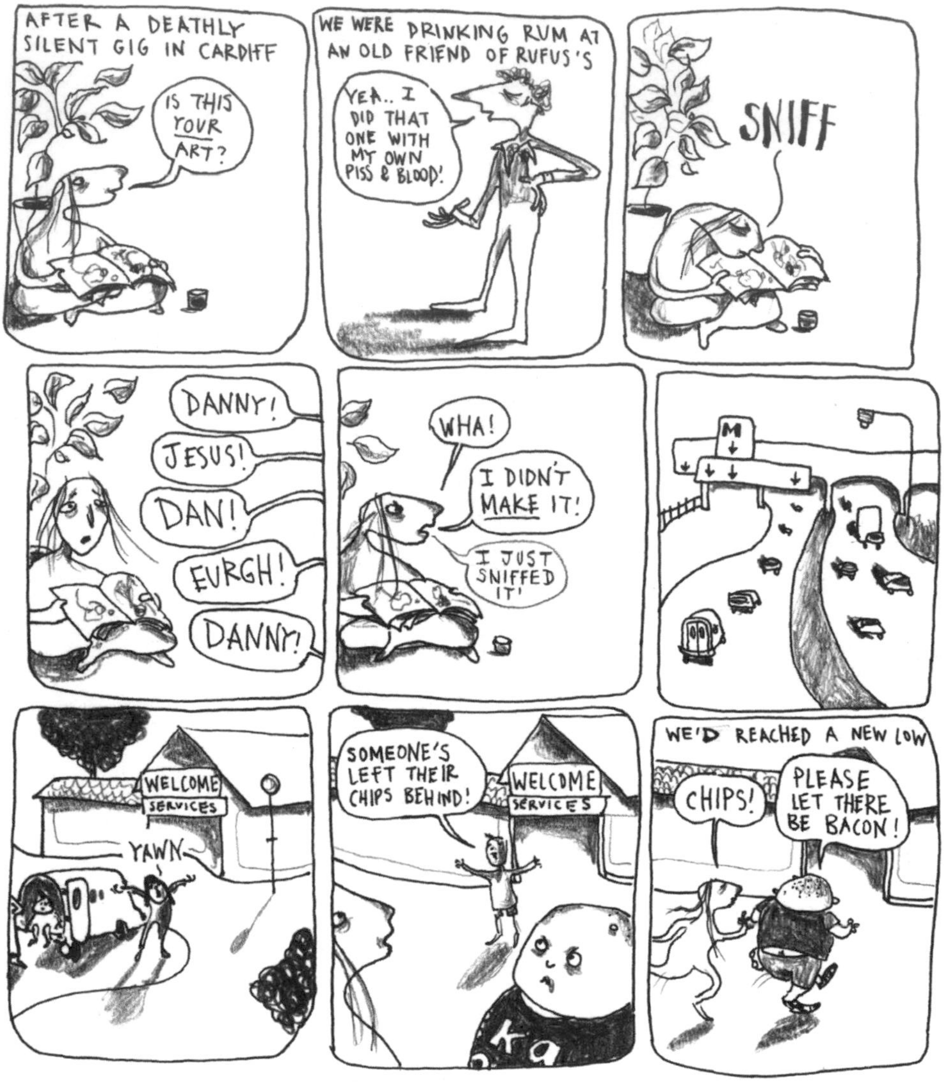
AFTER A DEATHLY SILENT GIG IN CARDIFF
IS THIS YOUR ART?
WE WERE DRINKING RUM AT AN OLD FRIEND OF RUFUS'S
YEA.. I DID THAT ONE WITH MY OWN PISS & BLOOD!
SNIFF
DANNY!
JESUS!
DAN!
EURGH!
DANNY!
WHA!
I DIDN'T MAKE IT!
I JUST SNIFFED IT!
M
WELCOME SERVICES
YAWN
SOMEONE'S LEFT THEIR CHIPS BEHIND!
WELCOME SERVICES
WE'D REACHED A NEW LOW
CHIPS!
PLEASE LET THERE BE BACON!

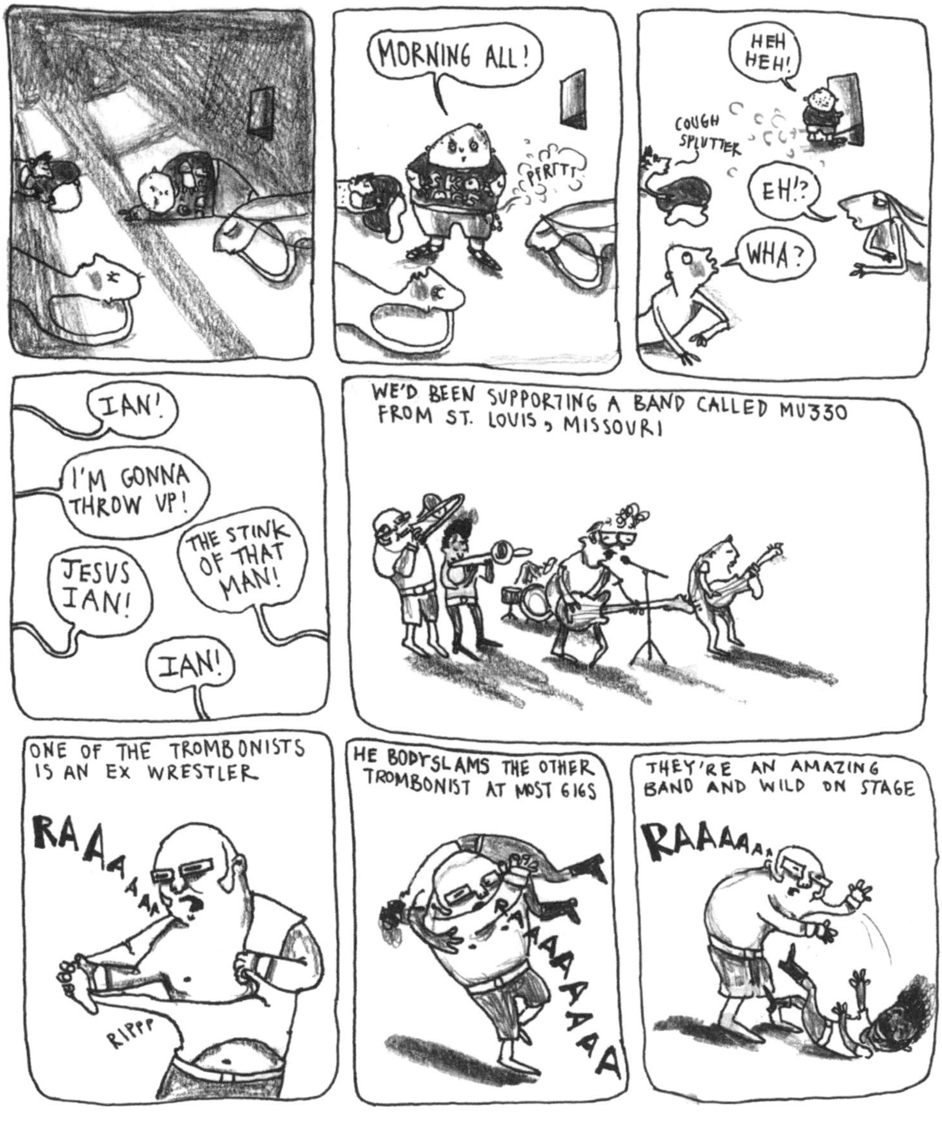
MORNING ALL!
PFRTTT
HEH HEH!
COUGH SPLUTTER
EH!?
WHA?
IAN!
I'M GONNA THROW UP!
JESUS IAN!
THE STINK OF THAT MAN!
IAN!
WE'D BEEN SUPPORTING A BAND CALLED MU330 FROM ST. LOUIS, MISSOURI
ONE OF THE TROMBONISTS IS AN EX WRESTLER
RAAAAA
RIPPP
HE BODYSLAMS THE OTHER TROMBONIST AT MOST GIGS
RAAAAAAAAA
THEY'RE AN AMAZING BAND AND WILD ON STAGE
RAAAAAA

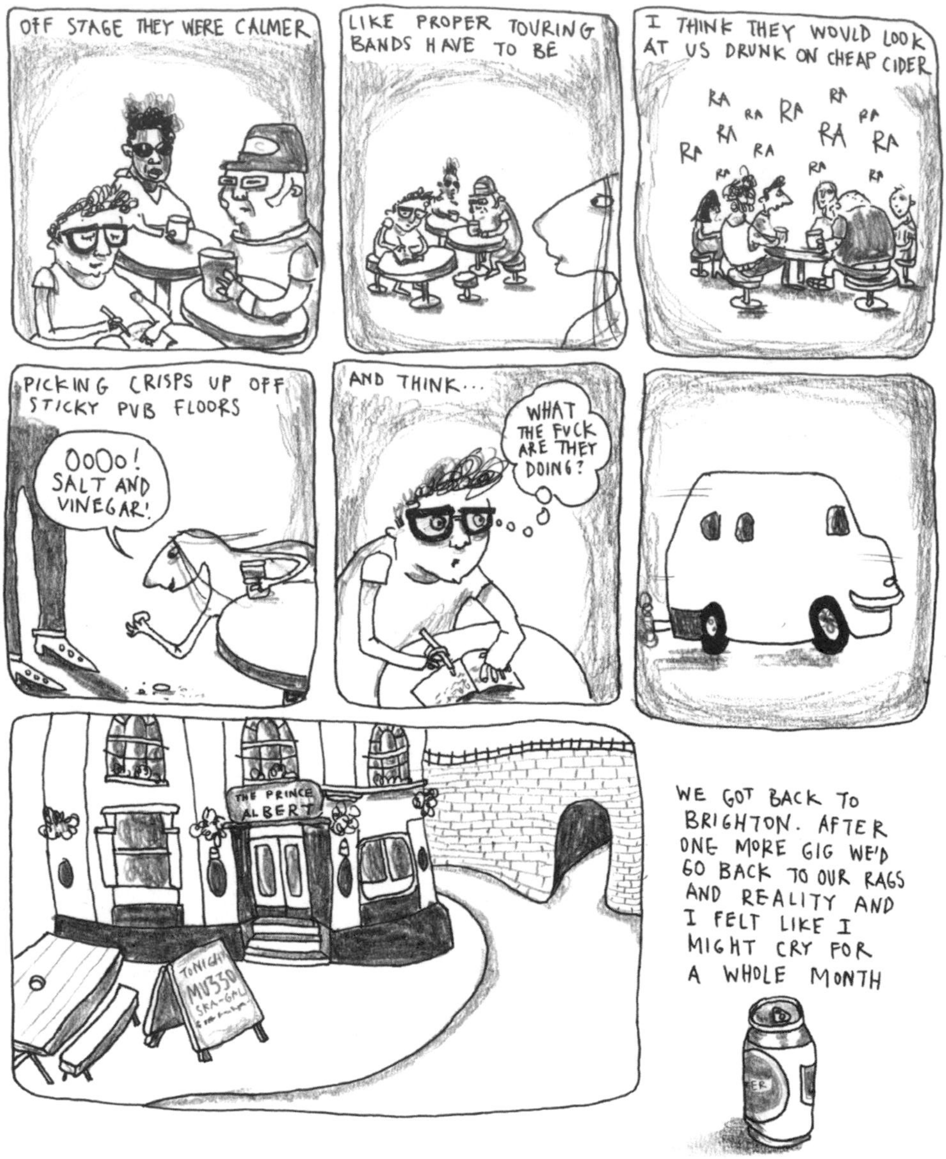
OFF STAGE THEY WERE CALMER
LIKE PROPER TOURING BANDS HAVE TO BE
I THINK THEY WOULD LOOK AT US DRUNK ON CHEAP CIDER
RA RA RA RA RA RA RA RA RA RA RA RA RA RA
PICKING CRISPS UP OFF STICKY PUB FLOORS
OOOo! SALT AND VINEGAR!
AND THINK...
WHAT THE FUCK ARE THEY DOING?
THE PRINCE ALBERT
WE GOT BACK TO BRIGHTON. AFTER ONE MORE GIG WE'D GO BACK TO OUR RAGS AND REALITY AND I FELT LIKE I MIGHT CRY FOR A WHOLE MONTH

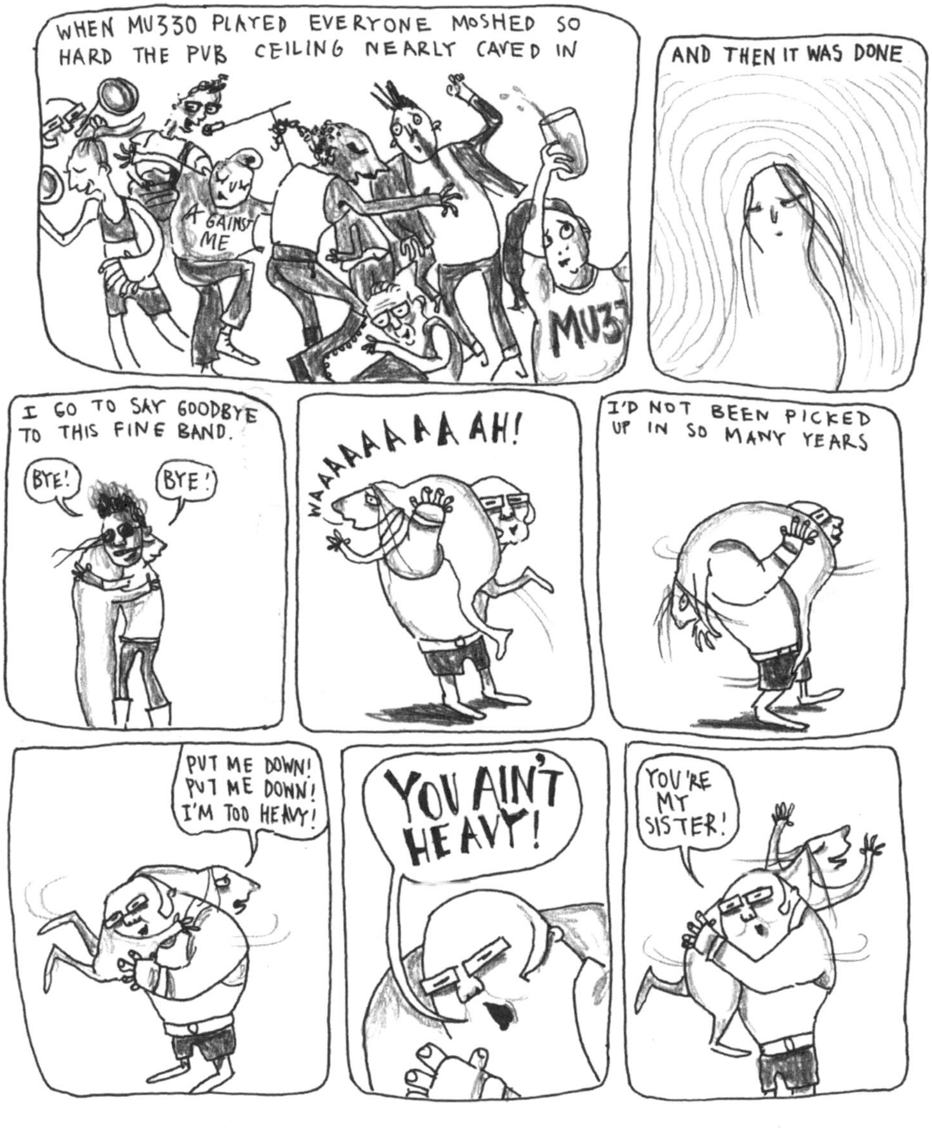

WHEN MU330 PLAYED EVERYONE MOSHED SO HARD THE PUB CEILING NEARLY CAVED IN
AGAINST ME
MU33
AND THEN IT WAS DONE
I GO TO SAY GOODBYE TO THIS FINE BAND.
BYE!
BYE!
WAAAAAAAAAAH!
I'D NOT BEEN PICKED UP IN SO MANY YEARS
PUT ME DOWN! PUT ME DOWN! I'M TOO HEAVY!
YOU AIN'T HEAVY!
YOU'RE MY SISTER!

CHAPTER 12
MILK IN THE SUGAR BOWL

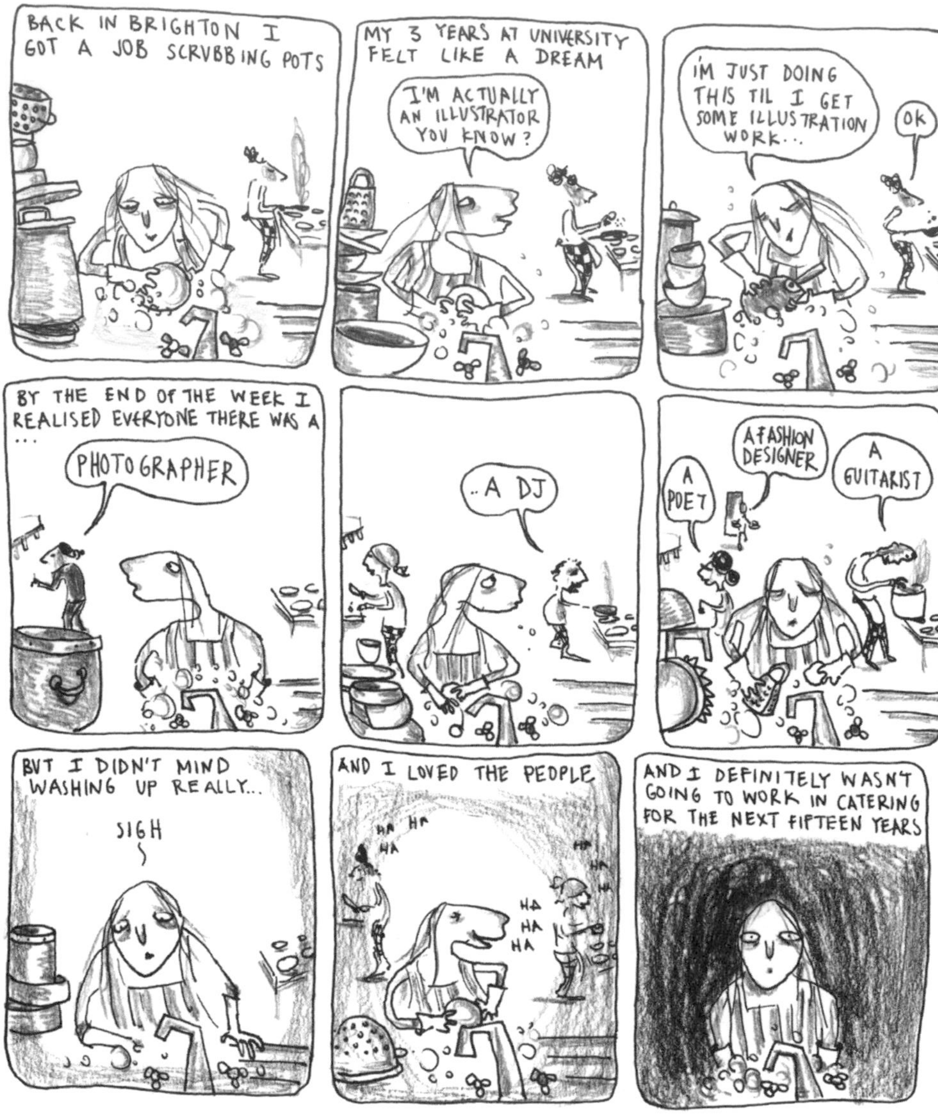
BACK IN BRIGHTON I GOT A JOB SCRUBBING POTS
MY 3 YEARS AT UNIVERSITY FELT LIKE A DREAM
I'M ACTUALLY AN ILLUSTRATOR YOU KNOW?
I'M JUST DOING THIS TIL I GET SOME ILLUSTRATION WORK...
OK
BY THE END OF THE WEEK I REALISED EVERYONE THERE WAS A ...
PHOTOGRAPHER
..A DJ
A POET
A FASHION DESIGNER
A GUITARIST
BUT I DIDN'T MIND WASHING UP REALLY...
SIGH
AND I LOVED THE PEOPLE
HA HA HA
HA HA HA
AND I DEFINITELY WASN'T GOING TO WORK IN CATERING FOR THE NEXT FIFTEEN YEARS

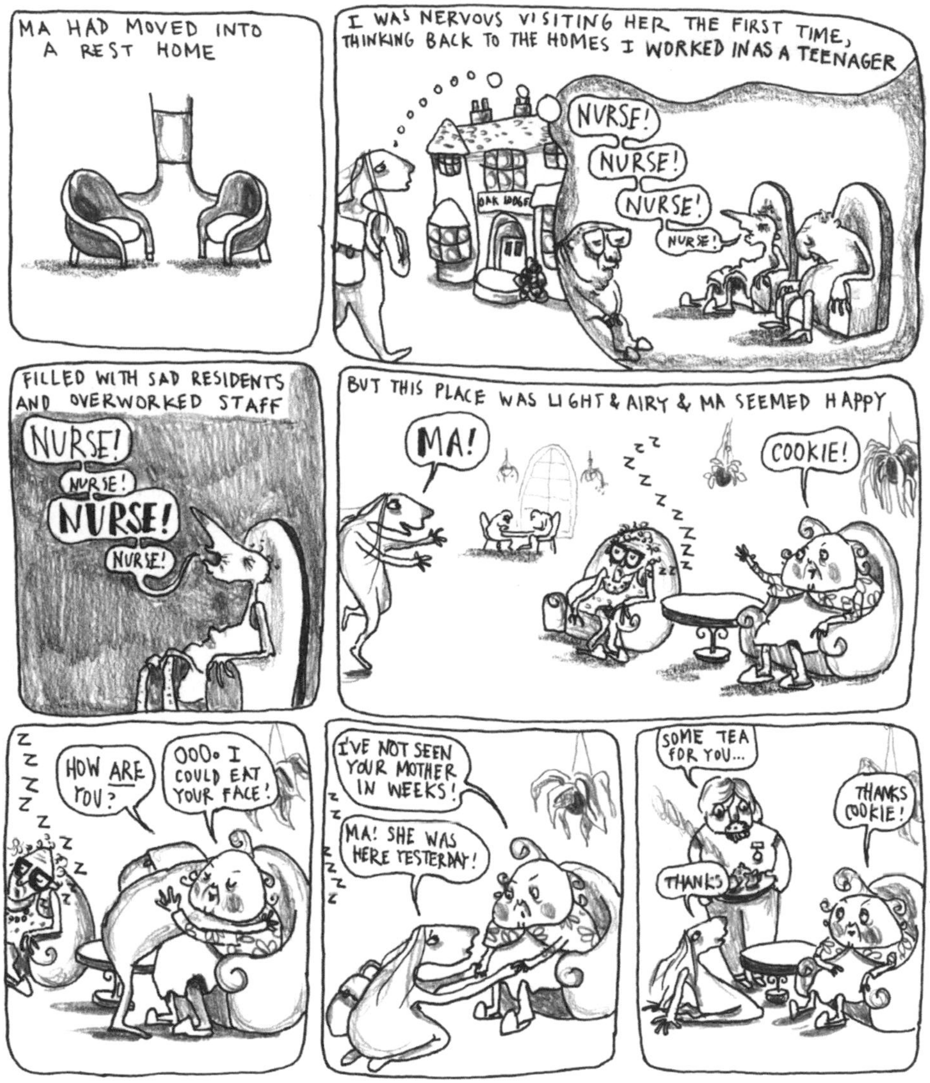
MA HAD MOVED INTO A REST HOME
I WAS NERVOUS VISITING HER THE FIRST TIME, THINKING BACK TO THE HOMES I WORKED IN AS A TEENAGER
OAK LODGE
NURSE!
NURSE!
NURSE!
NURSE!
FILLED WITH SAD RESIDENTS AND OVERWORKED STAFF
NURSE!
NURSE!
NURSE!
NURSE!
BUT THIS PLACE WAS LIGHT & AIRY & MA SEEMED HAPPY
MA!
COOKIE!
HOW ARE YOU?
OOO. I COULD EAT YOUR FACE!
I'VE NOT SEEN YOUR MOTHER IN WEEKS!
MA! SHE WAS HERE YESTERDAY!
SOME TEA FOR YOU...
THANKS
THANKS COOKIE!

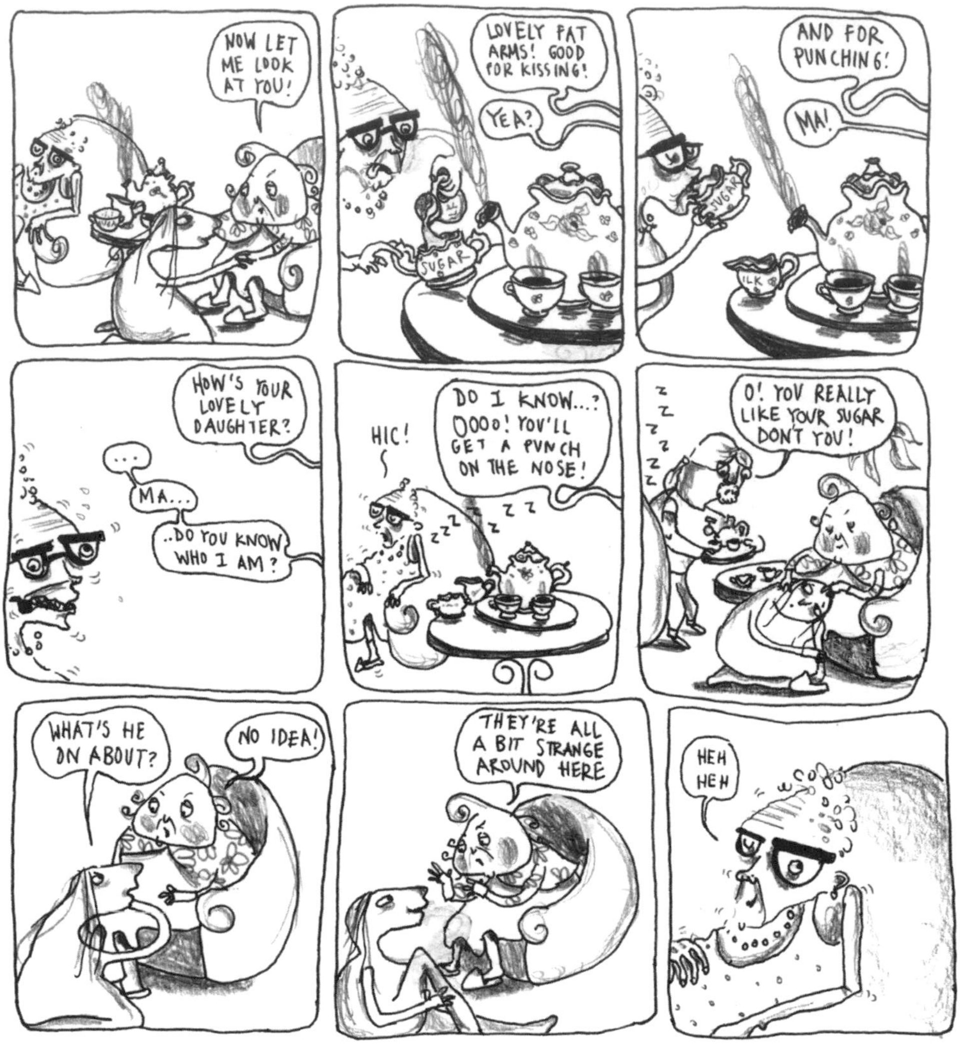
NOW LET ME LOOK AT YOU!
LOVELY FAT ARMS! GOOD FOR KISSING!
YEA?
SUGAR
AND FOR PUNCHING!
MA!
SUGAR
ILK
HOW'S YOUR LOVELY DAUGHTER?
...
MA...
..DO YOU KNOW WHO I AM?
HIC!
DO I KNOW...? OOOO! YOU'LL GET A PUNCH ON THE NOSE!
O! YOU REALLY LIKE YOUR SUGAR DON'T YOU!
WHAT'S HE ON ABOUT?
NO IDEA!
THEY'RE ALL A BIT STRANGE AROUND HERE
HEH HEH

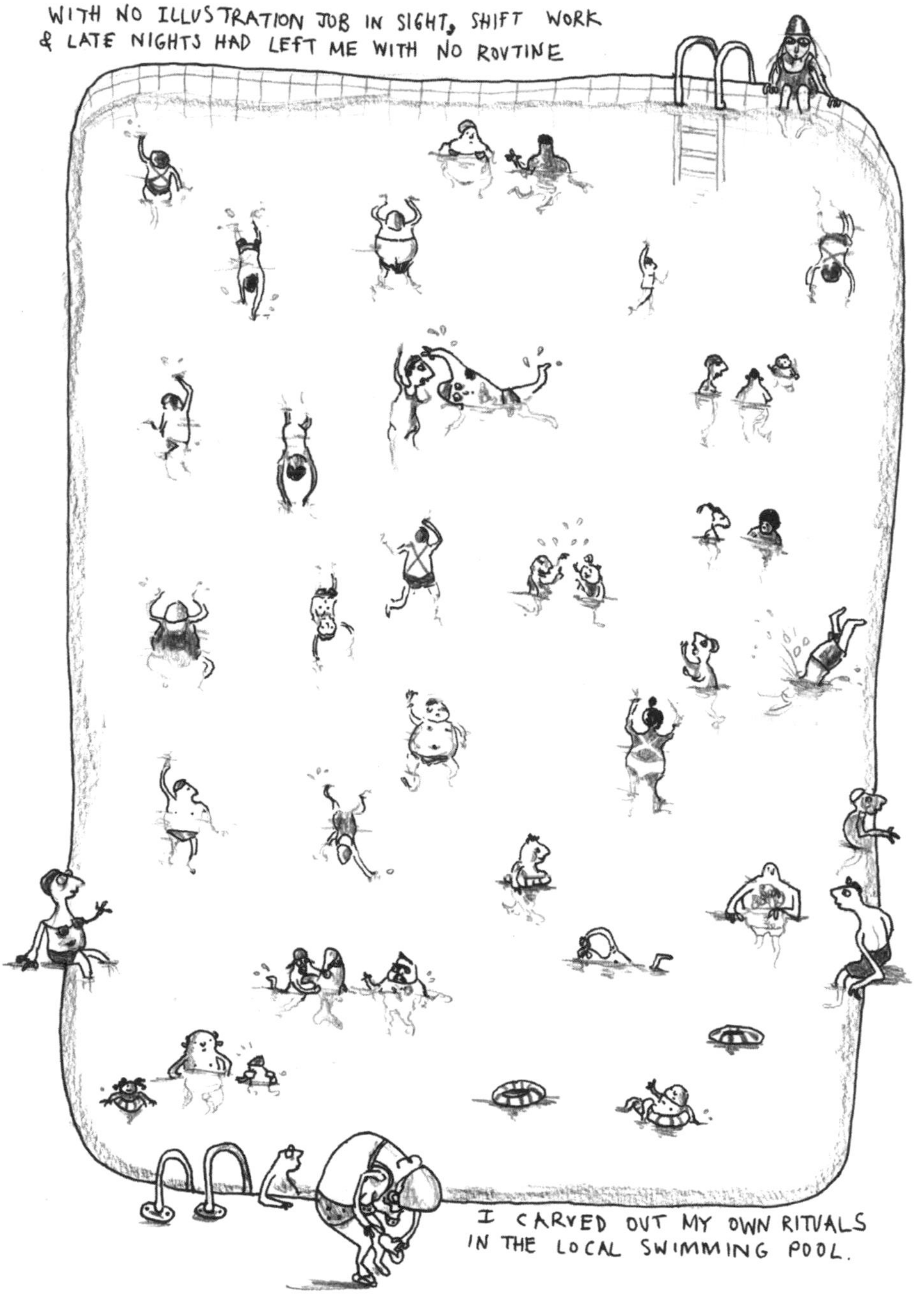
WITH NO ILLUSTRATION JOB IN SIGHT, SHIFT WORK
& LATE NIGHTS HAD LEFT ME WITH NO ROUTINE
I CARVED OUT MY OWN RITUALS
IN THE LOCAL SWIMMING POOL.

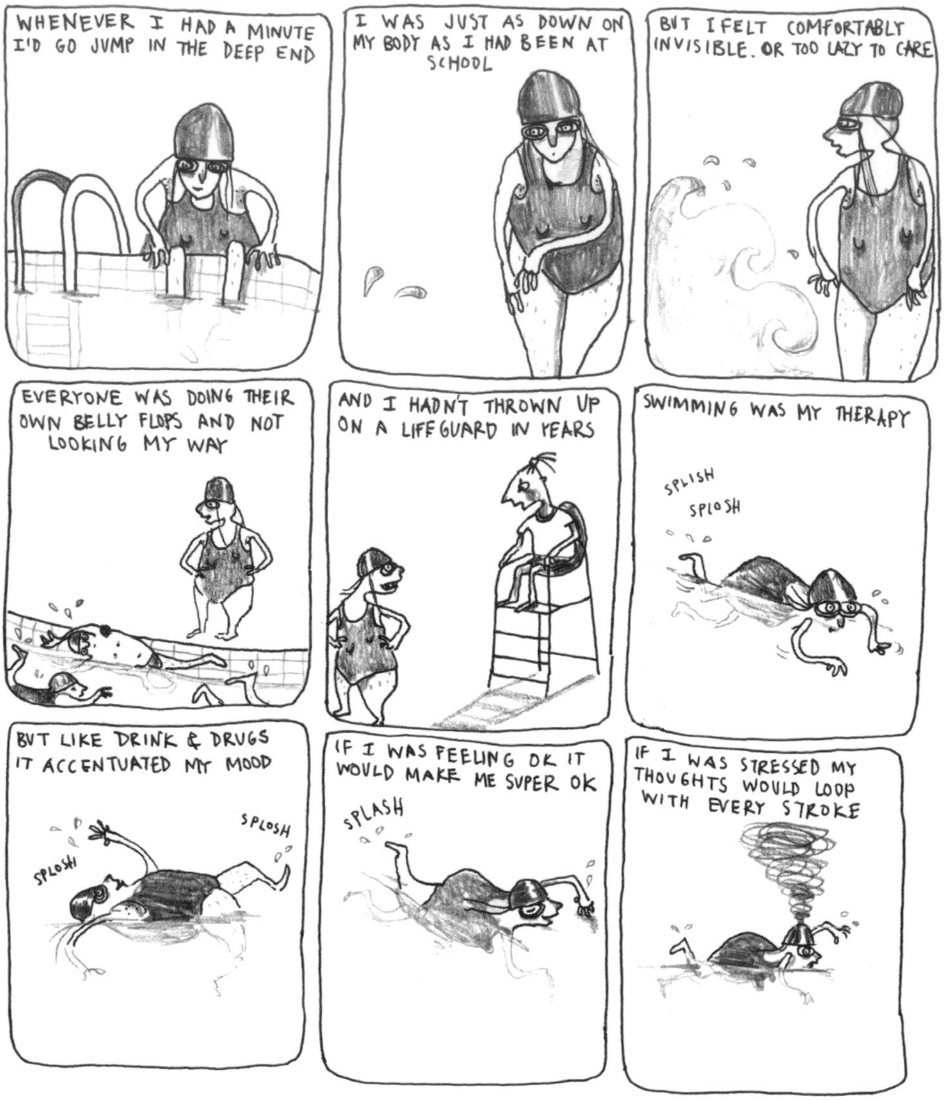
WHENEVER I HAD A MINUTE I'D GO JUMP IN THE DEEP END
I WAS JUST AS DOWN ON MY BODY AS I HAD BEEN AT SCHOOL
BUT I FELT COMFORTABLY INVISIBLE. OR TOO LAZY TO CARE
EVERYONE WAS DOING THEIR OWN BELLY FLOPS AND NOT LOOKING MY WAY
AND I HADN'T THROWN UP ON A LIFEGUARD IN YEARS
SWIMMING WAS MY THERAPY
SPLISH
SPLOSH
BUT LIKE DRINK & DRUGS IT ACCENTUATED MY MOOD
SPLOSH
SPLOSH
IF I WAS FEELING OK IT WOULD MAKE ME SUPER OK
SPLASH
IF I WAS STRESSED MY THOUGHTS WOULD LOOP WITH EVERY STROKE

AND I'D PULL MYSELF OUT THE POOL COVERED IN CHLORINE & FURY

BUT ON THE WHOLE MOVEMENT CALMED ME DOWN AND WATER, LOVELY WATER IS LIFE.

SIGH

MY FAVOURITE MEDICINE WAS GOING TO THE MOVIES.

I WORSHIPPED AT THE CHURCH OF CINEMA

EVEN DELIGHTING IN HATING THE TALKERS, THE KISSERS AND THE POPCORN MUNCHERS

CRUNCH MUNCH
CRUNCH
CRUNCH

MMM M M M

HE SAID

YEA

YEA

CRUNCH MUNCH
RUSTLE
CRINKLE
CRUNCH

MMM M M M

RUSTLE

AND THEN

YEA

AND THEN I SAID TO HIM WHAT DO YOU MEAN YOU DON'T LIKE BLOW JOBS!?

YEA

YEA

YEA

153

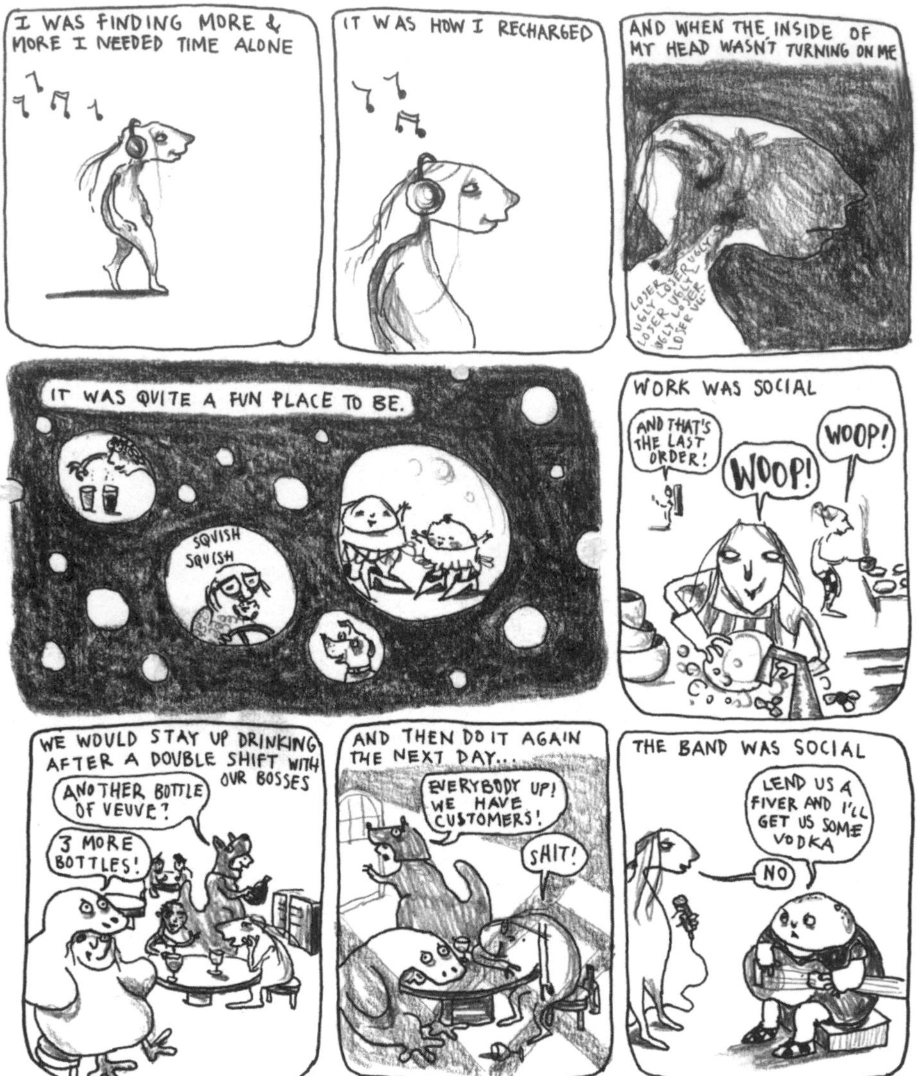
I WAS FINDING MORE & MORE I NEEDED TIME ALONE
IT WAS HOW I RECHARGED
AND WHEN THE INSIDE OF MY HEAD WASN'T TURNING ON ME
IT WAS QUITE A FUN PLACE TO BE.
SQUISH SQUISH
WORK WAS SOCIAL
AND THAT'S THE LAST ORDER!
WOOP!
WOOP!
WE WOULD STAY UP DRINKING AFTER A DOUBLE SHIFT WITH OUR BOSSES
ANOTHER BOTTLE OF VEUVE?
3 MORE BOTTLES!
AND THEN DO IT AGAIN THE NEXT DAY...
EVERYBODY UP! WE HAVE CUSTOMERS!
SHIT!
THE BAND WAS SOCIAL
LEND US A FIVER AND I'LL GET US SOME VODKA
NO

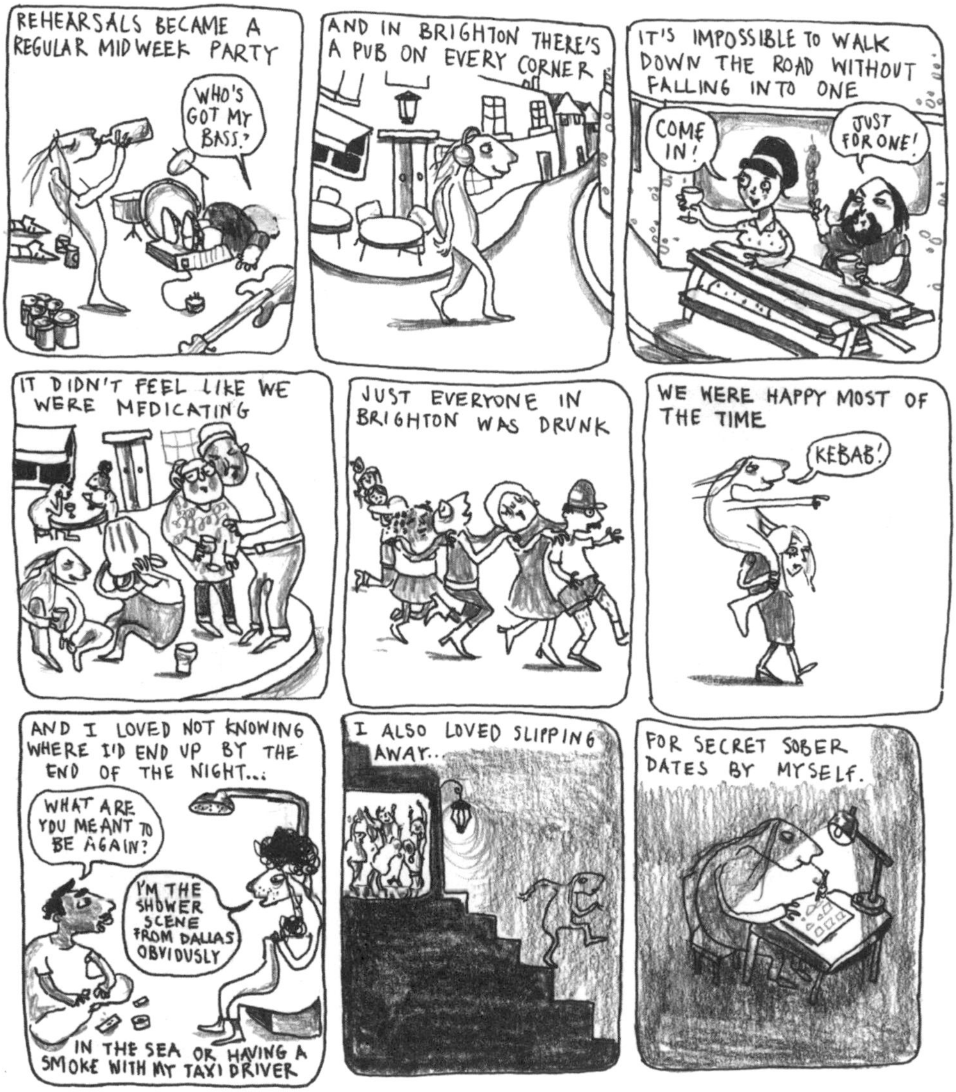
REHEARSALS BECAME A REGULAR MIDWEEK PARTY
WHO'S GOT MY BASS?
AND IN BRIGHTON THERE'S A PUB ON EVERY CORNER
IT'S IMPOSSIBLE TO WALK DOWN THE ROAD WITHOUT FALLING INTO ONE
COME IN!
JUST FOR ONE!
IT DIDN'T FEEL LIKE WE WERE MEDICATING
JUST EVERYONE IN BRIGHTON WAS DRUNK
WE WERE HAPPY MOST OF THE TIME
KEBAB!
AND I LOVED NOT KNOWING WHERE I'D END UP BY THE END OF THE NIGHT...
WHAT ARE YOU MEANT TO BE AGAIN?
I'M THE SHOWER SCENE FROM DALLAS OBVIOUSLY
IN THE SEA OR HAVING A SMOKE WITH MY TAXI DRIVER
I ALSO LOVED SLIPPING AWAY..
FOR SECRET SOBER DATES BY MYSELF.

CHAPTER 13

HIGH LEG KICKS IN THE SILVER DRESS

GRANDMA MIN WAS WAY MORE STYLISH THAN ME
HOW'S THE BAND DARLING?
OOO! WE'RE RECORDING AN EP!
SO I OFTEN PILLAGED HER WARDROBE
?
IT FITS!
CLAP CLAP
O YOU LOOK LOVELY DARLING!
HOW DOES IT FIT?! I'M 3 TIMES BIGGER THAN YOU!
I BOUGHT IT IN 1967 WITH MY WAGES FROM THE PERFUME COUNTER IN BOOTS
I USED TO CLEAR THE TABLES AND DO MY HIGH LEG KICKS
LIKE THIS?
LOOK AT THESE VEINS NOW!
GRANDMA! YOU ARE BEAUTIFUL!
BYE DARLING! HAVE FUN.
BYE GRANDMA

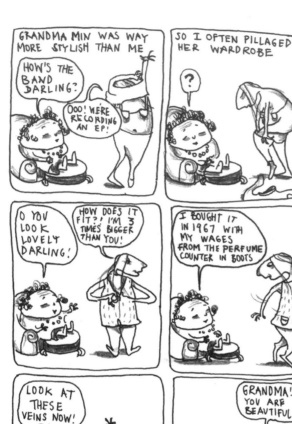

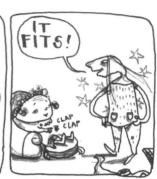

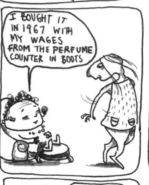

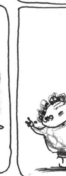

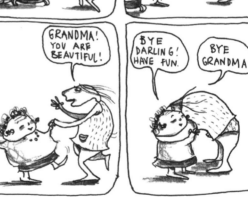

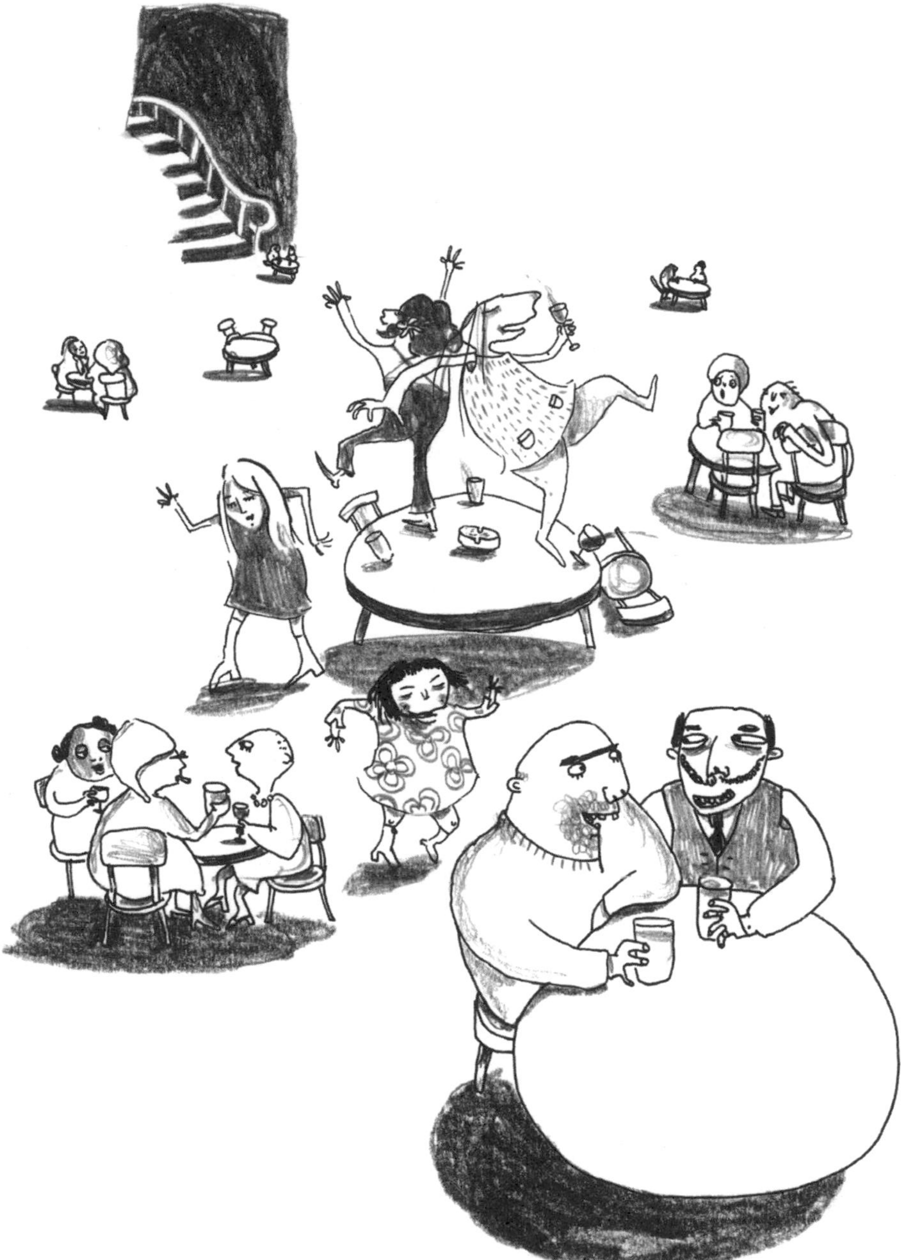

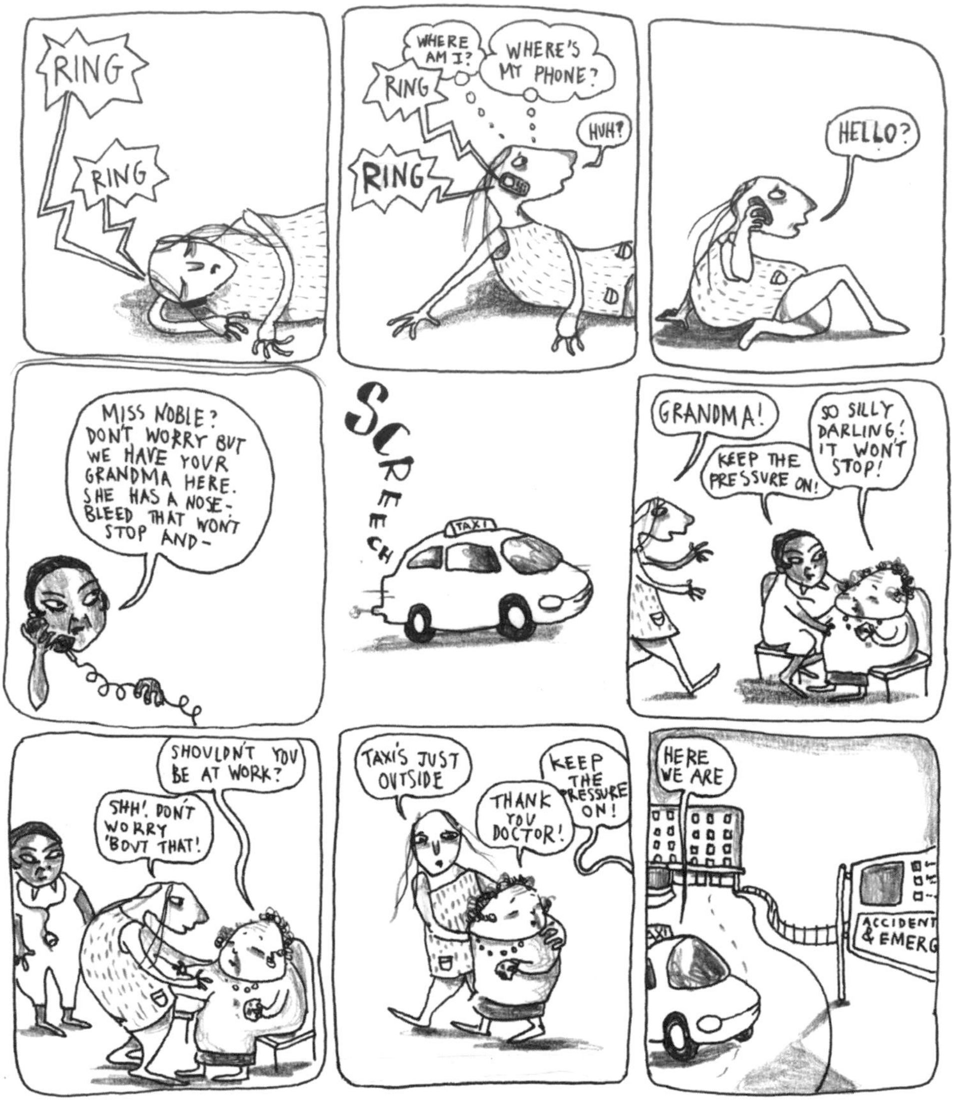
RING
RING
WHERE AM I?
WHERE'S MY PHONE?
RING
RING
HUH?
HELLO?
MISS NOBLE? DON'T WORRY BUT WE HAVE YOUR GRANDMA HERE. SHE HAS A NOSE-BLEED THAT WON'T STOP AND-
SCREECH
TAXI
GRANDMA!
KEEP THE PRESSURE ON!
SO SILLY DARLING! IT WON'T STOP!
SHOULDN'T YOU BE AT WORK?
SHH! DON'T WORRY 'BOUT THAT!
TAXI'S JUST OUTSIDE
THANK YOU DOCTOR!
KEEP THE PRESSURE ON!
HERE WE ARE
ACCIDENT & EMERG

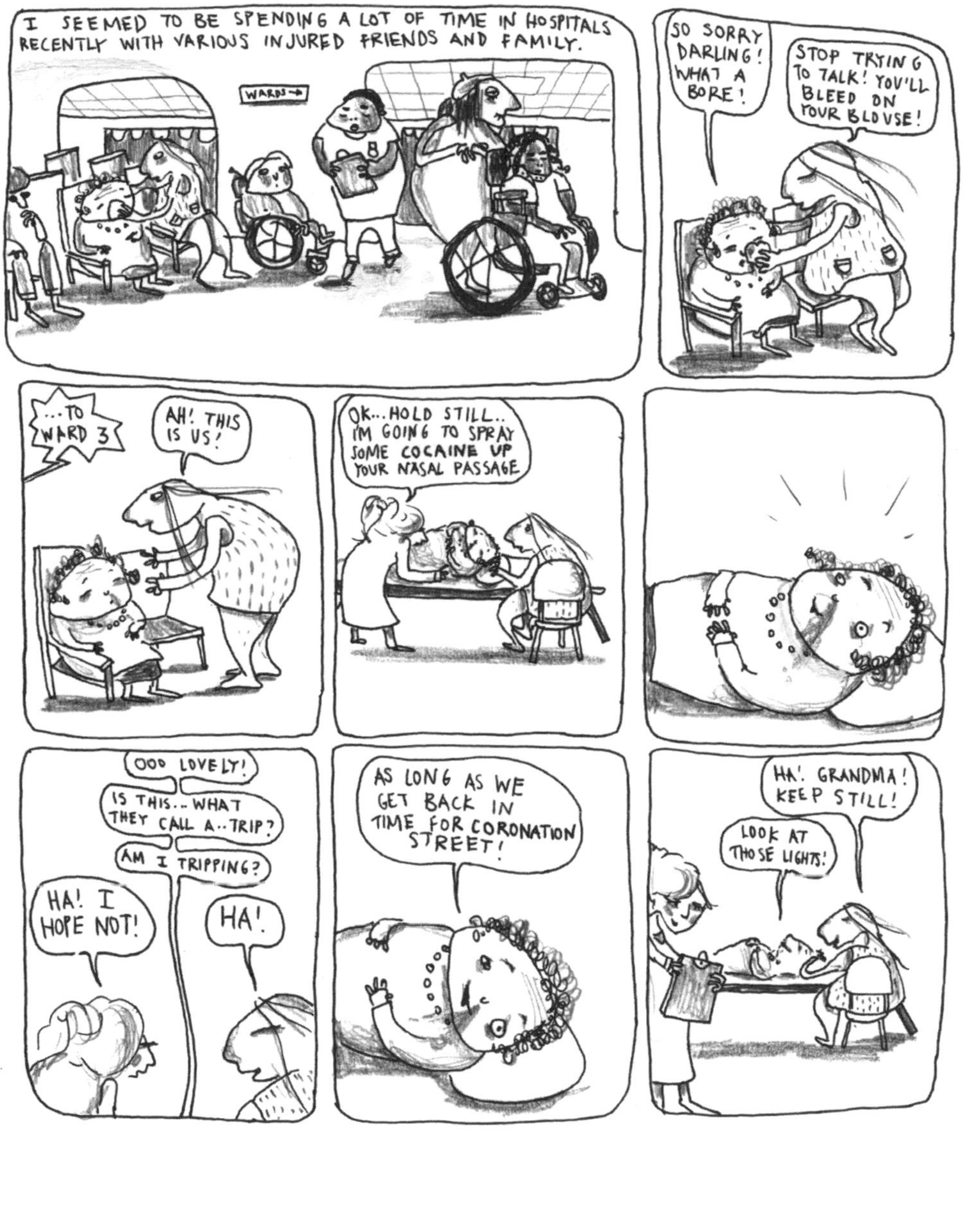
I SEEMED TO BE SPENDING A LOT OF TIME IN HOSPITALS RECENTLY WITH VARIOUS INJURED FRIENDS AND FAMILY.
WARDS →
SO SORRY DARLING! WHAT A BORE!
STOP TRYING TO TALK! YOU'LL BLEED ON YOUR BLOUSE!
...TO WARD 3
AH! THIS IS US!
OK... HOLD STILL.. I'M GOING TO SPRAY SOME COCAINE UP YOUR NASAL PASSAGE
OOO LOVELY!
IS THIS... WHAT THEY CALL A.. TRIP?
AM I TRIPPING?
HA! I HOPE NOT!
HA!
AS LONG AS WE GET BACK IN TIME FOR CORONATION STREET!
HA! GRANDMA! KEEP STILL!
LOOK AT THOSE LIGHTS!

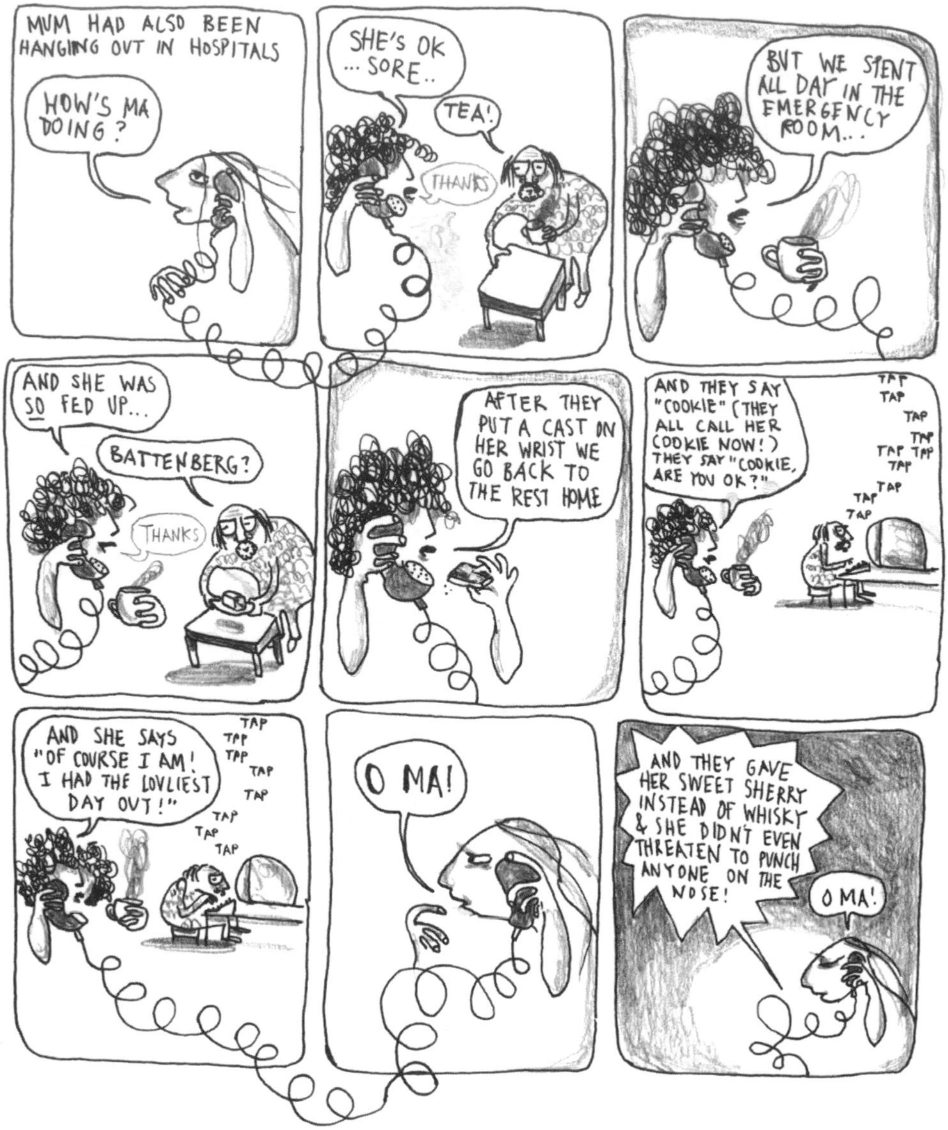
MUM HAD ALSO BEEN HANGING OUT IN HOSPITALS
HOW'S MA DOING?
SHE'S OK ... SORE..
TEA!
THANKS
BUT WE SPENT ALL DAY IN THE EMERGENCY ROOM...
AND SHE WAS SO FED UP...
BATTENBERG?
THANKS
AFTER THEY PUT A CAST ON HER WRIST WE GO BACK TO THE REST HOME
AND THEY SAY "COOKIE" (THEY ALL CALL HER COOKIE NOW!) THEY SAY "COOKIE, ARE YOU OK?"
TAP TAP TAP TAP TAP TAP TAP TAP TAP
AND SHE SAYS "OF COURSE I AM! I HAD THE LOVLIEST DAY OUT!"
TAP TAP TAP TAP TAP TAP TAP TAP
O MA!
AND THEY GAVE HER SWEET SHERRY INSTEAD OF WHISKY & SHE DIDN'T EVEN THREATEN TO PUNCH ANYONE ON THE NOSE!
O MA!

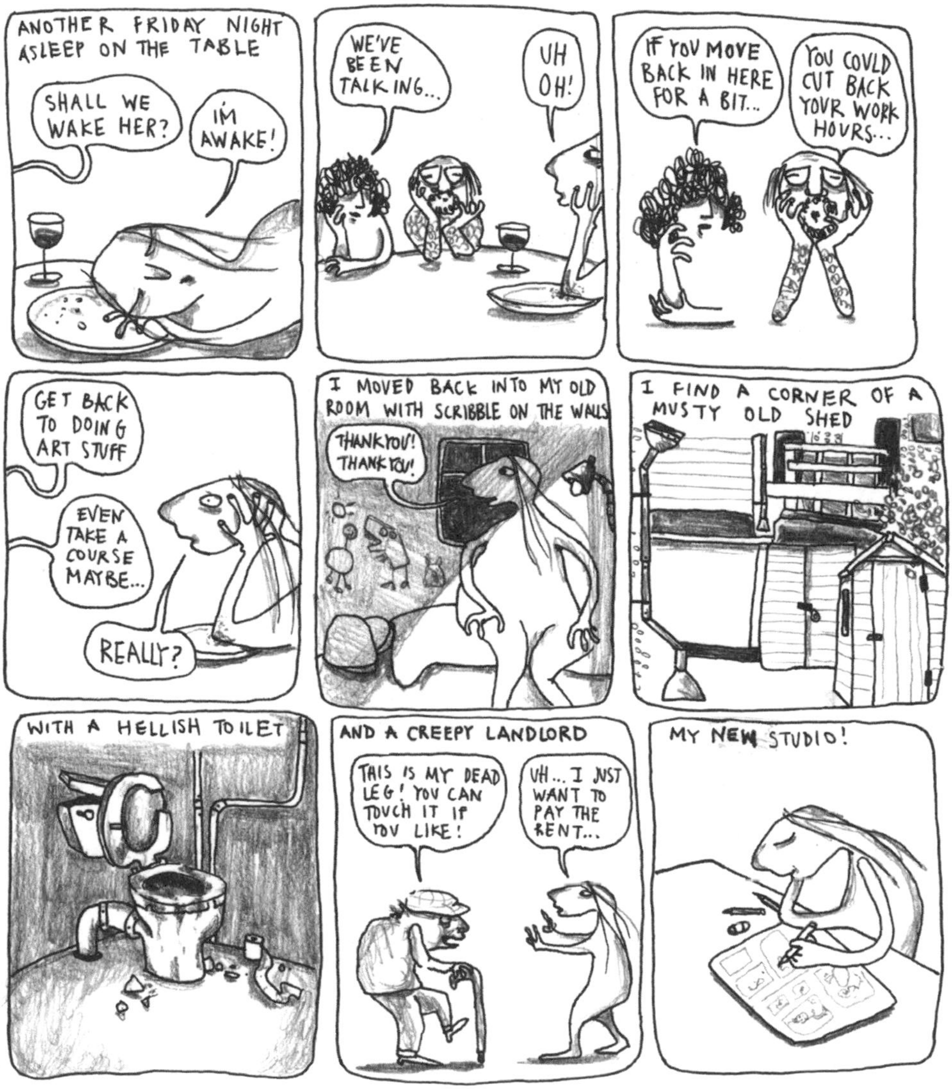
ANOTHER FRIDAY NIGHT ASLEEP ON THE TABLE
SHALL WE WAKE HER?
I'M AWAKE!
WE'VE BEEN TALKING...
UH OH!
IF YOU MOVE BACK IN HERE FOR A BIT...
YOU COULD CUT BACK YOUR WORK HOURS...
GET BACK TO DOING ART STUFF
EVEN TAKE A COURSE MAYBE...
REALLY?
I MOVED BACK INTO MY OLD ROOM WITH SCRIBBLE ON THE WALLS
THANK YOU! THANK YOU!
I FIND A CORNER OF A MUSTY OLD SHED
WITH A HELLISH TOILET
AND A CREEPY LANDLORD
THIS IS MY DEAD LEG! YOU CAN TOUCH IT IF YOU LIKE!
UH... I JUST WANT TO PAY THE RENT...
MY NEW STUDIO!

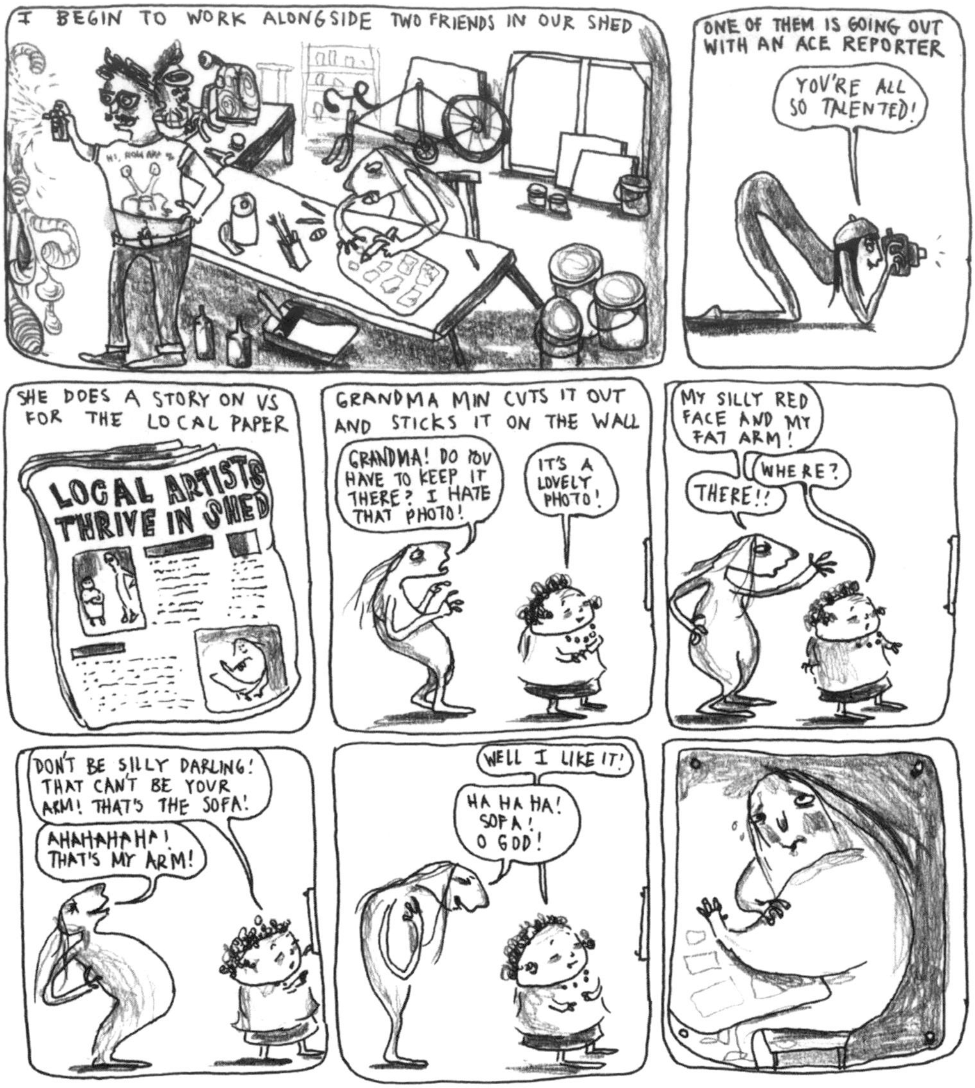
I BEGIN TO WORK ALONGSIDE TWO FRIENDS IN OUR SHED
ONE OF THEM IS GOING OUT WITH AN ACE REPORTER
YOU'RE ALL SO TALENTED!
SHE DOES A STORY ON US FOR THE LOCAL PAPER
LOCAL ARTISTS THRIVE IN SHED
GRANDMA MIN CUTS IT OUT AND STICKS IT ON THE WALL
GRANDMA! DO YOU HAVE TO KEEP IT THERE? I HATE THAT PHOTO!
IT'S A LOVELY PHOTO!
MY SILLY RED FACE AND MY FAT ARM!
WHERE?
THERE!!
DON'T BE SILLY DARLING! THAT CAN'T BE YOUR ARM! THAT'S THE SOFA!
AHAHAHAHA! THAT'S MY ARM!
WELL I LIKE IT!
HA HA HA! SOFA! O GOD!

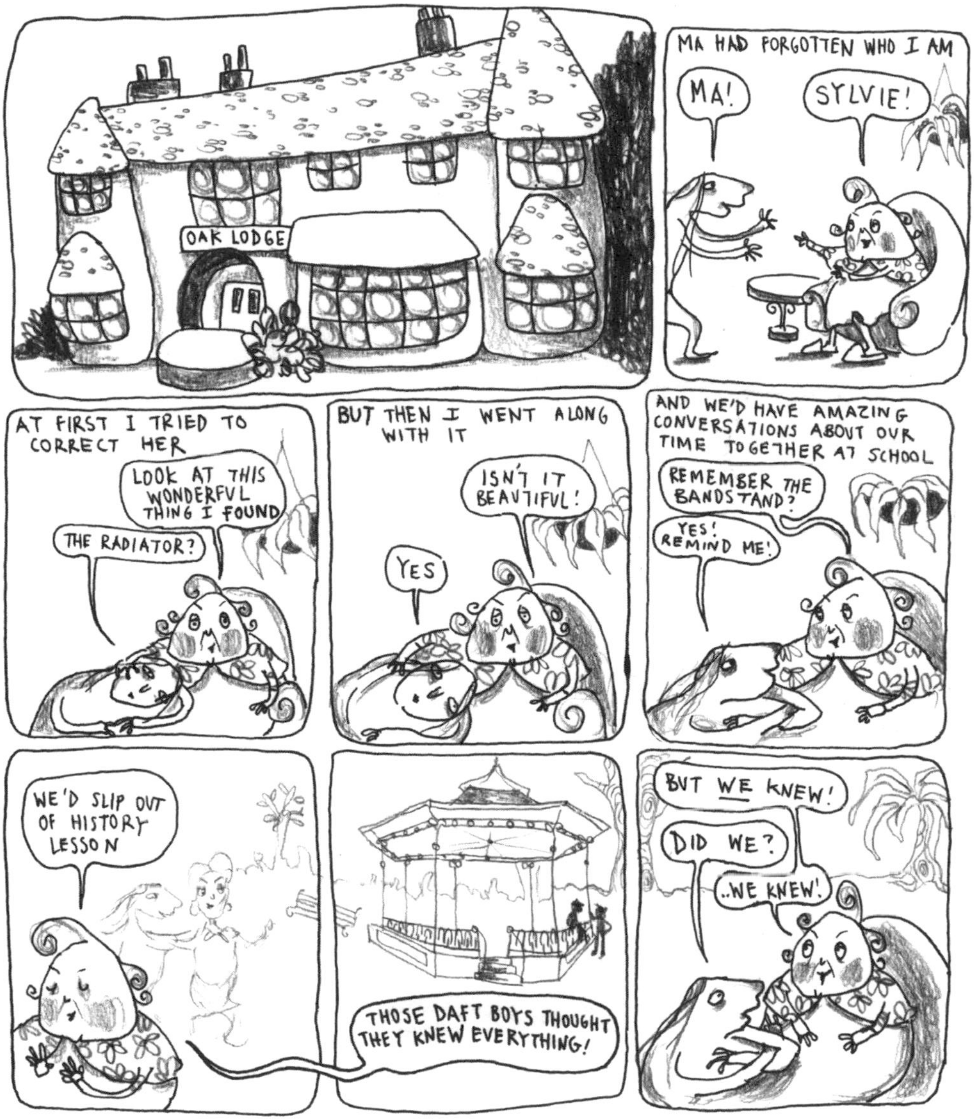
OAK LODGE
MA HAD FORGOTTEN WHO I AM
MA!
SYLVIE!
AT FIRST I TRIED TO CORRECT HER
LOOK AT THIS WONDERFUL THING I FOUND
THE RADIATOR?
BUT THEN I WENT ALONG WITH IT
ISN'T IT BEAUTIFUL!
YES
AND WE'D HAVE AMAZING CONVERSATIONS ABOUT OUR TIME TOGETHER AT SCHOOL
REMEMBER THE BANDSTAND?
YES! REMIND ME!
WE'D SLIP OUT OF HISTORY LESSON
THOSE DAFT BOYS THOUGHT THEY KNEW EVERYTHING!
BUT WE KNEW!
DID WE?
..WE KNEW!

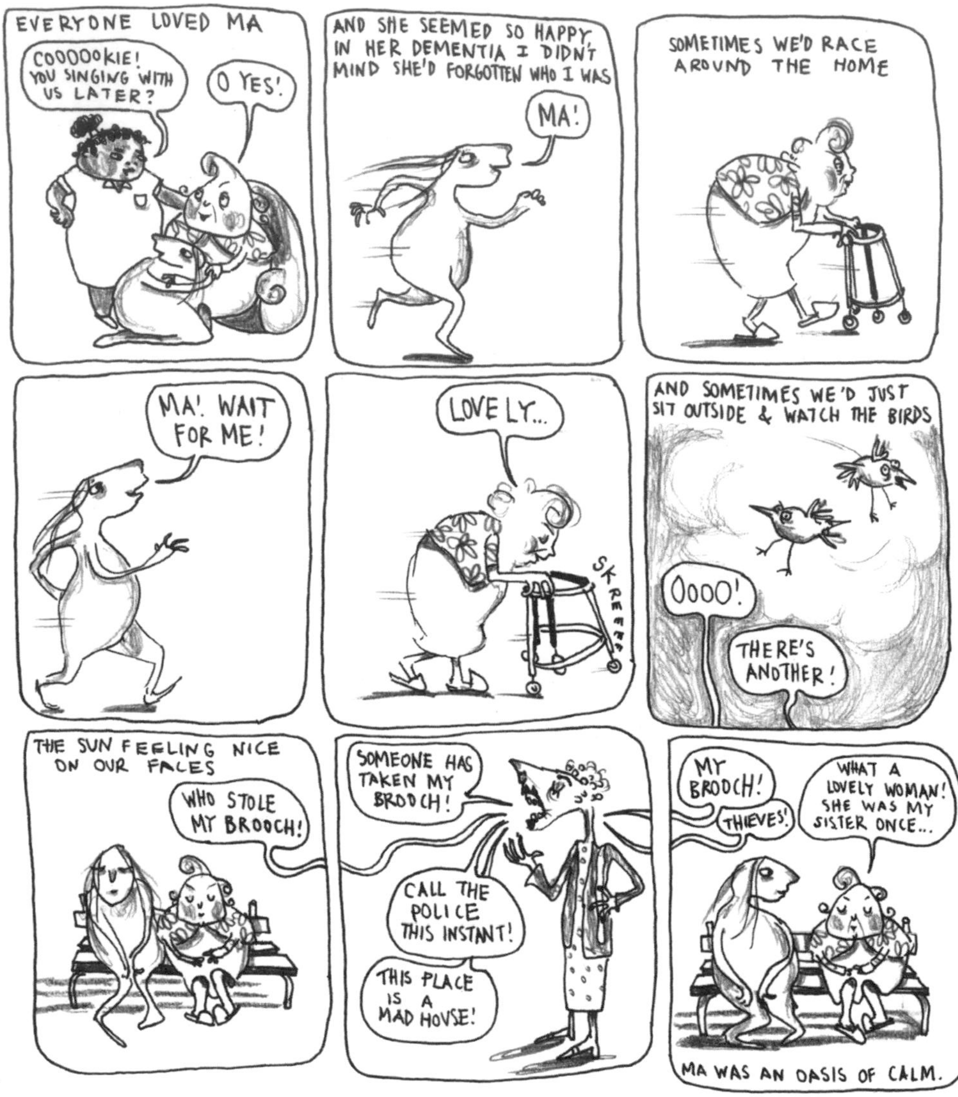

EVERYONE LOVED MA
COOOOOKIE! YOU SINGING WITH US LATER?
O YES!
AND SHE SEEMED SO HAPPY, IN HER DEMENTIA I DIDN'T MIND SHE'D FORGOTTEN WHO I WAS
MA!
SOMETIMES WE'D RACE AROUND THE HOME
MA! WAIT FOR ME!
LOVELY...
SKREEEE
AND SOMETIMES WE'D JUST SIT OUTSIDE & WATCH THE BIRDS
OOOO!
THERE'S ANOTHER!
THE SUN FEELING NICE ON OUR FACES
WHO STOLE MY BROOCH!
SOMEONE HAS TAKEN MY BROOCH!
CALL THE POLICE THIS INSTANT!
THIS PLACE IS A MAD HOUSE!
MY BROOCH!
THIEVES!
WHAT A LOVELY WOMAN! SHE WAS MY SISTER ONCE...
MA WAS AN OASIS OF CALM.

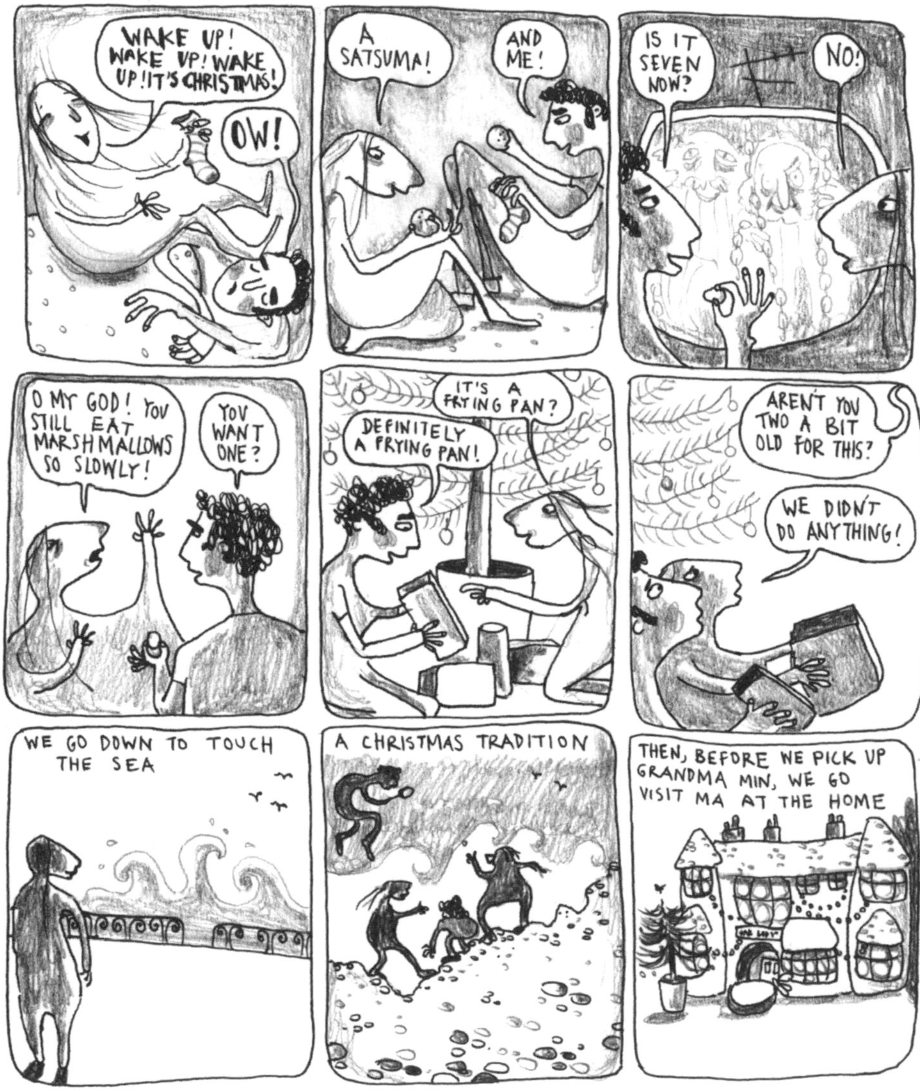
WAKE UP! WAKE UP! WAKE UP! IT'S CHRISTMAS!
OW!
A SATSUMA!
AND ME!
IS IT SEVEN NOW?
NO!
O MY GOD! YOU STILL EAT MARSHMALLOWS SO SLOWLY!
YOU WANT ONE?
IT'S A FRYING PAN?
DEFINITELY A FRYING PAN!
AREN'T YOU TWO A BIT OLD FOR THIS?
WE DIDN'T DO ANYTHING!
WE GO DOWN TO TOUCH THE SEA
A CHRISTMAS TRADITION
THEN, BEFORE WE PICK UP GRANDMA MIN, WE GO VISIT MA AT THE HOME

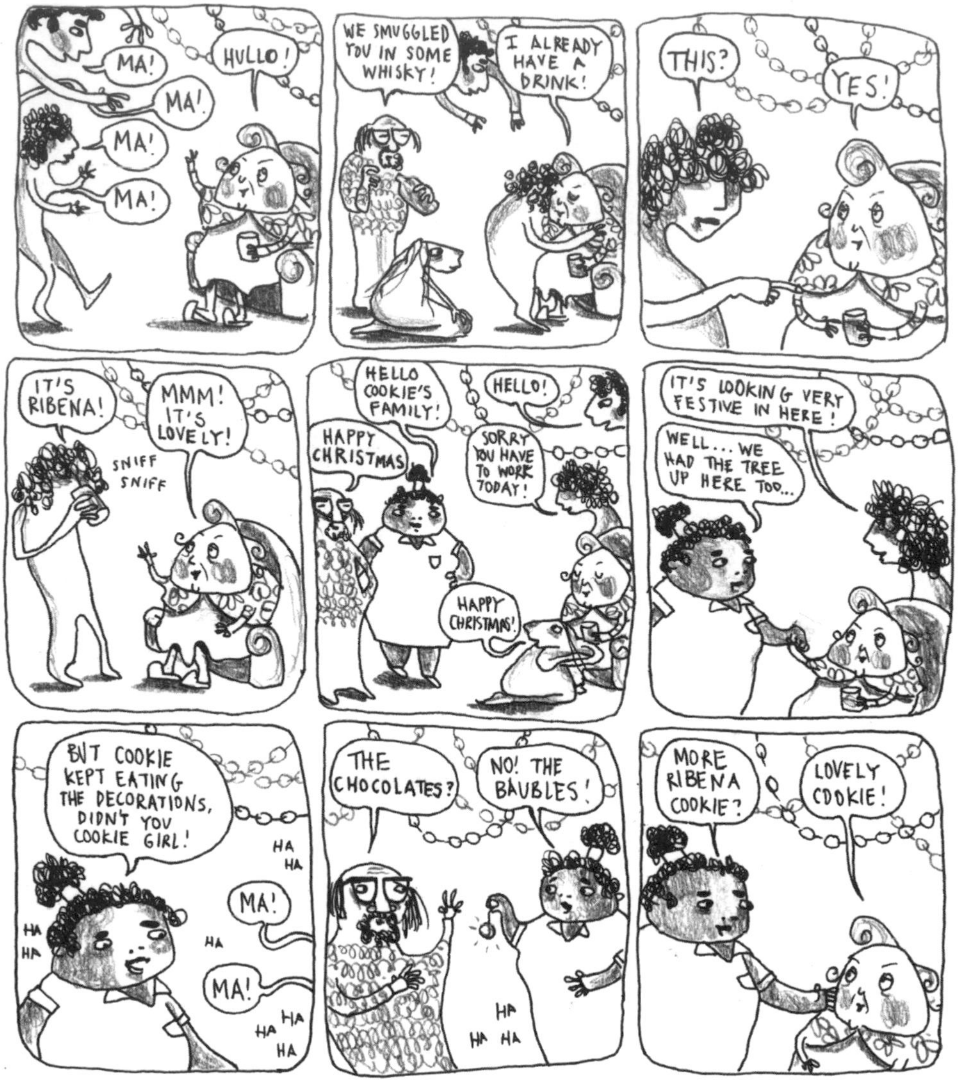
MA!
MA!
MA!
MA!
HULLO!
WE SMUGGLED YOU IN SOME WHISKY!
I ALREADY HAVE A DRINK!
THIS?
YES!
IT'S RIBENA!
SNIFF SNIFF
MMM! IT'S LOVELY!
HELLO COOKIE'S FAMILY!
HELLO!
HAPPY CHRISTMAS
SORRY YOU HAVE TO WORK TODAY!
HAPPY CHRISTMAS!
IT'S LOOKING VERY FESTIVE IN HERE!
WELL... WE HAD THE TREE UP HERE TOO...
BUT COOKIE KEPT EATING THE DECORATIONS, DIDN'T YOU COOKIE GIRL!
HA HA
HA HA
HA
MA!
MA!
HA HA HA
THE CHOCOLATES?
NO! THE BAUBLES!
HA HA HA
MORE RIBENA COOKIE?
LOVELY COOKIE!

CHAPTER 14
HEARTS & THE THINGS THEY DO

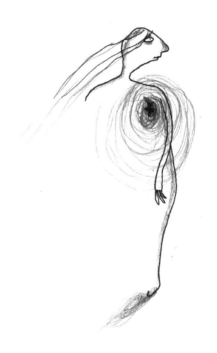

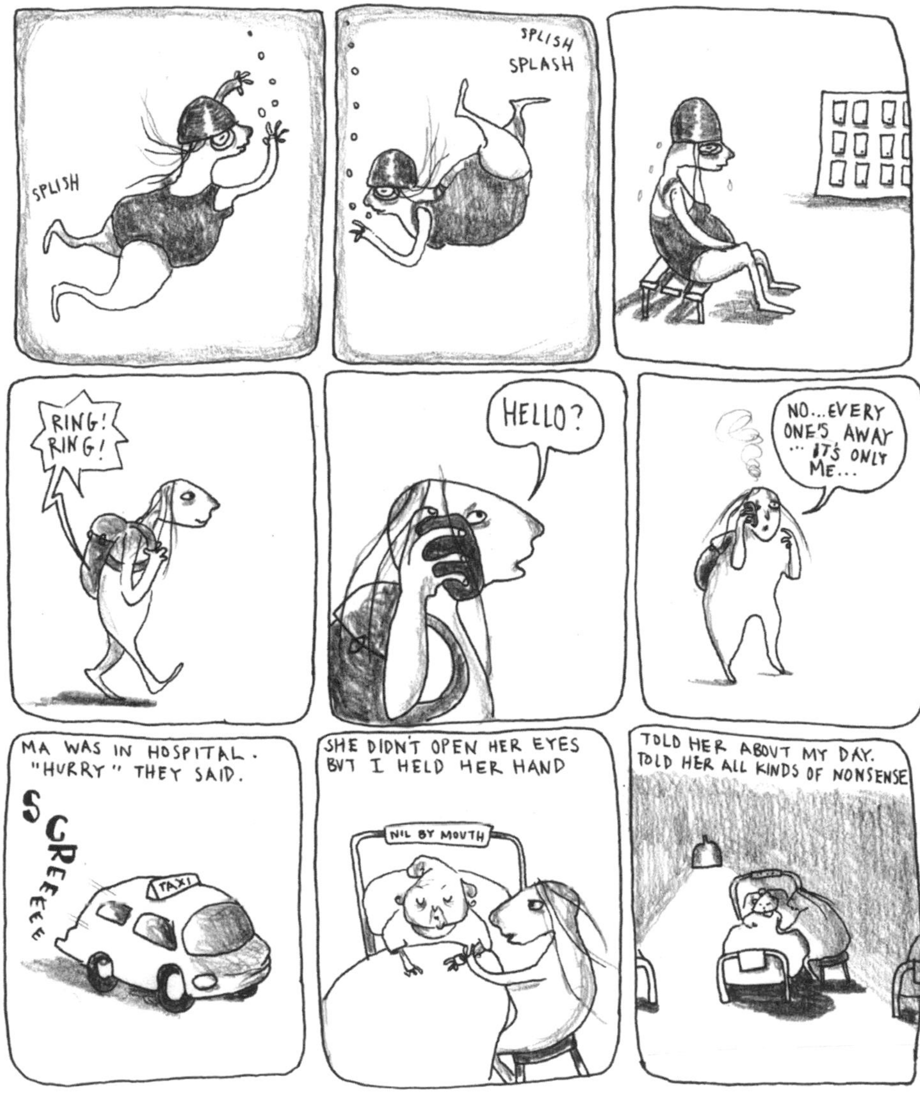
SPLISH
SPLISH
SPLASH
RING! RING!
HELLO?
NO...EVERY ONE'S AWAY ... IT'S ONLY ME...
MA WAS IN HOSPITAL. "HURRY" THEY SAID.
SCREEEEEE
TAXI
SHE DIDN'T OPEN HER EYES BUT I HELD HER HAND
NIL BY MOUTH
TOLD HER ABOUT MY DAY. TOLD HER ALL KINDS OF NONSENSE

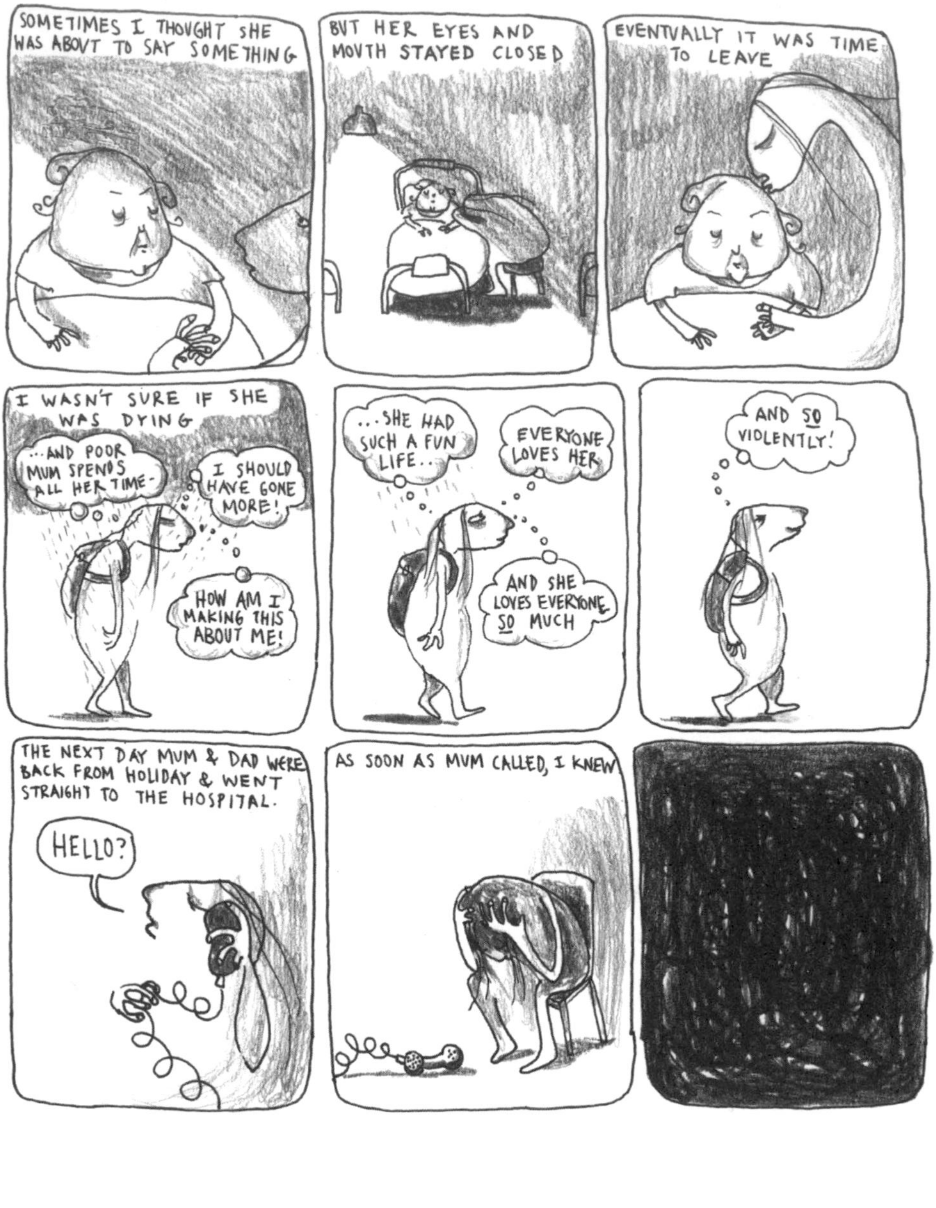

SOMETIMES I THOUGHT SHE WAS ABOUT TO SAY SOMETHING
BUT HER EYES AND MOUTH STAYED CLOSED
EVENTUALLY IT WAS TIME TO LEAVE
I WASN'T SURE IF SHE WAS DYING
...AND POOR MUM SPENDS ALL HER TIME-
I SHOULD HAVE GONE MORE!
HOW AM I MAKING THIS ABOUT ME!
...SHE HAD SUCH A FUN LIFE...
EVERYONE LOVES HER
AND SHE LOVES EVERYONE SO MUCH
AND SO VIOLENTLY!
THE NEXT DAY MUM & DAD WERE BACK FROM HOLIDAY & WENT STRAIGHT TO THE HOSPITAL.
HELLO?
AS SOON AS MUM CALLED, I KNEW

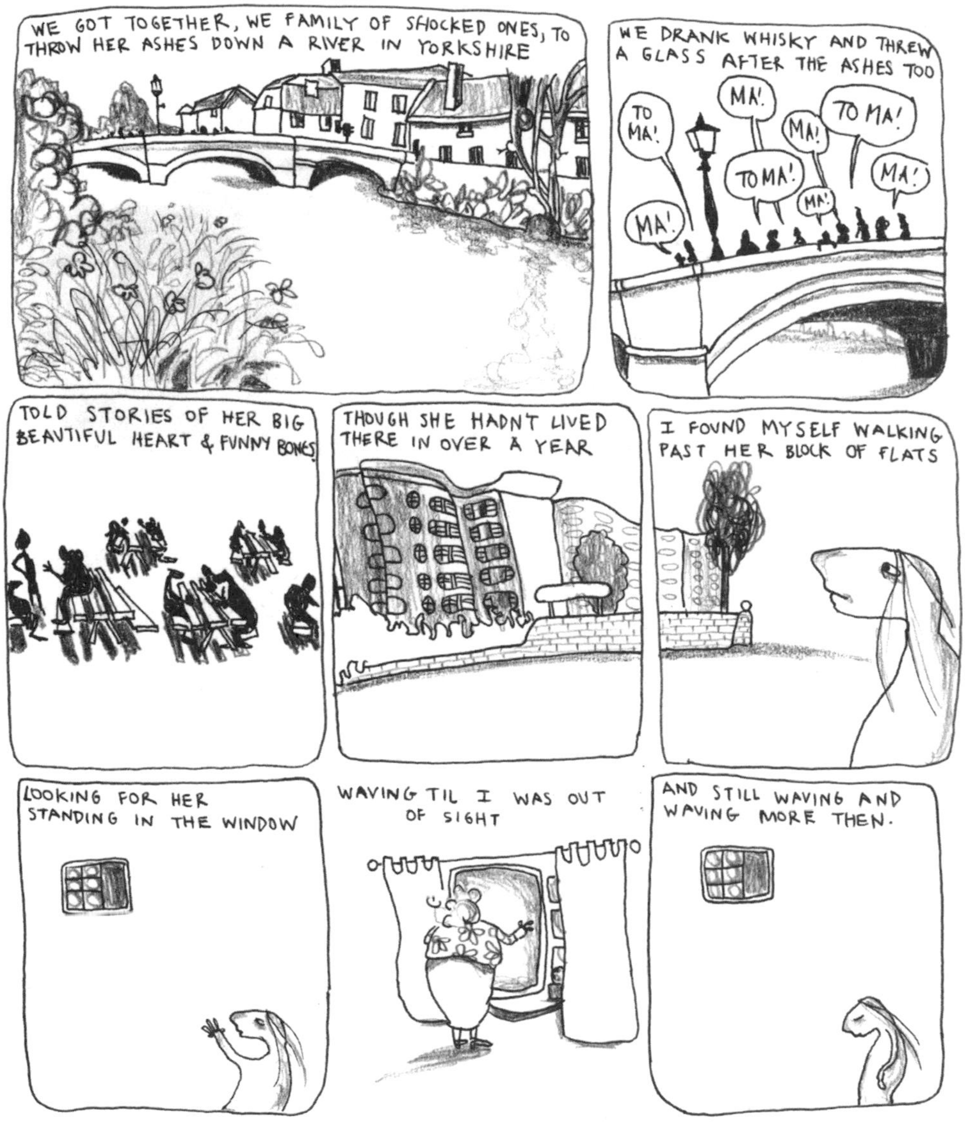
WE GOT TOGETHER, WE FAMILY OF SHOCKED ONES, TO THROW HER ASHES DOWN A RIVER IN YORKSHIRE
WE DRANK WHISKY AND THREW A GLASS AFTER THE ASHES TOO
TO MA!
MA!
MA!
TO MA!
TO MA!
MA!
MA!
MA!
TOLD STORIES OF HER BIG BEAUTIFUL HEART & FUNNY BONES
THOUGH SHE HADN'T LIVED THERE IN OVER A YEAR
I FOUND MYSELF WALKING PAST HER BLOCK OF FLATS
LOOKING FOR HER STANDING IN THE WINDOW
WAVING TIL I WAS OUT OF SIGHT
AND STILL WAVING AND WAVING MORE THEN.

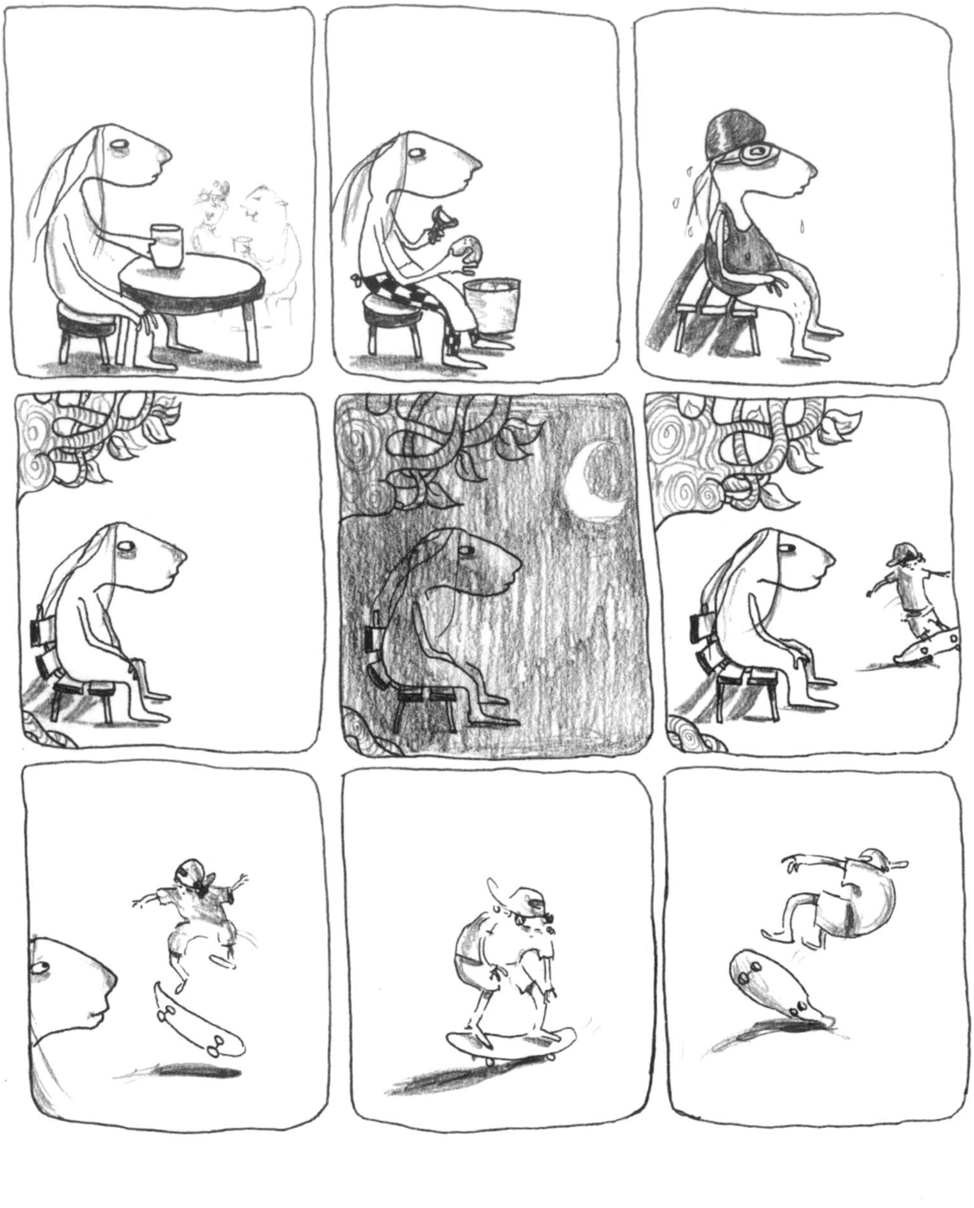

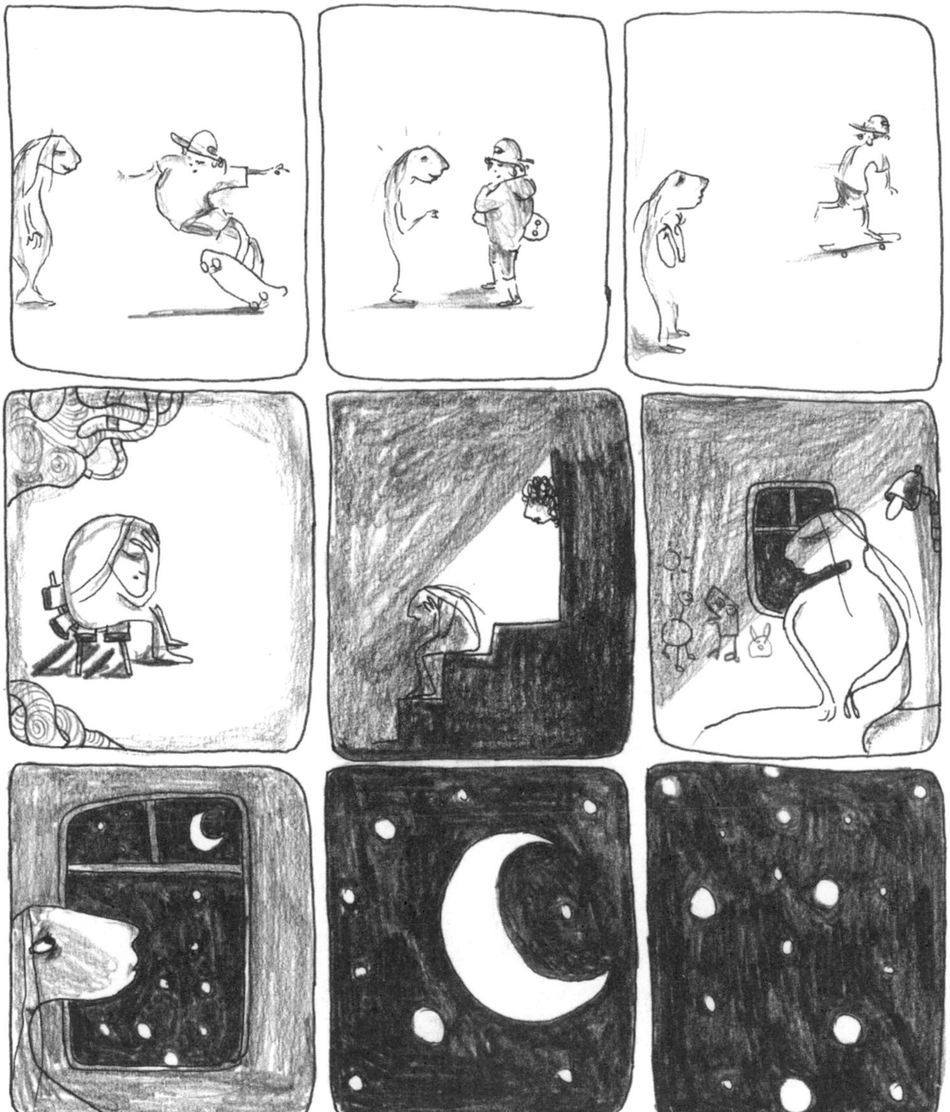

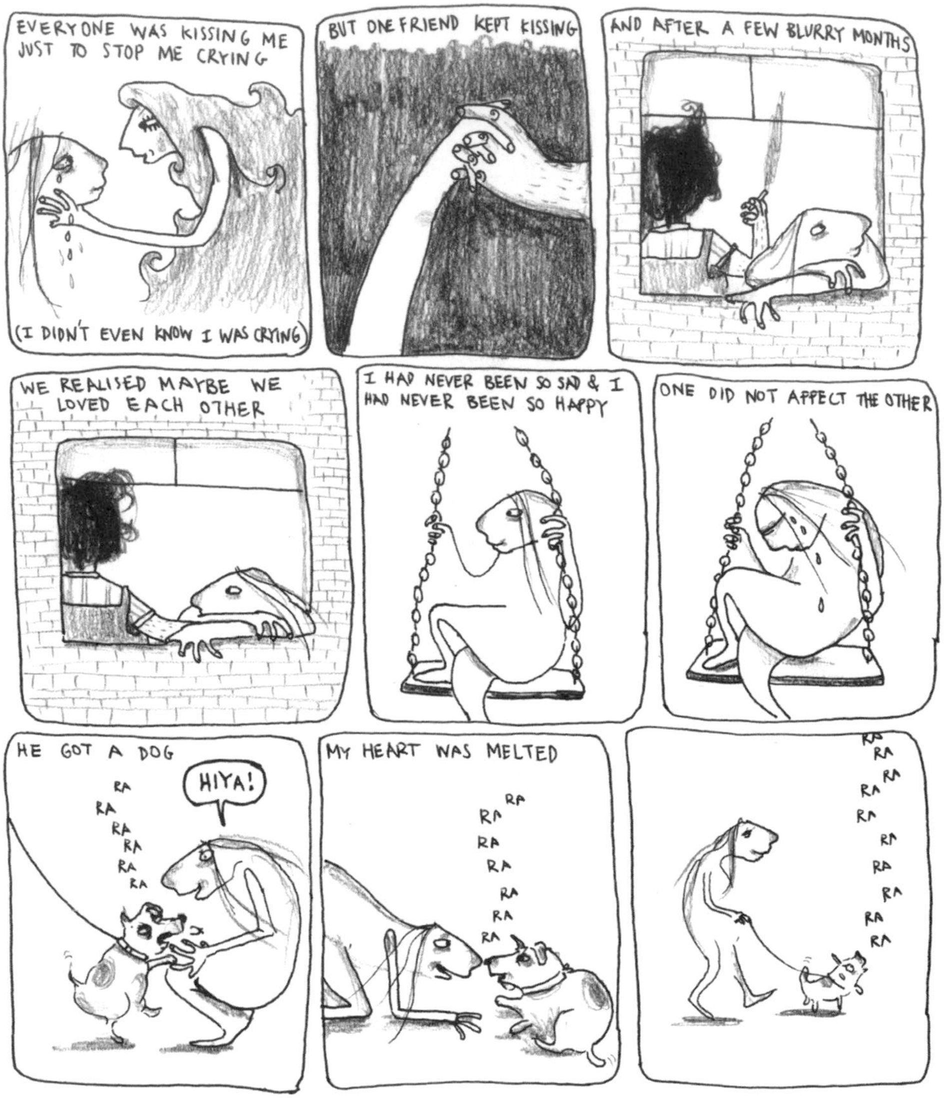
EVERYONE WAS KISSING ME JUST TO STOP ME CRYING
(I DIDN'T EVEN KNOW I WAS CRYING)
BUT ONE FRIEND KEPT KISSING
AND AFTER A FEW BLURRY MONTHS
WE REALISED MAYBE WE LOVED EACH OTHER
I HAD NEVER BEEN SO SAD & I HAD NEVER BEEN SO HAPPY
ONE DID NOT AFFECT THE OTHER
HE GOT A DOG
HIYA!
RA RA RA RA RA RA
MY HEART WAS MELTED
RA RA RA RA RA RA RA
RA RA RA RA RA RA RA RA RA RA RA

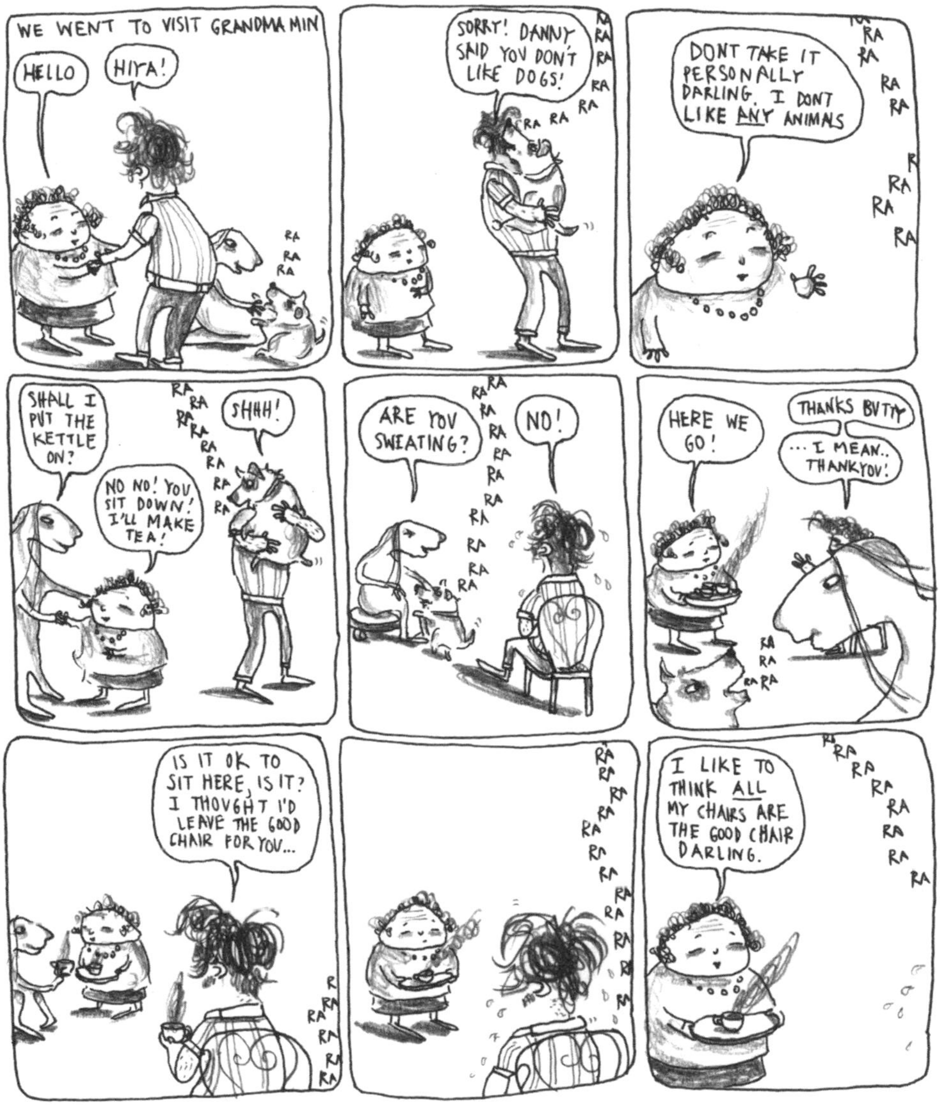

WE WENT TO VISIT GRANDMA MIN
HELLO
HIYA!
RA RA RA
SORRY! DANNY SAID YOU DON'T LIKE DOGS!
RA RA RA RA RA RA RA RA
RA RA
DONT TAKE IT PERSONALLY DARLING. I DONT LIKE ANY ANIMALS
RA RA RA RA RA RA RA
SHALL I PUT THE KETTLE ON?
NO NO! YOU SIT DOWN! I'LL MAKE TEA!
RA RA RA RA RA RA RA RA RA
SHHH!
ARE YOU SWEATING?
RA RA RA RA RA RA RA RA RA RA RA
NO!
HERE WE GO!
THANKS BUTTY
... I MEAN.. THANKYOU!
RA RA RA RA
IS IT OK TO SIT HERE, IS IT? I THOUGHT I'D LEAVE THE GOOD CHAIR FOR YOU...
RA RA RA RA
I LIKE TO THINK ALL MY CHAIRS ARE THE GOOD CHAIR DARLING.
RA RA RA RA RA RA RA RA

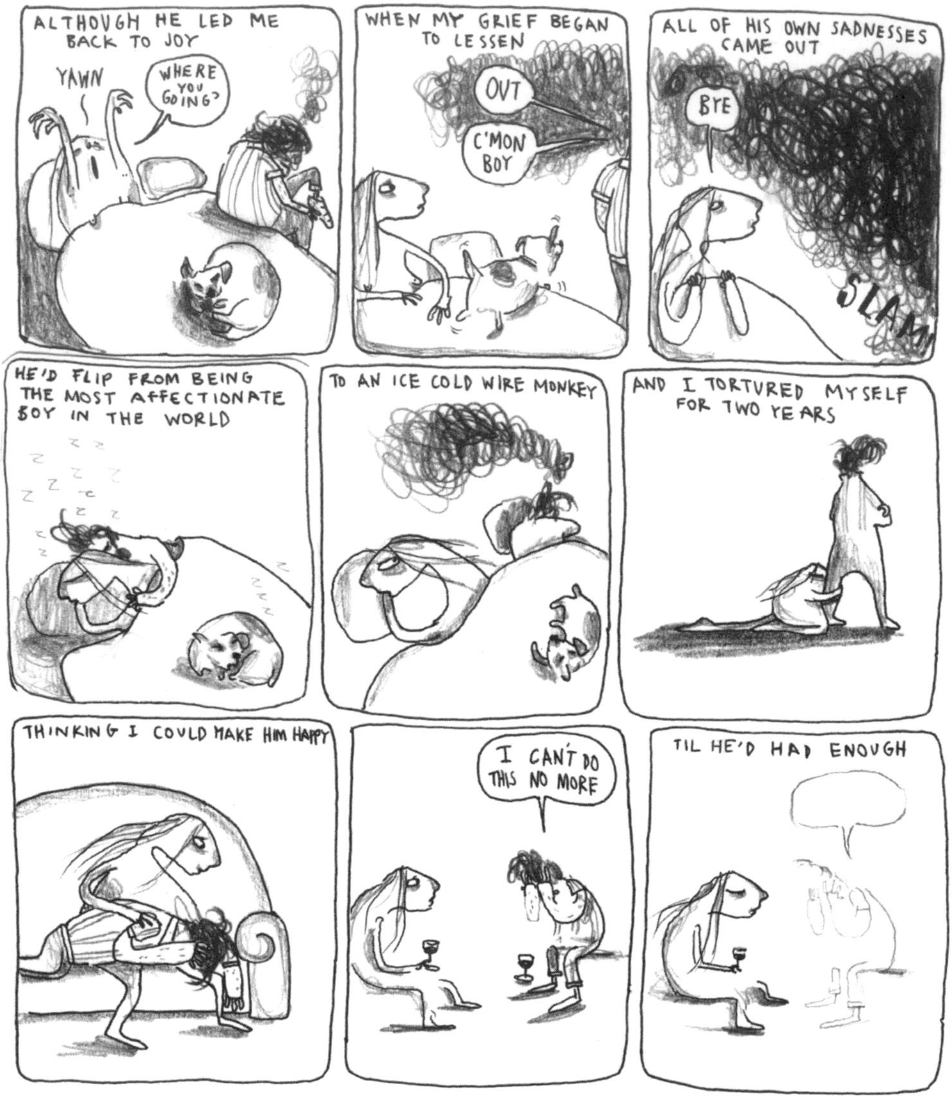
ALTHOUGH HE LED ME BACK TO JOY
YAWN
WHERE YOU GOING?
WHEN MY GRIEF BEGAN TO LESSEN
OUT
C'MON BOY
ALL OF HIS OWN SADNESSES CAME OUT
BYE
SLAM!
HE'D FLIP FROM BEING THE MOST AFFECTIONATE BOY IN THE WORLD
TO AN ICE COLD WIRE MONKEY
AND I TORTURED MYSELF FOR TWO YEARS
THINKING I COULD MAKE HIM HAPPY
I CAN'T DO THIS NO MORE
TIL HE'D HAD ENOUGH

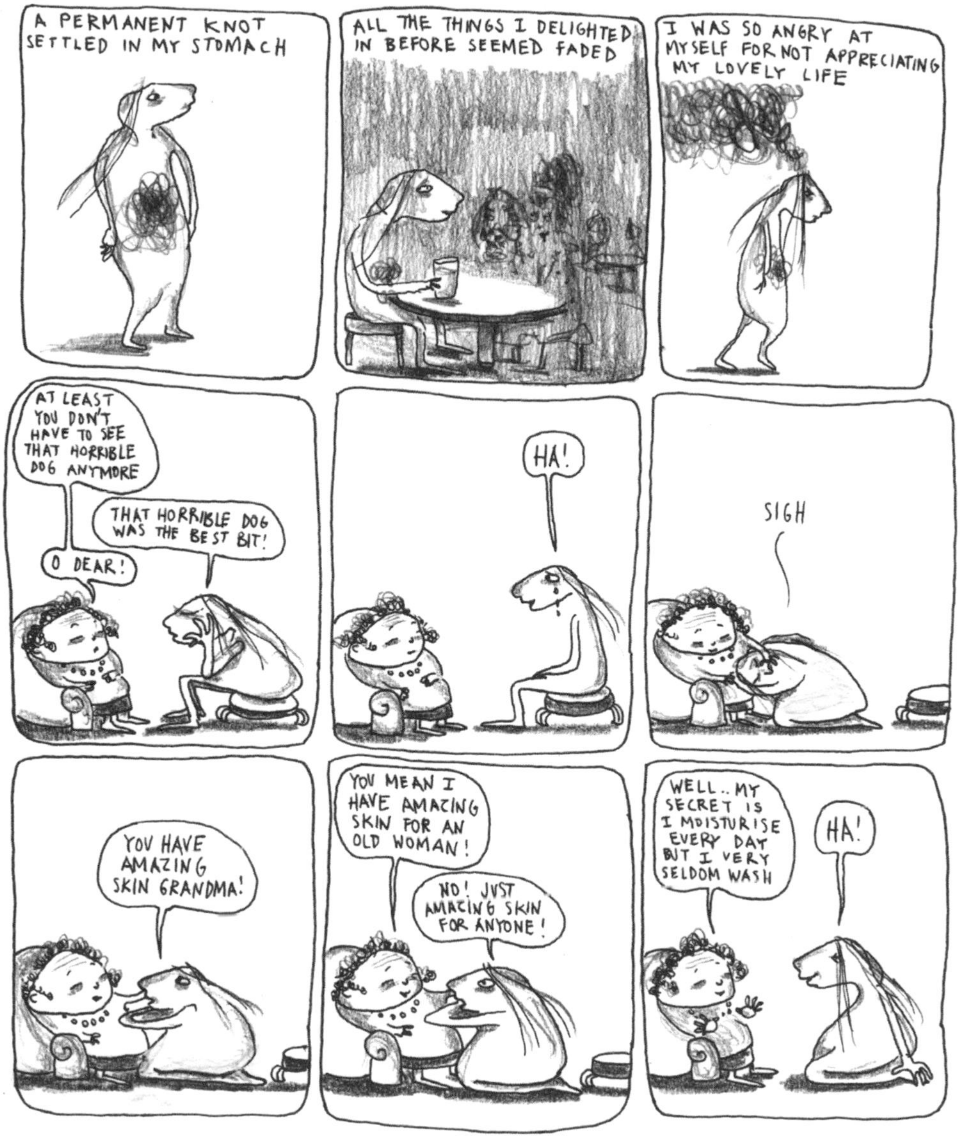
A PERMANENT KNOT SETTLED IN MY STOMACH
ALL THE THINGS I DELIGHTED IN BEFORE SEEMED FADED
I WAS SO ANGRY AT MYSELF FOR NOT APPRECIATING MY LOVELY LIFE
AT LEAST YOU DON'T HAVE TO SEE THAT HORRIBLE DOG ANYMORE
THAT HORRIBLE DOG WAS THE BEST BIT!
O DEAR!
HA!
SIGH
YOU HAVE AMAZING SKIN GRANDMA!
YOU MEAN I HAVE AMAZING SKIN FOR AN OLD WOMAN!
NO! JUST AMAZING SKIN FOR ANYONE!
WELL.. MY SECRET IS I MOISTURISE EVERY DAY BUT I VERY SELDOM WASH
HA!

CHAPTER 15

"LIGHTS OUT"

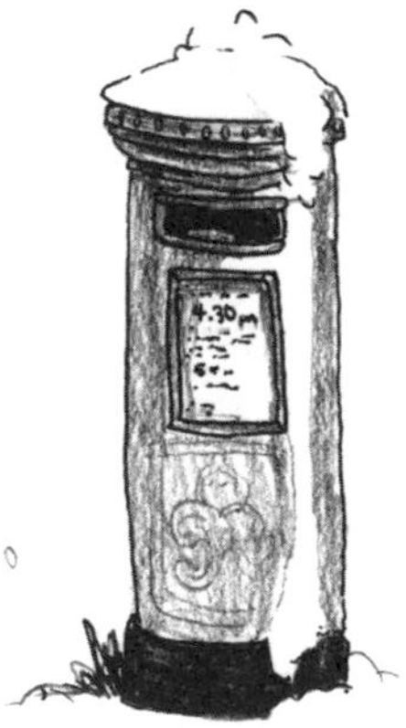

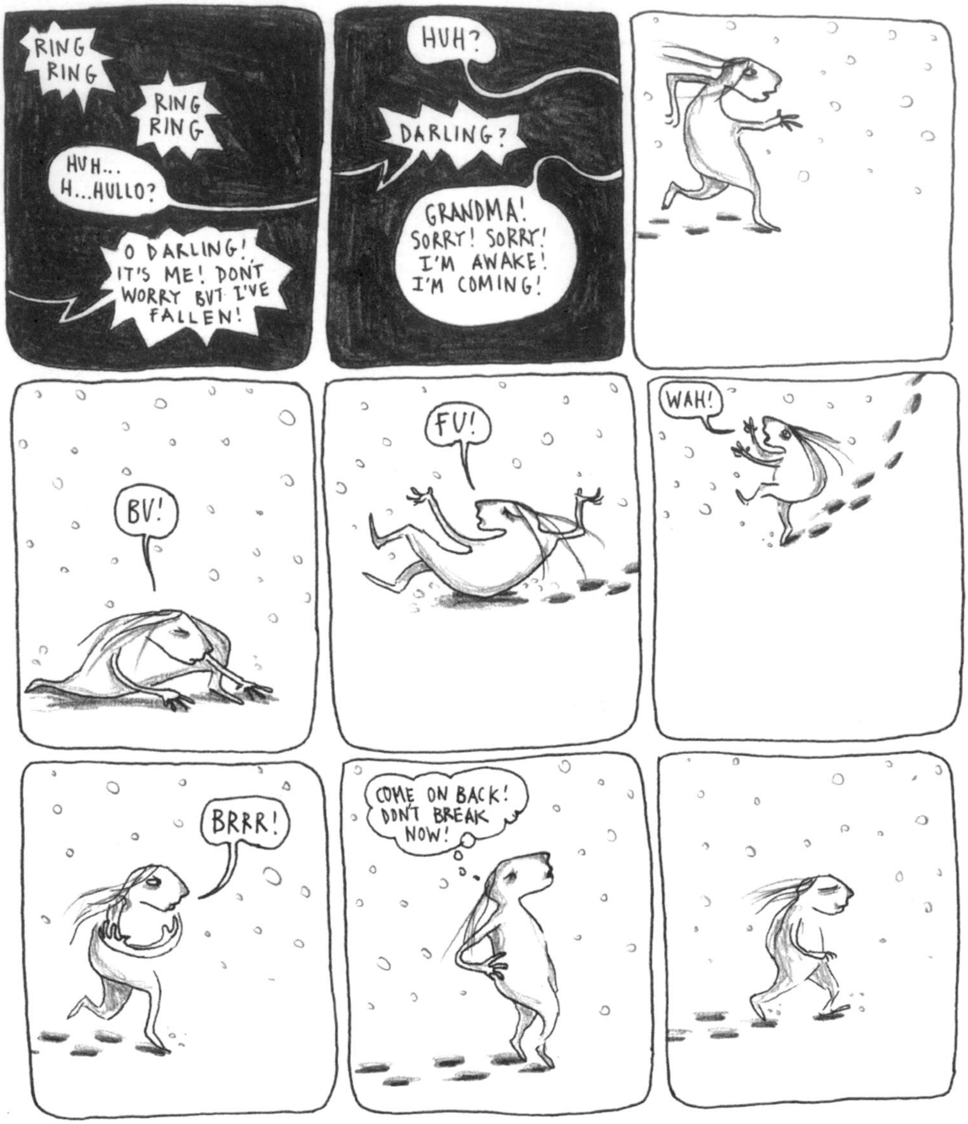
RING RING
RING RING
HUH... H...HULLO?
O DARLING! IT'S ME! DON'T WORRY BUT I'VE FALLEN!
HUH?
DARLING?
GRANDMA! SORRY! SORRY! I'M AWAKE! I'M COMING!
BV!
FU!
WAH!
BRRR!
COME ON BACK! DON'T BREAK NOW!

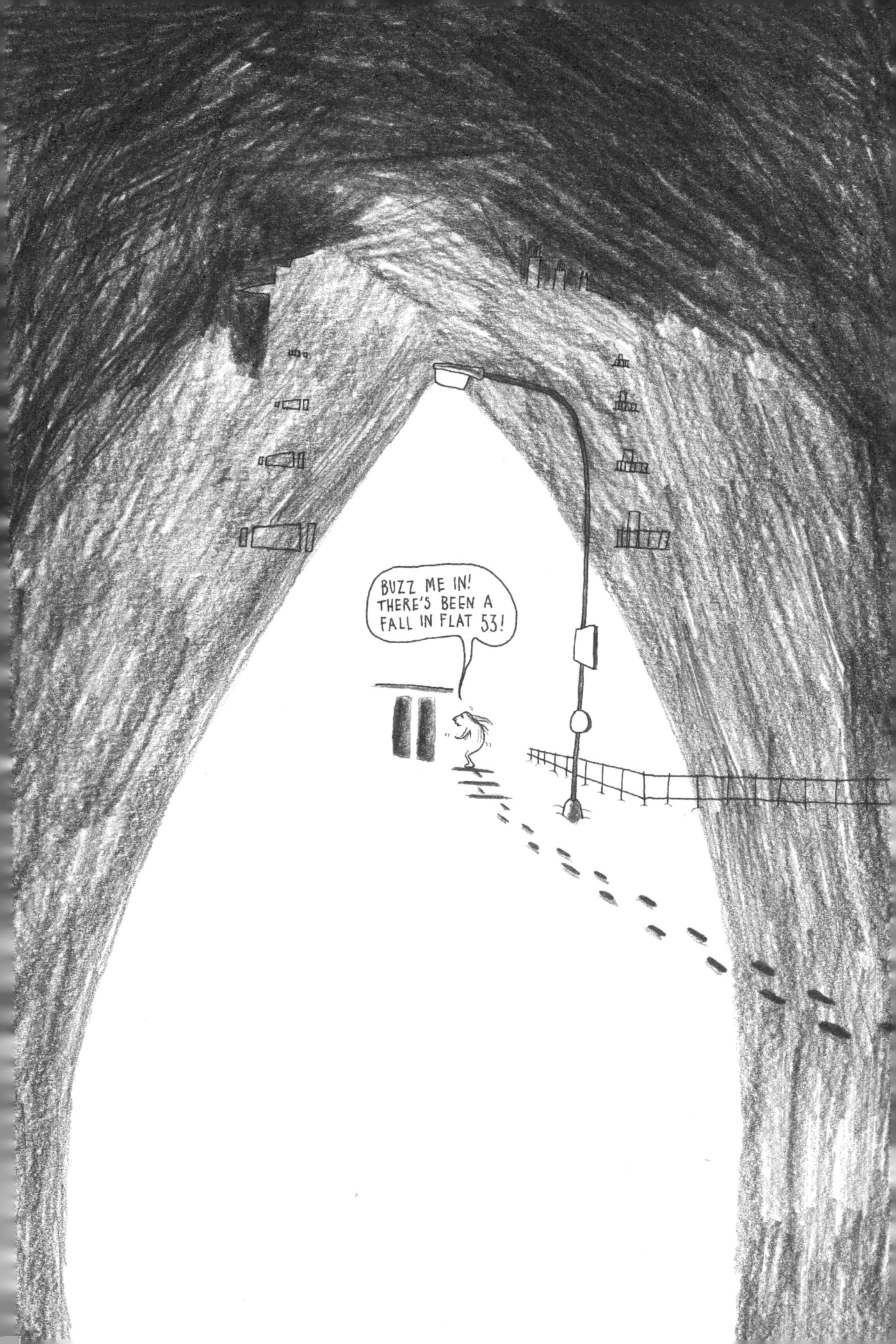
BUZZ ME IN!
THERE'S BEEN A
FALL IN FLAT 53!

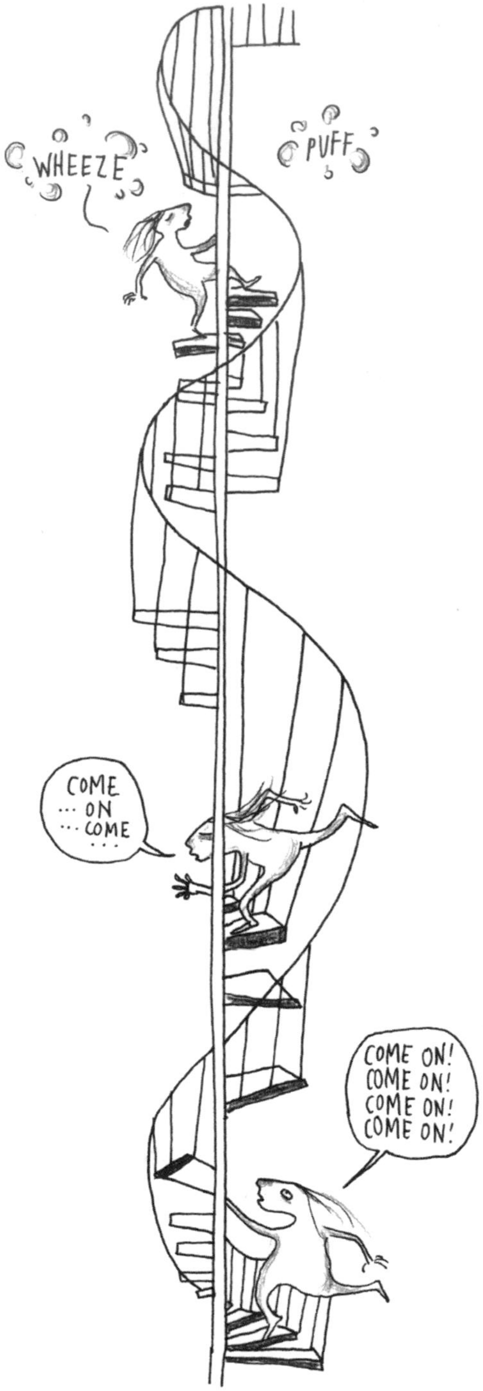
WHEEZE
PUFF
COME ... ON ... COME ...
COME ON! COME ON! COME ON! COME ON!

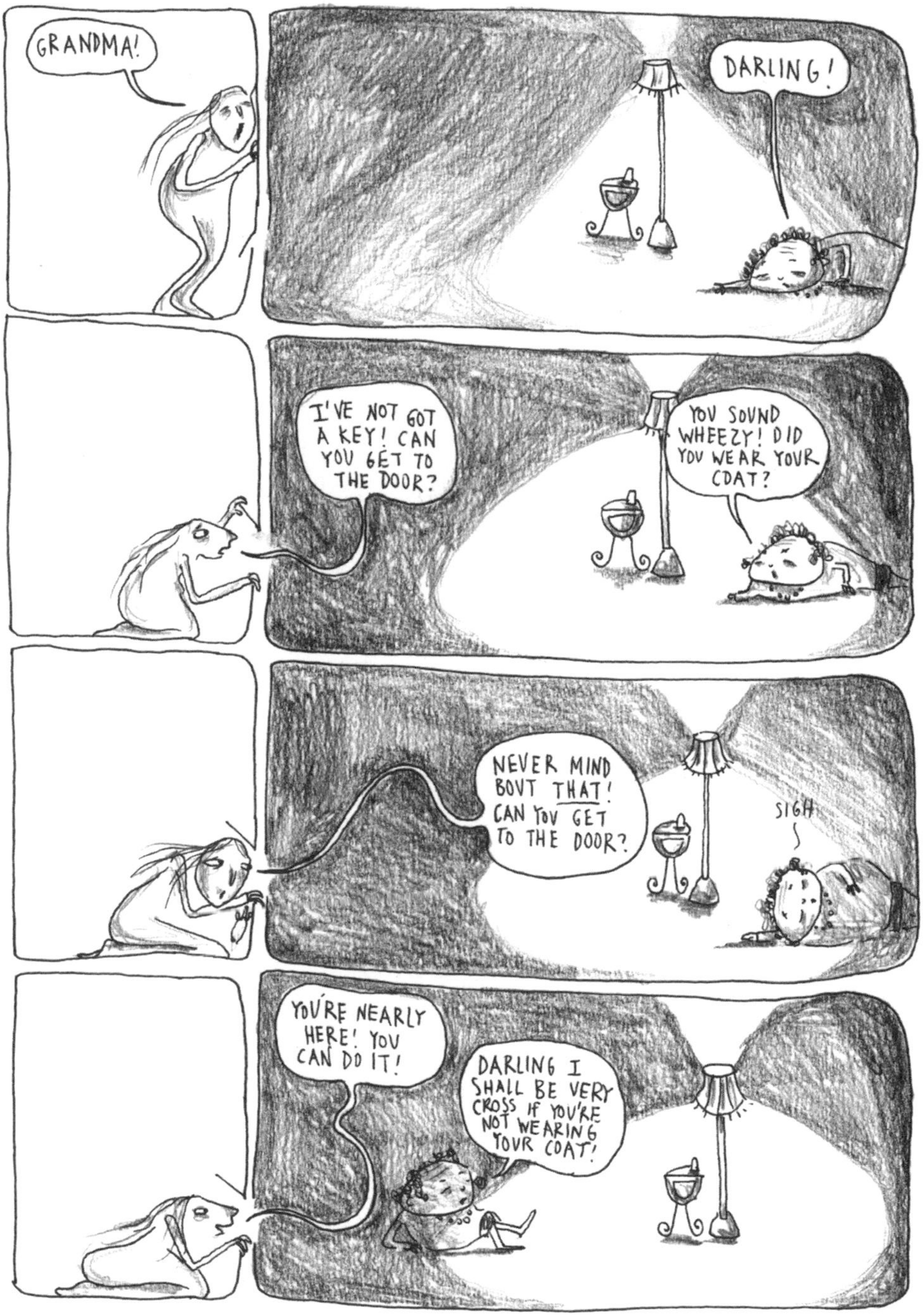
GRANDMA!
DARLING!
I'VE NOT GOT A KEY! CAN YOU GET TO THE DOOR?
YOU SOUND WHEEZY! DID YOU WEAR YOUR COAT?
NEVER MIND BOUT THAT! CAN YOU GET TO THE DOOR?
SIGH
YOU'RE NEARLY HERE! YOU CAN DO IT!
DARLING I SHALL BE VERY CROSS IF YOU'RE NOT WEARING YOUR COAT!

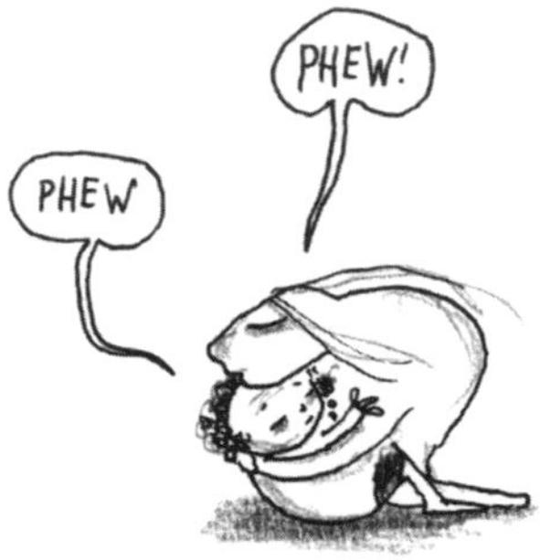
PHEW
PHEW!

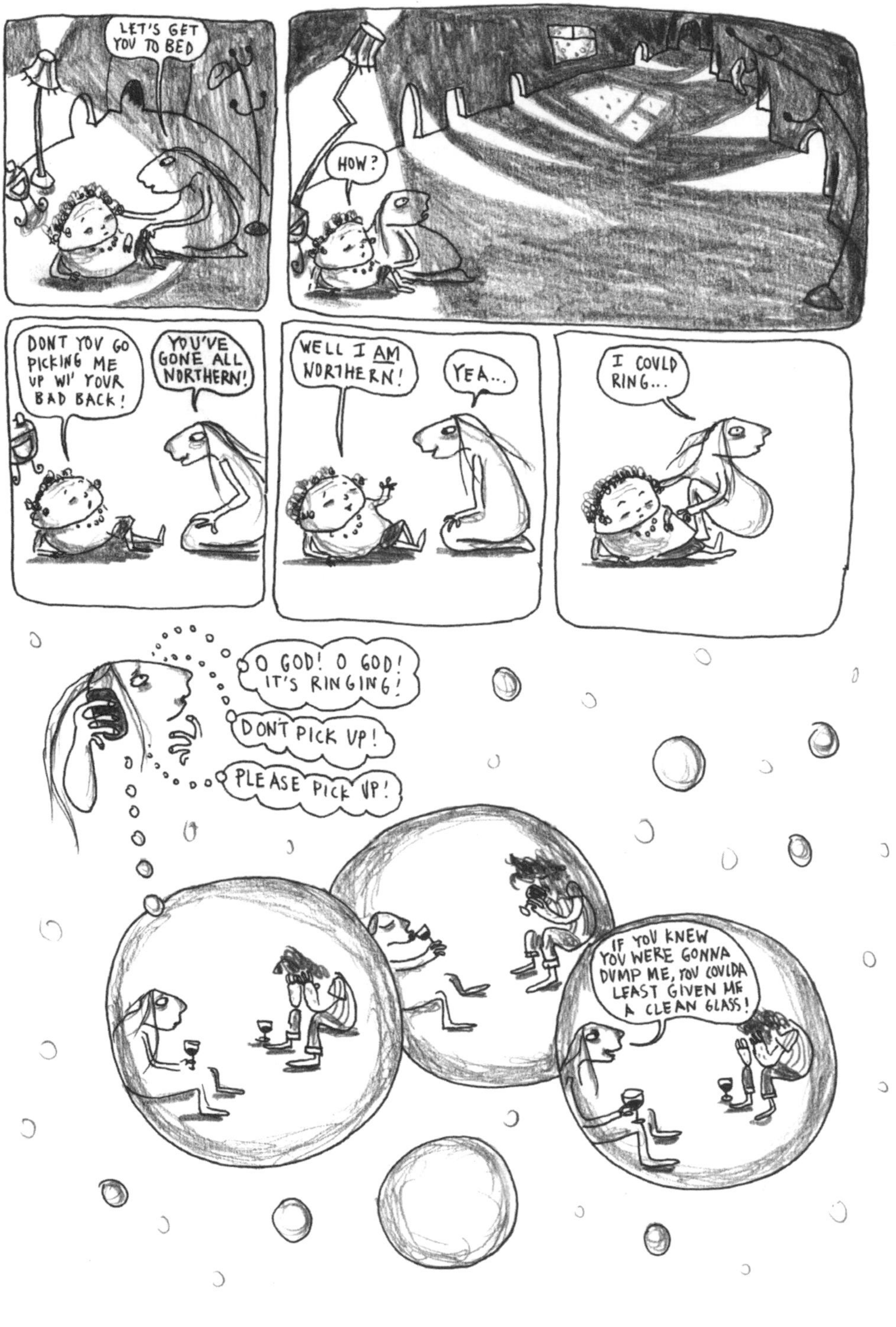
LET'S GET YOU TO BED
HOW?
DONT YOU GO PICKING ME UP WI' YOUR BAD BACK!
YOU'VE GONE ALL NORTHERN!
WELL I AM NORTHERN!
YEA...
I COULD RING...
O GOD! O GOD! IT'S RINGING!
DON'T PICK UP!
PLEASE PICK UP!
IF YOU KNEW YOU WERE GONNA DUMP ME, YOU COULDA LEAST GIVEN ME A CLEAN GLASS!

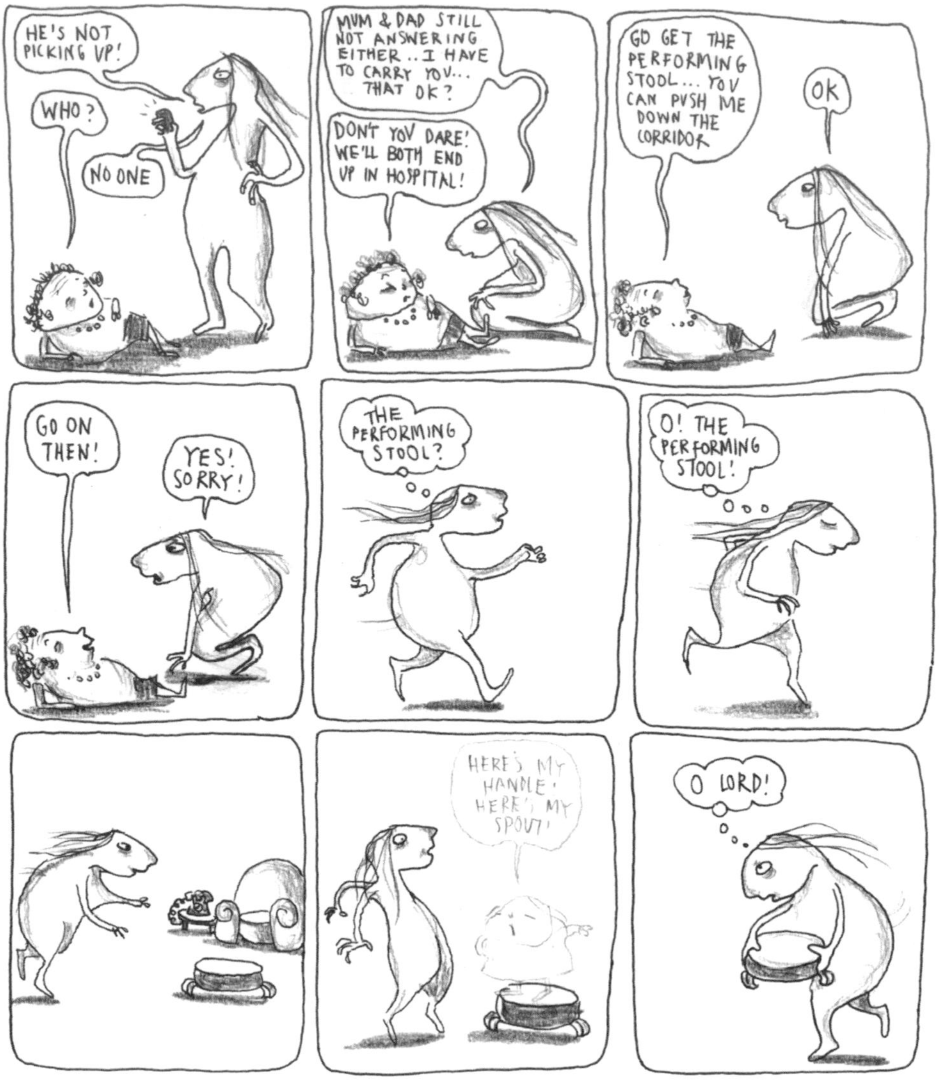

HE'S NOT PICKING UP!
WHO?
NO ONE
MUM & DAD STILL NOT ANSWERING EITHER.. I HAVE TO CARRY YOU... THAT OK?
DON'T YOU DARE! WE'LL BOTH END UP IN HOSPITAL!
GO GET THE PERFORMING STOOL... YOU CAN PUSH ME DOWN THE CORRIDOR
OK
GO ON THEN!
YES! SORRY!
THE PERFORMING STOOL?
O! THE PERFORMING STOOL!
HERE'S MY HANDLE! HERE'S MY SPOUT!
O LORD!

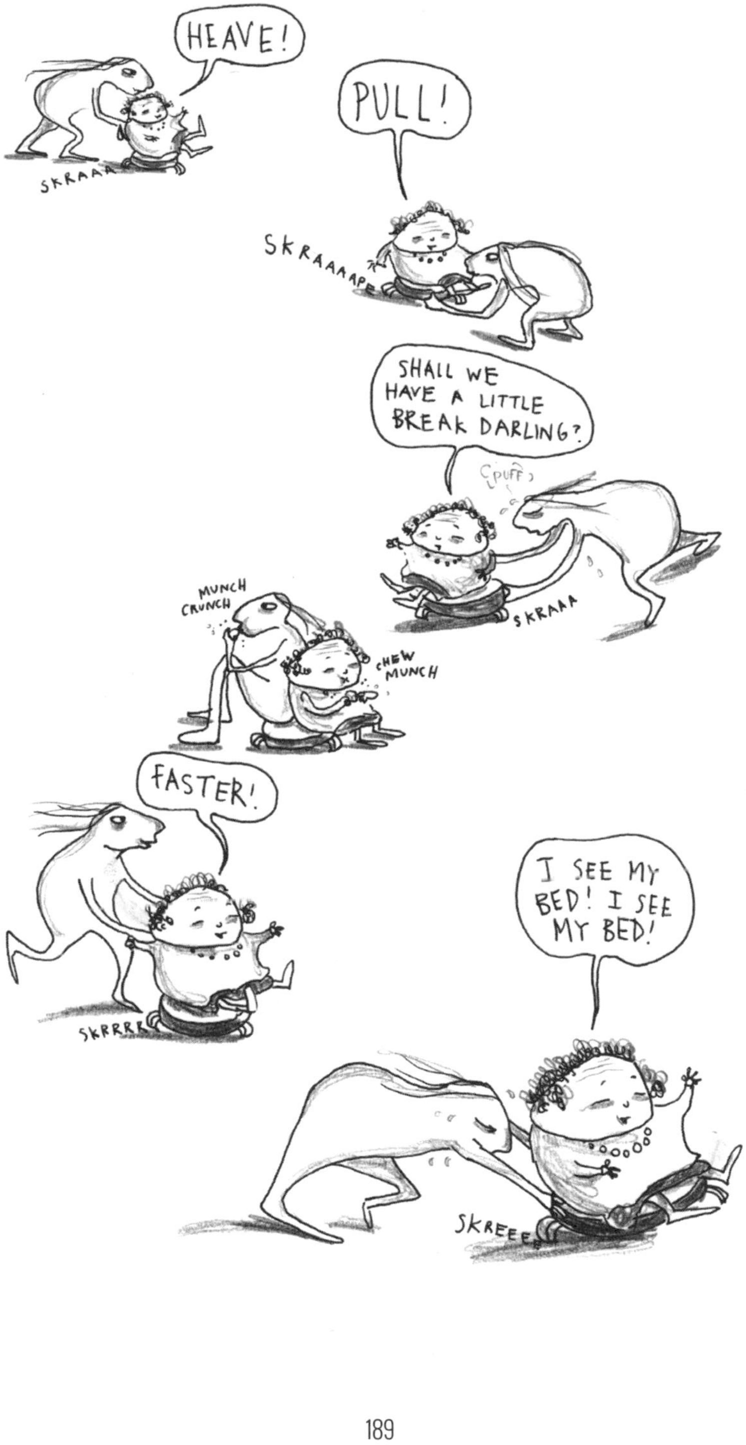
HEAVE!
SKRAAA
PULL!
SKRAAAAAPE
SHALL WE HAVE A LITTLE BREAK DARLING?
PUFF
SKRAAA
MUNCH CRUNCH
CHEW MUNCH
FASTER!
SKRRRR
I SEE MY BED! I SEE MY BED!
SKREEE

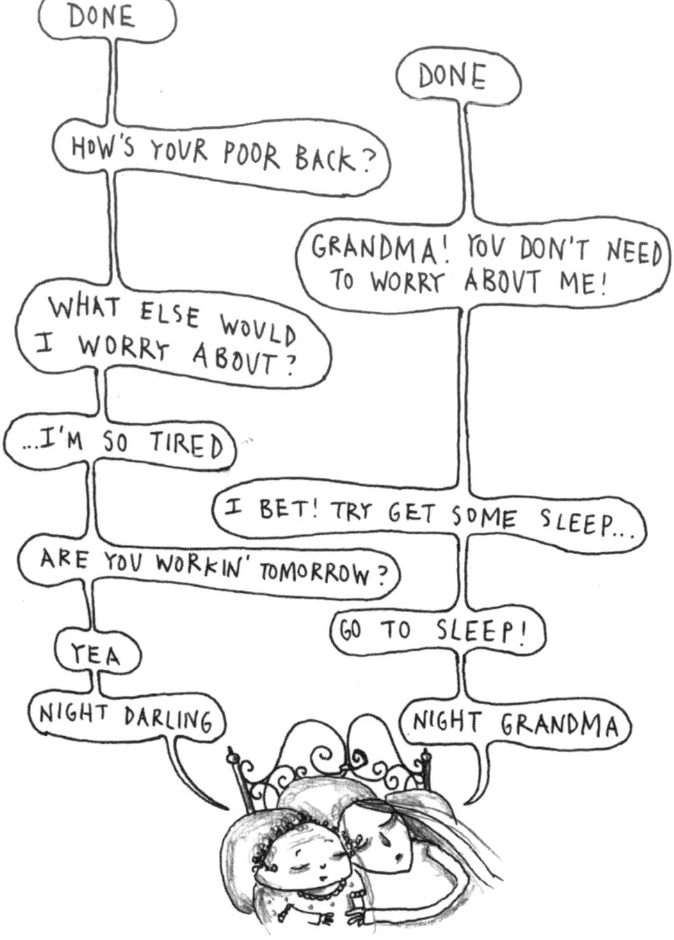
DONE
HOW'S YOUR POOR BACK?
WHAT ELSE WOULD I WORRY ABOUT?
...I'M SO TIRED
ARE YOU WORKIN' TOMORROW?
YEA
NIGHT DARLING
DONE
GRANDMA! YOU DON'T NEED TO WORRY ABOUT ME!
I BET! TRY GET SOME SLEEP...
GO TO SLEEP!
NIGHT GRANDMA

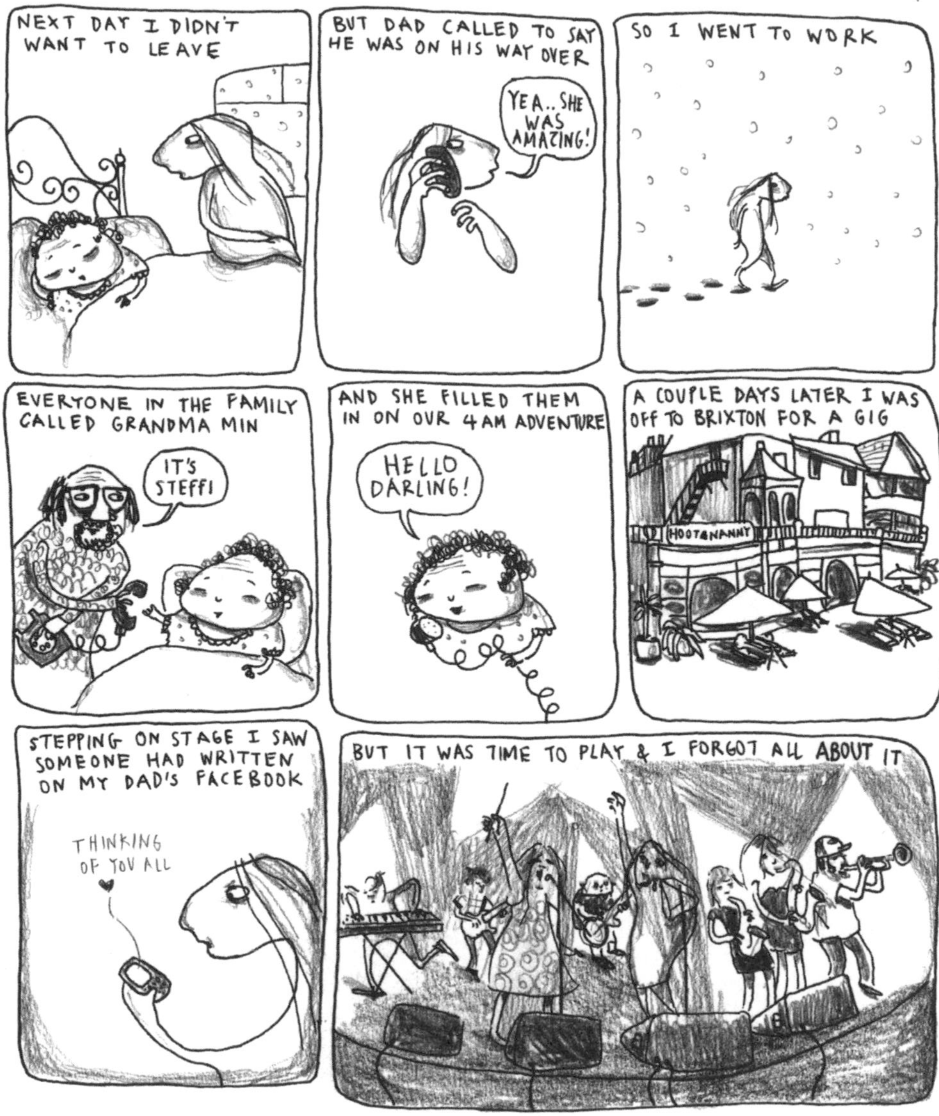

NEXT DAY I DIDN'T WANT TO LEAVE
BUT DAD CALLED TO SAY HE WAS ON HIS WAY OVER
YEA.. SHE WAS AMAZING!
SO I WENT TO WORK
EVERYONE IN THE FAMILY CALLED GRANDMA MIN
IT'S STEFFI
AND SHE FILLED THEM IN ON OUR 4AM ADVENTURE
HELLO DARLING!
A COUPLE DAYS LATER I WAS OFF TO BRIXTON FOR A GIG
HOOTANANNY
STEPPING ON STAGE I SAW SOMEONE HAD WRITTEN ON MY DAD'S FACEBOOK
THINKING OF YOU ALL
BUT IT WAS TIME TO PLAY & I FORGOT ALL ABOUT IT

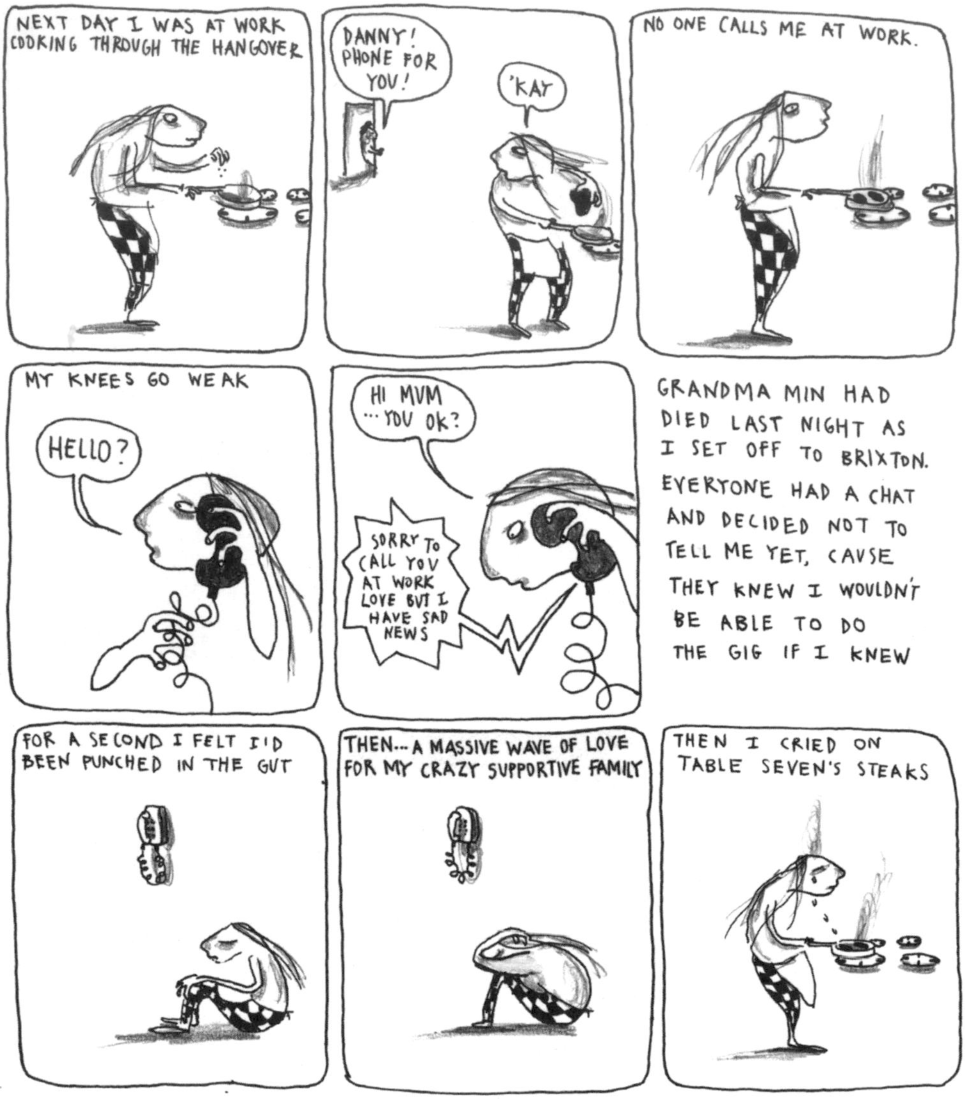
NEXT DAY I WAS AT WORK COOKING THROUGH THE HANGOVER
DANNY! PHONE FOR YOU!
'KAY
NO ONE CALLS ME AT WORK.
MY KNEES GO WEAK
HELLO?
HI MUM ...YOU OK?
SORRY TO CALL YOU AT WORK LOVE BUT I HAVE SAD NEWS
GRANDMA MIN HAD DIED LAST NIGHT AS I SET OFF TO BRIXTON. EVERYONE HAD A CHAT AND DECIDED NOT TO TELL ME YET, CAUSE THEY KNEW I WOULDN'T BE ABLE TO DO THE GIG IF I KNEW
FOR A SECOND I FELT I'D BEEN PUNCHED IN THE GUT
THEN... A MASSIVE WAVE OF LOVE FOR MY CRAZY SUPPORTIVE FAMILY
THEN I CRIED ON TABLE SEVEN'S STEAKS

AFTER THE FUNERAL ME & MY COUSIN TIMNA DOUSED OURSELVES IN GRANDMA'S CLOTHES

I REFUSED TO WEAR ANYTHING ELSE FOR WEEKS

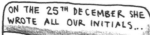

BREATHING DEEP TO HOLD ON TO HER SMELL

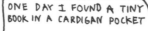

ONE DAY I FOUND A TINY BOOK IN A CARDIGAN POCKET

IT WAS A DIARY

ON THE 25TH DECEMBER SHE WROTE ALL OUR INITIALS...

Friday 25th Dec.
Christmas
R.M.D.A.N.
...and me!

THE EXCLAMATION AFTER THE "ME"! LIKE SHE WAS SURPRISED TO EVEN HAVE BEEN INVITED!

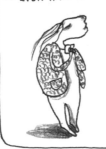

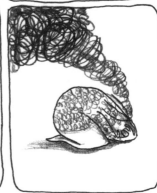

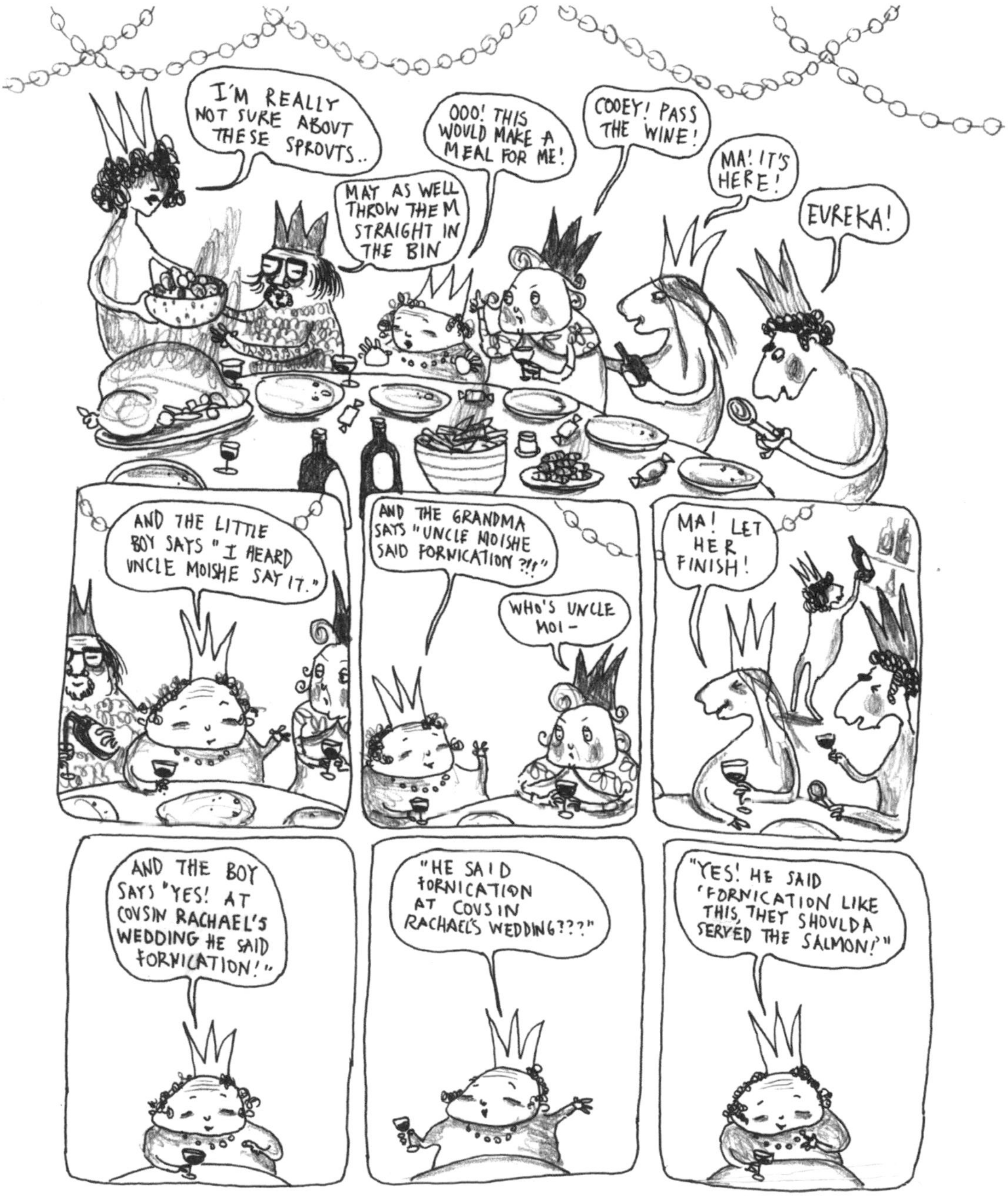
I'M REALLY NOT SURE ABOUT THESE SPROUTS..
MAY AS WELL THROW THEM STRAIGHT IN THE BIN
OOO! THIS WOULD MAKE A MEAL FOR ME!
COOEY! PASS THE WINE!
MA! IT'S HERE!
EUREKA!
AND THE LITTLE BOY SAYS "I HEARD UNCLE MOISHE SAY IT."
AND THE GRANDMA SAYS "UNCLE MOISHE SAID FORNICATION ?!!"
WHO'S UNCLE MOI-
MA! LET HER FINISH!
AND THE BOY SAYS "YES! AT COUSIN RACHAEL'S WEDDING HE SAID FORNICATION!"
"HE SAID FORNICATION AT COUSIN RACHAEL'S WEDDING???"
"YES! HE SAID 'FORNICATION LIKE THIS, THEY SHOULDA SERVED THE SALMON!'"

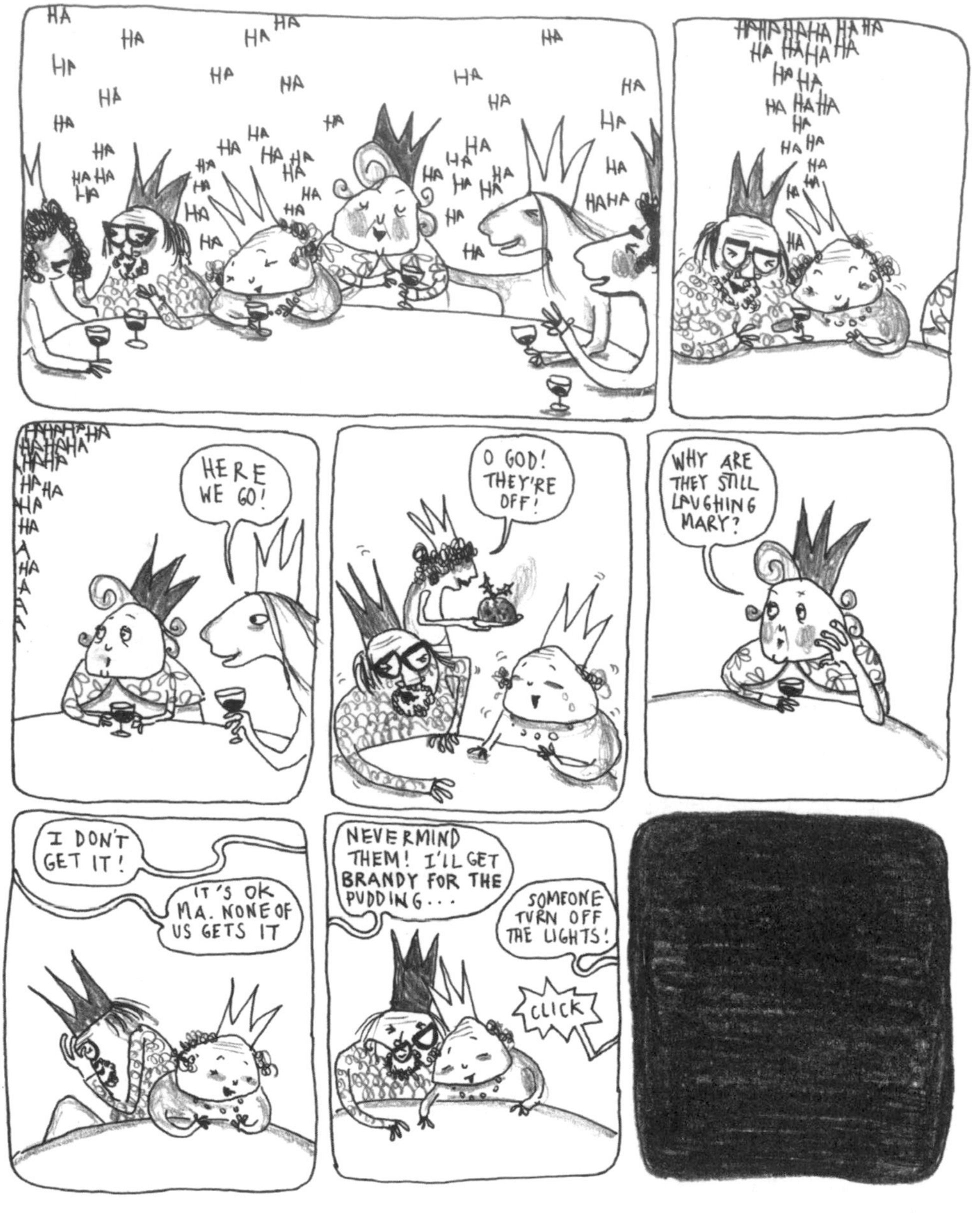

HA HA HA HA HA HA HA HA HA HA
HAHAHAHAHA HAHA
HAHAHA
HERE WE GO!
O GOD! THEY'RE OFF!
WHY ARE THEY STILL LAUGHING MARY?
I DON'T GET IT!
IT'S OK MA. NONE OF US GETS IT
NEVERMIND THEM! I'LL GET BRANDY FOR THE PUDDING...
SOMEONE TURN OFF THE LIGHTS!
CLICK

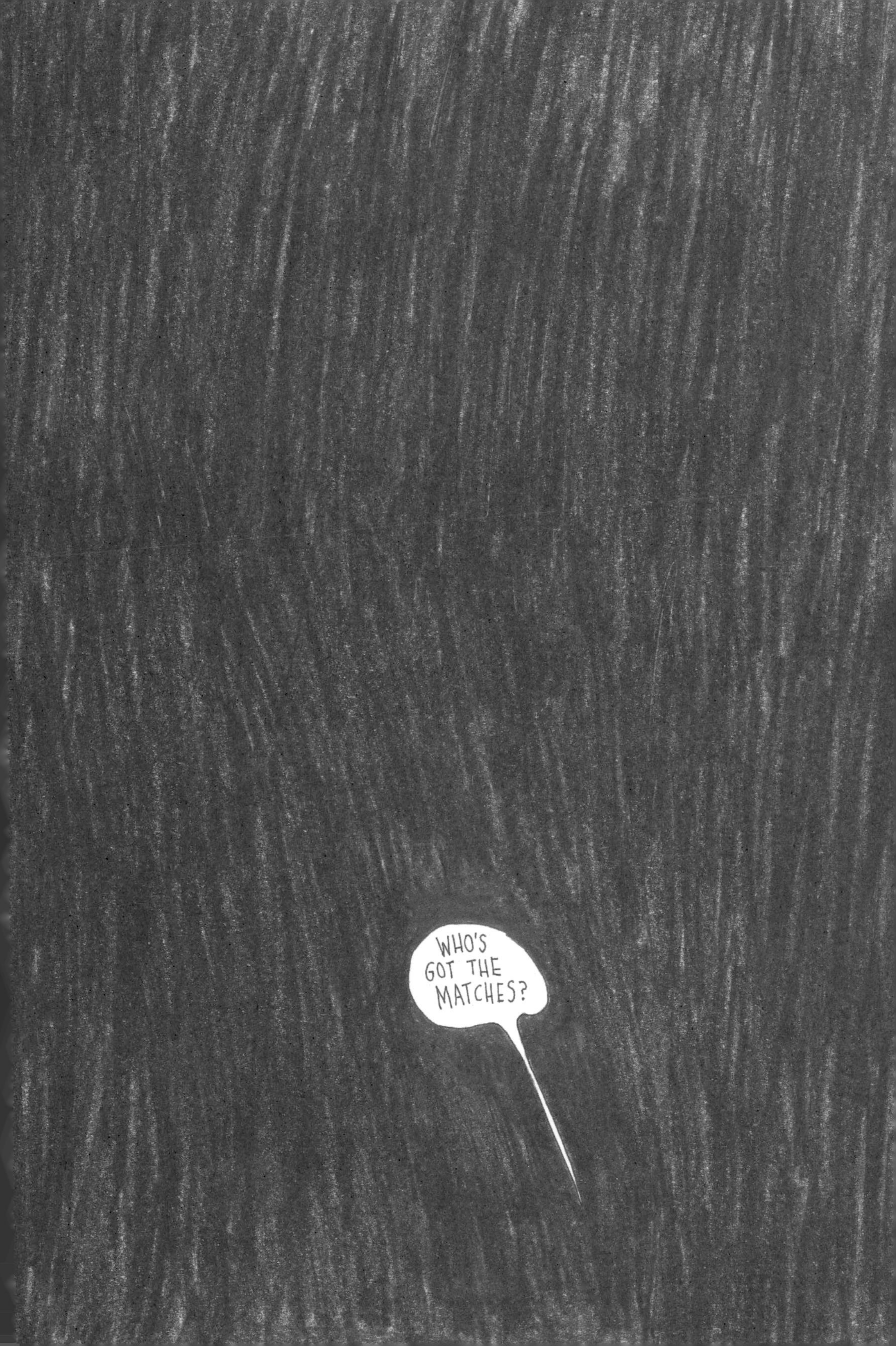
WHO'S GOT THE MATCHES?

GLOSSARY

ARSE - ASS, A BACKSIDE OR AN UNPLEASANT PERSON

BATTENBERG - AN AMAZING PINK & YELLOW SPONGE CAKE COVERED IN MARZIPAN. LOOKS LIKE A CHECKERBOARD

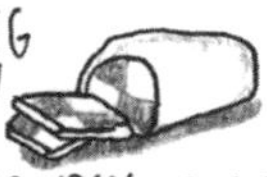

BIN MEN - GARBAGE COLLECTORS

BUNKED OFF - PLAYING HOOKEY, SKIPPING SCHOOL

BUSK - PLAY MUSIC ON THE STREET FOR MONEY

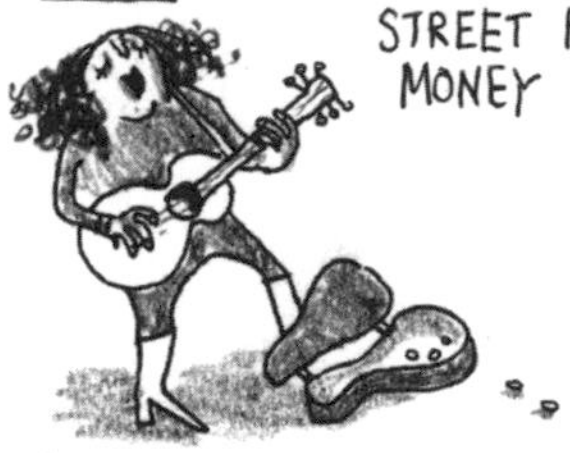

BUTTY - A CASUAL WELSH SLANG WORD MEANING FRIEND, BUDDY, PAL

CASHPOINT - ATM

CHIPS - FRIES!

CIDER - AN ELIXIR OF THE GODS! ALCOHOLIC FERMENTED APPLES, AND THE CAUSE OF MANY OF MY MISADVENTURES

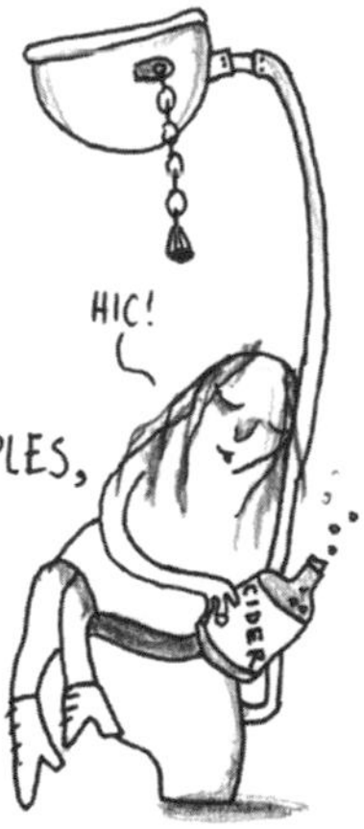
HIC!
CIDER

CLIFF RICHARD - WAS SOLD TO US AS THE BRITISH ELVIS. WAS DEEPLY UNCOOL

CONKERS - THE LARGE NUT-LIKE SEEDS FROM THE HORSE CHESTNUT TREE. IN THE OLD DAYS, BEFORE SMART PHONES, BRITISH CHILDREN WOULD COLLECT CONKERS, DRILL A HOLE IN THEM & THREAD A ROPE THROUGH. THEN THEY WOULD SMASH THEIR CONKER AS HARD AS THEY COULD AGAINST ANOTHER KID'S CONKER & THE CONKER TO SMASH LAST WAS THE WINNER. IT'S PLAYED LEFT OFTEN NOW AS EYES WERE DAMAGED & FIGHTS WERE FOUGHT, BUT I'M PLEASED TO REPORT, BY SOME COMPLETE FLUKE, I WAS THE CONKER CHAMPION AT OUR SCHOOL IN 1987. LAST THING I EVER WON!

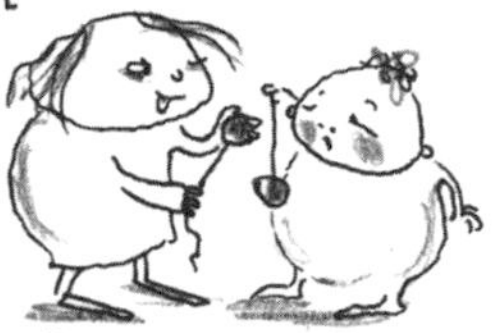

CORONATION STREET - BRITAIN'S LONGEST RUNNING T.V. SOAP OPERA

CRISPS - POTATO CHIPS

DUNGAREES - OVERALLS

FLATS - APARTMENTS

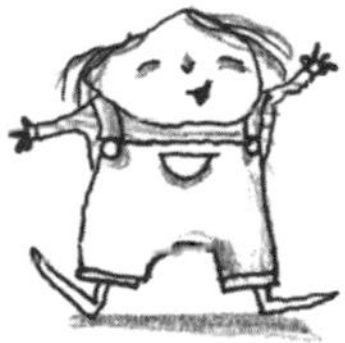

FLYPOSTING - PASTING UP POSTERS, OFTEN UNDER COVER OF DARKNESS AS NOT 100% LEGAL

HOCKEY - FIELD HOCKEY, PLAYED ON GRASS NOT ICE, BUT EQUALLY AS VICIOUS

JUMPERS - PULLOVER SWEATERS, NOT TO BE CONFUSED WITH CARDIGANS

KIT - GYM UNIFORM

"LIVING DOLL" - AN INCREDIBLY UNCOOL SONG

LOO ROLL - TOILET PAPER

MODS & ROCKERS - TWO RIVAL BRITISH YOUTH GROUPS OF THE 60s AND 70s

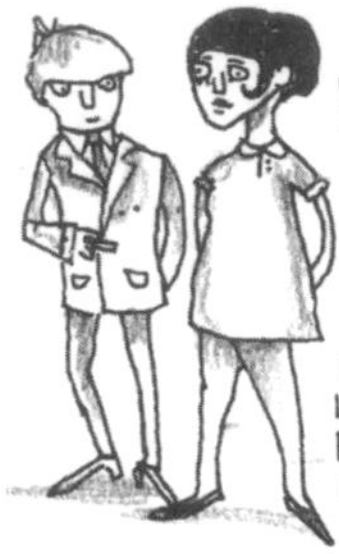

MODS WOULD DRESS SUPER SHARP & DANCE ALL NIGHT TO NORTHERN SOUL ON AMPHETAMINES. ROCKERS WOULD DRESS IN DENIM AND LEATHER, RODE MOTORBIKES AND LISTENED TO 1950s ROCK n' ROLL. THE TWO FACTIONS WOULD MEET UP ON BRIGHTON BEACH ON BANK HOLIDAYS & BEAT EACH OTHER UP, SPARKING WIDESPREAD MORAL PANIC AROUND THE COUNTRY

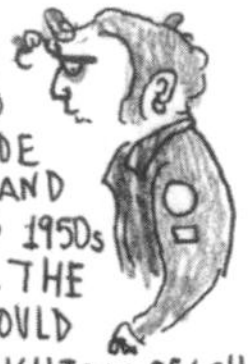

NORTHERN - RESIDENTS OF THE NORTH OF ENGLAND, OFTEN IN POSSESSION OF NICE, WARM TRUSTWORTHY ACCENTS.

PALWINS NUMBER 10 - A DISGUSTING SYRUPY WINE DRUNK ONLY AT PASSOVER. VERY APPEALING TO YOUNG CHILDREN

PANTS - UNDERWEAR

POIROT - A GENIUS BELGIAN DETECTIVE CHARACTER WRITTEN BY FAMOUS MURDER MYSTERY WRITER AGATHA CHRISTIE FAMOUS FOR HIS MOUSTACHE & BRAIN CELLS. LIVED IN A BEAUTIFUL ART DECO APARTMENT

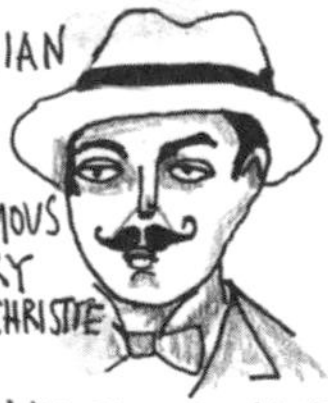

QUIFF - AN ELVIS-STYLE HAIRCUT, A POMPADOUR

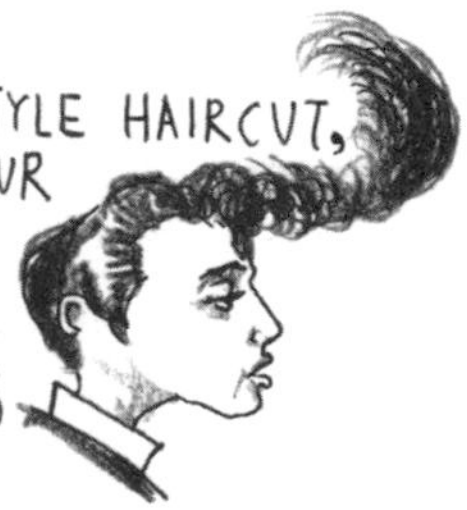

REVISION - STUDYING FOR EXAMS

RIBENA - DELICIOUS SUGARY BLACKCURRANT SYRUP ADDED TO WATER TO MAKE A BEVERAGE

ROLLIES - D.I.Y. CIGARETTES

SATSUMA - A CLEMENTINE BUT BETTER

SKINNING UP - ROLLING A JOINT

SMARTIES - LIKE M&Ms, ONLY BETTER

SNAKEBITE & BLACK - A LETHAL COMBINATION OF ALCOHOLIC CIDER, BEER & BLACKCURRANT CORDIAL. MANY PLACES REFUSE TO SELL IT & IT MAKES YOUR EYES SPIN

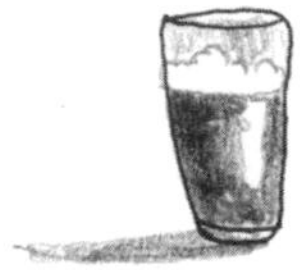

SPORT - PHYS ED

SUBBUTEO - A VERY INTENSE TABLETOP GAME IN WHICH PLAYERS FLICK TINY WOODEN SOCCER PLAYERS AROUND A CLOTH & TRY & SCORE GOALS. WHAT WE DID BEFORE SMART PHONES

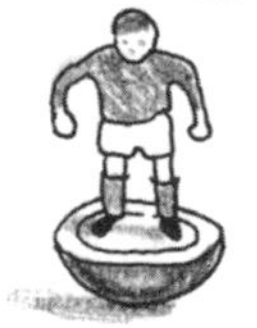

VERRUCA SOCK - A PROTECTIVE SOCK WORN IN SWIMMING POOLS TO PREVENT KIDS FROM PICKING UP PLANTAR WARTS, GROSS & PAINFUL WARTS ON THE FEET

VERVE CLIQUE - A TYPE OF CHAMPAGNE WE SOLD AT WORK WHICH MY BOSSES WOULD CRACK OPEN AFTER A BUSY DAY

WASHING UP - DISHWASHING

WODGES - LARGE PIECES, LUMPS, CHUNKS. IN THIS CASE, MY PARENTS HAD SCRUNCHED UP BALLS OF TOILET PAPER IN THEIR EARS TO PROTECT AGAINST MY BAND'S MUSIC

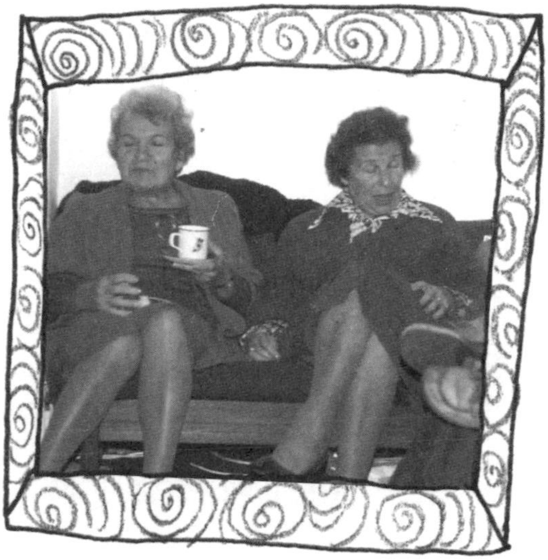

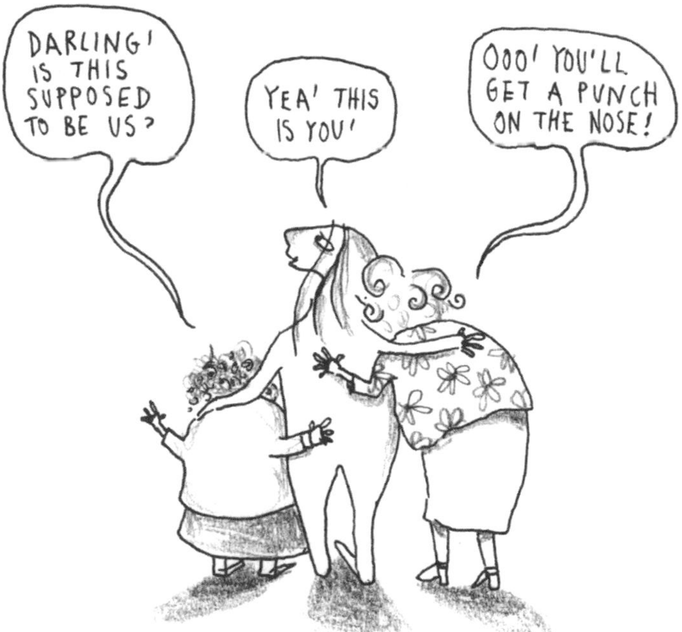
DARLING! IS THIS SUPPOSED TO BE US?
YEA! THIS IS YOU!
OOO! YOU'LL GET A PUNCH ON THE NOSE!

THANKS TO MY FRIENDS & FAMILY FOR
ALL THE FUN. TO LIZ FOR TAKING A CHANCE
ON A GRUBBY GIRL, AND TO ADA & CHARICE
FOR YOUR CARE & ATTENTION TO MY BOOK
BABY. THANKS TO DAD & TOM FOR BEING THE
MOST PATIENT & BRILLIANT PHOTOSHOP
COACHES TO THIS UNWILLING TECHNOPHOBE.
MOST OF ALL THANKS TO MUM & DAD FOR
MAKING THE WORLD A MAGICAL PLACE,
AND TO ADAM FOR ALL THE MARSHMALLOWS
AND FOR PUTTING UP WITH MY CRAP.